Jane Austen and Representations of Regency England

Jane Austen and Representations of Regency England

Roger Sales

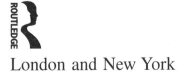

London and New York

First published 1994
Paperback edition published 1996
by Routledge
11 New Fetter Lane, London EC4P 4EE

Simultaneously published in the USA and Canada
by Routledge
29 West 35th Street, New York, NY 10001
Routledge is an International Thomson Publishing company

© 1994, 1996 Roger Sales

Typeset by Computerset, Harmondsworth, Middlesex
Printed in Great Britain by TJ Press (Padstow) Ltd,
Padstow, Cornwall

British Library Cataloguing in Publication Data
A catalogue record for this book is available from the British
Library.

Library of Congress Cataloging in Publication Data
A catalogue record for this book has been requested.

ISBN 0-415-109213

For William and Jessica with love

Contents

Acknowledgements

I began writing this book during the summer of 1987 when I was teaching on exchange at the English Institute of the Free University of Berlin. I was still working on it during the summer of 1991 when I was a visiting professor of Cultural Studies at the English Institute of the University of Munich. Teaching in Germany has played a very important part in the book's development partly because being there provided me with many more opportunities for sustained writing and research than were available at the time in Britain. The students whom I taught, particularly those in Munich, contributed a great deal to my thinking about Austen.

I am particularly grateful to my old friends Elfi Bettinger and Irmgard Maassen for helping to make an exceptionally wet summer in Berlin such a successful one for me, my wife Anne and our children. I would also like to thank all those in Munich who made us equally welcome during another wet summer. My special thanks are due to Elizabeth Bronfen for her intellectual support and to Werner von Koppenfels who was both a very stimulating and hospitable colleague as well as being my saviour when it came to filling out forms. I gave my colloquium paper on Austen and benefited from responses to it.

I would also like to acknowledge the help that I have received from other English and Cultural Studies teachers, past and present, at East Anglia: David Aers, John Ashworth, Ros Ballaster, Charles Barr, Sarah Beckwith, Robert Clark, Jon Cook, Roger Fowler, Andrew Gasoriek, Andrew Higson, Patricia Hollis, Su Kappeler, Allan Lloyd-Smith, Tim Marshall, Lorna Sage and Peter Womack. My special thanks are due to Janet Todd who generously helped me with advice on a number of topics, particularly letter writing and theatre history. I am also grateful to her as head of department for allowing me to do a substantial amount of teaching on Austen and related areas while I was completing the book. My research students and others at East

Anglia who have also helped me include: Glen Creeber, Penny Farrow, Bill Hughes, Jenny Jones and Jane Rondot. Very special thanks are due, as always, to Anne Sales. Many of the ideas developed here have their origins in the undergraduate seminars on Austen that I have taught and I would like to take this opportunity to thank all the students who have participated in them over the years. I acknowledge the importance of a study leave term that was granted to me in 1990, during which I worked on some of the later chapters, and also the assistance of the limited amount of extra funding that was made available to me by my department for library visits.

Those working at other universities in Britain and elsewhere who have helped directly with this particular project usually either by producing readers' reports, or else by inviting me to deliver papers on Austen, include: Joan Fitzpatrick Dean, Jonathan Dollimore, Richard Johnson, Philip O'Neill, David Punter, Helen Taylor and Alan Sinfield. I have benefited from the responses to visiting lectures that I have given on Austen at universities in Germany and Spain and, where appropriate, would like to thank the British Council for its support. I have also been helped by sound advice from my publishers: Claire L'Enfant made some very helpful suggestions when the book was still at a relatively early stage and Talia Rodgers's comments led to a number of improvements later on. One of the anonymous reports commissioned by the publishers before I embarked upon the final draft was particularly useful because while acknowledging what had already been achieved, it calmly yet supportively identified what remained to be done. Last but by no means least, my thanks are due yet again to the librarians at East Anglia and Cambridge for helping me to locate some of the material used here. It should go without saying that, while I want others to share in the success of the book, I am entirely responsible for what might be regarded as its failings. It is dedicated with love to our children, William and Jessica, who have enriched my life so much and therefore also I believe my work.

Textual note

Many academic studies use the texts as edited by R. W. Chapman for the Oxford University Press. I have broken with this convention because I wanted to work with one of the paperback editions that is widely used, certainly in Britain and elsewhere in Europe, by students. Quotations from Austen's novels are therefore taken from the Penguin English Library editions, subsequently re-issued as Penguin Classics. Austen's spelling in both the letters and the novels has sometimes been corrected. Standard abbreviations have been used for the major works:

E   *Emma* (1815/16)
MP   *Mansfield Park* (1814)
NA   *Northanger Abbey* (1818)
P   *Persuasion* (1818)
PP   *Pride and Prejudice* (1813)
S   *Sanditon*
SS   *Sense and Sensibility* (1811)

I have also used abbreviations for some of the other texts that are discussed reasonably frequently in order to avoid unnecessary notes:

AL   Jane Austen and Another Lady, *Sanditon* (Book Club Associates, London, 1976)
B   Edward, Lord Brabourne (ed.), *Letters of Jane Austen*, (Richard Bentley & Son, London, 1884), 2
L   R. W. Chapman (ed.), *Jane Austen's Letters to Her Sister Cassandra and Others* (Oxford University Press, Oxford, 1952 edn)
LV   *Lovers' Vows: A Play in Five Acts, as Performed at the Theatre Royal, Covent-Garden; Altered from the German of Kotzebue by Mrs Inchbald* (Longman, Hurst, Rees and Orme, London, 1798)

M   R. W. Chapman (ed.), *Memoir of Jane Austen by her Nephew James Edward Austen-Leigh* (Clarendon Press, Oxford, 1951)

MW   R. W. Chapman (ed.), *The Works of Jane Austen* (Oxford University Press, Oxford, 1987), 6, 6, *Minor Works*

Abbreviated references followed by a page number are given in the text of the argument itself. Daily newspapers together with weekly publications are also referenced in the argument itself through their date of publication. Almost all other references are contained in notes which appear at the end of the volume. While most of these notes merely provide the basic information, some are of a more descriptive nature. Although difficult to generalise, there are usually two reasons for the inclusion of a longer note. First of all, they are employed to show that the connections that I am making between Austen and history are based on detailed research. Secondly, I use them to give students a wider sense of developments in Austen criticism than it is sometimes possible to do within the confines of the argument itself. I have still not thought it appropriate in such a book, however, to reference all of my own reading in this area. The existence of these reasonably detailed notes means that there is no real need for a full bibliography. I offer instead a very short, highly selective list of the studies of both Austen and Regency England that I have found particularly useful. Some students might want to consult this list first, before gathering other suggestions for further reading from the notes. There is an introduction that sets out my aims and objectives, as well as explaining the structure of the argument. I have not provided a conclusion since all of the chapters, together with many of the sub-sections within them, contain summaries of the points that have been established. There is an appendix which summarises the plot of Elizabeth Inchbald's version of *Lovers' Vows*. I have added an Afterword that deals with the 1995 television adaptation of *Pride and Prejudice*.

Introduction

I have written this account of Jane Austen's later, or Regency, writings mainly for undergraduates at all levels who are studying the literature and history of this period. The material on the Austen industry at the beginning may also be of interest to those who are working on contemporary British culture. This is not then a specialist monograph aimed primarily at other scholars, even though it is based on detailed research and advances its own distinctive arguments. It nevertheless obviously needs to win the broad support of other Austen specialists. These opening statements will therefore explain to them and others both the aims and organisation of the arguments. I have chosen, at this preliminary stage, to refer to general patterns within both Austen criticism and social history rather than to anticipate the more detailed references and citations that are provided later.

The book is divided into four unequal parts. The first one consists of a single chapter which considers the origins and growth of the Austen industry. It probably requires a little more explanation than any of the subsequent chapters since it could be argued that the facts about Austen's Victorian biographers are too well-known to bear repetition. My own particular experience has been that this is not a familiar story, or mouldy tale, for many students in Britain and elsewhere. This may be the result of the fact that some of the relevant texts are not always easily available to those who do not enjoy access to good research libraries. The main reason, however, for starting with the origins of the Austen industry is that the early biographers often tried to suppress the very connections between her writings and the Regency period which form the main subject of this study. The short survey of their anxieties about Regency values therefore provides a necessary introduction to the more detailed account of the period that follows.

This opening chapter also considers some of the mythologies that circulate around the figure of Austen in contemporary British culture.

It looks briefly at the bicentenary celebrations of 1975, at newspaper articles and one television adaptation. The reason why this modern material is included in a book that is primarily concerned with early nineteenth-century literature and history, and relationships between them, is that it too carries definitions of Regency values. As they are often different from those to be found in the Victorian biographies, it is possible for students to gain a sense of historiographical difference and debate while at the same time becoming aware of at least some of the complexities that surround Austen's changing cultural status.

The treatment of the Austen industry is historical rather than polemical. Although I return to modern mythologies at the very end of the book when considering one of the completed versions of *Sanditon* as a way of identifying what is distinctive about Austen's own text, I do not dwell on them elsewhere. My fundamental disagreements with what I call the heritage version of Austen are too obvious to sustain the kind of detailed arguments that students are entitled to expect from this kind of book. I am much more concerned with locating my arguments within recent academic criticism on Austen, as well as with showing how they are informed by new developments in cultural and social history. I argue nevertheless that there are still some occasions when these popular representations of Austen can help academic criticism to recover meanings from the texts themselves.

The second part of the book consists of two chapters designed to provide a more detailed account of Regency England. The first of these deals with Austen's letters, which are probably still the single most neglected historical source for this period. They are used not just in this chapter, but also in many of the subsequent ones. As it may still be suggested by a few specialists that this chapter on the letters also covers old ground, I should say my own experience has been that most students are in fact only familiar with various selected editions of the letters. Opinions and experiences are obviously going to differ here. My sense is of some exciting critical work beginning to emerge around letters and related forms of writing in this period that may not yet have had the impact at undergraduate level that it deserves. I have always found the letters quite difficult to teach, which is why I wanted to write on them as a way of trying to clarify some of their problems. My necessarily limited contribution to this new work is to read the letters alongside those of other Regency women, some of whom may not be familiar to students of English literature. I also establish, albeit briefly, some of the material conditions under which letters were produced in this period. Another reason for this chapter is that it introduces a theme that will become important in the subsequent readings of the Regency novels themselves. To put the argument as simply as possible at this stage, it is suggested that there are times in the letters when Austen, like other women letter writers, is able to lose the 'countenance', or face, that she is expected to wear in public. The readings of the novels identify an often impatient narrator who also alternates between keeping and losing her countenance.

The second chapter on Regency England provides an account of the Regency Crisis of 1810/11, before looking more generally at the scandalous reputations of both the Prince Regent himself and other members of the Royal Family. The Crisis was precipitated by George III's illness and eventually resolved when his eldest son became head of state, at first for a probationary period and then more permanently. Many historical sources are used to reconstruct these public events, and Austen's letters are among them. The Regency period, defined precisely, runs from 1811 through to 1820 when George III finally died. A more general, but nevertheless still acceptable, definition would include the decade immediately before the Crisis as well as George IV's reign, which lasted until 1830. Although in fact I am primarily concerned with the tighter of these two chronologies, I have not felt inhibited from introducing some earlier materials into the argument, particularly when dealing with Austen's letters.

The Regency Crisis, sometimes referred to by historians as the second one to differentiate it from the events of 1788/9 when the King's illness first precipitated a constitutional crisis, is given such a prominent place in this study in order to suggest the need for establishing new contexts for Austen's writings. There are a number of influential readings of the novels that place them very productively within the ideological debates of the 1790s. It is accepted here that these debates provide crucial contexts for the earlier writings which are seen as including the Juvenilia, 'Lady Susan', *Northanger Abbey*, *Sense and Sensibility* and *Pride and Prejudice*. Opinions still differ as to how extensively *Pride and Prejudice* was revised for its eventual publication in 1813. It is seen here as belonging more to the historical moment of its original composition in the 1790s than to that of its publication in 1813. I suggest that the debates of the 1790s may not be quite so crucial as far as the later writings are concerned, or at least that it is dangerous to read the novels that were produced during and after the second Regency Crisis exclusively in terms of events that took place ten or more years earlier.

The details of Austen's literary life are obviously much more complicated and contentious than this rather rigid separation between the earlier and later writings implies. There are clearly continuities and connections between the two periods, as well as literary activities in the intervening years. It is still the case, however, that two important and previously unconnected events took place at the same time. Austen moved from Southampton to Chawton in 1809 and was able to establish herself, if not as a truly professional writer, then at least as a published author with professional aspirations. This was happening at the same time as there was a major constitutional, but also much wider cultural, crisis. At this stage, the possibility of a connection between these two events only needs to be noticed rather than explored. It is important to stress here that this work is envisaged as extending rather than replacing those studies that tend to read the later writings in terms of the debates of the 1790s. It is clear that these debates continue to reverberate throughout Austen's Regency texts. The point that will be established here is that other, more specifically Regency, contexts are also available.

My concentration on the later writings obviously means that students are not being offered a conventional study that devotes a chapter to each of the major novels. The argument contains some references to the Juvenilia and earlier novels and, because the television adaptation chosen is of *Pride and Prejudice*, there is a more detailed treatment of this particular text. The lack of sustained readings of the texts produced, if not published, in the 1790s nevertheless means that this book will not cater for all students' needs. I believe nevertheless that contextual work should be detailed rather than merely tokenistic and the concentration on a limited number of Austen's texts facilitates this. This is not to imply that some of the more conventionally structured studies do not contain important historical work but, rather, to indicate that my own particular version of historicism benefits from the imposition of certain chronological restrictions. The book is conventional, however, in that it devotes a chapter to each of the Regency novels rather than adopting a more thematic approach. One of the main reasons for this is that I am particularly concerned to suggest the precarious and often contradictory nature of resolutions, and such arguments work best when developed alongside a reading of the text as a whole.

Some cultural historians have suggested the existence of a long eighteenth century that stretches from the Restoration through to the Regency period. They do not propose an unchanging *ancien régime* but rather a dynamic, commercially expanding society that in terms of its institutional structures nevertheless retains certain common features. Many students in my experience have a good sense of Restoration mentalities, while exhibiting much vaguer notions about Regency ones.

This is understandable since the later part of this long century has traditionally been associated in literary histories with Romanticism rather than with the Regency, a fact which has hindered work on Austen's later writings. Students are not helped, however, by the surprising number of Austen critics who convert her Regency writings into early Victorian ones simply because they are not familiar enough with cultural developments that took place in the earlier decades of the nineteenth century. This casual approach needs to be differentiated quickly from the one that suggests that the later writings can be located within what historians have described as a Victorian prelude in which movements such as Evangelicalism took root. Although I argue strongly against such interpretations, they deserve to be taken more seriously because they are at least grounded in a version of the history of the Regency period.

The analysis of the Regency Crisis ends with a study of Beau Brummell and dandyism, given that at the time it seemed highly likely that the Prince Regent would allow the dandies to take control of his father's political house. It is argued more generally that an analysis of the contradictory nature of dandyism, which was both exclusively aristocratic and subversively democratic, helps to identify important features of Regency mentalities and their double countenances. This paves the way for the readings of the dandies who are represented in the later writings such as Henry Crawford, Frank Churchill and Sir Walter Elliot. I suggest that as far as the younger characters are concerned their dandyism is revealed through mode of address, and its accompanying gestures, rather than through dress itself. I also argue that these representations reveal a fascination with the dandy which often contradicts other messages about the need for more professional standards and lifestyles. Here and elsewhere, I am concerned to show that the texts are capable of wearing different countenances.

Austen's explorations of different masculine identities have not received enough critical attention. It could be argued that this is as it should be since the novels are primarily concerned with the education of heroines. A vital part of this education is nevertheless to acquire the ability to read, as correctly as possible on the limited information that is available, the mysterious motives and actions of dandies, eldest sons, fathers, sportsmen and other Regency males. There are inevitably times here when the development of individual arguments about masculine identities leads to the apparent marginalisation of heroines. They and their concerns are, however, still one of the central themes in the overall structure of the argument except possibly in the chapter on *Mansfield Park*.

The third part of the book consists of a long chapter on *Mansfield Park*, which makes original connections between the novel itself and the events and debates that formed the Regency Crisis. Sir Thomas Bertram's extended visit to Antigua produces a form of regency crisis at Mansfield Park. Critics who use general terms such as custodianship miss the novel's topicality. The recognised regents are Tom and Edmund Bertram, although I also argue that there is an important debate about the rival claims of Mrs Norris and Fanny Price for the job. The debates on the Regency Crisis involved the question of female government since there was an attempt to invest Queen Charlotte with some of the Regent's powers. It was a commonplace of the period for accounts of the government of a house and estate to be seen as offering commentaries on the government of the state itself. I make no claims that Austen's novel offers a precise, literal or indeed intentional representation of these historical events. I show instead that new meanings and messages become available when it is read in the light of them.

The argument here and elsewhere is organised to some extent around the idea that modern readers ought to be aware of the terms of reference that it can be assumed that at least some Regency readers brought with them to the novels. This historicist approach is certainly not new, as will be clear from what has already been said about those critics who read Austen's novels in the context of the political debates of the 1790s. I am not, however, just interested in the wars of ideas that took place in literary, philosophical and other written texts. I am also concerned at times to move beyond an essentially literary idea of history towards placing the Regency novels within a more obviously material and politicised social history. To take a relatively easy example, characters are often associated with particular places which may not always be represented directly in the texts themselves. The association is a kind of shorthand that would have been understood by Regency readers but which may remain either unnoticed, or else cryptic, for modern ones. Research into the social, as opposed to the intellectual or literary, history of the period can nevertheless recover the reputations that were acquired by particular locations. The historicism practised here fills out seemingly marginal contexts such as place names, as well as concentrating on more central but still neglected ones such as the Regency Crisis itself.

I follow many other critics in arguing that to try to understand *Mansfield Park* it is necessary to unravel some of the complexities that surround the rehearsals of *Lovers' Vows*. I try to recover the reputation that this play and its author might have had for Regency readers. I also

deal with theatre history more generally, establishing the ambiguous social status of the professional actress at this time as well as considering the significance of events such as the 'old price' riots at Covent Garden in 1809. Once again, I am concerned to show that Austen's text is capable of wearing different countenances. It is, at times, more radical than the play text and, if there is a critique of theatricality, then it is paradoxically a highly theatrical one. The critics whose work I admire most also concentrate on contradictions within the Regency texts. There was a period in the earlier 1980s which produced a polarisation between those who claimed Austen as an ideologically conservative writer and those who demonstrated her connections with Enlightenment feminism. It is now beginning to be recognised that there may be debates within the texts themselves between these two positions. Although I certainly show the availability of conservative messages, one of my main concerns has been to highlight how they are always in competition with another countenance.

Aspects of medical history are referred to directly, or more indirectly, in all of the opening chapters. The Austen industry often offers sentimental images of the dead, or dying, woman but her own letters challenge this particular kind of sentimentality, in addition to providing equally sharp comments on the related cult of female invalidism. The Regency Crisis was initially a medical one that was concerned with the constitution of the King, before it broadened out into debates about the constitution of the state. Some attention is devoted to Tom Bertram's nearly fatal illness after the end of the regency period at *Mansfield Park*. The fourth and final part of the book, while continuing to explore themes such as dandyism and theatricality, offers a more sustained account of invalidism in the wider context of medical history. It consists of three chapters, one on each of the novels that were written after *Mansfield Park*: *Emma*, *Persuasion* and the unfinished *Sanditon*.

Austen's representations of health and the body are, like her letters, increasingly becoming seen as important subjects for academic study. It is necessary therefore to identify the particular approach that is being taken towards them here. I am not primarily concerned with reading Regency texts in the light of more modern clinical and psychoanalytic theories, nor do I deal in any significant detail with the medical theories about nervous and other diseases that were available to Regency medical men. I am mainly interested in exploring the more purely social, or material, structures of the expanding health and leisure industries in this period. Two related examples will help to clarify the point. What I take as being important about the representation of Mr Perry in *Emma* is that the debates over the nature of his social status were

written and first read at precisely the same time as the status of the apothecary was being debated in Parliament and elsewhere. Just as I argue that *Mansfield Park* can be read originally and productively in relation to the Regency Act of 1811, so I show the possibilities that are opened up by reading *Emma* in relation to the Apothecaries' Act of 1815. Similarly, I set the role of Nurse Rooke in *Persuasion* in the related debates that were taking place in this period about the status of the midwife. I use these and other examples to show that Austen's Regency novels are often highly topical. Although this topicality is usually denied quite emphatically by the Austen industry, I am much more concerned to show that academic criticism with its emphasis on forms of literary history has not registered all of its manifestations. This is indeed my main thesis.

The discussion of the related theme of leisure involves a continuation of the reconstruction of the associations that particular places, in this case watering places, might have had for Regency readers. The ones considered include Southend, Cromer, Weymouth, Lyme Regis and Cheltenham. The chapter on *Emma* also identifies the mentality of the watering place by looking at its representatives, such as Frank Churchill and Mrs Elton. As they are both specifically linked with Frenchness, it can be shown that the debates over the rival merits of the watering place and the village are part of much wider ideological debates about national identities. It is, once again, possible to show the topicality of Austen's Regency novels, although the argument here will initially be a reasonably familiar one to other Austen specialists. I go on to argue, however, that the debate is always unresolved and thus that there is a countenance that favours the French over the English. As the characters from watering places are further defined by their mobility, there is a discussion of the politics of movement. This involves a consideration of the experiences of Regency women, as well as of the way in which Austen's text itself also draws attention to the gendered control of transport. One example that is highlighted is the reaction to Jane Fairfax's walks to the post office which, in turn, leads to a treatment of the significance of letters and letter writing in the novel as a whole. This builds on the previous work that has been done on Austen's own letters.

The chapter on *Persuasion* concentrates on representations of dandyism, invalidism and leisure. It also includes some work on naval history, using material about the lower decks as well as sources from the upper decks. This fills out previous arguments about masculine identities, as well as initiating new ones. It is shown, for instance, that Mrs Croft's proposal that wives ought to be encouraged to accompany

their husbands on operational vessels is a potentially radical one. The representation of Mrs Musgrove sighing over the loss of her son in the war is used as one of the examples to illustrate the way in which the Regency novels, like the letters, alternate between keeping and losing their countenance. This particular novel is seen as offering both radical and more conservative responses to the Condition-of-England question. Here and earlier on I argue that the endings of Austen's Regency novels perpetuate rather than resolve debates and difficulties. There are no settled conclusions to the fate of the various estates which in turn stand for the state itself.

Sanditon, which remained unfinished at Austen's death in 1817, has sometimes been seen as a Victorian novel by critics with an erratic sense of history. Those who suggest, by contrast, that it is her only quintessentially Regency text deserve to be taken much more seriously. My argument is, however, that all of the later writings can be considered as a whole since they represent invalidism and leisure, together with relationships between them, at a particular historical moment. I concentrate here on both Mr Parker's plans to market a new watering place and the invalidism that is exhibited by other members of his family. Although I consider the possibility of a submerged text associated with the figure of the 'mad' woman doctor, I have generally avoided joining other critics in the search for camouflaged meanings. This is because I see Austen as a more openly Condition-of-England writer than is generally recognised. This is another of my main arguments. As indicated, this chapter is concluded with a reading of a finished version of the text that was published in 1975 and carries many of the assumptions of the Austen industry. The reason for this is that the modern text highlights the centrality of the specifically Regency themes of the original in the very act of trying to suppress them. Brief connections are made between such texts and the kind of academic criticism that insists that Austen herself would have rewritten the satirical parts of *Persuasion* and most of *Sanditon* if she had lived longer.

I have already said a bit about what the book does not attempt to cover when explaining the omission of a sustained discussion of the earlier writings from it. Although there are certainly references to many of the other well-known women writers from this period, only Mary Wollstonecraft, Maria Edgeworth and Elizabeth Inchbald are treated in any detail. As will become apparent, some of the best recent criticism on Austen has been concerned with locating her writings within traditions of writing by women so that she can no longer be regarded as a splendidly isolated figure. One of my concerns, however, has been to relate her Regency writings to those by women who tend not to have a prominent place in literary histories because they did not use one of the recognised genres. This is particularly true of the chapter that deals with letter writing, although elsewhere I have often used other forms of marginalised writing such as diaries and autobiographies in preference to taking examples from novels by women writers. Many critics have already shown that Austen is an intensely parodic writer whose works are full of literary allusions and echoes. I have therefore felt able to concentrate instead on locating topical allusions.

There are also some omissions as far as Austen criticism is concerned. It will become clear that my own work in general has its origins in the critical debates about Austen and history that began in the 1970s. It will be seen, more particularly, that I have been most influenced by the readings offered by feminists whose approach is materialistic rather than more purely psychoanalytic as well as by those of other historicists. I provide students both in the argument itself and in the notes with commentaries on what I consider to be the most significant pieces of modern criticism, irrespective of whether I am in agreement with them or not. There will, inevitably in a book of this length on this subject, be a few gaps. I have not ignored the views of earlier critics altogether. My first chapter references the work of some of the first writers on Austen whom I would have liked to have dealt with in more detail and, later on, I occasionally discuss the views of critics who wrote before the 1970s where they seem relevant to the argument. Just as I do not show each and every time how my readings differ from those offered by the heritage version of Austen, so it seemed redundant to keep pointing out where some earlier critics had missed opportunities to historicise their arguments. The other reason why there is not a full survey of the earlier criticism is because it is important for a book of this nature to create as much space as possible for its own historical work.

Part I
The Regency reproduced

1 Rewriting the Regency

FLEAS, NAKED CUPIDS AND BAD BREATH

Henrietta Keddie was an extremely prolific professional writer from Scotland who published under the name of Sarah Tytler. Her book on Austen, *Jane Austen and Her Works*, came out in 1880. The problem that she encountered when writing it is one which, in less exaggerated form, has beset many later writers. The only full version of Austen's life that was in circulation when she wrote the more purely biographical parts of her book was one that was, in accordance with Victorian conventions, carefully policed by Austen's family. Her difficulty was that she heard some voices in Austen's novels and letters which she was politely, but firmly, told did not exist.

Austen's brother, Henry, had published his 'Biographical Notice' in 1818 in the posthumous first edition of *Northanger Abbey and Persuasion*. It was a short, elegantly written account that emphasised his sister's domesticity and piety. Any anxieties that might have been felt about the satirical nature of her writings were meant to be calmed by reassurances that, almost faultless herself, 'she always sought in the fault of others, something to excuse, to forgive or forget' (P, p. 31). Henry also gave his own impression of some of the Regency qualities of his sister's writing when he drew attention to their charm, polish and finish. Austen's nephew, the Reverend James Edward Austen-Leigh, continued to emphasise her domestic virtues in his much more substantial biographical notice, *Memoir of Jane Austen*, which was first published in 1870. Its popularity led to a second edition the following year and can be seen as launching the Austen industry.

Tytler certainly follows some of the guidelines that had been set out for her by Austen's brother and nephew. She too represents Austen as a person who was content to be everything to her family and nothing to the world. She echoes Austen-Leigh's praise for his aunt's sewing:

She sewed and embroidered, as she did everything else, with exquisite finish. She was great in satin-stitch. She spent much of her time in sewing – not being above making her own clothes, as well as those of the poor.[1]

There are times, however, when this picture of domestic perfection is at odds with her own reading of the novels and the limited range of letters that were available to her. She finds a different kind of writer: proud, intolerant, impatient and cynical. She pictures Austen as being a 'brilliant, rather hard girl' and is sometimes unable to reconcile this view with the image of quiet docility that had been carefully cultivated by the family:

It would have been little short of a miracle if she could have conducted herself with such meekness, in her remote rural world, or during the visits she paid to the great English watering-place – while she was all the time laughing in her sleeve – so as not to provoke any suspicion of her satire, or any resentment of what might easily be held her presumption.[2]

The watering place referred to here is Bath. Tytler is unable at this particular point in her argument to make an act of faith and accept the gospel preached by Austen's family. Meek and mild Austen becomes, albeit momentarily, satirical and presumptuous Austen.

One of the most disconcerting things about Austen-Leigh's *Memoir* is that it actually provides a lot of the evidence that challenges his own cosy account of his sainted aunt. He quotes her businesslike correspondence over the dedication of *Emma* to the Prince Regent and yet still asserts that she was an unpresumptuous writer who only wrote to amuse herself and her family. He introduces extracts from *Sanditon*, an unfinished text that satirises the Regency culture of invalidism, while claiming that its author never meddled with medicine in her novels. He produces for the first time the whole of *Lady Susan*, an epistolary novella, without appearing to be at all troubled by the way in which its heroine might turn literary and social conventions upside down. Lady Susan Vernon is a powerful widow who enjoys having dominion over others. She achieves this by wearing one countenance, or face, in public while plotting in private to manipulate and manoeuvre everybody to her own advantage. As Patricia Meyer Spacks notes, she only uses fashionable theories about how women ought to conduct themselves as a mask.[3] She does not expect men to be constant and demands the same privilege. She has no time for maternal feelings and her daughter, Frederica, is by turns sent away, confined and bullied.

Although events do not go entirely according to her plans, she is not severely punished for all her disruptive finesses and masquerades.

Austen-Leigh does not register the subversive qualities of *Lady Susan* itself, although he raises the question of his aunt's satire at a more general level. He reflects upon her dealings with her neighbours who, in his version of realism, are destined to become her characters:

> She was as far as possible from being censorious or satirical. She never abused them or *quizzed* them – *that* was the word of the day; an ugly word, now obsolete; and the ugly practice which it expressed is much less prevalent now than it was then. (M, p. 93)

A 'quizz' was either an eccentric person or an outlandish object. The habit of 'quizzing', perfected by both Regency dandies and high society hostesses, involved staring at people in a haughty way that was meant to make them feel utterly ridiculous. The repetition of 'ugly' in relation to a custom particularly associated with the Regency period hints that, behind the seemingly calm and emphatic reassurances to the contrary, Austen-Leigh may still have been worried by the possibility that his aunt had been infected by some of the practices of her age.

It can be argued that Austen-Leigh tries to allay such anxieties about his aunt's Regency associations by transforming her into a Victorian proper lady. As Margaret Kirkham suggests, this can be clearly demonstrated by contrasting Cassandra Austen's portrait of her sister with the one commissioned by Austen-Leigh for the *Memoir*. Although this second portrait is inspired by the earlier one, both the look and the colour scheme are much softer and smoother. Kirkham argues that what she calls the 'received biography' came into existence as an attempt to dissociate Austen from the kind of controversy that surrounded Mary Wollstonecraft's writings after her death in 1797 and the publication of William Godwin's biographical memoir in the following year.[4] Jan Fergus draws attention to the ambiguous cultural status of most women writers at this time as a way of explaining, more generally, why Austen's brother and nephew were so keen to deny that she had any professional aspirations as a writer. Only women who self-consciously presented themselves to the reading public as deserving cases for charity were authorised to write for money.[5]

Austen-Leigh's written text offers a more complicated relationship between Victorian and Regency values than is apparent in his visual text. At one level, he nostalgically evokes a world that has been lost. The Victorian home is represented as being cluttered with furniture, technology and servants. It is contrasted with fond memories of

simpler, more functional Regency interiors. The opposition to technology runs throughout the text. One of the reasons why Austen's sewing
is praised is because it is remembered as being almost as good as that
produced by machines. Deborah Kaplan identifies an 'antiquarian
sensibility' that pervades Austen-Leigh's recollections.[6] He paints a
highly romanticised picture of cottage industries such as spinning,
which are presented as having become the victims of industrialisation.
This pastoral perspective is nevertheless at odds with the way in which
he also declares his distaste for the Regency period and its ugly
practices. This more critical perspective surfaces in relation to religion.
It is claimed that neither Edmund Bertram in *Mansfield Park* nor
Henry Tilney in *Northanger Abbey* 'had adequate ideas of the duties of
a parish minister' (M, p. 154). This surprising judgement on Edmund is
based on the conviction that he belonged to a world that was as yet still
untouched by the religious revivals, High Church as well as Evangelical, that had shaped Victorian beliefs.

Austen-Leigh does not in fact reposition Austen by placing her in a
Victorian home. He confines her to a Regency one, which he does his
best to reassure readers was largely free from the coarseness that was
still prevalent in this period. The closeness of her confinement obviously needs to be related as Fergus suggests to male anxieties about
the status of the woman writer but, more specifically, it is part of
Austen-Leigh's attempt to protect her from the contaminating effects
of Regency society. He almost hermetically seals her off from it. His
version of realism is also designed to protect her from any accusations
that she might really have been part of this ugly, coarse society: 'These
writings are like photographs, in which no feature is softened; no ideal
expression is introduced, all is the unadorned reflection of the natural
object . . .' (M, p. 153). Anything that is felt to be less than perfect in
her writings can only be attributed to the imperfections of her period.

The *Memoir* voices some prejudices against Regency values, while
leaving others unspoken. A sense of what really troubled Austen-
Leigh about his aunt and her writings can be obtained by considering
some of the silent alterations he made to them. It is only necessary to
look briefly at three of the letters printed in chapter six to become
familiar with the basic techniques that were employed in constructing
the mythology. The chapter ends by appearing to quote the whole of a
letter written by Austen to her sister Cassandra and dated 2 March
1814. It describes the last stage of a journey to London with Henry.
Omissions nevertheless include: a level-headed description of financial
transactions; the hope that somebody would not be 'cruel enough to
consent' (L, p. 378) to an invitation to dinner and an inquiry as to

whether Cassandra has had time to discover if there is anybody who is more boring than a certain Sarah Mitchell. Austen-Leigh is not just denying his aunt's rationality and playfulness, but is also concerned to cover up what he takes to be her Regency coarseness. The full text should read: 'Give my love to little Cassandra! I hope she found my Bed comfortable last night and has not filled it with fleas' (L, p. 378). The *Memoir* removes the reference to the fleas.

A similar pattern emerges when the two versions of the preceding letter are briefly considered. This one, which also describes a journey to London with Henry, is dated 20 May 1813. Omissions include: Austen complaining to a tradesman about the quality of some currant bushes that had been purchased earlier; the fact that it was Henry rather than she who was fatigued by the journey; and some confidently given advice for one of her other brothers on the best roads to travel when coming to London. The editing denies her strength, both of purpose and of physique, as well as not allowing her to display knowledge of the world beyond home. The letter ends with an account of a call on Charlotte Craven, who was at school in London:

> I was shewn upstairs into a drawing-room, where she came to me, and the appearance of the room so totally unschool-like, amused me very much; it was full of all the modern elegancies – & if it had not been for some naked Cupids over the Mantlepiece, which must be a fine study for Girls, one should never have smelt instruction. (L, pp. 308–9)

The 'naked Cupids', together with the playful remarks about their educational role, are silently removed from the version of the letter that appears in the *Memoir*.

The final letter to be considered shows that Austen-Leigh was not just an editor who suppressed examples of what he considered to be Regency coarseness. He was also actively engaged in re-arranging his aunt's writings. The letter that he purports to be printing is one that is dated 9 February 1813. His text starts with a heavily edited version of this particular letter and then material from an earlier one, dated 24 January 1813, is spliced into it. It continues to move freely between these two original Austen texts. This is an attempt to manufacture a letter that sticks as far as possible to a single theme, namely books. References to the writing, reading, publishing, discussing and lending of books are culled from the two original letters and then arranged in such a way that the 'forgery' passes for the genuine article. Austen-Leigh shows that he is worried that his aunt's letters will be seen as being too gossipy and discursive. He believes, like Henry Tilney, that women's letters do not contain enough full stops. He therefore imposes his own masculine definition of order and theme on what he takes to be the chaos of her writing.

Austen's great-nephew, Lord Brabourne, consolidated the 'received biography' when he published two volumes of *Letters of Jane Austen* in 1884, dedicating them to Queen Victoria. The Dedication acknowledges the existence of 'a very few omissions which appeared obviously desirable' before going on to hope that the letters would 'interest or amuse your Majesty' (B, 1, p. v). Brabourne continues the praise for Austen's domestic virtues: 'In truth, the chief beauty of Jane Austen's life really consisted in its being uneventful: *it* was emphatically a home life, and *she* the light and blessing of a home circle' (B, 1, p. 5). Over-emphasis characterises his style. His purpose, as a member of the family, is to share his inside information with readers so that they can 'feel at home' (B, 1, p. 6) with the people who are discussed in the letters. He tells a few genial, clubland anecdotes which might have put a few readers at their ease. His antiquarian parade of the minute details of local and family history nevertheless has the effect of making Austen's letters seem to be both difficult and remote. Mrs Humphrey Ward found the opening chapters 'ponderous' as they were full of 'endless strings of names'.[7]

Brabourne, like Austen-Leigh, confronts the issue of satire by asserting that, if there are traces of it, then they must be essentially good-natured because his great-aunt was that kind of person:

> Indeed, it should always be borne in mind during the perusal of these letters that, although, as I have before pointed out, a vein of good-natured satire might generally be found, alike in the letters and conversations of many of the Austen family, it always was good natured, and no malice ever lurked beneath. No one, I imagine, was in reality ever more kind-hearted and considerate of the feelings of others than Jane Austen, and certainly no one was ever better loved or more sorrowfully lamented by the relations whom she left behind her. (B, 1, p. 47)

The repetition of emphatic words such as 'always' and 'ever' is designed to suppress any opposition. Brabourne has more doubts about the spiritual messages of the writing. He admits that he is not able to consider the novels as being specifically 'religious' ones and yet is still confident that they can be read without too much harm. This is because:

> There is a purity of thought as well as of style, an undercurrent of refinement, and an imperceptible suggestion of good which have not

improbably had more salutary effects than any 'religious' novels that have ever been written. (B, 1, p. 110)

An emphatic, patrician style is being used once again to close down discussion.

Brabourne can only maintain this image of the essentially 'good-natured' tone of the letters by tampering with the evidence. He plays down the conflicts that existed within Austen's family by removing the passages that contained criticisms of particular individuals such as James Austen and Mrs Knight. He is generally squeamish over anatomical details and more specifically removes some of Austen's angry comments on the way in which women were forced to breed incessantly. He is, like Austen-Leigh, troubled by Regency coarseness and edits out what he takes to be its worst excesses. Lady Susan O'Brien commented in 1818 on the way in which Regency frankness was already being replaced by a more euphemistic language:

> No one can say 'breeding' or 'with child' or 'lying in', without being thought indelicate. 'In the family way' & 'confinement' have taken their place. 'Cholic' & 'bowels' are exploded words. 'Stomach' signifies everything.[8]

Brabourne imposes his own sense of delicacy on the letters.

Two examples will be sufficient to suggest the more general anxieties that Brabourne had, in private, about the coarseness of the letters. They both come from a letter dated 20 November 1800 where Austen provides Cassandra with an account of a ball at Hurstbourne Park and which will be discussed in more detail in the next chapter. Austen is introduced to some of the other guests and, in her own dramatisation of the event, 'was as civil to them as their bad breath would allow me' (L, p. 92). Brabourne has Austen say, for the benefit of Queen Victoria and his other readers, that she 'was as civil to them as circumstances would allow me' (B, 1, p. 243). The second example comes a little bit earlier and concerns a particularly grotesque description of Mrs Warren. As will become more apparent during the more detailed reading of the letters that follows, Austen gains power in these texts by playing the part of an impatient dramatist who places characters on her stage only to dismiss them briskly and contemptuously. Her description of Mrs Warren's brief appearance on this stage is as follows:

> Mrs. Warren, I was constrained to think a very fine young woman, which I much regret. She has got rid of some part of her child, &

danced away with great activity, looking by no means very large. (L, p. 91)

Brabourne retains the first sentence, but renders the second one as 'She danced away with great activity' (B, 1, p. 243). He was obviously shocked by Austen's implication that the selfish Mrs Warren had lopped and cropped bits off her unborn child so that she is able to dance and be admired for her beauty at the ball.

Sarah Tytler was able to discover a satirical, Regency Austen because her nephew reproduced examples of this kind of writing while firmly maintaining that it did not exist. She was nevertheless unable to argue her case in relation to the letters with any sustained confidence because some of the evidence that she needed had either been suppressed altogether or else rewritten. Brabourne continued the family tradition by seeking to deny the specifically Regency Austen. Both men were working within the conventions for Victorian literary biography and, as Ian Hamilton's study of this genre shows, their suppressions and alterations were not as outrageous as some of those that were undertaken to preserve the reputations of other writers.[9] Yet, of the biographies that were constructed by the Victorians, Austen's is probably the one that has proved to be most resistant to forms of historical contextualisation. As will be shown next, there are still cultural pressures at work to dissociate Austen from a detailed history of the Regency period. There are still attempts to deny that she ever wrote about fleas, naked Cupids and bad breath.

THE MOST ENGLISH AUTHOR

The texts that have just been considered are mainly from the 1870s and 1880s. It is clear that there have been important shifts of emphasis in the Austen industry since then. There has been less concern recently about whether her religious views were entirely safe and sound. Variations on Austen-Leigh's pastoral representations of the Regency period can still be found. There is however another picture which stresses the splendour of Austen's world by foregrounding stately homes, gardens and well-crafted artefacts. This view had its origins in turn-of-the-century studies by Constance Hill and others.[10] Regency England has increasingly been rediscovered as an age of refinement and elegance, which means that there is a tendency to rank Austen higher in class terms than was the case so that she can become part of this high society world. It is eminent Victorians such as Austen-Leigh and Brabourne who are now in danger of being represented as lacking taste. Perhaps the most important change that has taken place concerns the way in which Austen is used, much more explicitly and directly, to promote particular ideas of Englishness. This interpretation began to be asserted in the biographical studies that followed in the wake of Brabourne's edition of the letters. G.E. Mitton declared in 1905 that Austen was the 'most thoroughly English' writer of fiction.[11] This association between Austen and Englishness is currently a particularly powerful one.

Although there have been important changes, the 'received biography' in its various popular forms has proved to be remarkably resistant to the challenges offered to it by both new texts and new critical approaches. It has survived more or less unscathed the publication of a much more complete and accurate edition of the letters in 1932. The publication of more of the Juvenilia has not had as much effect in changing cultural perceptions as it should have done. Austen-Leigh's version of his aunt still has the authority to determine what memories of the author many readers bring with them to the texts because, as will be seen, the portrait of her that he commissioned continues to have a wide circulation. Recent forms of feminist and historical criticism have certainly shown the foundations of this authority to be very insecure, particularly in relation to the continued pronouncements that the writings can be detached from their society. Such revisionist readings, in Britain if not elsewhere, may have helped to reinforce rather than replace the traditional mythology of Austen, which clearly derives a certain strength and self-importance from the opposition to it.

A sense of the gap between academic and more popular studies of Austen can be given by looking very briefly at what was published in 1975. This was the year in which Marilyn Butler argued that Austen's writings needed to be placed back in the context of the literary and political polemics against what were seen as being the excesses of Revolutionary and Napoleonic France. She claimed, more particularly, that the texts carried conservative or anti-Jacobin messages. Although this reading will be challenged here for, amongst other things, placing too much emphasis on endings or resolutions, it still represents one of the landmarks in Austen criticism.[12] Some earlier studies had also insisted upon the need to consider the writings in relation to society. Alistair Duckworth had anticipated some of Butler's conclusions by concentrating on the ideological nature of debates about landscape in this period.[13] Raymond Williams had argued the case for relating the novels to the emergence of new economic structures.[14]

This historically informed work was allowed to play little or no part in celebrations of the bicentenary of Austen's birth in 1975. Patrick

O'Donovan took readers of the *Observer Magazine* on a nostalgic pilgrimage to Chawton Village on 14 December 1975. He assured them that Austen could not possibly have been unhappy there because she lived in 'the sort of house that every civilised man in England now covets'. He associates the Regency period with civilisation rather than with coarseness and implies very strongly that civilisation in any period is a male preserve. All forms of conflict are seen as being alien to 'a society in which everyone seemed content'. O'Donovan acknowledges that this might in fact have been a rather snobbish society but hastens to add that it was only 'a sort of unhurtful, ordered snobbery to which all subscribed'. No historical evidence is offered to support such assumptions.

Wendy Monk invited readers of the December issue of the *Illustrated London News* on a similar journey to this mythological England. Her article was accompanied by an almost full-page reproduction of Austen-Leigh's portrait of his aunt. She represents Austen as a Regency country lady:

> Jane Austen, who was born 200 years ago on December 16, lived in a small world both geographically and socially. Disliking urban surroundings, she relied on the English countryside both for her own happiness and for the background to her novels, which mirrored a society still largely based on the feudal village and the rural life.

Forms of confinement and isolation are viewed positively, even though they may have been represented more negatively by Austen and other women from the period: 'At Chawton the Austen daughters slipped into contented spinsterhood, and, adorably aunthood. Their world was small and isolated. Journeys were slow and uncomfortable.' The Napoleonic Wars are mentioned but are not allowed to disturb the tranquillity of what is taken to be a quintessentially English scene: '. . . a place of woods and hills and muddy lanes and parsonages and seaside towns; a place to parody, and to love. Her England was by no means a "sad place".'[15] Elizabeth Vallance also claimed in the *Guardian* on 17 December that Austen's world was still essentially medieval and that its moral and social certainties provided 'welcome relief' for modern readers. The bicentennial allowed these and many other writers to produce what Patrick Wright calls, in his study of constructions of nostalgia, legends of forgetfulness.[16]

The way in which anything to do with Austen and the houses with which she was associated has become topical or newsworthy, means that it is difficult to select just one example to illustrate this development. Despite the recent coverage of the future of Chawton House,[17] the best example remains an article by Maureen Owen in the *Daily Mail* on 22 October 1987 which was based around the recent publication of Park Honan's biography of Austen. It deals more specifically with a marriage proposal that Austen received in 1802 from Harris Wither, the heir to the 'substantial acres' of Manydown Park. This event is discussed in many earlier biographies, although Honan is able to fill it out through his use of new sources. The *Daily Mail* is initially not concerned with shades of grey and so presents the proposal as a revelation. A come-hither banner headline announces: 'Revealed: The night Jane Austen said "Yes"'. This strongly suggests that the article will deal with more intimate matters than even a marriage proposal.

There is, almost inevitably, a reproduction of the portrait of Austen commissioned by Austen-Leigh below the headline. It has been put inside an oval frame to give it the appearance of a miniature. This obliquely, but nevertheless importantly, reinforces the view of Austen as a miniaturist who was only concerned with reproducing the details of domestic life. As indicated, the continual circulation of this portrait within contemporary British culture illustrates the power still retained by the 'received biography' to determine memories of Austen. *The Times* used a smaller version of it, within a square frame, on the front cover on 20 January 1992 to announce an article on an inside page about Book Aid to the former Soviet Union. The article itself, entitled 'Emma goes East', singles Austen out from all the other writers whose books have been donated as the representative of a particular kind of Englishness. It then seeks to establish contrasts, to which all readers will subscribe, between Austen's rural English gentility and the grim realities of life in the former Soviet states. The idea of *Emma* being a novel about provincial boredom, familiar enough in academic criticism, which may therefore have something in common with the Russian literary tradition, is not canvassed.

There is a caption beside the miniature of Austen in the *Daily Mail* article that reads: 'Jane Austen as we think of her in her spinster's cap; but as a girl she flirted her way through most of the Southern counties'. The revelation is, once again, not as shockingly new as it strives to be. It is based, as the article goes on to point out, on a story that was put into circulation by the mother of Mary Russell Mitford, who described the young Austen as being 'the prettiest, silliest, most affected, husband-hunting butterfly'. Austen-Leigh added a very severe postscript to the first edition of the *Memoir* that was devoted to trying to scotch a rumour that was 'so totally at variance with the modest simplicity of character which I have attributed to my aunt' (M, p. 210).

Some later admirers have not been so troubled by this story. David Rhydderch claims that there is 'nothing derogatory' about it, perhaps because this gives him permission to conduct his own flirtatious relationship with Austen. He agonises about which of her heroines he would like to marry and then decides that he 'will take Jane Austen, and possess them all'. He himself compares her to a peach rather than to a butterfly. Literature is a banquet at which the main courses are provided by male writers such as François Rabelais and Charles Dickens. It is then time for something much softer and sweeter: 'Jane Austen comes in among the sweets, and to the literary palate is as toothsome as a peach'.[18] A more restrained variation on this theme is provided by Lord David Cecil. He casts doubt on the authenticity of the story of Austen as flirt and yet is not prepared to reject it entirely:

> Altogether Mrs Mitford's account must be considered mainly worthless. Personally, I should be sorry to regard it as wholly worthless. I like to think there was a time in Jane Austen's life when she could be called a pretty butterfly. I know of no other woman writer of the first rank who has been similarly described.[19]

The *Daily Mail* article, with its promise to reveal intimate sexual details, panders to the way in which some male critics have transformed Austen into an object of desire.

The article nevertheless makes its initial play for the attention of readers by assuming that they all share a belief that the subjects of sex and sexuality are completely alien to the innocent, Austenesque world. It is an assumption that still pervades contemporary British culture. The *Sunday Telegraph* published an insensitively written article on 7 June 1992 about the way in which sex shops were trying to market themselves as friendly pharmacies rather than as dangerous distributors of pornography. It was accompanied by a cartoon that sought to juxtapose the subject of sex with a cultural icon that was universally acknowledged to be its complete antithesis. A twee, old-fashioned shopfront announces that it is 'Jane Austen's Sex Boutique' and the sign in the window says 'We're in the extremely chaste sex shop guide'. The example is offensive and yet it encapsulates the way in which Austen is often used to symbolise a lost innocence. At one level, it could be argued that modern Regency romances also represent a sexually innocent society. This view nevertheless underestimates the way in which writers like Barbara Cartland suggest links between the sexual mores of the Regency period and those of the 1960s. Both have to be reformed or rolled back, if only partially, by heroines who subscribe to Victorian values.[20] Other texts which associate the Regency period with forms of permissiveness, in a more open and celebratory way, include the 1979 BBC TV serial *Prince Regent*.[21] The continuing authority of the 'received biography' means that contemporary representations of Austen's England are often very different from other Regency reproductions.

Maureen Owen sets up a version of Austen as angel so that she can replace it with Austen as flirt, as if these were the only available alternatives: 'Jane Austen's secret is out at last. The most English author England has ever known, the ideal daughter, sister and aunt who died a spinster at 41, was once engaged – though only for one night.' Austen is described in terms of subordinate relationships with family, marriage and ultimately country. Her literary achievements are acknowledged and then denied at the end of the article where she is described as 'literature's most famous spinster'.[22]

Readers are also presented as miniaturists who are totally obsessed with detail for its own sake. The revelation of Austen's brief engagement is seen as exactly what they want:

> Such minute details are the breath of life to the Jane Austen Society in this country who meet regularly to discuss every aspect of their heroine's life. In America JASNA (the Jane Austen Society of North America) will be rushing news of the fully authenticated engagement into their monthly bulletin.

The bracketing together of these two Societies does a disservice to the North American one. Its journal, *Persuasions*, shows a healthy interplay between the pleasures of the fan club and a concern to promote historically informed critical readings. The English one, by contrast, has always been deeply suspicious of most forms of literary and historical criticism.[23]

Owen then retells the story of how Harris Wither, an aspiring dandy, proposed marriage to Austen. He was accepted only to be refused the next day. It is at this point that readers are given a clearer idea as to why Austen has been introduced as the quintessentially English writer:

> In the beautiful historical setting among lands as green as those she later pictured in Pride and Prejudice, Jane faced the longest night of her life as she began to consider what she had done. Jane's family had recently moved house and Harris's proposal . . . would take her

from Bath which she disliked and restore her to Hampshire which she loved.

Austen's Englishness, here and in some of the other examples that have already been considered briefly, is being defined in two related ways. First of all, it is geographically limited to the 'southern', or the perhaps significantly named Home, counties which are just assumed to stand for England. This misrepresents the geographical range present in the novels themselves, which becomes even wider if the Juvenilia is included. The presentation of Austen as our most English writer nevertheless depends more particularly upon the way that she can always be associated with a forever green and pleasant Hampshire. This is seen as being what Wright calls the real, or deep, England.[24] Secondly, Englishness is being defined in class terms. Owen's scene is set more specifically within the world of the Hampshire upper-gentry. Her story is as much about the status and authority of the country house, Manydown Park, as it is about Austen's own reputation. Although never quite brought to the surface, she seems genuinely puzzled that Austen should have turned down the opportunity to live in the kind of elegant house which would be coveted by modern readers.

Owen sets out to demolish the Victorian image of Austen and yet ends up reinscribing many of the most important parts of it. Austen is still defined and positioned as a spinster. Her personal life is, more generally, also given more importance than her public or literary life. Honan's biography starts uncertainly. Forms of religious dissent are conveniently banished from the village world of early nineteenth-century England. Readers are initially positioned with Frank Austen as he rides back into this green landscape after experiencing some of the harsh realities of the public sphere. Honan nevertheless goes on to demonstrate in some detail important connections between Austen's writings and a Regency society that has not been emptied of scandal. He suggests, and yet does not develop, the idea that *Mansfield Park* can be related to the Regency Crisis debates of 1810/11 that were precipitated when 'a good, self-disciplined King was succeeded by a fat, fair-haired Prince Regent'.[25] Here and elsewhere Austen's writings begin to emerge as being both specifically Regency and often highly topical. This is the real revelation and it is one that Owen, like Austen-Leigh and Brabourne before her, seeks to bury as quickly as possible.

MR COLLINS HUMBLY PRESENTS

The news that London Weekend Television was planning an adaptation of *Pride and Prejudice* that contained nudity caused *The Sun*, a tabloid newspaper not renowned for its previous interest in Austen criticism, to produce a short editorial on the subject on 25 October 1990. It was headlined 'Hanky Panky' and defied anyone to produce a single episode from the written text 'where there was even a stolen kiss or even a handkerchief was doffed'. There is currently some doubt about whether this adaptation will ever be made. The 1980 BBC TV adaptation of *Pride and Prejudice* will be considered here to illustrate the ways in which both Austen and the Regency period have become associated not just with the promotion of a general idea of Englishness but also, more specifically, with the marketing of heritage products.

Five fifty-five minute episodes were transmitted on BBC 2 on Sunday evenings with a repeat in an early evening slot on Wednesdays, which was designed to make the programmes more accessible to younger viewers. It is clear from the numerous editions of the novels that foreground their romance characteristics that Austen remains a best seller in the market that caters for young teenage girls. Broadcasting institutions often justify the quantity of adaptations, which in the earlier 1990s accounted for roughly a third of the drama output, by claiming that they bring new readers to the original texts. This disguises the fact that the writers who are used on a regular basis are the ones who can be relied upon to deliver their own audiences, both popular and educational. Austen's advantage as far as television-makers are concerned is that she is a culturally respected writer who also happens to be a bestseller. The listing of *Pride and Prejudice* in April 1993 as one of the recommended texts for fourteen- to sixteen-year-olds in the attempt to centralise the school curriculum led to an increase in sales. The *Daily Express* carried a feature article on 27 May 1993 that was headlined 'Austen and Hardy Top Sales Charts'. Such developments may help to prolong the already long shelflife of the 1980 television version of *Pride and Prejudice*.

The serial format that was used in the 1980 version is no longer so widespread in adaptations. Classic serials originally drew their inspiration from both radio and stage drama which meant that there was always a strong emphasis on the spoken word.[26] Austen texts were popular choices because they usually contained good dialogue. The letters were sometimes raided and reconstructed on the few occasions when the novels themselves proved to be inadequate. The way in which actors were encouraged to stand and deliver their lines often led to static, or at least stagey, productions. Recent adaptations, such as the

1987 BBC TV *Northanger Abbey*, have often abandoned serialisation altogether in favour of self-contained filmic narratives. This one uses some star performers, is fast-moving, employs both point-of-view and deep-focus shots and generally creates a look that is visually pleasurable. Some of these filmic conventions tend to be employed now, even if elements of the serial format are still retained. Although the television version of *Northanger Abbey* was innovative in many respects, it was also remarkably traditional or classical in the way in which it both heightened and eroticised Catherine Morland's vulnerability.

The text that has been chosen to show connections between Austen and the heritage industries is, then, already itself something of a period piece. It belongs to the same historical moment as The National Heritage Acts which were passed under the Thatcher Conservative Government in 1980 and 1983. As far as television history is concerned, it can be associated with other nostalgic adaptations such as *Brideshead Revisited* (1981) and *Jewel in the Crown* (1983). As far as feature films are concerned, it comes from the same historical period as *Chariots of Fire* (1981). These and the other similar texts that lovingly foregrounded heritage products have been seen, at one level, as essentially Thatcherite in their sympathies. Yet, just as Austen-Leigh's nostalgia takes the form of a rejection of the present as well as an endorsement of it, so these texts can offer contradictory responses to both past and present.[27]

One of the camera's main functions in the adaptation of *Pride and Prejudice* is to produce shots of highly polished Regency tables to complement the equally highly polished dialogues. It shows, and shows off, the various locations which have been chosen to enhance historical authenticity. Houses can be seen as being the star performers. The subdued colour scheme at Longbourn, together with its tastefully arranged Regency furniture, make it the kind of civilised period residence that O'Donovan might covet. It is then contrasted with the loud colours, overblown floral designs and cluttered objects at Netherfield. Lady Catherine de Bourgh holds court at Rosings on a plush pink sofa trimmed with gold. Both Netherfield and Rosings are shown to be florid and gaudy. The early shots of the interiors at Pemberley appear to capture some of the novel's emphasis on the way in which it may combine past with present, money with taste and prestige with responsibility. It is therefore very disconcerting to see Darcy later on entertaining guests in the kind of late Victorian drawing-room in which Austen-Leigh and Brabourne would have been very much at home. This is not to suggest for a moment that Austen adaptations must always be shot in period locations, but rather to indicate the way in which this particular one actively encourages such a close inspection of its historical details.[28]

Mr Bennet is in the library when the rest of the family return from the Meryton Assembly. He snuffs out the candles while Mrs Bennet tries in vain to interest him in gossiping about the dance. Candles are used throughout to light domestic interiors for scenes that take place in the evening. This also happens in the television version of *Northanger Abbey*. These adaptations thus follow Austen-Leigh by presenting Regency England as an essentially pre-industrial era. There is a category of popular Regency romance fiction called 'Candlelight Regency Specials'. Candlelight is used here to evoke a sense of historical difference and to prepare the way for a pleasurable escape from a harshly lit modern world. Horse-drawn transport is frequently foregrounded in order to provide the same compact, nostalgic visual images. As will be suggested during the reading of *Emma*, these glossy images, which are often based around James Pollard's coaching prints, deny the way in which transport owned by men could be seen by Regency women as symbolising their own powerlessness and confinement. As Robert Hewison has argued, we are usually encouraged to 'look back in nostalgia' rather than in anger.[29]

The snuffing out of the candles in the library is just one of the occasions when stage business is closely linked to the display of period objects. Earlier historical dramas, such as the 1940 Hollywood film of *Pride and Prejudice* and Gainsborough melodramas, tended to use costumes rather than objects or artefacts to signify the past.[30] One of the distinctive features of texts from the 1980s is the opening up of what Andrew Higson describes as 'heritage space'. He argues that the display of period objects has marginalised the telling of the story itself in the 'narrative space'.[31] Examples of this include Charlotte Collins cleaning the leg of a Chippendale chair while talking to Elizabeth and Mrs Bennet holding a Staffordshire pottery ornament, which needs to be arranged on a mantlepiece, for one of her entrances.

Adaptations have become television's equivalent of the coffee-table book. Susan Watkins claims in *Jane Austen's Town and Country Style* (1990) that the Regency gentry were a 'group of people of unsurpassed elegance and refinement'. The aim of her lavishly illustrated account is to allow readers 'to wander, to gaze and to gain an almost tactile understanding of this world'. She wants them to imagine 'the muffled clink of crystal touching mahogany'.[32] Nigel Nicolson's *The World of Jane Austen* (1991) is mainly concerned with Regency architecture and offers a guided tour of most of the houses with which Austen was associated. He is also concerned to represent the period more generally as one of unsurpassed craftsmanship:

> Objects of everyday use like crockery, clothes, tools, chairs, were beautifully made, and in making them the craftsmen shared in the pleasure of the better-off who bought them. What is almost inexplicable is their unerring sense of colour and proportion. Nothing in the middle-class house was strident, nothing ungainly, nothing shoddy. Never had the building and furniture trades been so efficient. Everything was made to last; everything functioned as intended. A man without natural discrimination need not worry how he furnished his house, for there was nothing on sale which could disfigure it.[33]

A fantasy of total perfection is projected back onto the Regency period so that it becomes a safe haven that is completely uncontaminated by what are taken to be the vulgarities of the modern world. Maggie Lane claims in *Jane Austen's England* (1989) that the Georgians 'were incapable of building anything ugly'.[34] Joanna Richardson's earlier study also sees this period as the last time that real craftsmanship was prized and artefacts were 'free of foreign influence, they were wholly English, they were part of the organic whole'.[35] Less strident versions of these cultural fantasies often control and mediate the way in which Austen texts are represented on television. This helps to explain the slow movement of such programmes which are designed, unlike the classical Hollywood film of *Pride and Prejudice*, to allow viewers to feel as if they are wandering through either period locations or museums.

One of the contradictions at the heart of this particular adaptation is that, while it retains some of the novel's critique of Mr Collins, it also celebrates his habit of enumerating the contents of a room and the courses of a meal. He draws up an inventory as soon as he arrives at Longbourn: 'The Hall, the dining-room, and all its furniture were examined and praised' (PP, p. 109). He is immediately 'much struck with the size and furniture of the apartment' (PP, p. 119) when he dines at Mrs Philips's house. He passes the carriage journey back to Longbourn 'enumerating all the dishes at supper' (PP, p. 127). When Elizabeth visits Hunsford Parsonage, she is forced by him 'to admire every article of furniture in the room, from the sideboard to the fender' (PP, p. 192). She is expected to be equally engrossed by 'his enumeration of the windows in the front of the house, and his relation of what the glazing altogether had originally cost Sir Lewis de Bourgh' (PP, p. 196) when they walk to Rosings.

Mr Collins quite literally gets his hands on Mrs Bennet's possessions when he first dines at Netherfield in the television version. He admires the way in which the dining-room chairs match, turns over the cutlery to check out the hallmarks and then pings his wineglass to make sure that it is the genuine article. The camera has its own ways of pinging a wineglass and enumerating all the objects, including the gleaming fenders, in a room. It also resembles Mr Collins in its obsessions with food. The party at Longbourn for the departing officers opens with a shot of a table groaning with pies and similar delicacies. The camera also enumerates some of the dishes that are served when Wickham and Lydia Bennet return to Longbourn. Game pie is the gentry equivalent of the ploughman's lunch in this world of heritage reconstructions. There is a reference to food in a letter that Austen wrote to Cassandra in February 1813 when she was correcting the proofs of *Pride and Prejudice*: 'There might as well have been no suppers at Longbourn; but I suppose it was the remains of Mrs Bennett's [*sic*] old Meryton habits' (L, p. 300). Although difficult to interpret with certainty, it appears as though she is conscious that the novel does not represent the Bennet family at mealtimes. The television adaptation, by contrast, more than makes up for such omissions. The spectacle of both the Regency and Edwardian upper classes eating was a particularly common one during the 1980s. The film versions of E.M. Forster's novels are almost patterned around scenes involving meals, as well as ones foregrounding travel and sport. It is no accident that the adaptation of *Northanger Abbey* creates a relatively long scene out of the brief description of Catherine's first dinner at the Abbey.

The camera finds its own way of embodying the 'monotonous solemnity' (PP, p. 113) of Collins's voice. Its obsequiousness captures not only the spirit of his deference towards Lady Catherine but also, by extension, television's deference towards a culturally respectable figure like Austen. The existence of this solemn, enumerating camera produces one truly astonishing shot. It is Collins's point-of-view of the five sisters as he enumerates them just as if they were like any of the other objects in the house.

The tendency of the adaptation to allow Elizabeth to become the 'elegant female' of conduct literature, seen at its most extreme when Collins is granted this particular point-of-view shot, is continued in some of its commercial spin-offs. The front cover of the 1982 Macmillan Students' Novels edition uses a production still of Elizabeth and Darcy in a rural setting. It is Darcy who is given the power of direct address, in other words of looking directly at the camera and therefore at the reader. Elizabeth is demurely looking down and is thus different from the female figures who appear on most academic, as opposed to popular romance, editions of Austen's texts who have a form of direct address. She is wearing a high-waisted white dress and a short velvet jacket. Her cloche hat sits neatly on top of carefully arranged ringlets. Her white gloves and satin parasol add the finishing touches to her elegant appearance. Illustrations inside the volume include the Austen-Leigh portrait of Austen and a picture of Manydown Park, which is described as 'a typical upper-class country house of the period'.[36]

Adaptation is a safe form of television not just because certain writers can always be relied upon to deliver the home audience, but also because it sells well abroad. This one was made in association with the Australian Broadcasting Commission. Overseas buyers, like the American producers of Masterpiece Theatre, have often been so convinced of the strength of British television's reputation in the field of heritage drama as to take a serial sight unseen. They know that they will eventually hear the reassuring sound of crystal on mahogany.[37]

The rules governing forms of public service broadcasting may prevent the open display of designer labels. There is nevertheless nothing to stop adaptations from providing a more general showcase for quality British products together with the heritage industries. The way in which Austen adaptations use historic homes and gardens for their principal locations obviously provides a good advertisement at home and abroad for the tourist industry. It may also help to stimulate the property market. The *Evening Standard* carried a story on 13 May 1992 about a Thatcherite tycoon who had recently purchased Ashe Park in Hampshire. His financial investment is seen as being enhanced by the Austen connection: 'As something of a bonus there is a literary association – Jane Austen, the daughter of the local rector was a frequent visitor and apparently based some of her novels on events at Ashe Park.' The fact that, according to one way of reading the relevant letter, Austen was once trapped in a room here while the owner harassed her is not mentioned because it is in conflict with images of civilisation and refinement. The present owner uses the house to entertain overseas business clients, who think it is 'quaint'. He also has plans to market a product called Ashe Park Spring Water. The article suggests that advertising the bottles will present no problem: 'Jane Austen would probably have been quite happy to have had them on her dining table'. Austen's name is also used in adaptations to associate an elegant lifestyle with particular products.

The furniture, particularly that used at Longbourn, provides a showcase for the Regency reproduction industry. A lot of the china is

Wedgwood. General Tilney's view, rendered as dialogue in the television text of *Northanger Abbey* to fill out the dinner scene, that people should purchase their pottery from Staffordshire rather than from Dresden as a way of stimulating the national economy is one that is emphatically endorsed in heritage television. Russell Davies noticed in his review in *The Sunday Times* on 27 January 1980 that Elizabeth and Jane's dresses were 'very Laura Ashley'. It could also be argued that Austen adaptations provide welcome publicity for all those products and services which choose to associate themselves with the Regency period. British telephone directories show that the label Regency is frequently linked to leisure activities: eating, drinking, dancing, travelling and gambling. Connotations of leisure are overlaid with more specific messages about exclusivity. The term is most frequently traded under by hairdressers. It sets up in this context expectations not just of leisure and exclusivity, but also of elegance, refinement and personal service. Hair will be arranged rather than merely cut.

It has been argued that this adaptation is concerned to promote heritage in general and heritage products in particular. It would be dangerous, however, to imply that the kind of social tourism that is an integral part of the promotion of heritage is totally alien to the novel itself. The lack of detailed information about Austen's Regency readership has meant that too much weight has probably been placed upon the opinions which she herself collected from family and friends about the reception of *Mansfield Park* and *Emma*. Some of these views perhaps inevitably give the impression of novels for the gentry by one of the gentry. Mrs Pole enjoyed reading them because 'they are so evidently written by a Gentlewoman'. She went on to affirm that everything about them 'clearly evinces the Writer to *belong* to the Society whose Manners she so ably delineates' (MW, p. 435). This does not register the way in which Austen was positioned both inside and outside the world of the greater gentry.[38] The other problem with Mrs Pole's comments is that they tend to rule out the possibility that for many Regency readers the pleasures of *Pride and Prejudice* might have been to do with the way in which, rather than preserving exclusive worlds, it made them more inclusive. In other words, the guided tour of Pemberley which is given to Elizabeth and the Gardiners may need to be seen as only the most explicit instance of the way in which the novel itself guided some of its readers around unfamiliar locations.

This period witnessed, if not quite the birth of forms of domestic tourism, then certainly their rapid expansion and commercialisation. A lot of material will be provided later on about the growth of watering places as this is a major, although still neglected, theme in Austen's writings. Ian Ousby is right, however, in his study of the historical evolution of tourism in England to insist that watering places need to be considered alongside the development of other attractions such as country houses, ruins and picturesque landscapes. Austen's representations of country houses as potential tourist attractions should be related to such wider social developments.[39] The way in which her writings were associated with a narrow form of domestic realism, not just by members of her family but also by some of the earlier publishers, has tended to prevent these connections with tourism and therefore with movement from being made. Richard Bentley's complete edition of the novels in 1833 declared that 'she is emphatically the novelist of home'.[40] This was meant to differentiate her quite clearly from the 'silver-fork' novelists of the period whose popularity was based on the way in which they allowed readers through-the-keyhole access to an often scandalous high society world. The argument here and later on is that there may be some similarities, as well as many differences, between Austen and such novelists. Television adaptations badly overstate the case by making a fetish of the silver fork itself and yet, with all their faults, they may still be capable of recovering some important themes.

Monica Lauritzen records a revealing detail about the design of the 1972 BBC TV version of *Emma*. The institutional emphasis on providing 'heritage space' for period objects, present then and intensified since, meant that there had to be a reproduction of Harriet Smith's riddle-book, which is described in the novel as just being 'a thin quarto of hot-pressed paper' (E, p. 95). The person who was given the task of making this prop went off and did some research. This probably involved looking at period pictures and visiting museums. This in turn led to the creation of what Lauritzen describes as a 'beautiful volume decorated with pressed flowers and a variety of pictures'.[41] It was the kind of quality product that the mythical Austen would have been only too happy to have had on her elegant table. The problem was that this sumptuous and substantial Regency reproduction looked far too good. Harriet's thin book should indicate the flimsiness of her character. This anecdote illustrates Lauritzen's main thesis that television invariably celebrates elegant surfaces whereas Austen's novels are much more concerned to explore discrepancies between surfaces, particularly conversational ones, and substance.

The reproduction of Harriet's riddle-book suggests that adaptations are authored by all those who translate the institutional commitment to promote heritage into practice. They can be seen, more particularly, as being a set designer's medium. Such a view of collective, or institutional, authorship is nevertheless frequently denied by adaptations themselves. The individuals who are credited as the authors of the television version of *Pride and Prejudice* are Austen herself and Fay Weldon. Weldon published *Letters to Alice on First Reading Jane Austen* four years after the adaptation was first transmitted. Austen emerges from this account as a somewhat reticent supporter of feminism in a society that is characterised by extreme forms of both mental and physical cruelty towards women. Weldon writes particularly effectively about medical history, which is a topic that will also be dealt with in some detail later on here. Although there is a short gap between these two texts, the question still remains as to why their versions of Austen are so different.[42]

One answer, which has been emphasised here, is that the institutional commitment to promoting heritage means that, irrespective of the views of the credited adaptor, the heirs of Mr Collins will always be allowed to hold the camera. Another response is to see the television text as being made up of conflicting and contradictory interpretations. It encourages viewers to see Elizabeth as an 'elegant female', despite her own comments during the proposal scene with Mr Collins, while at the same time drawing attention to some of the arguments in the written text about the social position of women. The themes of sisterhood and female friendship are visualised in scenes involving Elizabeth and Jane. There are also recurring shots of one or more of the Bennet sisters looking out of a window, perhaps inspired not just by the written text itself but also by some of the paintings of the period. They watch events from which they are excluded, such as the departure of Mr Bennet for Netherfield and the arrival of Bingley to return the call. They wait for events to happen over which they have no control, such as the delivery of letters from men to explain their mysterious movements and motives. These shots, which are rarely accompanied by dialogue, have a visual and thematic density that works against the emphasis on surfaces. Heritage images of historic homes and gardens lose some of their conservative meanings if these homes are also visualised as genteel prisons. The adaptation goes some way towards suggesting that an elegant sash-window can be looked at, and looked through, in very different ways.

CONCLUSIONS

The origins, growth and remarkable survival of the Austen industry are complex cultural developments that have had to be approached here, for reasons of space, through a limited range of central texts. These have been a family memoir, a newspaper article and a television serial. The final chapter will add another text to this list by considering the way in which a modern writer has completed one of Austen's unfinished novels. Although the main emphasis of this study of the Regency writings will be on relationships between them and their immediate historical contexts, these texts from later periods have been introduced early on in the argument as a way of showing at least some of the different associations that the term Regency has acquired from the Victorian period through to the present day. It has been variously represented as being a pastoral idyll, an era of ugly coarseness, a feudal society, a period of unsurpassed elegance, the age of craftsmanship, a time of scandal and a world of innocence. Despite this seeming variety, the particular reproductions of the Regency that have acquired a cultural authority in relation to Austen are ones that seek to distance her writings from most aspects of a society that when looked at historically resists reduction to these single catchphrases and labels. This is why such reproductions merit some attention here.

Popular modern texts are relevant to the academic study of Austen since readers construct an idea of the author, and therefore of her works and their historical period, from the materials that are readily available within a particular culture at a particular time. It would be very arrogant indeed to assume that all those who teach or study Austen are necessarily exempt from, rather than implicated in, this cultural process. Another point that needs emphasising is that popular modern texts can recover some important meanings, at the same time as they are attempting to close down others. The only example that there has been room to discuss here in any detail is the possibility that television adaptations may help to alert readers, more than academic criticism has done until recently, to the ways in which the novels offer the pleasures of social tourism. A number of other examples could have been considered. As mentioned, one of the reasons why Austen's novels are adapted on such a regular basis is because of the theatrical nature of her writing. Academic criticism has not been silent on this issue and yet, as the profusion of simplistic readings of *Mansfield Park* as an anti-theatrical novel indicates, it could still learn something from these more popular texts. The attempts to visualise some of the male characters, on the covers of popular editions and in girls' annuals as well as on television, draw attention to the ways in which the novels may be debating dandyism, which is another subject that does not figure prominently in academic criticism. Austen-Leigh did his best to distance his aunt from the Regency period itself. Those who believe that she should also be sealed off from the Regency reproductions that circulate freely within modern cultures are in danger of following his lead.

Part II
The Regency rediscovered

2 The letters: Keeping and losing her countenance

INTRODUCTION

This chapter begins the process of establishing Regency contexts for Austen's writings, as well as situating them within critical debates. Cassandra Austen has often been blamed for destroying some of her sister's letters which may have contained forthright opinions on family and wider matters. It seems likely that she did indeed burn letters and other documents in the years just before her death in 1845. Jo Modert nevertheless suggests that there are also other explanations as to why some of the letters did not survive. Other members of the family such as Henry Austen and his connections suppressed the collections that were in their possession. Some letters held by the family may have been dispersed later on in the century to provide collectors with autographs.[1] One of the arguments here and later on is that the surviving letters should be seen as being both an important literary text and a historical source rather than as a collection that always has to be read with disappointment because of what it might have contained.

The aim of this particular chapter is not to dwell too much on biography but, rather, to concentrate more on some of the thematic and stylistic features of the letters which are repeated in the Regency novels. The first section explores the way in which the letters alternate between keeping and then losing what Austen and her contemporaries called countenance, as a way of contributing to the critical debate about their abusiveness. This is followed by a closely related argument which brings out their highly theatrical qualities and thus their Regency tone. The third section suggests that the representation of themes such as invalidism needs to be seen as being both sustained and political. These sections discuss the letters as a whole, whereas the final one offers a reading of a single letter in order to fill out some of the previous points, as well as to look more closely at thematic movement and structure. Contexts that are established by the chapter include the material conditions for letter writing in this period, as well as letters written by other Regency women.

FORCED TO BE ABUSIVE

Marilyn Butler argues that Austen's letters were not written to please other people but, rather, 'to resist, to challenge, and, in her private mental universe, to master them'.[2] Warren Roberts discovers a more divided author who alternates between socially acceptable remarks and 'eruptions of ill feeling and verbal malice'.[3] Other critics have, like Butler, found essentially narcissistic narratives that celebrate self and challenge those who threaten its supremacy. Joseph Kestner sees the main theme as being 'the self contemplated, particularly the self contemplated at the moment', a view that is also developed more historically by James Thompson.[4] Butler's remarks provide a useful starting point for a reading of the letters, even if her assumptions about the rigid differences between them and the novels have to be rejected straightaway. Other necessary qualifications will be indicated during the course of the argument.

Austen spent the autumn of 1813 staying with two of her elder brothers. She visited Henry in London and saw lots of plays, as well as the 'naked Cupids' in the schoolroom. She then journeyed to stay at Godmersham, the country house in Kent which Edward had inherited. She wrote to Cassandra at the end of October to share a joke about a visit that a party from the big house had paid to a Mrs Milles and her daughter Molly:

> Miss Milles was queer as usual, and provided us with plenty to laugh at. She undertook in *three words* to give us the history of Mrs. Scudamore's reconciliation, and then talked on about it for half-an-hour, using such odd expressions, and so foolishly minute, that I could hardly keep my countenance. (L, pp. 360–1)

Mr Scudamore, sometimes abbreviated to Scud, was the medical man in attendance at Godmersham. It seems probable that Molly is gossiping about matrimonial problems, since the letter goes on to make it reasonably clear that Mrs Scudamore has been reconciled with her husband. Austen's public behaviour is inhibited in the sense that she just about manages to keep a straight face while having to endure a rambling account of the Scudamores' personal difficulties. This part of the letter to Cassandra provides her with an opportunity to lose the public countenance which she has to wear to please other people.

It is possible then to follow Butler and see Austen's letters as representing a potentially unrestrained space in which she did not always have to keep her countenance, or wear an acceptable mask. Such a reading is also available as far as other women letter writers of the Regency period are concerned. Dorothy Jordan attended Methodist services when she was playing at theatres in Lancashire, partly out of a curiosity to see the type of people who sent her letters denouncing the wickedness of the theatre. She wanted to laugh out loud at what she took to be the ridiculous antics of the preachers and their congregations, but had to reserve her laughter for her letters back home.[5] Mary Shelley, in a letter written in 1825, noticed the way in which she was able to remain silent in public only to 'gallop over fence & ditch without pity for my reader' when the pen was in her hand.[6]

It still has to be remembered, however, that letters were frequently treated in this period as being like newspapers, to be read and widely discussed throughout a particular social circle. This was especially true for the Austens as far as those that contained naval intelligence were concerned. Jane also used to open and reply to letters for Cassandra when her sister was away. D.W. Harding is right to suggest that families as well as neighbourhoods were full of what Henry Tilney describes as 'voluntary spies' (NA, p. 199).[7] Princess Charlotte's letters contain a number of references to her fear that she herself was being spied on and that her letters might also be under surveillance.[8] The connections between letter writing and espionage are dealt with very skilfully by Mary A. Favret, who shows that this was a period in which an embattled state maintained itself by intercepting and sometimes fabricating the correspondence of its enemies both at home and abroad. The radical Corresponding Societies of the 1790s were subjected to this kind of surveillance, despite their attempts to maintain that letters as opposed to newspapers ought to be treated as private documents. Some male radicals tried to evade the attentions of government spies by using female subjects such as dress-making as a coded language for conspiracy. Favret's study also provides important reminders of the way in which political debates were frequently conducted in the form of open letters. Her work indicates that it is much too simplistic just to equate the letter with private space.[9]

Austen's letters to mere acquaintances appear to have been written with a more or less straight face. A Miss Irvine wrote to her in 1807 when she was living at Southampton with a reproach for being a slow correspondent. She gives Cassandra a quick sketch of Miss Irvine's epistolary style: 'the first page is in her usual retrospective, jealous, inconsistent style, but the remainder is chatty and harmless'. She then outlines how she had responded to Miss Irvine's rebukes:

> I have answered her letter, and have endeavoured to give something like the truth with as little incivility as I could, by placing my silence to the want of subject in the very quiet way in which we live. (L, p. 171)

Civility was not always so necessary in at least some of the letters that were written to Cassandra, Martha Lloyd and, later on, to the nieces. Austen's letters to all of them are certainly chatty but not always harmless, although Roberts's view that there is usually an alternation within a single letter between the polite and the abusive still needs to be taken seriously.

The want of a subject often appears to be the subject in Austen's letters, as it is in those of most other Regency women. Some critics have, however, taken her more playful confessions that she was not overburdened with subject matter a little too literally. She uses it after all as a convenient, conventional excuse when writing to Miss Irvine. Lady Louisa Stuart appears to do the same when, after having kept a letter in her pocket for a month by mistake, she claimed that 'leading an uniform life and having little to say must be my excuse for not writing sooner'.[10] There were certainly occasions when Austen had to construct a 'smartish' (L, p. 181) letter out of what appeared to be nothing. She often succeeded in doing so. Ellen Weeton, a Regency governess, described such letters as being much ado about nothing. Hester Piozzi quoted directly from Shakespeare's play itself when she labelled these kind of letters as being 'all mirth and no matter'.[11] The novelist Susan Ferrier referred to them as 'parish news' letters.[12] Only aristocratic political hostesses such as Lady Bessborough could escape from the necessity for such letters. Even she complained on occasions that she had nothing to say because the evening papers had already published all of her news.

Austen declares in one of her letters: 'I am forced to be abusive for want of subject, having nothing really to say.' She had just treated Cassandra to the opinion that Sir Brook Bridges, a widower with three children, 'has no right to look higher than his daughter's Governess' (L, p. 186) when considering another marriage. She plays the powerful part of the match-maker here and elsewhere in the letters. Abuse, as Butler implies, nevertheless needs to be seen as a main theme, rather than as something that only occurs when there is apparently nothing left to say. Molly Milles is after all abused in the middle of a letter that has plenty of other things, civil as well as uncivil, to say. Austen's abusiveness in the letters can, with qualifications, be seen in terms of a temporary loss of the countenance that has to be worn publicly, in the letters themselves as well as in more obviously social situations. The individual examples can be related to a central theme. The letters as a whole provide her with opportunities to fashion events and people into a script over which she has control or 'mastery'. She is forced to be abusive in order to gain and retain this control. She becomes a powerfully impatient dramatist, who only just has time to abuse characters, before contemptuously dismissing them from her stage.

The material conditions under which letters were written in this period can, to some extent, be held responsible for Austen's impatient tone. The government raised money for the war against France by putting up postage charges on a regular basis: in 1801, 1805 and then again in 1812 when a penny was added to the mileage rates that were charged for letters outside London. The cost of letters had always been one of their main themes. Lady Sarah Lennox complained in 1784 of the way in which 'Mr Pitt's vile postage regulations' might force her 'to write just as the servants do, once a quarter or so, to say "I hope you are as well as I am, etc"'.[13] Such complaints became particularly acute during the war years. Lady Sarah Spencer tried to write every day to her brother, who was a midshipman. She commented on the cost of this habit in 1808: 'Why didn't you tell me before that my letters cost you 15d a piece – 8 shillings and 9d a week! How very hard on a poor middy'.[14] Ferrier told Charlotte Clavering in 1809 that she had had to pay nine shillings for just two of her friend's letters.

As will already be clear, letters in this period were usually paid for by the recipient rather than by the sender. The number of sheets that they contained, together with the distance carried, was used to calculate the charge. The recipient not only had to pay the high charges but was also usually expected, particularly in rural areas, to collect letters from the post office.[15] One of Austen's earlier letters apologises for the fact that she has not used all of the available space: 'Do not be angry with me for not filling my sheet' (L, p. 53). She was conscious later on of the difference between her 'wide lines' (L, p. 228) and Cassandra's more densely packed scripts. A later letter ends by saying that economy must take precedence over news: 'I must finish it now, that I may save you 2d' (L, p. 441). It was fairly standard practice for letters to be 'crossed', or written both horizontally and vertically, in order that they might remain as cheap as possible. According to Miss Bates in *Emma*, this was what Jane Fairfax usually did: 'in general she fills the whole paper and crosses half' (E, p. 171). There were, then, strong economic pressures on most letter writers to write succinctly and they may well have played their part in the creation of Austen's impatient, dismissive tone. It has to be said, however, that not all writers faced with the same pressures produced this kind of letter.

Ellen Weeton's letters, to take just one main example, are similar to Austen's in that they use abuse to gain control but they are also different in that they lack an impatient, dismissive tone. Weeton enjoyed playing at imaginary conversations in which she '*always* comes off victorious in every argument'.[16] Her letters, like those of other Regency women, are an extended series of such imaginary conversations. She was employed by Edward Pedder in 1809 to be a governess for his daughter by a previous marriage and moved to Dove's Nest in the Lake District. Pedder's second wife had been a dairymaid and was much younger than him. He emerges from Weeton's letters as an unpleasant Regency bully, who prefers drinking with the servants to talking to his wife. He locks her out of the house on the slightest provocation and is mean with money. One of the ways in which he demonstrates his power is by insisting that both his wife and governess eat meals only when it suits him to do so. This means that they have to put up with late breakfasts and dinners. Weeton's revenge is to use her letters, as well as a journal, to record all of his many weaknesses.

The child whom Weeton was supposed to look after burnt herself to death by standing too close to a fire. Pedder's manner of grieving becomes another item that is entered in the catalogue of his crimes. Weeton describes this in a letter to her brother in 1810:

> The afternoon before the corpse was taken away, thinking perhaps he should be accused of want of feeling, he went, completely drunk, into the room where the body lay, and worked himself up into almost a complete frenzy; lying down by the side of the coffin, getting astride of it, pulling and mawling the body, till the servants attending durst stay no longer in the room, expecting every moment he would have it out of the coffin.

This is part of a longer description. Lest her brother should feel any sympathy for Pedder who had, it could be argued, employed a governess to stop his daughter from having such accidents, he is informed that this display of grief was clearly theatrical because her employer 'thought more of the expense of the funeral than the loss of his child'.[17]

Weeton abuses Pedder and yet is reluctant to dismiss him, or to let go of him. After reading Austen's letters, hers often seem very long-winded. This is perhaps because she appears to have written with publication in mind, being careful to keep copies of all the letters that she sent. Her description of a local painter, Mr Green, has Austen-esque touches but it is much too long and contrived:

> Green is a man of good size, rather inclining to corpulent, and good, solid, thick legs. His eyes are black and somewhat small, and he does peep so queerly with them! His eyes both look one way, to be sure, but I can seldom catch them looking straight forward. A stranger that was addressed by him, would imagine he was talking to some-one else; or if no other person was in the room, would stare about him, wondering what the fellow was talking to. Green talks a good deal in an inflated style, and always looks sideways at the object he is speaking to; when he looks directly forward, it is at some piece of furniture or other inanimate object, still talking all the while. I have much ado to keep my countenance when I hear and see him, though really the man means well; . . .[18]

This comes towards of the middle of a lengthy, self-conscious character study. Weeton, like Austen, can keep one countenance in public and at times another in the relative privacy of her letters. Unlike Austen, however, her need to be abusive usually takes the form of extended essays on character. A squinting painter might only have merited a line or two in Austen's letters, just as Dorothy Jordan does not waste too much time on a squinting actor with whom she was once offered the chance to work. She was given a choice between this actor and one whom she claims had no nose:

> I had indeed the choice of two, but the other was *stone deaf* and squinted so *intolerably* that it would be *impossible* to look in his face without laughing. The other is a melacholy sight and I shall at least keep my countenance.[19]

Countenance usually had to be kept both on the stage itself and in the stage-play world of Regency society. There were, however, some opportunities to lose it when writing letters.

The writers of influential eighteenth-century conduct manuals such as James Fordyce and John Gregory were particularly concerned that a woman's countenance should always reveal her true character. Fordyce declared that a blush could be read as 'the precious colouring of virtue'. He was disgusted by the idea that some women could wear a virtuous face in public even though they had no right to do so, which is just how Austen's Lady Susan is allowed to behave. He wanted them to be 'put out of countenance', or made to appear as who they really were.[20] Gregory was also attracted by blushing, claiming that 'when a girl ceases to blush, she has lost the most powerful charm of beauty'. He went on to contrast faces that openly displayed modesty with the 'unabashed countenance' that seemed to defy society and its conventions.[21] Some parts of the letters written by Austen and other Regency women confirm the worst fears of the conduct writers.

Lady Bessborough described in a letter written in 1810 how one of her aristocratic acquaintances proceeded to abuse people just as soon as they had left the room:

> Nothing escapes: character, understanding, opinions, dress, person, age, infirmity – all fall equally under the scalping knife, and no sooner has the wretched person closed the door than the shouts of laughter proclaim to him that he is under the dissection he has witnessed of others, and which you felt assured will be your lot as soon as you also quit the room.[22]

As Ruth Richardson has shown, anxieties about dissection were widespread in early nineteenth-century society. The surgeons regarded the legitimate supply of corpses from the gallows as being insufficient for their purposes and so lent silent support to the activities of the bodysnatchers who raided the graveyards for more bodies. One of Richardson's most interesting sources for the Regency period itself is the diary of a bodysnatcher, Joshua Naples.[23] The male surgeons were greatly feared, particularly in working-class communities, because they exerted power over dead as well as live bodies. Austen could not become a surgeon and yet her letters, as will become more apparent, provide some opportunities for a series of metaphorical dissections, with abuse often being used as the knife.

THE IMPATIENT DRAMATIST

Austen appears to have been an avid reader of newspapers, even though she may have sometimes had difficulty getting hold of them. She referred in 1813 to 'our newspaper' (L, p. 297), although on other occasions it is clear that she had to borrow them from men. She occasionally alluded to some of their more sensational stories: a family who were almost frozen to death in a blizzard and a madwoman who escaped from confinement. Alison Sulloway notes that the letters as a whole contain 'inventories of one poor woman after another'.[24] Austen was also particularly interested in what the newspapers had to say about high society scandals, naval intelligence and forthcoming marriages. Mrs Powlett's elopement caught her eye in 1808:

> This is a sad story about Mrs. Powlett. I should not have suspected her of such a thing. – She staid the Sacrament I remember, the last

time that you & I did. – A hint of it, with Initials, was in yesterday's Courier; and Mr Moore guessed it to be Ld Sackville, beleiving [*sic*] there was no other Viscount S. in the peerage, & so it proved – Ld Viscount Seymour not being there. (L, p. 197)

The religious reference and tone early on certainly accord with the saintly version of Austen produced by her family. She then changes her countenance and reveals the delight that she and Moore, who was a clergyman, took in deciphering the riddles of the gossip column.

Naval news was eagerly scanned in order to gather any details about the movements of her two brothers, Charles and Frank, when they were on active service. Sarah Spencer describes how every time she picked up a newpaper she 'flew as usual to the ship-news'.[25] Jane passed on some news to Cassandra in 1800 that had been gathered from Mr Holder's newspaper:

Mr Holder's paper tells us that sometime in last August, Capt: Austen & the Petterell were very active in securing a Turkish ship (driven into a Port in Cyprus by bad weather) from the French. – He was forced to burn her however. – You will see the account in the Sun I dare say. (L, p. 87)

Mr Holder, the owner of Ashe Parke, made 'infamous puns' (L, p. 85) and it may be that his general behaviour towards women was infamous as well. Austen told her sister in 1801 of how she found herself unwittingly trapped in a room with him:

Your unfortunate sister was betrayed last Thursday into a situation of the utmost cruelty. I arrived at Ashe Park before the Party from Deane, and was shut up in the drawing-room with Mr Holder alone for ten minutes. I had some thoughts of insisting on the housekeeper or Mary Corbett being sent for, and nothing could prevail on me to move two steps from the door, on the lock of which I kept one hand constantly fixed. (L, p. 117)

The evidence, if read literally, certainly suggests that Mr Holder might have harassed her. There may, alternatively, be elements of literary parody here that depend upon there being a comic discrepancy between Holder and a Richardsonian villain.

Austen sometimes seems to have been left clutching at straws in much the same way as the Bennet women in *Pride and Prejudice* have to ascertain Mr Bingley's movements through rumour and surmise. She passed on some news that was at least third-hand to Cassandra in 1801: 'Eliza talks of having read in a Newspaper that all the Ist Lieuts of the Frigates whose Captains were to be sent into Line-of-Battle ships were to be promoted to the rank of Commanders' (L, p. 113). Although this looks like wishful thinking, there were in fact promotions throughout the navy at this time as a result of the union between Great Britain and Ireland.

Austen clearly also spent time reading the coverage of engagements and marriages in the newspapers. She declared to Anna Lefroy in an undated letter that 'one may as well stay single, if the wedding is not to be in print' (L, p. 422). She spotted details of the Reverend Samuel Blackall's marriage in a newspaper and wrote to her brother Frank in 1813 to see whether he could supply any further gossip:

> I wonder whether you happened to see Mr Blackall's marriage in the Papers last Jany. *We* did. He was married at Clifton to a Miss Lewis, whose Father had been late of Antigua. I should very much like to know what sort of Woman she is. He was a piece of Perfection, noisy Perfection himself which I always recollect with regard. (L, pp. 316–17)

Blackall is usually seen by biographers as being one of Austen's early admirers. Two years earlier she picked up from the newspapers a more scandalous account of the marriage of one of her cousins and relayed it to Cassandra:

> You certainly must have heard before I can tell you that Col. Orde has married our cousin, Margt. Beckford, the Marchess. of Douglas's sister. The papers say that her father disinherits her, but I think too well of an Orde to suppose that she has not a handsome independence of her own. (L, p. 280)

Margaret Beckford was the daughter of William Beckford, who built perhaps the ultimate Regency folly at Fonthill Abbey. The comedy is closer to the surface here than it is at other points in the letters: Austen affects to think well of Orde for being a fortune-hunter. A personal or family connection with a particular wedding was important, but not absolutely essential, for it to become part of the gossip between the two sisters. Austen was amused in 1808 by an item that she had read in a Salisbury newspaper:

> On the subject of matrimony, I must notice a wedding in the Salisbury paper, which has amused me very much, Dr. Phillot to Lady Frances St. Lawrence. *She* wanted to have a husband I suppose, once in her life, and *he* a Lady Frances. (L, p. 227)

The particular joke is more buried here but it seems, as so often in the letters and more occasionally in the novels, to be based around names.

Austen had affected to be shocked when she had read about the marriage between the Reverend Edward Bather and Miss Emma Halifax, claiming that 'he does not deserve an Emma Halifax's maid Betty' (L, p. 157). Phillot and Bather were presumably names that did not have any gentry associations as far as she was concerned. Her irritation at the way in which Henry Wigram had virtually invited himself to stay at Godmersham produced a much coarser joke about names. He did not deserve the name of Henry, one of her favourites, as she has 'seen many a John & Thomas much more agreable [*sic*]' (L, p. 348) than him.

Second marriages held a particular fascination for Austen. She told Cassandra in 1799 about the marriage of Dr. Gardiner to 'Mrs Percy and her three daughters' (L, p. 69). The following year she passed on the news that 'Mrs Estwick is married again to a Mr Sloane, a young Man under age' (L, p. 95). Mrs Lyford's second marriage was commented on at the beginning of 1801:

> Mrs. John Lyford is so much pleased with the state of widowhood as to be going to put in for being a widow again; – she is going to marry a Mr. Fendall, a banker in Gloucester, a man of very good fortune, but considerably older than herself & with three little children. (L, p. 105)

Both Mrs Estwick and Mrs Lyford appear to have had the power to play the marriage market to their own advantage. Perhaps second marriages interested Austen because they could involve the exercise of a widow's power, as well as the apparent sacrifice of it.

Lady Sondes was another widow who was anxious to qualify for the position again. Austen gains power by only giving her very guarded approval to the forthcoming match with Sir Henry Montresor even though, of course, neither of the parties ever bothered to consult her:

> Lady Sondes' match surprises, but does not offend me; had her first marriage been of affection, or had there been a grown-up single daughter, I should not have forgiven her; but I consider everybody as having a right to marry *once* in their lives for love, if they can, and provided she will now leave off having bad headaches and being pathetic, I can allow her, I can *wish* her, to be happy. (L, p. 240)

Austen's tone was even sharper after the wedding had taken place:

> Lady Sondes is an impudent Woman to come back into her old Neighbourhood again; I suppose she pretends never to have been married before – & wonders how her Father & Mother came to have her Christen'd Lady Sondes. (L, p. 262)

Lady Sondes's behaviour does not appear to be nearly as shocking as it is made out to be. The facts are not allowed, however, to prevent an opportunity for gaining power through abuse.

As has been suggested, the family biographies of Austen try to distance and detach her from a coarse and scandalous Regency world. Biographers such as Honan, as well as many of the critics who have written on the letters, suggest that this was not the case. The letters show not only that she read about such a world in the newspapers but also that, particularly during her residence in Bath, she was a part of it. They show furthermore that she sometimes derived pleasure from observing or 'quizzing' it, despite affectations to the contrary. She alluded to two men who were known to have taken mistresses: Lord Craven and Lord Lucan. She told Cassandra in 1801 how she had spent time at a party in Bath identifying and then observing an adulteress:

> I am proud to say that I have a very good eye at an Adultress, for tho' repeatedly assured that another in the same party was the *She*, I fixed upon the right one from the first. – A resemblance to Mrs. Leigh was my guide. She is not so pretty as I expected; her face has the same defect of baldness as her sister's, & her features not so handsome; – she was highly rouged, & looked rather quietly & contentedly silly than anything else. (L, pp. 127–8)

Austen's acquaintances at this particular party do not appear to have had inhibitions about discussing adultery. The letter allows her to be even more open about it, although it is the writer herself and her pride which is at the centre of the stage.

The use of rouge provides the subject matter for one of the best jokes in the letters. Austen spent much of the earlier part of a letter to Cassandra in 1807 detailing improvements to the house and garden in Southampton. She was still on this subject when an unlikely opportunity for abuse occurred. The change of countenance is quite abrupt, although the joke still depends upon the laconic way in which it is delivered:

> Our Dressing-Table is constructing on the spot, out of a large Kitchen Table belonging to the House, for doing which we have the permission of Mr Husket Lord Lansdown's Painter – domestic Painter I Shd call him, for he lives in the Castle. – Domestic Chaplains have given way to this more necessary office, & I suppose whenever the Walls want no touching up, he is employed about my Lady's face. (L, p. 178)

Austen's abuse is aimed once again at a woman who occupies a higher social position than herself. Lord Lansdowne was another well-known eccentric of the period, who built his own castle in Southampton. He was an admirer of the French Revolution and collected portraits of Robespierre, Napoleon and others. Lady Bessborough visited the castle in 1811 after his death and noted how Lady Landsdowne's eccentric clothes, which included a veil, attracted the 'astonish'd gaze' of people in the street.[26]

Austen 'quizzed', or had a good eye at, fashions which came to be regarded as scandalous by the Victorians. She commented in 1801 on Mrs Powlett's appearance. This appears to be a different Mrs Powlett from the one who eloped in 1808: 'Mrs. Powlett was at once expensively & nakedly dress'd; we have had the satisfaction of estimating her Lace & her muslin; & she said too little to afford us much other amusement' (L, p. 105). Mrs Powlett is allowed a brief appearance on Austen's stage as there is some 'amusement' to be gained from the fact the little she wears costs a lot. She is then briskly dismissed in the hope that a new character will provide either more entertainment or scandal. Austen allows Mrs John Lyford to enter next so that she can tell the joke about the widow who wants to become one again. James Thompson argues that Mrs Powlett's brisk dismissal needs to be read in the context of the many other letters which reveal how the Austen sisters increasingly had to dress as economically as possible.[27]

Miss Langley is also only allowed a brief, walk-on part when Austen dramatises a particularly dull party at Bath for Cassandra's amusement in 1801: 'Miss Langley is like any other short girl with a broad nose & wide mouth, fashionable dress, & exposed bosom' (L, p. 129). Austen's power is demonstrated not just by the way in which she abuses both Mrs Powlett and Miss Langley, but also by the contemptuous manner in which they are bundled off the stage. She describes the party at Bath as being 'stupid' and 'intolerable' (L, p. 128), mainly because it was far too small. Those who were present talked 'nonsense to each other' (L, p. 129). As some of the guests played cards throughout the evening, it seems likely that Austen was unable to escape from having to exert herself and make polite conversation to Miss Langley. Her revenge, both against particular individuals and social situations that she did not control, is to rewrite the script. She becomes a powerfully impatient dramatist, who only just has time to abuse characters, before losing all interest in them.

Admiral Stanhope makes his main appearance on the stage after Miss Langley has been dismissed from it: 'Adm: Stanhope is a Gentlemanlike Man, but then his legs are too short, & his tail too long (L,

p. 129). His 'tail' refers to his tail-coat, although perhaps a coarser meaning is available. This may also be the case with the explanation that is offered for his wife's absence: 'I fancy she had a private appointment with Mr. Chamberlayne' (L, p. 129). Mrs Chamberlayne, unlike her husband, attended the party. She can therefore be quickly damned with some very faint praise: 'I respect Mrs Chamberlayne for doing her hair well, but cannot feel a more tender sentiment' (L, p. 129). Austen's stage is crammed with women who, either playfully or more seriously, are cast as being impudent and scandalous. They may be dismissed individually as being silly or boring but, as a type, the scandalous woman holds the attention of the dramatist.

Austen's letters, like others from the Regency period, are open about the pleasures and problems associated with alcohol. Austen begins one to Cassandra in 1800 with an apology:

> I beleive [*sic*] I drank too much wine last night at Hurstbourne; I know not how else to account for the shaking of my hand today; – You will kindly make allowance therefore for any indistinctness of writing by attributing it to this venial Error. (L, p. 90)

This can either be read quite literally, or else as another example of the way in which Austen the dramatist rewrites a script to empower herself. Young women were certainly not expected to get drunk at balls. Such behaviour nevertheless was tolerated as far as young men were concerned. Master Lucas declares in *Pride and Prejudice* that, if he had as much money as Mr Darcy, he 'would keep a pack of foxhounds, and drink a bottle of wine every day' (PP, p. 67). Although he is warned against such a lifestyle, his aspirations nevertheless illustrate the way in which boys were socially conditioned to expect to be allowed to drink alcohol. By claiming to be drunk at the ball, Austen may be asserting her right to a specifically masculine privilege. One of the ways in which the Juvenilia may express dislike for the restrictions imposed on women is by allowing heroines to get drunk. Alice Johnson in 'Jack and Alice' is always, like the rest of her family, 'heated by wine' (MW, p. 15) and often 'dead drunk' (MW, p. 14). She flies to the bottle once again when she discovers that Charles Adams is going to marry Lady Williams rather than herself.

Regency drunks like Edward Pedder followed the example set by the Prince Regent himself. Sarah Spencer warns her brother not to behave like the Prince when the two of them are at a dinner together, as this would mean that he would inevitably 'be too drunk to write next day'. She goes on to contrast the Prince's notorious lifestyle with that of a patriotic naval officer, anticipating the themes of *Persuasion*:

Of course you'll tell us if *the* Prince spoke to you or was decently civil to any of the naval officers, he being in general terms famous for having too much of the effeminate milksop, or rather winesop, about his august character, to be fond of a real manly brave man, like a sailor, at least so they say. [28]

The Prince's drunken countenance was a subject which many others dealt with in the relative privacy of a letter. Mary Berry described it more succinctly than most in 1811 when she noticed his 'muddled complexion'.[29]

When Austen wrote to Cassandra in 1813 she affected to be reconciled to the fact that her dancing days were over: 'By the bye, as I must leave off being young, I find many Douceurs in being a sort of Chaperon for I am put on the Sofa near the Fire and can drink as much wine as I like' (L, p. 370). This was written from Godmersham where, if read literally, she liked to 'drink French wine, & be above vulgar economy' (L, p. 209). French wines, unlike those from Portugal, carried high import duties and were therefore luxury items. Drunks are sometimes given permission to perform comic turns in Austen's theatre. The adulteress's acquaintances at the gathering in Bath include the Badcocks:

> Mrs Badcock & two young Women were of the same party, except when Mrs Badcock thought herself obliged to leave them to run round the room after her drunken Husband – His avoidance, & her pursuit, with the probable intoxication of both, was an amusing scene. (L, p. 128)

She is presumably intoxicated by the chase, whereas he continues to get his pleasure from the drink. The drunken husband is treated here as a figure of fun in an 'amusing scene', but is seen as a much more threatening type when Austen wrote to Cassandra in 1807 about a recent marriage:

> Miss Jackson is married to young Mr. Gunthorpe, & is to be very unhappy. He swears, drinks, is cross, jealous, selfish & Brutal; the match makes *her* family miserable, and has occasioned *his* being disinherited. (L, pp. 180–1)

The severity of this judgement forced Brabourne to blank out the names when he reprinted this letter.

It has been suggested that Austen raided the newspapers as well as her own experience in order to produce an open-ended, or continuous, Regency drama. She was both the imperious playwright and the star performer. She often gained this power over her characters by abusing

them when they were on stage and then by haughtily and contemptuously dismissing them quickly from her regal presence.

DETERMINED TO BE WELL

Austen's letters were accused of triviality when they were first published in a scholarly edition. H.W.Garrod was clearly irritated at
having to listen to what he considered to be idle gossip about petticoats
and drawing-room curtains.[30] E.M. Forster declared that the letters
were characterised by 'triviality, varied by touches of ill breeding and
of sententiousness'.[31] Such accusations, which still persist, are broadly
similar to ways in which modern television soap operas are denigrated
for their emphasis on personal and domestic issues. What needs to be
established as far as the letters are concerned is that they too are
capable of dealing with such issues in ways which can assert their
seriousness. The particular 'personal' issue that will be discussed here
is health. Others that could have been chosen to show the way in which
the letters can politicise the 'personal' include travel and transport.

Personal and family health was a major topic in letters between
Regency women. Lady Sarah Napier described her letters to Lady
Susan O'Brien as being essentially a 'bulletin of family health'.[32] She
records the deaths of her daughters, her husband's attempts to find a
cure for severe chest complaints and her own serious problems with her
face and eyes. She eventually underwent eye surgery in order to try to
save her sight. Lady Susan had an even more terrifying encounter with
the surgeon's knife since she survived an operation for breast cancer.
Both operations would have been performed without anaesthetics as
we understand them today.

Some parts of Austen's letters, such as her account of her father's
death, are straightforward but also moving bulletins of family health
along the same lines as those written by Lady Napier. The difference is
that Austen juxtaposes such descriptions with a sustained critique of
imaginary invalids like Lady Sondes, who need to have headaches in
order to feel important. Lady Williams is taken to task in 1813: 'Lady
W. has taken to her old tricks of ill-health again, & is sent for a couple
of months among her friends. Perhaps she may make *them* sick' (L, p.
304). Frank was told later on in the same year about the antics of Mrs
Edward Bridges:

> They have been all the summer at Ramsgate, for *her* health, she is a
> poor Honey – the sort of woman who gives me the idea of being
> determined never to be well – & who likes her spasms & nervous-
> ness & the consequence they give her, better than anything else.

Austen may have remembered that she was writing to Frank rather than to Cassandra when she adds a disclaimer: 'This is an ill-natured sentiment to send all over the Baltic!' (L, p. 339). She still sent it.

It was not just middle- and upper-class women who were forced to play at being ill in this period. Ann Moor worked as a domestic servant and a labourer before becoming too old to support herself. Although genuinely ill, she nevertheless transformed herself into a professional patient. She abstained first from food in 1807 and then from liquids in the following year. Her fast attracted local interest and soon tourists started to visit Tutbury to see her rather than the castle where Mary, Queen of Scots, had been held prisoner. Pamphlets were written to excite more curiosity and, according to Joan Jacobs Brumberg, they eventually established Moor's fame in America.[33] Although they followed the conventions of the conversion narrative by stressing the way in which Moor had changed her allegedly immoral habits and was now bearing her illness with religious fortitude, it was the body rather than the soul of the sick woman that was foregrounded. Suspicions that she might be tricking visitors out of money, and anxieties that illness was in fact allowing her to become too powerful, led to the establishment of a panel in 1813 to investigate her claims. She had already managed to satisfy an earlier investigation. This second panel consisted of magistrates, medical men and clergymen. Moor was kept under constant surveillance by these men until it was eventually discovered that she was taking liquids through handkerchiefs. Her stained undergarments were regarded as incriminating evidence. Her story suggests that illness could become the profession of working as well as more leisured women.

Austen's mother may have had some of the characteristics of the imaginary invalid. Cassandra was treated in 1798 to a highly theatrical representation of this particular invalid's triumphant and long-awaited entrance from the sick-room:

> My mother made her *entrée* into the dressing-room through crowds of admiring spectators yesterday afternoon, and we all drank tea together for the first time these five weeks. She has had a tolerable night, and bids fair for a continuance in the same brilliant course of action to-day . . . (L, p. 34)

The following year Austen responded to a question from her sister about the state of their mother's health:

> She is tolerably well – better upon the whole than she was some weeks ago. She would tell you herself that she has a very dreadful

cold in her head at present; but I have not much compassion for colds in the head without fever or sore throat. (L, p. 57)

Biographers such as John Halperin have used these and later references to suggest that there was a long-running family feud between Austen and her mother. This seems to exaggerate the available evidence. If there was a feud, it was with her eldest brother James rather than with her mother.[34]

The letters show an awareness, which is serious and political rather than trivial, that invalidism was a part that women were encouraged to play. Their frail bodies were seen by the conduct writers and others as complementing their fragile minds. Austen's hostility towards this sentimental cult of the sick woman may have owed something to a reading of Wollstonecraft and perhaps also of Mary Hays. Wollstonecraft's *A Vindication of the Rights of Woman* (1792) ridicules Fordyce and Gregory both through apt quotation and devastating mimicry.[35] The views of these male conduct writers seem to intrude upon Austen's responses to the early death of Marianne Mapleton in 1801, possibly from 'billious fever' (L, p. 128):

You will be sorry to hear that Marianne Mapleton's disorder has ended fatally; she was believed out of danger on Sunday, but a sudden relapse carried her off the next day. – So affectionate a family must suffer severely; and many a girl on early death has been praised into an Angel I believe, on slighter pretensions to Beauty, Sense & Merit than Marianne. (L, p. 133)

She keeps her countenance while telling Cassandra the news and expressing her sympathy for the family, whom she was later to visit to express her condolences. She then switches quite abruptly to an attack on the sentimental literary and social eulogies that were read out over a young woman's dead, or dying, body.[36] Although the point is obviously a difficult one to illustrate through short quotations, this movement between polite and more abusive remarks runs throughout the letters.

Austen herself playfully confessed to acting the part of the sick woman when staying at Lyme in 1804: 'It was absolutely necessary that I should have the little fever and indisposition which I had: it has been all the fashion this week in Lyme' (L, p. 139). She nevertheless emerges from the letters as somebody who was absolutely determined to be well, despite the playful statements to the contrary. Cassandra was told about a thinly populated ball at the end of 1798:

There were twenty dances, & I danced them all, and without any fatigue. I was glad to find myself capable of dancing so much, and with so much satisfaction as I did; from my slender enjoyment of the Ashford balls (as assemblies for dancing) I had not thought myself equal to it, but in cold weather and with few couples I fancy I could just as well dance for a week together as for half an hour. (L, p. 44)

Although the supply of partners did not affect her enjoyment at this particular ball, other letters comment sharply on the scarcity of men who were 'good for much' (L, p. 24).

Austen's stage is often crammed with both male and female characters who are determined never to be well. These characters frequently become caricatures who are seen just in terms of one part of their grotesque bodies: a big nose, an exposed bosom and a bald face. Mrs Warren is speedily removed from the stage in the representation of the Hurstbourne Park Ball in 1800 to make way for a fresh supply of grotesque bodies:

> Her husband is ugly enough; uglier even than his cousin John; but he does not look so *very* old. – The Miss Maitlands are both prettyish; very like Anne; with brown skins, large dark eyes, & a good deal of nose. – The General has got the Gout, and Mrs. Maitland the Jaundice. (L, pp. 91–2)

These caricatures are in turn rapidly replaced with Miss Debary and her party, to whom Austen was as civil 'as their bad breath would allow me' (L, p. 92).

Austen mourned the death of Marianne Mapleton, while drawing attention to the way in which others would sentimentalise it. If she disliked people she refused to mourn for them, as she made clear in a number of letters. For example, she told Cassandra in 1813: 'Only think of Mrs. Holder's being dead – Poor woman, she has done the only thing in the World she could possibly do, to make one cease to abuse her.' (L, p. 350). The anecdote about Mrs Hall and the death of her child in 1798 is frequently quoted. One of the reasons for dealing with it towards the end of this reading of the letters is to suggest that the way in which it moves abruptly from the conventional to the abusive is not particularly exceptional. Cassandra was staying at Godmersham when she received the news: 'Mrs. Hall, of Sherbourne, was brought to bed yesterday of a dead child, some weeks before she expected, owing to a fright. I suppose she happened unawares to look at her husband' (L, p. 24). The implication is that Mrs Hall had evolved a way of keeping her countenance, or being able to look at her husband without seeing his frightful qualities. One day she made the mistake of forgetting to put on the mask. She did not keep her countenance and so lost her child.

Austen had strong views on the dangers to which women were exposed as a result of multiple pregnancies. Two of her sisters-in-law died in childbirth: Elizabeth Knight in 1808 after the birth of her eleventh child and Frances Austen in 1814 giving birth to a fourth child. Her objections, although hardened by these events, were probably in place before they happened. The dishevelled state of another sister-in-law, Mary, after giving birth in 1798, discouraged her from wanting 'to lay in myself' (L, p. 35). She commented to Cassandra in 1801 on the way in which Mrs Dyson's pregnancies did not enhance domestic happiness: 'The house seemed to have all the comforts of little Children, dirt & litter. Mr. Dyson as usual looked wild, & Mrs. Dyson as usual looked big' (L, p. 121). Austen expressed her astonishment to Cassandra in a letter written just before Elizabeth Knight's death at the news that Mrs Tilson was pregnant again: 'Mrs. Tilson's remembrance gratifies me, & I will use her patterns if I can; but poor Woman! how can she be honestly breeding again?' (L, p. 210). Once again, there is an abrupt movement from mere news to a potentially angry comment on it. A later letter describes Mrs Tilson, who appears to have had twelve children, as 'quite a wretch – always ill' (L, p. 427). Austen commented to Fanny Knight in 1817 on the birth of what seems to have been Mrs Deedes's twelfth child: 'I hope she will get the better of this Marianne, & then I Wd recommend to her & Mr. D the simple regimen [*sic*] of separate rooms.' The letter then moves briskly on to other matters of 'Scandal & Gossip' (L, p. 480). Yet Austen returned to the theme in a later letter to Fanny Knight in which she lamented the fate of her niece, Anna: 'Poor Animal, she will be worn out before she is thirty. – I am very sorry for her. – Mrs. Clement too is in that way again. I am quite tired of so many Children. – Mrs. Benn has a 13th.' (L, p. 488). An earlier letter notices the way in which Anna is expected to go straight from weaning one child to conceiving the next (L, p. 254). One of Lady Napier's letters shows that some of those who were involved in breeding shared Austen's concerns about it. She writes of one pregnancy: 'I wish with you that I was not in the same way, as I have just as many children as I wish to have, but I am afraid that I am breeding again'.[37]

Austen seems to have believed that the sick woman was not just the product of the social acceptance of the sentimental construction of weakness. Sick and dead women were also created by the ways in which multiple pregnancies and large families were normalised. The imaginary invalids, such as Lady Williams and Mrs Bridges, and the genuine ones, such as Marianne Mapleton and Elizabeth Knight, all played parts in somebody else's play. The script, over which they appeared to have no control, determined that they should never be well. Austen's determination to be well gave her power not just over her own body, but also over the bodies of all the grotesque caricatures and poor animals who littered her stage.

Austen continued to mock the figure of the sick woman almost to the end. She described her state of health in March 1817 to Fanny Knight in the famous letter in which she dismisses 'pictures of perfection':

> I have had a good deal of fever at times & indifferent nights, but am considerably better now, & recovering my Looks a little, which have been bad enough, black & white & every wrong colour. I must not depend upon being ever very blooming again. Sickness is a dangerous Indulgence at my time of Life. (L, p. 487)

Her final illness meant that she quite literally lost her countenance. She affects to be indulging in an illness over which in reality she probably knew that she had little control. Her letters in general are adamant that it was dangerous to play at being ill at any age. She wrote in an earlier letter to Fanny about how she was trying to fight her sickness rather than giving in to it and encouraging others to feel sorry for her:

> I am got tolerably well again, quite equal to walking about & enjoying the Air; and by sitting down & resting a good while between my Walks, I get exercise enough. I have a scheme however for accomplishing more, as the weather grows springlike. I mean to take to riding the Donkey. It will be more independent & less troublesome than the use of the carriage . . . (L, pp. 484–5)

She is determined to use physical activity to avoid becoming like Lady Williams and all the others who used real and imaginary illnesses to increase their importance.

CONSTRAINED TO THINK

Several quotations from Austen's letter of 20 November 1800 to Cassandra about the Hurstbourne Park Ball have already been discussed. She possibly plays at being drunk, certainly abuses most of the other guests and passes on the gossip that Mrs Estwick has snapped up a much younger man. When considered more fully as a complete text, this particular letter, like many others, reveals some of the social constraints that were imposed upon Austen as well as the ways in which letter writing allowed her to evade some of them.

The letter was begun on the morning after the ball, added to that evening and then finished off the next day. Although its contents can also be divided into three sections, there are a number of recurring themes. One of them concerns the way in which Austen's own movements are dependent upon the travel plans of her brothers. Charles Austen appears to have arrived much later than planned to escort her to the Ball: 'Naughty Charles did not come on tuesday; but good Charles came yesterday morning. About two o'clock he walked in on a Gosport Hack' (L, p. 90). Austen is unable in the middle part of the letter to tell Cassandra what her own travel plans might be for the following week because there is still some uncertainty over whether Charles means to come back to escort her to another ball. Charles's own movements are shown to be dependent in turn, to some extent at least, upon those of Henry Austen.

A related form of dependency becomes apparent in the description of the ball. Austen notes that Charles 'danced the whole Evening' (L, p. 90), whereas she had to miss three of the twelve dances because she did not have the power to select her own partners. She names four of her partners for the evening, which presumably meant that they were already known to both her and Cassandra. She may have danced with some of them more than once or, alternatively, have partnered relative strangers for the other dances. Her ability to form such new relationships would have been dependent on formal introductions and yet the letter also implies that she was aware of the need to attract admiring gazes in the first place. She completes the description of the ball by seeming to mock her own appearance at it, just as she was later to damn Mrs Chamberlayne with faint praise: 'I wore my aunt's gown and handkerchief, & my hair was at least tidy, which was all my ambition' (L, p. 92). It is not absolutely clear whether this is the same gown that is referred to in the middle section of the letter which recounts how she and her appearance were very closely scrutinised by the family. It seems likely, however, that it is:

> Miss Summers has made my gown very well indeed, & I grow more and more pleased with it. – Charles does not like it, but my father and Mary do; My mother is much reconciled to it, and as for James, he gives it the preference over everything of the kind he ever saw; in proof of which I am desired to say that if you like to sell yours, Mary will buy it. (L, p. 93)

Mary was James's first wife. The letter represents, either directly or more indirectly, a world in which young women are gazed at in the home as well as in the ballroom. They are dependent upon gaining approval. It is revealed in the final section of the letter that Charles changes his mind about the gown, so a connection is made between his unpredictable movements and his unsettled opinions on his sister's appearance.

Charles's initial reluctance to compliment Jane on her appearance contrasts with the way in which James is emphatic in his praise. Although not quite stated explicitly, the implication is that his words are empty. Even in what critics have generally seen as being Austen's most abusive letter countenance is sometimes kept. The middle section of the letter also deals with the way in which the absent Cassandra has been praised by an admirer:

> I think he must be in love with you, from his anxiety to have you go to the Faversham Balls, & likewise from his supposing, that two Elms fell from their grief at your absence. Was it not a gallant idea? – It never occurred to me before, but I dare say it was so. (L, p. 93)

The letters provide a space in which sentimental compliments can be mocked, in this case quite gently.

The two sisters are also dependent in the sense that they often have to build up their knowledge of what is happening from gossip. This is shown here to be an unreliable source:

> The young lady whom it is suspected that Sir Thomas is to marry, is Miss Emma Wabshaw . . . He is certainly finishing his house in a great hurry. – Perhaps the report of his being to marry a Miss Fanshawe might originate in his attentions to this very lady; the names are not unlike. (L, p. 92)

The middle section of the letter deals with a visit to Ashe Park. It is here that Austen learns that Mrs Heathcote has made 'a great blunder' (L, p. 93) about the identities of the couple in another forthcoming marriage. Such misunderstandings occur throughout the letters.

There is, then, one text that highlights some of the constraints that helped to render women dependent as far as movement, approval and knowledge were concerned. This is in sharp contrast, although closely related, to the other text in which Austen displays an impatient, abusive independence. Here it is her gaze that is active, mobile and capable of fragmenting and objectifying bodies. She finds her own way of dissecting them. Mrs Blount was admired by others at the ball for her beauty and was presumably openly complimented on it. Austen casts herself as a predatory character who, instead of waiting passively to be selected as a partner, roams around the ballroom selecting which reputations to destroy. She quickly and contemptuously runs her eye over Mrs Blount from top to toe: 'She appeared exactly as she did in September, with the same broad face, diamond bandeau, white shoes, pink husband, & fat neck' (L, p. 91). The husband is one of the least important fashion accessories. Necks, like noses, momentarily hold the attention. Sir Thomas Champneys's daughter briefly enters the field of vision only to be dismissed from it for being 'a queer animal with a white neck' (L, p. 91). The social constraints that forced Austen to keep her countenance and agree with the opinion that Mrs Blount, Mrs Warren and others were elegant females can be dispensed with in the letter. The ball was given by Lord Portsmouth, one of whose sons had been educated for a time by Austen's father. She was a guest and therefore on terms of rough equality with everybody else. There is also a sense, however, in which socially she might have been quite a marginal figure at such an event, a spy who had to keep her own opinions carefully concealed. The letter nevertheless allows her to hold the centre of the stage.

There are some broad similarities between the representation of the ball and the way in which the party at Ashe Park is dramatised. As already noted, many of the guests at the ball suffered from diseases such as gout and jaundice as well as being afflicted with bad breath. The guests at Ashe Park appear to be much healthier, although disease makes its appearance with the description of how 'James & Mrs. Augusta alternately read Dr. Jenner's pamphlet on the cow pox' (L, p. 93). This is part of the construction of an amusing scene that depends upon contrasts between the world of romance and that of a more grotesque reality. These two characters read about the new cure for smallpox, while two more 'made love'. Another character has fallen asleep and the dramatist herself regally 'bestowed my company by turns on all' (L, p. 93). She once again casts herself in the most active part.

CONCLUSIONS

Letter writing was a relatively private activity that could at the same time be an extremely public one. There were established codes and conventions, which Austen was quick to recognise when they were employed by Miss Irvine. Most letters were either read, or at least discussed, by a wide range of people. One of the reasons for this public circulation was that the government, to raise money for the war against France, had helped to transform letters into expensive items. Recipients were usually keen to get their money's worth. The war also intensified the links that had always been made between letter writing and forms of espionage. Political debate was often conducted through the publication of open letters. Such developments warn against any simplistic equation between the letter and a private space. It is nevertheless still possible to read Austen's letters, and those of other Regency women, as offering opportunities for resistance to social constraints as Butler has suggested. Some letters, such as the one that has just been considered, need to be seen as sustained bids for mastery. It is more usual, however, for the writer to alternate between keeping and losing her countenance within the space of a single letter. It will be seen that the same double movement takes place in Austen's Regency novels. Another reason for considering the letters alongside these novels is that they share common themes such as invalidism.

3 The Prince, the dandy and the Crisis

INTRODUCTION

This chapter begins by providing an account of the second Regency Crisis. It then expands upon this by considering some of the scandals associated with the Prince Regent and other members of his family. This is followed by a section that deals with the career of Beau Brummell and his relationship with the Prince. The basic aim of the chapter is to describe, at the level of historical narrative, certain events that may not be familiar to many students of literature. Austen's letters are one of the sources used. The more ambitious intention is to use topics such as scandal and dandyism to move beyond a factual account of the Regency period towards one which concentrates more on moods and mentalities. The section on scandal ends by anticipating very briefly how the material discussed throughout the chapter is going to be used in the readings of the novels that follow as a way of emphasising its relevance.

CHANGING THE FURNITURE

Austen told Cassandra, in a letter from Chawton dated 10 January 1809, that she had been devoting time to the question of whether the rule of George III would have to be replaced by that of the Prince of Wales: 'The "Regency" seems to have been heard of only here; my most political correspondents make no mention of it. Unlucky that I should have wasted so much reflection on the subject' (L, p. 246). George III's erratic health meant that the Regency question was never very far away from the political agenda. Legislation had eventually been framed back in 1788/9, after much delay and party feuding, to enable the Prince of Wales to assume a strictly limited number of his father's prerogatives and privileges. It was in the event not needed as the King's health improved.[1]

Although some modern studies of the royal malady have suggested that the King was in fact suffering from a physical or metabolic disorder known as porphyria, contemporaries increasingly came to diagnose his condition in terms of either madness or melancholia. A wide range of medical opinion was canvassed in the search for explanations and cures, as was customary in this period. It was however a 'mad doctor', the Reverend Doctor Francis Willis together with members of his family, who gradually took control of the situation after he was summoned to Windsor in December 1788. Willis owned a private asylum in Lincolnshire, where he attempted to cure patients by taming them. He tried to master or mesmerise them through the power of his presence and gaze, but when these failed he resorted to the straight-waistcoat. His apparent success in curing the King in 1788/9 gave some credence to his methods. Regency 'mad doctors' continued to rely on the straight-waistcoat even though it often produced circulatory problems. They still believed in restraint and, although new treatments were beginning to emerge, a range of gothic implements such as neck-irons and leg-locks continued to be used on the inmates of the asylums.[2]

Despite the King's recovery, the spectre of the libertine Prince destroying his father's political house continued to haunt the country. His defiant friendships with Charles James Fox, Richard Brinsley Sheridan and other leading Whig politicians meant that Tories were particularly agitated by the prospect of a Regency that seemed certain to deprive them of place and power. There were anxious periods in both 1801 and 1804 when it looked as though the King's health was breaking down again. Yet he demonstrated on both occasions what Sidney Smith, a Whig, referred to as his 'deplorable knack of re-covering'.[3] It was not in fact until the Autumn of 1810, after the celebrations to mark the fiftieth anniversary of his accession to the throne, that the Regency question became once again the central political issue. Austen's letter shows that she did not remain detached from the major events of her day and was, on this occasion, well in advance of public opinion.

The King's relapse in October 1810, seen by contemporaries as being aggravated by the illness and eventual death of Princess Amelia, meant that politicians were forced to reconsider the question of what limitations ought to be placed on the powers of the Prince of Wales if he had to become the temporary head of both the state and the state church. The Tory government, reasonably well led on this particular issue by Spencer Perceval, was in no hurry. Time was spent examining the doctors and their conflicting accounts helped to sow confusion.

Even Lady Bessborough, who prided herself on being better informed than any newspaper, had to admit in December that she did not know whether the King was 'at the last gasp' or not.[4] Then members of Parliament were encouraged to chew over the vexed constitutional issue of whether it was actually in their power to pass legislation, or if the correct way of proceeding was to issue a more generalised invitation or address to the Prince. This produced the insoluble riddle of whether the Prince was able to sign the legislation that actually empowered him to sign legislation. The need to ransack history for useful precedents was also very time-consuming.

When the King showed no signs of improving, these filibusters eventually had to stop. The government returned to the principles of 1788/9 and remained adamant that a limited Regency was all that was required. The Prince was to become Regent for a limited, or probationary, period on the assumption that his father would eventually stage yet another dramatic recovery. His powers were also limited, particularly in areas of patronage such as the creation of new peers. His supporters, such as Samuel Whitbread, claimed that deprived of real power he would be 'a mere pageant' or just a player king.[5] Perhaps he was always destined to play this part.

Fear of a libertine Regent even forced some Tories to explore the possibilities of abandoning a commitment to male lines of descent in this particular instance. *The Courier*, a government newspaper, supported the case on 31 December 1810 for allowing Queen Charlotte, advised by a council, to act as Regent. Although this proposal, which formed the fifth resolution of the Bill, did not find its way into the Act itself, the Queen was nevertheless given complete control of the government of the King's household. Her correspondence with Perceval indicates that the King himself was adamant that his son should never be allowed the 'power to place or displace any of the members of his Household'.[6] Princess Charlotte indicated that, in reality, the Queen's influence probably extended beyond the government of the household since the Prince was *'quite governed'* by his mother.[7] *The Examiner*, at this stage firmly on the side of the Prince, described these arrangements for the household on 6 January 1811 as an insult to him. The Prince's supporters in Parliament were equally dismissive of any manoeuvres to invest the Queen with authority. Essentially conservative attempts to limit the Regent's powers nevertheless opened up controversial issues such as the political position and power of women.

The Regent was officially sworn into office on 6 February 1811. He used the occasion to indulge his passion for dressing up in military uniforms and appeared in the fullest of regimentals. Dorothy Jordan was in Coventry at the end of this month and noted that the milliners had got 'Regency caps and gowns', while the riband weavers were producing other Regency emblems.[8] Radicals in Coventry obviously believed that the Regent was going to initiate political change. Most newspapers remained optimistic about the chances for the King's recovery during the early months of the Regency, even though old age and blindness were now beginning to complicate his medical condition. It was feared, however, that he might be dying during the Summer. Some of those on small incomes decided it was time to get their mourning clothes ready before the rush produced inflated prices. Austen had commented on the expense of going into mourning for Royal funerals in 1807, after the death of the Duke of Gloucester had been reported in the newspapers, when she asked Cassandra if it was really necessary to buy lace. She was part of a shopping expedition for mourning clothes in June 1811:

> I had just left off writing & put on my Things for walking to Alton, when Anna & her friend Harriot called in their way thither, so we went together. Their business was to provide mourning, against the King's death; & my Mother has had a Bombasin bought for her. (L, p. 291)

The King in fact gasped again, although it was becoming increasingly clear that he was never going to be able to resume any of his duties. The Regency, which had originally been a grudging, temporary measure that was to last for a year at most became a political fact of life.

There is no easy explanation as to why the Prince did not create opportunities to bring the Whigs back into office, as most contemporaries expected him to do. He was incapacitated for quite long periods during his first year. He twisted his ankle in November while unwisely demonstrating how to dance a highland fling. The Duke of Cumberland bluntly declared that it was his head rather than his ankle that required treatment. He was frequently unable to attend to the business of government as a result of the excessive consumption of either laudanum or alcohol. He had always been associated with conspicuous consumption, perhaps most notably by James Gillray in a caricature of 1792 entitled 'A Voluptuary under the Horrors of Digestion'. It may still be true, however, that it would have been difficult for him to have taken initiatives during the early months of the Regency. Yet he could have played a more decisive part in politics when his powers were extended at the beginning of 1812. Decisiveness had never been one of his strengths and it gradually became more and more apparent that his support for the Whigs had in fact been a largely theatrical act of defiance towards his father rather than the product of any deep commitment. Depth had also never been one of his strong points.

The assassination of Perceval on 11 May 1812 by Henry Bellingham, who harboured a personal grudge against the government, nevertheless presented the Regent with the kind of opportunity that he had been reluctant to create for himself. A month of political wheeling and dealing ensued during which some of the Whig leaders were invited to become members of a new administration, although on terms that were calculated to meet with their suspicion. Francis Horner MP captures the feeling of uncertainty that prevailed: 'The apparent changes of conduct succeeded each other so rapidly that the story of one day looked nothing but a contradiction of that before it.'[9] Lord Liverpool eventually agreed to head another Tory administration on 8 June and two days later *The Star* informed its readers that 'the ministerial arrangements may now be regarded as settled'.

The Prince had revealed that the Whig colours were just another theatrical costume that he had worn when it had suited him to do so. His latest preference was for the military uniforms which his father had always tried to prevent him from wearing. Although he had been allowed to perform the essentially ceremonial functions of Colonel of the Tenth Light Dragoons, a more active and distinguished military career was to elude him. It was his younger brother, the Duke of York, who was appointed Commander-in-Chief of the army. Friction on this issue between the Prince and his father became so acute in 1803/4 that he caused a scandal by telling his side of the story to the press. It was very common in this period for the eldest and only sons of both gentry and aristocratic families to lack any sort of profession. The Prince was also forced to devote himself almost entirely to the profession of pleasure. This helps to explain why indulging himself by dressing up and playing the part of a king proved to be more important than either rewarding old friends or taking political decisions.

It soon became clear that the Prince was more interested in changing his furniture than in altering his government. As Sarah Spencer noted: 'He changes the furniture so very often that one can scarcely find time to catch a glimpse at each transient arrangement before it is all turned out for some other'.[10] The poet Tom Moore also drew attention to the way in which this player king devoted his energies to converting Royal residences into elaborate theatrical sets. Moore, who was still confident that the Whigs would gain office and that he in turn would benefit from such a move, was one of the many guests at a fête that was held at Carlton House on 19 June 1811. The Prince, resplendent in what appeared to be a field marshal's uniform, was playing host to the

French Royal Family. He used the occasion to display the heightened theatricality and conspicuous consumption that were to become such distinctive features of his rule:

> Nothing was ever half so magnificent; it was in *reality* all that they try to imitate in the gorgeous scenery of the theatre; and I really sat for three quarters of an hour in the Prince's room after supper, silently looking at the spectacle, and feeding my eyes with the assemblage of beauty, splendour, and profuse magnificence which it presented.[11]

Moore is both an actor in this Regency spectacular as well as an equally privileged on-stage spectator of it. He takes pleasure from 'just looking' at the theatrical set that has been created by close attention to the arrangement of the furniture and the other opulent stage props.

A. D. Harvey does not exaggerate when he claims that the Regency Crisis produced widespread fears amongst the politically enfranchised that 'the whole structure of oligarchic rule . . . was on the point of collapse'.[12] Such fears were fuelled by the way in which policies such as Catholic emancipation and limited parliamentary reform, to which some but by no means all Whigs subscribed, were seen as being capable of shaking the foundations of George III's political house. There were also widespread anxieties about the progress of the war, which were not helped by the way in which some Whigs such as Whitbread declared their intention of negotiating an immediate and perhaps unconditional peace treaty with France.

Much parliamentary time was devoted in the earlier part of 1810 to recriminations over the Walcheren expedition, which had set sail from Portsmouth and elsewhere at the end of July 1809 to try to open up a front against Napoleon in Holland after what many felt was a badly delayed start. Lord Gower described the conduct of the expedition as disgraceful and William Windham called it an 'unparalleled disaster'.[13] The attempt to prevent the press and other 'strangers' from hearing the full extent of this failure, when the matter was debated in parliament, indicated a serious crisis of confidence. William Cobbett argued in *The Political Register* that the government was anxious to cover up the delay in sending medical aid, which had led to malaria and typhoid decimating the troops. He also declared that the decision to evacuate was taken much too late. A radical apothecary, John Gale Jones, objected to closed government and was promptly confined in Newgate by order of Parliament. Sir Francis Burdett, a radical member of Parliament, was sent to the Tower of London for two months for questioning the legality of Jones's treatment. He had shocked most other members by declaring that they ought to be guided by the voice of the people, earlier on during the debates on the Regency Act.[14]

The campaign in the Iberian Peninsula appeared to be having little or no effect during the first year of the Regency. It was associated at this time in the public mind with Sir John Moore's death at Corunna in December 1808 rather than with the Duke of Wellington's victories. The retreat to Corunna was a tactical one designed to draw the army of occupation away from its bases, thus preventing the likely conquest of southern Spain. If looked at retrospectively purely in terms of military history, the campaign can be regarded as a success.[15] Public opinion at the time, however, tended to equate Moore's death with the failure of his tactics. Austen wrote to her sister on 24 January 1809, after probably reading about the retreat in a newspaper: 'This is grievous news from Spain. – It is well that Dr. Moore was spared the knowledge of such a son's death' (L, p. 288). Cassandra probably told her that Moore's mother was still alive, which produced on 30 January 1809 a further reflection on the 'grievous news':

> I am sorry to find that Sir J. Moore has a mother living, but tho' a very Heroick son, he might not be a very necessary one to her happiness.– . . . I wish Sir John had united something of the Christian with the Hero in his death.– Thank Heaven! we have had no one to care for particularly among the Troops– no one in fact nearer to us than Sir John himself. (L, pp. 261–2)

The tone of this letter, and a later one that also expressed relief that she did not care for any of the casualties, has led to suggestions that she was unconcerned about events that were taking place outside of her own allegedly small family world. This does not register that she found the news 'grievous' in the first place, or that her relief at scanning the casualty lists and finding nobody she knew there might have been very genuine. Her brother Frank was at one time on stand-by to help in the evacuation of what remained of Moore's army. Other women letter writers often adopted a similar tone. After describing the bustle in Portsmouth at the time of the Walcheren expedition, Sarah Spencer declared 'How thankful we are that we have no relations in it'.[16]

It was not until July 1812, with the unexpected victory at Salamanca, that memories of Corunna faded and were replaced by more optimistic views on the war. It still required a further victory the following year at Vittoria, together with the news of the consequences of the disastrous French campaign in Russia, to convince many people that there was a possibility of winning the war. Austen implies that the prospects for peace were sunnier after Vittoria, which once again she probably read about in a newspaper: 'What weather! & what news! – We have enough to do to admire them both.– I hope you derive your full share of enjoyment from each' (L, p. 372). Military successes eventually allowed the Prince to attract some of the popularity that had eluded him during the first two years of his rule.

Battles were also being fought on the home front. More troops were deployed to contain the Luddite movements of 1811 and 1812 in midland and northern counties than were being used in Spain and Portugal at this time. The *Leeds Mercury* painted a picture in December 1811 of a country plunged into civil war: 'the Insurrectional state to which this country has been reduced for the last month has no parallel in history, since the troubled days of Charles the First'.[17] The *Mercury* had some sympathy for the Luddites, blaming the war together with the failure of the Regent's ministers for the high level of discontent. Although Luddism is sometimes seen as just being a movement against new machinery, it was in fact also a more broadly based series of protests including food riots against the effects of the wartime economy. It also involved the revival of primitive forms of community protest. Mr Lloyd of Stockport reported to the Home Office the existence of gangs who went about 'levying contributions in the country at Gentleman's houses'.[18] The fact that the Regent had not brought in a reforming government meant that during the last phases of Luddism he became a much hated figure, particularly it seems in Yorkshire. Rewards were offered for his head and he was described in a letter to a Yorkshire Luddite as being a 'blackgard drunken whoreing fellow'.[19] Seventeen Luddites were tried and executed at York in January 1813 for carrying out what were described as 'daring acts of tumultuous outrage, violence and rapine'. Their bodies were eventually 'dissected and anatomised'.[20]

The voices of the opposition, both within and outside Parliament, were increasingly stifled. *The Morning Chronicle*, a newspaper that supported the Whigs, was taken to court at the beginning of the Regency for seeming to declare that the Prince ought to initiate a 'total change' of the political system.[21] This particular case, tried in London, was thrown out by the jury, but other journalists and editors were not so fortunate. Cobbett was fined and imprisoned for two years a few days before the Carlton House Fête for an article that had criticised the way in which German troops had been allowed to flog militiamen in Ely for protesting about how their pay had been docked to cover the cost of equipment. Militiamen were conscripts often chosen by ballot. Military punishments, referred to by their opponents as military tortures, became one of the main grievances for radicals when it began to become clear that the Prince was not going to preside over even minor changes to the political system. *The Examiner* ran a sustained campaign on this issue, which involved championing the case of John Drakard, the editor of *The Stamford News*, who had been fined and imprisoned for writing about military despotism on 24 August 1810.[22]

Cobbett himself had been rumbling away about the crime of punishment for some time before an article in *The Courier* caught his eye and he decided to mimic a reactionary voice that supported the German soldiers at Ely:

> *Five hundred lashes each*! Aye, that is right! Flog them; flog them; flog them! They deserve it, and a great deal more. They deserve a flogging at every meal-time. "Lash them daily, lash them duly". What, shall the rascals dare to *mutiny*, and that, too, when the German legion is so near at hand! Lash them, lash them, lash them! They *deserve* it. O, yes; they merit a double-tailed cat. Base dogs! What, mutiny for the sake of *the price of a knapsack*! Lash them! flog them! Base rascals![23]

Cobbett then proceeds to lash the inhabitants of Ely for, according to his simplistic reconstruction of events, allowing themselves to provide a passive audience for this particular spectacle of suffering. He allows his readers to make a connection which nevertheless is tactfully left unstated in the article itself. The way in which the alien German soldiers assaulted the native population can be seen as being similar to the tyranny of the Royal Family that was Germanic in origin. Such associations were not the only ones available to those who were looking for ways of attacking the Prince. His expensive collection of French furniture, together with his desire to honour the French Royal Family, meant that he could be cast not as a reforming Whig but rather as an upholder of the old order or *ancien régime*. His increasing preference for oriental designs and decor also allowed stereotypes of oriental despotism to cling to him.

The Examiner launched a full-scale attack on the Regent throughout March 1812. Every one of its leading articles for this month risked prosecution, and it was eventually taken to court for one on 22 March which ridiculed the ways in which journalists played the part of the domestic painter and touched up all the Regent's blemishes with rouge. Leigh Hunt saw this 'Adonis in loveliness' as being just a 'corpulent man of fifty':

> – in short, this *delightful, blissful, wise, pleasurable, honourable, virtuous, true,* and *immortal* PRINCE, was a violator of his word, a libertine over head and ears in debt and disgrace, a despiser of

domestic ties, the companion of gamblers and demireps, a man who has just closed half a century without one single claim on the gratitude of his country or the respect of posterity!

Hunt's earlier support for the Regent has been replaced by contempt for the self-indulgent voluptuary who prefers changing the furniture to making political decisions. Hunt was put in prison for two years for advancing such opinions.

Events such as the Carlton House Fête certainly allow the early years of the Regency to be seen as an age of elegance, even though extravagance and excess might be the more appropriate terms. Yet, as will be clear, it was also a time of acute anxiety. The King's illness produced a major constitutional crisis, perhaps the most serious one since the 'Glorious Revolution' of 1688/9. Fears about the safety and security of the state were heightened by what at the time seemed to be the inconclusive battles that were being fought both at home and abroad. It will be argued that Austen's Regency writings need to be read in the context of these particular anxieties, as well as in relation to the ideological debates of the 1790s.

THE BREATH OF SCANDAL

Accounts of the Prince's early life, or the rake's progress, are in danger of making Hunt's comments seem almost moderate and understated . The Prince conducted a well-publicised affair with a married actress, Mary 'Perdita' Robinson, when he was seventeen. The affair did not last long and Robinson was made a reasonably generous secret financial settlement on the understanding that she would not cause a scandal. Bad health forced her to rely more on her talents as a writer in later years. In addition to poetry and fiction, she published more polemical works on the subject of women's education. Her radical reputation was such that she was denigrated in the backlash against women writers that followed the death of Wollstonecraft.[24] The Prince went on to have more discreet affairs with other married actresses.

The Prince's name became synonymous with scandal. He became a prominent patron of racing and won the Derby in 1788 with a horse named Sir Thomas. It has been estimated that his racing activities cost him at least thirty thousand pounds a year and thus contributed to his financial problems. He was forced to retire from the turf in 1791 as a result of a scandal that surrounded the running of another of his horses, Escape, during the October meeting at Newmarket. Escape, ridden by Sam Chifney, lost badly on 20 October only to romp home the next day when the odds were obviously a lot longer. Foul play was suspected although never proven.[25]

A much bigger and more long-lasting scandal was occasioned earlier on by the Prince's relationship with Maria Fitzherbert. The Royal Marriages Act of 1772 stated unequivocally that there could be no possibility of marriage between them. Maria was a Roman Catholic who had been widowed twice and the Prince was still under twenty-five. A secret wedding ceremony took place in London on 15 December 1785. Although the precise details of the ceremony itself were to remain shrouded in a certain amount of secrecy, the fact that it had taken place was soon a very open secret. Gillray and other satirists gleefully added it to their catalogues of the Prince's vices. Gossipy articles, of the type read by Austen herself as well as by Mr Price in *Mansfield Park*, flourished. *The Morning Post* published a knowing question from a reader on 10 October 1788:

> What is the reason that Mrs. Fitzherbert, who is a lady of fortune and fashion, never appears at court? She is visited by *some* ladies of high rank, has been in public with them, and yet never goes to the Drawing-rooms at St. James's.[26]

The fact that the Prince was known by many people to have made a constitutionally unacceptable marriage helps to explain the delaying tactics that were used during both of the Regency crises.

The Prince and Maria Fitzherbert established their own court in London and then more particularly in Brighton, to where the Prince retreated in a vain attempt to limit his spending. Although this relationship was to last much longer than the one with Robinson, the Prince's name also became associated with those of a number of other married women, notably with that of Lady Jersey. He also attempted to start an affair in 1809 with Lady Bessborough, although she was not at all impressed by the sight of 'that immense, grotesque figure flouncing about half on the couch, half on the ground'.[27]

The Prince, although secretly married, decided to undergo a more open and conventional ceremony with Caroline of Brunswick on 8 April 1795. She had been conveyed to England by Frank Austen's squadron and was met on arrival by both Lady Jersey and Beau Brummell. Mercenary motives were uppermost in the Prince's mind since he wanted members of Parliament both to clear some of his debts and to provide him with a larger allowance in future. They in turn wanted him to provide an heir. Although this official marriage certainly helped to ease, if not to solve, some of his financial problems, it did nothing to put a stop to the breath of scandal that seemed to accompany everything he did. The new couple were living apart within a year, each of them embarking on a series of well-publicised relationships. This was the most conspicuous and public example of a marriage without affection that had been entered into by one of its partners for mercenary motives. Regency readers might have brought memories of it to the purely mercenary marriages that they encountered in fiction.

The libertine Prince was emulated by his rakish younger brothers. The Duke of Clarence also fell in love with an actress, Dorothy Jordan. The couple settled down together and had ten children. Jordan continued gruelling theatrical tours in order to provide for her large family. Clarence nevertheless brought the relationship to a very abrupt end in 1811 because he felt that he would be better off financially if he went through an official marriage ceremony with a young heiress. After years of making a fool of himself at watering places such as Ramsgate and elsewhere trying to captivate such an heiress, he eventually settled in 1818 for marriage to a German princess. Parliament dutifully paid his debts and increased his personal allowance. Jordan had died in poverty in France in 1816. The Duke of Kent left the woman he had been living with for over twenty years, Madame St Laurent, in order to make another dynastic marriage in 1818.

The Duke of York married the almost statutory German princess relatively early on in his career and then took a number of mistresses. One of them, Mary Ann Clarke, whom he may first have met at a watering place in 1803, brought further scandal to the Royal Family when accusations were made in Parliament in 1809 about the way in which she had used her position to make money out of the sale of army commissions. This particular scandal reverberated throughout 1809 and helps to account for the demoralised state of the country at the beginning of the Regency. Lord Holland, a leading Whig, declared that: 'There had never hitherto (at least in our time) been any measure hostile to the Court so popular as the inquiry and censure of the Duke of York.'[28] It became reasonably clear that Clarke had been feathering her own nest, which was just as well since she appears not to have been as well treated financially as Mary Robinson had been when the relationship ended. Questions remained unanswered about whether her former lover, who was now involved with a Mrs Carey, had known about her activities and had encouraged them. Cobbett and others nevertheless hinted darkly that the evidence of the Duke of York's involvement was carefully suppressed. The Commander-in-Chief resigned, although he was reinstated during the early months of the Regency. *The Examiner* claimed on 2 June 1811 that this rehabilitation was 'felt as a blow given to all the better reason and feeling of the nation'. The Prince did not make many decisions and when he did so they were usually unpopular ones.

The Royal Family also became associated, albeit briefly, with a potential homosexual scandal in May 1810 when the Duke of Cumberland's valet, Joseph Sellis, was found dead after allegedly trying to murder his master. One of the theories that was advanced was that Cumberland may have been blackmailed by Sellis or others about his own homosexuality. Anxieties about the conduct of the war led to increased surveillance of sexual conduct particularly amongst servicemen. A month after Sellis's mysterious death a molly house, or male brothel, was raided in Vere Street. Six of those seized eventually had to face an exceptionally ferocious crowd when they were placed in public pillories, before being imprisoned for two years. Two others, one of whom was a serviceman, were hanged in March 1811.[29] There is no evidence that Austen herself read the newspaper coverage of such events, or that she was aware that the 'unnatural crime of Sodomy' had taken place on one of Frank Austen's ships.[30] It is possible nevertheless that Mary Crawford's outrageous remark in *Mansfield Park* about the admirals she had met – 'Of *Rears*, and *Vices*, I saw enough' (MP, p. 91) – needs to be set in the context of Regency anxieties about the sexual conduct of the armed forces.

Austen's letters show that she was certainly familiar with at least some of the Royal scandals of the period. Prince Augustus had secretly married Lady Augusta Murray in Rome. They went through a more public ceremony back in England in the hope of placating the King. Augustus nevertheless was forced to return to Europe in disgrace and was transported to Lisbon by Austen's brother Charles. The news was circulated around the family: 'They were very well satisfied with their Royal Passenger, whom they found fat, jolly & affable, who talks of Ly Augusta as his wife and seems much attached to her' (L, p. 120). Augustus, used to being ostracised, was to lend some support later on to Princess Caroline.

Those who opposed the Prince Regent also often lent their support to his estranged wife, Princess Caroline. Austen did not remain detached from this particular royal scandal. She wrote to Martha Lloyd on 16 February 1813 to express her disgust at the Prince's conduct, or rather misconduct, towards Caroline. She comments specifically on a letter which Caroline had written to him and which was subsequently published by her Whig supporters in *The Morning Chronicle*. His own conspicuous pursuit of pleasure did not prevent him from declaring that Caroline was not a fit and proper person to be a mother and therefore from seeking to impose restrictions on their daughter's visits to her. Austen was angered by such a blatant example of double standards:

> I suppose all the World is sitting in Judgement upon the Princess of Wales's Letter. Poor woman, I shall support her as long as I can, because she *is* a Woman, & because I hate her Husband – but I can hardly forgive her for calling herself 'attached & affectionate' to a Man whom she must detest – & the intimacy said to subsist between her & Lady Oxford is bad – I do not know what to do about it; but if I must give up the Princess, I am resolved at least always to think that she would have been respectable, if the Prince had behaved tolerably by her at first. (L, p. 504)

Lady Oxford courted a rakish reputation by boasting that she had lost count of the names of the various fathers of her children. She added Lord Byron to her list of lovers and he visited Cheltenham in 1812 to be close to her. Austen may be objecting to such scandalous behaviour in a woman. Lady Oxford was also actively involved in radical politics. Her promotion of Caroline was meant to embarrass the Regent and her involvement with the foundation of Hampden Clubs linked her to the movement for constitutional reform. It could be argued that Austen's objections to Lady Oxford are political ones, which renders the voice in the letter that of the Tory gentry which is deeply suspicious of the Whig aristocracy. Yet Austen herself emphasises the gendered rather than party political nature of her response: she supports Caroline as 'a Woman' and is probably suspicious of what is taken to be Lady Oxford's unwomanly behaviour.[31]

Austen's letter to Martha Lloyd appears to contradict the sentiments expressed in the Dedication to the Prince Regent at the beginning of *Emma*, as does one written to Cassandra in June 1814. This was written when visiting heads of state were celebrating what was thought to be the final victory over Napoleon. The Prince and his guests were able to spend a lot of time dressing up in military and ceremonial costumes. The *Annual Register* described the arrival of the Emperor of Russia at Carlton House on 9 June:

> At a quarter past three, the Emperor of Russia arrived in state, in the Regent's carriage, escorted by a party of the Bays, and was received with military honours. His Majesty was dressed in an English uniform, and wore the Order of the Garter. He was met at the door of Carlton-house by the Prince Regent, in regimentals of blue and gold. His Royal Highness conducted the Emperor to his closet, where they held a conference for some time, and were dressed in the robes of the Garter.[32]

The round of enormous banquets was occasionally broken up by the need to conduct reviews of the troops. Lady Bessborough commented on another occasion that the Prince inspected the uniforms rather than the troops themselves. The high point of these festivities was a review of the navy at Portsmouth. The Prince spent two days showing off the dockyards as a prelude to the staging of a mock sea battle on 25 June. Cobbett described how the sea was covered 'with shows of the most expensive decoration, the Prince Regent going in person with all the parade capable of being furnished by his extravagant government'.[33] The battle was followed by a banquet at Government House. Thomas Cross, a local coachman, describes how these festivities attracted huge crowds: ' not only the town, but every village and hamlet within reach, was crowded with visitors. Strangers daily poured in from all quarters.'[34]

Cassandra Austen was staying in London at this time and received a letter dated 14 June from her sister that commented on these events:

> Take care of yourself, and do not be trampled to death in running after the Emperor. The report in Alton yesterday was that they would certainly travel this road either to or from Portsmouth. I long to know what this bow of the Prince's will produce. (L, p. 389)

The sense is difficult to recover, although it seems probable that Austen did not think that these festivities would produce very much. They were, after all, orgies of consumption. The way in which the Prince becomes his 'bow' and that this is all that there is to him may be related to the way in which Cobbett associates him with 'parade'. Although this letter is clearly not as openly hostile as the earlier one to Martha Lloyd, it does not appear to offer a flattering representation of the Regent.

The existence of these two letters raises questions about the sincerity of the Dedication of *Emma* to the Regent. This unlikely event came to pass as a result of Austen's visit to London in 1815 to help to nurse her brother Henry through a serious illness. His physician, Charles Haden, had connections at court and this was probably how Austen's presence in London was brought to the attention of the Regent. He issued an invitation to her through his librarian, James Stanier Clarke, to visit Carlton House. Clarke gave her a guided tour on 13 November and appears to have told her that his master kept copies of her novels in all of his residences. *Sense and Sensibility* had been popular amongst those who moved in court circles. Clarke claimed that the Regent himself had actually read her published novels rather than just using them to furnish rooms. He hinted that the dedication of any new novel to his master would be acceptable.

Austen was clearly unsure about either the precise status of this request, or else the wisdom of accepting it. She therefore asked for clarification. Clarke's reply left little doubt that the Regent's wish must become her command. So 'HIS ROYAL HIGHNESS'S dutiful and obedient humble servant'(E, p. 5) ever so respectfully had to dedicate one of her novels to the very man whom she had denounced as hateful and detestable less than three years earlier. She was forced to bow down, figuratively, before the man whom she appears to have described as being no more substantial than his bow. As mentioned, the Regent's popularity began to improve a little as a result of the victories against Napoleon but this does not provide an adequate explanation of the discrepancy between the private statements and the public dedication to the Regent. The Dedication may be best read as an ironic statement and therefore placed alongside the mock-dedications that were such a distinctive feature of the Juvenilia. Alternatively, it can be read more literally since, as will be argued later on, *Emma* celebrates as well as repudiates Regency values. The Prince was apparently pleased with his '*handsome*'(L. p. 453) copy, although it is not known whether it was handsome enough to tempt him to read it. Some Victorian editions of the novel did not reproduce the Dedication, perhaps because of the Regent's scandalous reputation.

It will be shown that the Regency Crisis of 1810 to 1812, together with the scandals associated with the Regent over a longer period, provide an important but neglected context for Austen's Regency writings. This is most apparent as far as *Mansfield Park* is concerned, which was written during these years and contains its own regency crisis when Sir Thomas Bertram has to visit his plantations in the West Indies. Edmund Bertram becomes the first regent because Sir Thomas takes his eldest son, Tom, with him. Tom takes over from his brother when he returns from the West Indies well in advance of his father. The arrival of the Crawfords together with the visit to Sotherton happen during the first period of regency and the rehearsals for *Lovers' Vows* take place during the second one. Edmund is shown to be the best qualified of the two sons for the post, whereas Tom's style of rule has some similarities with that of the Prince Regent. He too is an eldest son who follows the profession of pleasure and thus runs up debts. He gambles on the horses and so ends up gambling with both his own and Edmund's inheritance. His heavy drinking shortens the odds on his living long enough to inherit anything. He is a voluptuary who is associated with the conspicuous consumption of food as well as drink.

When he becomes regent, he is only interested in the ceremonial and theatrical aspects of government. He too moves the furniture about in order to create an elaborate theatrical set.

As noted, the Regency Crisis generated some important debates about the political position of women. *Mansfield Park* does not just debate the rival claims and merits of the two male regents. Power increasingly belongs to Mrs Norris who, although nominally subject to the rule of her nephews, is able to tighten her grip upon the reins of government during Sir Thomas's absence. She actively promotes all the 'noisy pleasures'(MP, p. 201) and 'unsafe amusements' (MP, p. 204) of the regency period, whereas Fanny Price opposes many of them. It can therefore be argued that women emerge during the regency period as the most effective figures of both misrule and rule. The novel's apparent answers to the regency question are potentially subversive ones: the younger son is a better regent than the legal heir and the poor female relation is superior to both of them.

Although *Mansfield Park* provides a particularly complex representation of a specific regency crisis, Austen's other later writings continue to explore many of the issues that were keenly contested between 1810 and 1812. They also explore scandalous elopements and engagements and, more particularly, responses to them. It will be suggested that the debate about the Prince Regent's profession of pleasure is continued around the figures of Frank Churchill in *Emma*, Sir Walter Elliot in *Persuasion* and Tom Parker in *Sanditon*. Despite differences of age, Churchill and Elliot can both be seen as representations of the Regency dandy. Dandyism is also an important theme in *Mansfield Park* since the house is invaded by dandies such as Henry Crawford and Mr Yates during the regency period. A fuller sense of the topicality of all of these later writings can therefore be recovered through a consideration of the career of Beau Brummell and his relationship with the Prince.

HOVERING ON THE VERGE OF INSOLENCE

Beau Brummell was a member of the Prince of Wales's pet regiment, the Tenth Light Dragoons, during the 1790s. Like the Prince, he enjoyed dressing up and playing at soldiers in Brighton but, according to the legend, resigned his commission in 1798 when the regiment was ordered to go to Manchester. Although all the stories about him have to been taken with a large pinch of snuff, this one is at least true to the spirit of dandyism. He was unwilling to move from one play, where all was splendour and profusion, to another which might have involved him in performing in a theatre of punishment and military torture. Manchester had an active radical movement and also experienced a series of food riots in the years immediately before the Prince's regiment was ordered to station itself there.[35]

Brummell stationed himself instead in Mayfair and, until he decamped to France in 1816 to avoid his creditors, playfully punished those whom he considered to lack style. He had a reasonably comfortable private income since his father had been private secretary to Lord North, the Prime Minister at the time of the American War of Independence. Nevertheless he was out of his financial depth when mixing with most members of the aristocracy. He relied increasingly on gambling to pay for his lifestyle and it was eventually his gaming debts that forced him to bow out of the high society world which he had dominated for so long.

Dandyism was inextricably linked with gambling since it was the ultimate game of chance in which it was crucial both to have a nerve and to know how to hold it. Success involved keeping one's countenance. Brummell established himself as the emperor of an exclusive, or exquisite, cult that was committed to preserving social distinction, discrimination and distance. As Jules Barbey D'Aurevilly suggests, he won this particular game of chance, or hazard, because he used charm combined with terror as his weapons. He was a butterfly with a sting, who had to amuse his spectators as well as abuse them. The dandies certainly terrorised members of high society, while at the same time mocking and disrupting their own credentials as arbiters of taste.

D'Aurevilly expands upon this central contradiction by indicating that 'dandyism . . . plays with the regulations, but at the same time pays them due respect'.[36] The dandy only just manages to keep a straight face when he is laying down the law. As J.B. Priestley suggests, the dandy's countenance often displayed 'poker-faced impudence'.[37] Ellen Moers also concentrates on the subversive, mocking elements that often lay just beneath the elegant surface, or façade, of the dandy. The fact that Brummell himself, despite his schooling at Eton and a brief period at Oxford, did not quite come from the top social drawer was ultimately not as important as the clothes that he kept in his own top drawer. He was aristocratic in everything but his background, allowing dandyism to stand for at one and the same time both social mobility and rigidity.[38] Dandies disdainfully despised commerce and those poor 'insects' who were forced to have to work for a living, yet they themselves can be seen as commodities. They lounged in the bow windows of their exclusive clubs displaying themselves and their clothes. They were advertising the fact that high social status was a commodity that could be purchased, if only you knew the secret of which tailor to patronise.

The Regency dandy is described in W.E. Henley and Robert Louis Stevenson's play *Beau Austin*, which was first performed in 1884 but was set in 1820, as being a 'private gentleman by birth, but a kind of king by habit and reputation'.[39] As will be seen, Brummell himself mounted a challenge to the Prince's leadership of high society, and the nicknames of some of the other dandies, for instance Prince Boothby and Prince Lascelles, suggest that such mockery and mimicry of authority was a distinctive feature of dandyism. Virginia Woolf very neatly captures these potentially subversive qualities when she sums up Brummell's own style: 'That was his style, flickering, sneering, hovering on the verge of insolence, skimming the edge of nonsense, but always keeping within some curious mean.'[40] The dandy was both the embodiment of the aristocratic principle as well as the insolent threat to it. Woolf's comment can also be applied to the way in which Austen's writings alternate between keeping and losing their countenance.

As has been indicated, the Prince Regent surprised most people by rejecting the Whigs when he finally took control of his father's political house. His rejection of Brummell was part of the same pattern. Dandies and Whigs were in fact often closely related. Captain Jesse, Brummell's first biographer, describes his hero's appearance during the long period of exile in France: 'He stood to his Whig colours to the last. His dress on the evening in question consisted of a blue coat with a velvet collar . . . a buff waistcoat, black trousers and boots.'[41] This particular uniform has some similarities with that worn by the American revolutionaries. The Prince's cultivation of Whigs and dandies was designed to irritate his father, who had been forced to preside over the loss of the American colonies and was haunted by this failure throughout his life. Although Brummell wore the 'Whig colours' and mixed with Whig grandees, he appears to have had little interest in party politics. Some of his letters indicate a distaste for Tory policies such as income tax as well as a dislike of some leading Tory ministers such as Lord Castlereagh, although both were familiar positions. It is thus difficult not to conclude that he preferred the Whigs because they gave the best dinners and parties. He was attracted towards the conservative Legitimists when he was in France for the same reason. Other dandies, for instance Scrope Davies and Sir Henry Mildmay, were much more actively involved in the radical politics of the day. Davies devoted some of his energy to the campaigns to get radical members elected to

Parliament, and Mildmay, himself one of the members for Hampshire, was involved with extra-parliamentary pressure groups.

All descriptions of Brummell's appearance confirm Moers's point that the Regency dandy, unlike many of his successors, dressed down at the same time as he dressed up. The style, as Jesse's portrait illustrates, was certainly plain and understated. Despite Brummell's playful assurances to the contrary, part of the game was nevertheless to allow understatement to hover dangerously close to overstatement. Dandies affected to believe that they were badly dressed if their clothes, or uniform, attracted comments but they would in fact have been mortified if none were made. Dandyism made a profession out of idleness. Brummell's own regime, or routine, was almost military in its precision. He got up late when the day was well aired, spent hours getting dressed and then went on parade in the clubs and parks. It was then time to dress again for evening social engagements such as dinner parties, dances and visits to the theatre. It was hard work being the idlest man in London.

Getting dressed was both a private activity so that the dandy did not reveal all his secrets to others, and a very public ritual. It could be both these things since, although few were allowed into the inner sanctum of the dressing-room itself, Brummell left the door open so that he could carry on conversations with his callers. The legend is that the Prince of Wales frequently attended the court of King Brummell. Jesse felt privileged to spend over two hours watching the old master at work:

> In the morning visits that I sometimes paid him at his lodgings, the door of his bedroom being always left a little open to carry on the conversation, the secrets of his dressing-table were, much to my entertainment, revealed in the glass upon the mantlepiece of his *salon*.[42]

As the passage goes on to indicate, Jesse took voyeuristic pleasure in peeping at the almost naked Brummell even though he used a comic tone to disguise his feelings.

Brummell's sexuality was enigmatic. He clearly enjoyed displaying his naked as well as clothed body to other men and probably arranged the mirror specially to give Jesse a better view of it. Nevertheless he also sent out frosty signals to both sexes that they were meant to gaze at him but never to touch him. He was not a 'drunken whoring fellow' and, unlike many other dandies, was not attracted by the dangerous intimacies of the underworld. He gambled in the smart clubs rather than in the gaming 'hells'.[43] Although he conducted some flirtatious relationships with women both in England and later on in France, they were usually cold and very stately social rituals. They were increasingly with women who were much younger than himself. The dandy mode of address was to affect to love all women and to be bored by all men though, at a suppressed level, the reverse may well have been closer to the mark in some cases.

Brummell is often represented in twentieth-century Regency romances, such as Georgette Heyer's *Regency Buck* (1935), as an amusing eccentric whose unthreatening attentions and hints on fashion help young heroines to establish themselves in high society. At a more general level, such texts recover important features of Regency society that tend to be ignored by more culturally respectable historical narratives. Their popularity can be partially explained by the way in which heroines, and therefore also readers, are able to inhabit a world in which it is quite legitimate for women to gaze at men. They are also alert to the ways in which Regency dandyism sanctioned the same-sex male gaze.[44]

Marriage might have saved Brummell from financial ruin. As Lord Glenthorn reflects in Maria Edgeworth's *Ennui* (1809), the extravagant gambler must come to matrimony as surely as the highwayman will end up on the gallows. Brummell nevertheless always affected to be unable to find the perfect partner. He let everyone know that he had been forced to reject one aristocratic candidate when he found out that she actually ate cabbage. He regarded eating vegetables as the height of vulgarity, although he was forced to make a mock-confession to the effect that he had once eaten a pea. Austen-Leigh told an anecdote about Brummell's disapproval of the habit of eating peas off a knife, as part of his reflections on the coarseness of habits before and during the Regency period. Brummell allegedly replied to a question about when he had last seen his parents by declaring that they must have cut their throats, since he last saw them eating peas with their knives (M, pp. 30–1).

While Brummell certainly set the tone of dandyism in many areas, his prim version of narcissism was exceptional. He invented the starched cravat and led what Regency people would have referred to as a starched life. Most dandies were associated with the kind of sexual excess practised by the Prince Regent. A satire published in 1796 on the Prince and his Brighton friends entitled *Twelve Golden Rules for Young Gentlemen of Distinction* indicates the deep levels of misogyny that permeated many forms of dandyism:

> All who are married must exhibit a public contempt for their wives in proportion to their rank in life . . . All bachelors must consider

the spinsters as their destined prey; and if they cannot enjoy their persons, they may make free with their reputations . . .[45]

The Prince, as has been seen, certainly kept the first of these golden rules.

William Hazlitt called Brummell 'the greatest of small wits'. He went on to suggest that the essence of dandyism lay in the story of how Brummell passed the time trying to decide which was his favourite leg.[46] Seemingly frivolous subjects were treated with great seriousness. Similarly, seemingly trivial social actions were elevated to a pinnacle of importance. One of Brummell's party pieces was to be able to employ one hand, perhaps his favourite one, to open a snuff-box. This nonchalant trick probably needed hours of practice in front of the mirror in order to perfect it. Brummell's mastery of it allowed him to affect a haughty contempt for those mere mortals who had difficulty opening a snuff-box. He had his off-the-cuff riposte carefully prepared when, according to the legend, Lord Liverpool actually tried to prise open one of his boxes with a knife: 'Confound the fellow, he takes my snuff-box for an oyster'.[47] Oysters were a plebeian rather than patrician delicacy in this period, so the future Prime Minister is being told, by the nobody who does nothing, that he is as vulgar as the aristocratic lady who eats cabbage. A similar story that went the rounds described how King Brummell once ordered a duchess to walk out of a ballroom backwards because he was offended by the sight of her back. He had the licence to abuse people to their faces, whereas Austen had to reserve her contempt for the other guests at Hurstbourne Park for her letter.

The art of the dandy mode of address lay in reversing categories. If Brummell was asked his opinion of a coat, he would claim not to be able to see one. If called upon to pronounce about a pair of shoes, he would declare after a well-timed pause that he thought they were slippers. When dining out and drinking what he considered to be a suspect champagne, he would ask for some more cider. The secret was of course never to explain how to open a snuff-box or how to recognise a good champagne. Brummell's rare pronouncements on fashion were brief and enigmatic. Shrugs, winces and 'quizzes' were seen as being more effective than words. Every feature was employed. He was very occasionally prevailed upon actually to tell an aspiring dandy that his trousers had 'bad knees' and yet remained studiously silent on the subject of what constituted good knees.

There are, inevitably, different accounts of Brummell's break with the Prince Regent. His minimal style of conversation allowed endless gossipy stories to be put in circulation about his activities and attitudes.

He became somebody of great consequence by doing very little and saying even less. It is reasonably clear that before the second Regency Crisis he and the Prince were intimate friends. They met frequently in London, Brighton and at various country house parties. They were both present for instance at the coming-of-age celebrations for the Duke of Rutland at Belvoir Castle in 1799. According to the legend, some of the local inhabitants mistook Brummell for the Prince and he did nothing to correct their mistake. He certainly enjoyed behaving like royalty when the end of the London season reluctantly forced him into the country. His dislike of rural society complemented his distaste for vegetables. He usually arrived late at houses to which he had been invited and got his valet to commandeer the best rooms even if they were already occupied.[48] He also occasionally enjoyed making dramatic entrances at houses where he was not on the guest list. Bewildered hosts and hostesses were placed in an impossible position: they might be socially damned if Brummell had decided that they were not worth visiting and yet they and their champagne would almost certainly be criticised when he did invite himself to stay. Harriette Wilson claimed that he was able to get away with such behaviour because everybody apart from her was afraid of his 'cold, heartless and satirical' manner.[49]

BEYOND THE EDGE OF NONSENSE

Before the Regency Crisis, Brummell was able to hover on 'the verge of insolence' in his relationship with the Prince and then appear to retreat to a more deferential position. This delicate mixture of insolence and deference no longer amused the Prince after he became head of state. Brummell's jests were seen as calling his dignity into question. The break may have been occasioned when Brummell called out rather too loudly one evening for 'Mistress' Fitzherbert's carriage. Cutting, or breaking, personal friendships was one of the most popular employments of the unemployed dandies, to be treated with the same degree of mock-seriousness as the cut of a coat. The Prince's vanity together with Brummell's pride nevertheless meant that what should have remained a game turned into a war, every bit as important to the participants and their many spectators as events in Spain. The Prince had probably joined in the joke at Belvoir when Brummell told the story of how their identities had been mistaken. Now he sat scowling in his carriage as he watched Brummell saunter down a London street and take a military salute that was intended for him.

The seriousness of the quarrel represented a problem for the organisers of the Dandy Ball at the Argyle Rooms in July 1813, an event which was paid for out of gambling winnings. Brummell himself was a member of the committee, together with Mildmay, Lord Alvanley and Henry Pierrepoint. It was decided to invite the uncharming Prince to the ball, even though he was known to be cutting Pierrepoint as well as Brummell. True to form, he refused to acknowledge Brummell when he arrived and was met by the 'unique four' who formed the committee. The emperor of fashion nevertheless was more used to cutting than being cut. He therefore turned to the stout Alvanley and asked him to identify his 'fat friend'. The question is a perfect example of the minimalism that both amused and exasperated Hazlitt. The Prince is cast as an obscure gatecrasher who may just be allowed in because he is one of Alvanley's less respectable friends. He has no identity other than as a hanger-on. Brummell, himself the real interloper, got away with voicing some of the same opinions that had landed Leigh Hunt in prison.

Brummell was not only able to survive the Prince's displeasure, but also at times to thrive upon it. According to the legend, he retaliated by threatening to go down to Windsor to bring the 'mad' George III, and perhaps the straight-waistcoat, back into fashion. He was, however, unable to survive the changes that began to take place in high society as the war drew to an end. He began to appear even more absurd and nonsensical in a world that was increasingly populated by returning officers and visiting heads of state. He was also becoming more and more dependent on gambling to finance the profession of idleness at a time when huge sums of money were changing hands every night in the London clubs. He had, like his fellow dandy Scrope Davies, many of the personal qualities necessary to take on and beat the heavy or deep gamblers. They both lacked money rather than countenance. Brummell had some investments in the West Indies, probably in slave plantations, but these failed to yield as much interest as they had done formerly. He claimed that play, or gambling, had been what had ruined him. Play and playfulness were also what had made him in the first place, as he admitted on one occasion to Lady Hester Stanhope.

When Brummell was forced to move from Chesterfield Street to a smaller residence in Chapel Street, his creditors began to get worried. He used to boast in his heyday that his patronage could be the making of tailors and tradespeople because others would flock to acquire the same commodities. It now seemed possible that it might ruin them if, in addition to not being able to pay his bills, he could no longer set the fashion. He responded like others to the archetypal Regency dilemma of how to live on nothing a year by borrowing large sums of money from his friends. When he fled to Calais in May 1816, he left his friends as well as many tradespeople to pick up the pieces. Regency society had created an elegant monster and yet, unlike Victor Frankenstein, it was never quite prepared to disown or discredit its creation.

Jesse records two parties that took place in Caen in the 1830s. Brummell had moved there in 1830 from Calais, where he had been one of the leading tourist attractions, on his appointment as British Consul. The post, however, was abolished soon afterwards, perhaps because he himself had disconcertingly informed his superiors in London that it was not necessary. He went back to scrounging free dinners which he often criticised, sponging off his friends in England, living on credit and flirting with much younger women. He was eventually thrown into the debtors' wing of the local prison in 1835 and remained there for nearly three months until his long-suffering friends in England came up with enough money to discharge him. The Duke of Clarence, by now King William IV, made a contribution to the fund. Exiled dandies were usually treated more sympathetically than rejected mistresses.

Brummell had always been afraid of being touched, even by his friends, and had taken great pains to distance himself completely, both mentally and physically, from strangers. This is why the underworld held no attractions for him. He once complained that he became ill when he stopped at an inn between Brighton and London to change horses and the landlord put him in a room with a damp stranger. He now shared a cramped building with a lot of damp strangers. His mood was generally depressed, although there were still moments when he seemed able to forget his surroundings. He trained one of the other prisoners to be an unpaid valet and spent an inordinate amount of time trying to get his folding boot-jack brought to the prison. He stood by his habit of confusing the serious and the trivial to the last.

A Legitimist, Baron de Bresmenil, who was only in the prison for a very short time, decided to hold a dinner party for selected inmates. Brummell's reputation secured him an invitation and he was allowed to plan the menu. He did not choose cabbage or peas. Although he was a shadow of his former self, having suffered at least two strokes since being very prematurely retired as consul, he managed to rise to this particular occasion. He regaled his host with his stock of threadbare anecdotes about the good old days of the Regency and did not call out for any cider. Three other inmates were employed as waiters. Everything went smoothly until it came to locating a bottle of brandy with which to round off the proceedings. It had, much to Brummell's annoyance, been drunk by one of the gaolers. This banquet in a debtors' goal may seem to be very far removed from the elegance of the Carlton House Fête. The earlier event can, however, be seen as a party that was held by a spendthrift in a country that for many of its poorer inhabitants resembled a debtors' prison. Brummell himself was an elegant monster and the Regency high society that he dominated also displayed a mixture of the classical and the grotesque.

The second party recorded by Jesse took place in Brummell's squalid hotel room, just before he was taken away to die in the Bon Saveur Lunatic Asylum in 1840. Tom Moore, who passed through Caen three years earlier, recorded that 'The poor Beau's head gone, and his whole looks so changed that I never should have recognised him. Got wandering in his conversation more than once during dinner'.[50] Alvanley noted at around the same time that 'Poor Brummell is become imbecile'.[51] Brummell gave a servant instructions, but probably no money, to announce the names of distinguished guests such as the Duchess of Devonshire. She was the sister of Lady Bessborough and had died as long ago as 1806:

> At the sound of Her Grace's well-remembered name, the Beau, instantly rising from his chair, would advance towards the door, and greet the cold air from the staircase, as if it had been the beautiful Georgiana herself. If the dust of that fair creature could have stood reanimate in all her loveliness before him, she would not have thought his bow less graceful than it had been thirty-five years before; for, despite poor Brummell's mean habiliments and uncleanly person, the supposed visitor was received with all his former courtly ease of manner, and the earnestness that the pleasure of such an honour might be supposed to excite.[52]

Having greeted his imaginary guests in this way, he then proceeded to exchange pleasantries with them. Any long silences were eventually terminated by the announcement of the names of any late arrivals at the party. The servant finally put an end to what Jesse described as a farce by announcing that the carriages had arrived to take the dead guests home.

Brummell had delighted and amused his contemporaries by 'skimming the edge of nonsense', to return to Woolf's description. His last years were increasingly spent, like those of George III, in a world of no sense. At one level, the imaginary parties in Caen can be seen as a pathetic travesty of a glittering golden age. A similar interpretation is possible of Lady Hester Stanhope's last days at Djoun in the Lebanon. Brummell was now mad, sad and no longer very dangerous either to know or not to know. The parties can be seen at another level, however, as encapsulating important features of a Regency mentality. Brummell's world was a looking-glass one in which narcissistic selves admired themselves, their clothes and their wit. The presence of other actors and spectators was important, although possibly not absolutely essential. Brummell had to manage without them in Caen as he hovered on the verge of insanity and senility, but perhaps he did not always see them when he ruled fashionable society in London. If they were in his field of vision, he was as likely as not to cut them and therefore to cut them out of the individualistic performance that he was staging. For the dandy dedicated to real exclusivity, the only possible society ultimately had to consist of himself alone.

Although there are inevitably few details about his last days, it seems almost certain that he carried on playing himself until the very bitter end. There was no need for him to claim to be Napoleon. Lord Byron had playfully declared that Brummell was more important than any other contemporary figure, himself and Napoleon included. When Lady Hester Stanhope met an English traveller after she had been residing in the Lebanon for some time, the two people she immediately asked after were Brummell and the Duke of Wellington. Brummell did not have to play at power by writing abusive letters, as it has been suggested with certain qualifications that Austen did. He was given leave to perform on a very public stage. There are at least two readings of his decline and fall that are available. The first one might concentrate on the dandy who was ruined by play and became mad towards the end of his exile. Alternatively, it could be argued that Brummell stayed more or less the same while conventions, mentalities and locations changed around him. What was applauded as amusing, abusive nonsense in his heyday increasingly came to be seen as no sense as he continued to play the part of the Napoleon of fashion. Regency high society therefore becomes inextricably linked not just to the world of the debtors' prison, but also to that of the lunatic asylum.

Austen's later writings, with the exception of the unfinished *Sanditon*, are not usually related by critics in any precise sense to the crises, anxieties and scandals of the Regency period. One of the main reasons for this has been the tendency to locate them primarily within the ideological debates of the 1790s. If they are considered in terms of their more immediate historical contexts, then they are often seen as being highly critical of Regency society. Scrope Davies's biographer, T.A.J. Burnett, confidently asserts that the world of rakes and dandies that has just been explored here is 'so different from the world of Jane Austen, so at odds with the rising tide of Methodism and Evangelicalism that was foreshadowing the Victorian age'.[53] If Austen-Leigh could have claimed his aunt for Evangelicalism, it would have solved a lot of the problems he had with her writing. Although not above tampering with the evidence, he felt unable to make such a claim. Some critics, as will be seen, follow the spirit of Burnett's remarks and read the later writings as offering an Evangelical critique of certain rather generalised aspects of Regency society. This reading is certainly available and yet it is always in danger of underestimating the contradictions within the texts themselves. Kate Fullbrook, dealing with the question of Austen's comedy, identifies the way in which she can herself speak 'precisely in the voice of the culture she mocks', a comment that could also be applied to the dandies.[54] This suggests the possibility that the later writings might be capable of celebrating Regency values even in the very act of repudiating them.

Part III

The political condition of Regency England

4 *Mansfield Park*: The Regency Crisis and the theatre

INTRODUCTION

Although some of the arguments developed in this long chapter have already been anticipated, its structure still needs to be outlined. The first section shows that it was commonplace for writers in the 1790s and later on to make connections between the government of the estate and that of the state itself. This allows *Mansfield Park* to be read as a Condition-of-England novel that debates topical issues such as the conduct of the war and the Regency Crisis. The second section concentrates on the neglected figure of Tom Bertram and his regency. He threatens to destroy his father's house by bringing into it attitudes and acquaintances acquired at watering places such as Ramsgate and Weymouth. It will be shown, more particularly, that he is associated with some of the transgressive forms of cross-dressing and masquerade common in the Regency period. The third section locates Henry Crawford in the contexts that have already been established for dandyism. Other areas that will be explored include the ideas of Portsmouth that Regency readers might have brought with them to the text. All of these sections comment on the period of the theatrical rehearsals, which is indeed the main focus of attention in the chapter as a whole. The final two sections provide more details about the complex relationships between *Lovers' Vows*, the play that is being rehearsed, and *Mansfield Park*. The contradictory attitudes of various characters to theatre and theatricality are explored in order to bring out this complexity. Historical contexts that are developed here include the cultural status of the actress in Regency society and the 'old price' riots at Covent Garden in 1809.

The function of all of these individual sections is to suggest what is being missed by those critics who read the novel exclusively in terms of its conservative messages. J. Steven Watson pictures England at the end of the Napoleonic Wars as having 'two faces, the one bacchanalian the other businesslike'.[1] The argument here is that the novel itself is capable of wearing both of these faces or countenances. In other words, it will be shown that forms of business are not always and inevitably being endorsed at the expense of forms of carnival.

THE POLITICAL HOUSE

The details concerning the composition and publication of *Mansfield Park* are relatively uncontroversial. It was probably begun in February 1811, completed sometime during the summer of 1813 and then published in 1814. Alternative timescales nevertheless have been proposed. Q.D. Leavis suggests that the text may have had its origins in an expanded version of *Lady Susan*, written in 1809 and subsequently lost. This seems unlikely and it will be assumed here that composition coincided with the second Regency Crisis.[2]

The possibility of making connections between the novel and this topical context depends to some extent upon a recognition of the familiar links that were made in this period between the estate and the state. Mary Evans's interesting study of *Jane Austen and the State*, which suggests that Austen offers a searching critique of a market economy, does not, despite its title, show how commonplace such connections were at this time.[3] *The Morning Post* launched an attack on the policies of the Whigs and Radicals on 3 June 1811:

> They want to pull down the old house about our ears, and, if we escape being knocked on the head by the fall of its massive timbers, we are to depend on some political talisman for the erection of a new one.

The 'old house' is the state. The article offers a simplified version of the arguments that were advanced by Edmund Burke in his *Reflections on the Revolution in France* (1790). He represented the state as a landed estate which needed to be protected from innovations so that it could be handed on intact to the next generation. The present owners were merely privileged custodians who needed to recognise, and reverence, their responsibilities to their ancestors as well as to their successors.

Wollstonecraft was one of the many writers who contested Burke's theory of the state. She drew attention in *A Vindication of the Rights of Men* (1790) to the way in which he had not been so absolutely wedded to established authority during the first Regency Crisis when, like most other Whigs, he had supported the cause of the Prince of Wales. She was more concerned to reveal the irrational sentimentality that lay at the heart of an argument that nevertheless purported to derive its authority from legal and historical precedents. She did not challenge Burke's basic idea of the state as an estate, seeking to show instead the danger to women that was caused when absolutist models of government were reproduced in the domestic sphere. One of the major themes of *A Vindication of the Rights of Woman* is the way in which husbands become absolute monarchs of their households who rule their wives and children through what is seen as a divine right. A national government, which is based on the existence of masters and slaves, is replicated in the government of the household so that 'every family might also be called a state'.[4]

This connection between the estate and the state was subscribed to by both conservatives and radicals in the Regency period. Cobbett's well-known commentary on the sale of a farmhouse in Reigate in 1823 is also an account of national decline. William Hone's *The Political House that Jack Built* (1819) continues not just the ideological debates of the 1790s but also, more specifically, a tradition of criticism of the Regent that was associated with Gillray, Leigh Hunt, Cobbett and, in private, Austen herself. The head of the political house is represented by Hone as a dandy who enjoys dressing up in military and other uniforms. His only claim to fame is that he can make an elegant bow:

> This is THE MAN – all shaven and shorn,
> All cover'd with Orders – and all forlorn;
> The DANDY of SIXTY, who bows with a grace,
> And has *taste* in wigs, collars, cuirasses and lace; . . .

A cuirass is a breastplate. It was probably the sound of the word, together with the rude puns that it provoked, that appealed to Hone. He goes on to remind readers of the great betrayal that took place during the Regency Crisis when the Prince refused to allow the Whigs back into office.[5]

There are a number of reasons why *Mansfield Park* has not been considered in relation to the Regency Crisis. Too many critics still want to read it as a Victorian text. Julia Prewitt Brown declares that it is 'the first great novel' of this later period.[6] There has also always been a tendency, amongst those who accept the need for more precise contextualisation, to see it as a historical rather than a topical text. R.W. Chapman's widely-used edition, which was first published in 1923, offers a chronology of the events that happen after the ball that is given for Fanny on 22 December 1808. Subsequent work by Avrom Fleishman on the earlier chapters has produced a chronology that runs from 1781, when Maria Ward marries Sir Thomas Bertram, through to 1809.[7]

Such work, although it is always in danger of encouraging very literal readings, can nevertheless help to provide reminders of important contexts. It becomes clear, if these chronologies are followed, that Sir Thomas's trip to the West Indies coincides with the economic disruption that was caused by the continental blockade. Antigua was particularly vulnerable because it had to import almost all of its food. This may have been why Sir Thomas is forced to attend to his plantations in person. The reason why he stays there longer than he originally intended may be connected with the abolition of the slave trade, which became law during the course of his visit. This measure, which was aimed at some of the practices rather than the principle of slavery, intensified the economic difficulties facing many plantation owners. The novel can therefore be seen as at least raising issues about the colonies alongside the more detailed consideration of the future of both the state, Mansfield Park, and the state church, Mansfield Parsonage.[8]

Chronologies with all their faults also act as general reminders of the need to consider the Revolutionary and Napoleonic Wars in relation to the novel. Sir Thomas is personally as well as economically at risk as a result of the war and some fears are expressed for his safety. Warren Roberts shows that the novel contains other references to the war. William Price is on active service in both the West Indies and the Mediterranean and tells stories about his adventures when he visits Mansfield. His father has been invalided out of the marines.[9]

Roberts's study is still very useful because it demonstrates the advantages of employing an idea of the historical that does not confine itself exclusively to forms of literary and philosophical history. Nevertheless he misses some of the most interesting references to the war. Many of these are associated with Henry Crawford. He plays the part of Frederick, a young but war-weary soldier, during the rehearsals for *Lovers' Vows*. Austen's text only refers to the fact that he would have worn a 'knapsack' (MP, p. 158). The stage directions for the play, together with dialogue that refers explicitly to his regimental costume, make it very clear that he would have had to wear a soldier's uniform. The part calls for him to draw his sword at one point. All the textual evidence suggests that the Mansfield production paid particular attention to costume. What Roberts has missed, in other words, is the way in which Henry plays the part of a soldier for his own enjoyment at a time when others had to fight against the Napoleonic armies in the Iberian peninsula and elsewhere. This juxtaposition between Henry's pursuit of pleasure and the conduct of the war is continued when he visits Portsmouth. Locations such as the dockyard and the Garrison Chapel, which were inextricably linked with the war effort and were thus used to celebrate what turned out to be a premature peace in the summer of 1814, become theatrical sets against which he stages a play to try to convince Fanny to accept his marriage proposal.

It could be argued that William Price performs his duty, while Henry merely performs. His lack of profession allows him to make professions of love when dressed in a military uniform, or else when walking around a naval dockyard. Although Roberts only gathers the more obvious references to the war, his argument is broadly similar to the one that has just been outlined. Business, in this case the business of war, requires the exclusion of the Bacchanalian. One of the problems with such readings, which are used to support the view of Austen as an exclusively anti-Jacobin writer, is that they do not pay sufficient attention to the text's fascination with Henry Crawford and its relative lack of interest in the much more marginal William Price.

Roberts does notice the way in which both Henry and Mary Crawford are associated with French manners and mannerisms. Henry refers to cash-in-hand as '*menus plaisirs*' (MP, p. 237), a phrase that Mary also uses later on in the same conversation. When she attempts to persuade Fanny that Henry's elopement with Maria Rushworth is not to be taken too seriously, she describes it as being the result of a 'moment's *etourderie*'(MP, p. 426) or thoughtlessness. The Crawfords, with their French phrases and salon morality, are seen by Roberts as representing the threat that is posed to the political house by a decadent ruling class. If the estate and therefore in turn the state are unable to resist their considerable charms, then there may be a revolution as there was in France. Such a reading sees them not so much as radicals but, rather, as characters whose selfish behaviour is always in danger of provoking radical responses. This could be supported as far as Mary is concerned by the way in which she associates herself, through an anecdote, with the court of Louis XIV. Henry's position is, however, more ambiguous. He is a dandy and therefore possibly a Whig and so may threaten, but also enliven, the political house with his own particular version of patrician radicalism. The Crawfords are difficult to place. They are associated with London as well as with fashionable watering places such as Bath, Cheltenham and Tonbridge. Raymond Williams is still right nevertheless to insist that they should also be seen as members of the rural gentry.[10]

The context of the Napoleonic Wars will be developed at certain points during the reading that follows, although it will not in fact be seen as being as important as that provided by the Regency Crisis. It may be necessary to state again, given the unnecessary polarisations that have occurred within Austen criticism, that the concentration on this particular context is not meant to preclude the use of others. Claudia Johnson has produced one of the best recent readings of the novel, even though she sees it as a text that is still animated primarily by the ideological debates of the 1790s. Her analysis makes two crucial points. First of all, she rejects quite emphatically the idea that the novel simply recommends the banishment of the Bacchanalian, or theatrical, in favour of the businesslike. She shows skilfully that the two categories are far from being mutually exclusive by looking at, amongst other things, the way in which Sir Thomas himself is an accomplished actor. Secondly, she argues that the resolution, or ending, is too short, precarious and possibly parodic to resolve many of the issues that have been extensively debated throughout. Roberts, like the critics whom he follows, such as Butler and Duckworth, tends to read the novel backwards. In other words, he locates what are taken to be stable anti-Jacobin resolutions and then proceeds to read the rest of the novel in terms of them. Johnson, by contrast, argues that even at the end an anti-Jacobin message is still in competition with others.[11]

The idea that Austen's novels might convey a range of different messages and meanings was popularised by Sandra Gilbert and Susan Gubar's very influential study.[12] Briefly, their two chapters suggested that Austen had to learn how to inhabit, and be comfortable in, the confined social and literary spaces that were available to her. This process inevitably produced conservative novels. Gilbert and Gubar nevertheless also proposed the existence of submerged, or camouflaged, meanings in which these restrictions were contested and resisted. Their arguments were badly flawed and yet still immensely exciting because of the way in which they focused, and continue to focus, attention on previously marginalised moments and characters. One of the problems concerned the lack of literary history. Austen was presented as a writer who had to invent the rules for herself because she was seen as not being part of any literary tradition. The work of literary historians such as Butler, Johnson, Janet Todd and Jane Spencer has shown up the dangers of this approach.[13] There was also a lack of a wider social and cultural history. This meant that, to all intents and purposes, Austen became indistinguishable from the Victorian writers who were considered later on in the book. Another set of problems attached themselves to the model of authorship that was being proposed. Austen emerged as an omniscient author who was almost miraculously in control of each and every part of her texts and was thus able very knowingly and self-consciously to bury some of her more subversive meanings. Gilbert and Gubar's refreshing radicalism was badly compromised at times by this remarkably traditional view of authorship.

It will be clear from what has just been said that the representation of the regency crisis at Mansfield Park will not be read as a self-consciously camouflaged script. Given the widespread existence of equations between estate and state in this period it can, alternatively, be seen as a reasonably open, if not a transparent, one. This obviously begs difficult questions. As has been seen, male writers like Cobbett and Leigh Hunt who openly criticised the Regent were fined and imprisoned for doing so. This suggests that others would have thought very carefully before embarking on a similar course of action. This would have been particularly true for women writers as they were not expected to deal directly with the political condition of England, except in connection with more specific debates around female education. There were certainly pressures on Austen not to produce a representation of a regency crisis. The fact that *Mansfield Park* contains one might suggest that an author's intentions do not always provide a reliable guide to what is eventually produced.

THE REGENT OF MANSFIELD PARK

Tom Bertram is generally seen, if at all, as being a very marginal character. W. A. Craik suggests that, as far as the Bertram family is concerned, he is the least important character. Tony Tanner does not even bother to list the various parts from *Lovers' Vows* that he rehearses in notes on this part of the novel. D. D. Devlin creates a hybrid character called Tom Yates who elopes with Julia Bertram.[14] Tom is the heir to Mansfield Park. The novel foregrounds his inheritance, while at the same time keeping him in the background except during the period of the theatrical rehearsals. He is, like the rest of his family, 'well-looking'(MP, p. 49). He enjoys 'merriment' (MP, p. 54), which includes teasing Fanny. He also enjoys reminding himself and everybody else of his own privileged position. He may tease Fanny and yet also showers her with presents of work-boxes and netting-boxes. Whereas Edmund takes the trouble to find out what she is thinking, he is only concerned that she should think well of him. His sisters, Maria and Julia, do not want Fanny's approval and so only give her critical looks and discarded toys.

This ostentatious habit of giving too many presents is part of Tom's 'careless and extravagant' (MP, p. 56) character which gets worse as he gets older. His debts prevent Sir Thomas from retaining the Mansfield living for Edmund and are thus responsible for its occupation by Dr

Grant and therefore also by the Crawfords. Sir Thomas tries in vain to make him realise the error of his ways and become more businesslike:

> Tom listened with some shame and some sorrow; but escaping as quickly as possible, could soon with cheerful selfishness reflect, 1st, that he had not been half so much in debt as some of his friends; 2ndly, that his father had made a most tiresome piece of work of it; and 3rdly, that the future incumbent, whoever he might be, would, in all probability, die very soon. (MP, pp. 58–9)

His cheerfulness is indicated by the way in which he proceeds to mimic his father's methodical mode of address. The Prince Regent was well-known for doing impersonations of his own father. Tom's debts include gambling ones and he calculates the odds in favour of the new incumbent not being too much of an encumbrance to Edmund's career. The fact that Dr Grant turns out to be 'a hearty man of forty-five' (MP, p. 59) does not undermine Tom's confidence that Edmund will get the living sooner rather than later. As if he were judging a horse before a race, he argues that Dr Grant 'was a short-neck'd, apoplectic sort of fellow, and, plied well with good things, would soon pop off' (MP, p. 59). Dr Grant does indeed die from gluttony in a relatively short space of time.

Tom ignores his father's advice and continues to absent himself from Mansfield in his pursuit of pleasure. Before Mary Crawford comes to live at the Parsonage, she has been aware of his presence at fashionable parties in London where she was impressed by his 'liveliness and gallantry'(MP, p. 80). Sir Thomas's scheme to take Tom with him to the West Indies is one of his unsuccessful educational experiments. As soon as Tom returns, he rushes off for a holiday in Ramsgate with his friend Sneyd instead of attending to the business of being regent of Mansfield Park.

Ramsgate was one of the many small fishing villages which had mushroomed into fashionable resorts, or watering places, during this period. Although it was not considered by some to be quite as fashionable as neighbouring Margate, it was still particularly popular with Londoners. *The Morning Post* reported on 18 September 1811 that the 'refined amusements here are card parties at private houses'. Private houses were also used for amateur theatricals. Other amusements included lounging on the famous pier, driving out to a gothic ruin for picnics and frequenting the Assembly Rooms. Such seaside resorts became notorious for the opportunities they offered for secret engagements and elopements. Ramsgate itself provides the location for George Wickham's unsuccessful attempt to elope with Georgiana

Darcy in *Pride and Prejudice*. The Duke of Clarence spent the autumn of 1811 here trying to captivate an heiress, after he had abruptly ended his relationship with Dorothy Jordan. Ramsgate catered for professional invalids as well as for professional lovers. As noted, Mrs Edward Bridges came here in 1813 to find a suitable stage on which to play the part of the sick woman.

Contemporary guide books pointed out that Ramsgate offered delightful views, or prospects, across the English Channel. When Tom took his holiday there Britain was still at war with France, so the prospect would have included signs of this conflict. Ramsgate had a naval garrison at which Frank Austen was stationed in 1803, when there were widespread fears of a French invasion. Caroline Powys, who visited the resort two years earlier, records in her diary how she heard the sound of Admiral Nelson's attack on Boulogne: 'The firing off Boulogne we heard very plain at Ramsgate that evening. He was said to be going from thence to do the same at Flushing, and took a great many men from Ramsgate and Margate to show them, as he had told them, some service.'[15] The possibilities that are open for a Condition-of-England reading, which contrasts Tom's pursuit of pleasure with the business of the war, are heightened by the fact that he stays at the significantly named Albion Place. This was a real location and yet it is not the only one that could have been chosen. The novel raises questions about how the sons of Albion ought to behave in a time of war.

Tom eventually returns to Mansfield, providing Mary Crawford with an opportunity to try to captivate the eldest son of a baronet. His advantages are listed according to Mary's perceptions of them:

> he had easy manners, excellent spirits, a large acquaintance, and a great deal to say; and the reversion of Mansfield Park, and a baronetcy, did no harm to all this. Miss Crawford soon felt, that he and his situation might do. She looked about her with due consideration and found almost every thing in his favour . . . (MP, p. 80)

Mary is more interested in Tom's potential property than in his propriety. He then leaves Mansfield to go to the races, where one of the horses that he has trained is due to run. Regency racecourses were not exclusively masculine preserves, although there were often restrictions imposed on women. They were supposed to stay inside their carriages at Newmarket, whereas men could roam about the course both on foot and on horseback. Tom enjoys acting the part of regent but quickly gets bored with its more mundane duties. Mary fears that she will miss this engaging and entertaining master of ceremonies, despite his lack of interest in her:

> In comparison with his brother, Edmund would have nothing to say. The soup would be sent round in a most spiritless manner, wine drank without any smiles, or agreeable trifling, and the venison cut up without supplying one pleasant anecdote of any former haunch or a single entertaining story about 'my friend such a one'. (MP, p. 84)

She associates Tom with food, drink and lively conversation. Edmund's regency, by contrast, is based upon order and method rather than on spectacle and gesture. Conspicuous consumption and heightened theatricality give way to a concern for estate management. The Bacchanalian is replaced by the businesslike. Edmund, like his father, spends his time 'talking to the steward, writing to the attorney, settling with the servants'(MP, p. 68).

The Crawfords' sexuality is conveyed through the seductive power of their voices. Marylea Meyershon also suggests that there are connections between passion and food as far as members of the younger generation are concerned.[16] The enjoyment of food indicates a willingness to participate in other pleasurable activities. Pleasure itself is something to be tasted and even 'devoured'(MP, p. 92). Tom gives all the correct signals that he is one of the sexually active characters and yet remains the only member of his generation who appears to remain free from attachments. It is suggested that Fanny might not have been able to resist Henry Crawford 'had not her affection been engaged elsewhere' (MP, p. 241). Her concealed love for Edmund prevents her from following her cousins and succumbing to Henry's power. Mary's sexuality is equally powerful which, as indicated, raises questions about how Tom is able to resist her quite so easily, particularly as there is no explicit reference to his own affections being otherwise engaged.

Those characters who shy away from food can also be seen as making statements about their other appetites. Fanny only manages to eat 'two mouthfuls'(MP, p. 50) of a gooseberry tart when she first arrives at Mansfield. Food or drink only really become acceptable to her as last resorts in her campaigns to remain silent. She swallows 'the greater part'(MP, p. 103) of a glass of madeira to avoid getting drawn into an argument between Edmund and Mrs Norris. It is implied that the sight of the 'solemn procession, headed by Baddely, of the tea-board, urn, and cake-bearers'(MP, p .341) is only a pleasant one for her because it prevents her from having to talk to Henry Crawford. She is hardly able to 'eat any thing'(MP, p. 307) at dinner on the day that

Henry proposes to her. The only exception to this general rule of restraint takes place during the ball for her at Mansfield. She appears to consume a certain amount of food and drink during it, for when Sir Thomas self-consciously orders her to go to bed she is 'feverish with hopes and fears, soup and negus' (MP, p. 286). He is staging a play to impress Henry Crawford with her obedience. This is just one of the examples that supports Johnson's claim that he is 'the most assiduous of actors at Mansfield Park'.[17]

Edmund eats sandwiches while he listens to Mary playing the harp and falls in love with her. When the Mansfield party arrive at Sotherton, they are almost immediately given something to eat:

> After the business of arriving was over, it was first necessary to eat, and the doors were thrown open to admit them through one or two intermediate rooms into the appointed dining-parlour, where a collation was prepared with abundance and elegance. Much was said, and much was ate, and all went well. (MP, p. 113)

This provides a fitting prelude for those characters who use the outing to try to free themselves from social and sexual restraints. The proposal to visit Sotherton, like the plan to stage a play, was itself the product of a dinner-table conversation. The party sit down again to eat just before their return to Mansfield. It is not revealed this time how much was eaten but Fanny, who consumes conversations in much the same way as her enemies consume food, notices the way in which Henry tries to use his elegant table-talk to smooth over resentments and to 'restore general good humour' (MP, p. 131). Henry certainly reveals that he has a good appetite when he visits her in Portsmouth. He eats two dinners at the Crown and the last one is referred to as 'the best dinner that a capital inn afforded' (MP, p. 404). Fanny shys away from food throughout her stay in Portsmouth, almost becoming a fasting woman. The representation of Tom as a regent who not only enjoys food and drink, but who also likes talking about them, carries messages about the real and potential licence that characterises his rule.

Tom's concern with his own pleasure meant that it was the gamekeeper who was the first to be informed that he was about to return home. His return to Mansfield after time spent at the races and at watering places appears to confirm Mary in her decision to prefer Edmund:

> by the end of August, he arrived himself, to be gay, agreeable, and gallant again as occasion served, or Miss Crawford demanded, to tell of races and Weymouth, and parties and friends, to which she might have listened six weeks before with some interest, and

altogether to give her the fullest conviction, by power of actual comparison, of her preferring his younger brother. (MP, p. 141)

Mary may be resolved not to like Tom any more, although she seems to be making a virtue of necessity:

his lengthened absence from Mansfield, without any thing but pleasure in view, and his own will to consult, made it perfectly clear that he did not care about her; and his indifference was so much more equalled by her own, that were he now to step forth the owner of Mansfield park, the Sir Thomas complete, which he was to be in time, she did not believe she could accept him. (MP, p. 141)

She is not as indifferent to Tom's title as she affects to be. She is still harping upon the subject when he is seriously ill and there is a chance that Edmund might get it after all. She only rejects Tom as a potential husband when his 'indifference' to her becomes too humiliating. When Henry is refused by Fanny, he pursues her with a renewed vigour because this is a new experience for him. Mary is also used to getting what she wants when she wants it, but she has to concede reluctantly that Tom is a lost cause as far as she is concerned.

Tom reassumes his position as regent and continues to play the part of a master of pleasurable ceremonies. The first of these is an impromptu, or unpremeditated, ball:

It was Fanny's first ball, though without the preparation or splendour of many a young lady's first ball, being the thought only of the afternoon, built on the late acquisition of a violin player in the servants' hall, and the possibility of raising five couple with the help of Mrs Grant and a new intimate friend of Mr Bertram's just arrived on a visit. (MP, p. 143)

The difference between Tom's style of government and that of his father becomes apparent when these casual arrangements are contrasted with the meticulous forward planning for Fanny's own ball. Tom's regency always runs the risk of making the servants and other employees at Mansfield discontented with their lot. He privileges the gamekeeper over the steward and selects a new servant to perform an important part at this ball. If all was well below stairs, perhaps there might not have been a new servant in the first place. The servants become even more discontented during the period of the theatrical rehearsals. Isobel Armstrong notices the way in which the servants often provide a potentially menacing audience for the actions of the main characters. One implication of this is that Mansfield Park is associated with forms of theatre long before the rehearsals for *Lovers' Vows* take place.[18]

Tom's behaviour during the impromptu ball confirms earlier impressions that he is uninterested in mixed company. Fanny, after dancing four times, has to sit out. She therefore adopts her familiar position as a listener, this time to a conversation between Mrs Norris and Mrs Rushworth. The topic is Mrs Norris's plan to make a marriage for Julia now that she has had such a triumph as far as Maria is concerned. Tom may fulfil some of the more symbolic and festive functions of a regent, although this conversation indicates that Mrs Norris has the real power. Fanny also has to watch Edmund dancing with Mary Crawford. She hopes to be rescued from these unpleasant sights and sounds by Tom's sudden appearance: 'He came towards their little circle; but instead of asking her to dance, drew a chair near her, and gave her an account of the present state of a sick horse, and the opinion of the groom, from whom he had just parted' (MP, p. 145). He is blind to Fanny's feelings and behaves just as he might do in a gentleman's club. His conversation continues to be more appropriate for the club than the ballroom. He fails to notice that Fanny, despite her polite protestations to the contrary, really wants to dance and then proceeds to tell her that a respectable married woman like Mrs Grant ought to take a lover. Scandalous conversation as well as behaviour is produced by the Mansfield environment itself as well as being brought in from outside by the Crawfords. The businesslike atmosphere necessarily creates the Bacchanalian impulse. The banishments and reformations at the end of the novel therefore need to be seen as only producing, at best, a temporary respite from the seeds of destruction that Mansfield and by implication England must always inevitably carry within itself.

Tom eventually dances with Fanny, although only as a way of escaping from a card game that Mrs Norris is trying to organise. His aunt displays her irresponsibility by attempting to interest him in gambling, giving him permission to 'bet half-guineas' (MP, p. 145) with Dr Grant. Sir Thomas would not have been pleased by this open encouragement of his eldest son's vices. Tom, who is used to playing for much higher stakes, has no intention of being trapped at a card table for two hours with such unprofessional players. He therefore selfishly takes advantage of Fanny to prevent his aunt from selfishly taking advantage of him. He complains about her lack of ceremony when his own conduct towards Fanny has been anything but ceremonious.

Tom forms a large number of male friendships in London and at fashionable seaside resorts such as Ramsgate and Weymouth. The Honourable John Yates, although only a casual acquaintance of ten days' standing, is regarded by Tom nevertheless as an 'intimate friend' (MP, p. 143) after they meet at Weymouth. The impromptu ball is given in his honour, making it as much a celebration of homosociablity as it is of heterosexuality and matchmaking. *Mansfield Park*, like *Emma*, is haunted by the consequences of a relationship that is formed in Weymouth. Sir Thomas, on his return, takes a particular dislike to the dandified, aristocratic Yates as well as to his eldest son's general habit of picking up a large number of what are seen to be undesirable male friends: 'Mr Yates's family and connections were sufficiently known to him, to render his introduction as the "particular friend", another of the hundred particular friends of his son, exceedingly unwelcome' (MP, p. 199). Tom's regency is characterised by sudden movement, for instance his own unpredictable entrances and exits together with events such as the impromptu ball. It is therefore entirely appropriate that Yates should make an unexpected entrance as a result of the fact that the aristocratic house party which he had been attending was brought to an abrupt end by a death in the family. He, like Tom, is a character who is always on the move in search of new pleasures to taste and devour.

Yates seeks to impress everyone with his dramatic tales of the theatricals at Ecclesford and Tom tries to impress this latest in the long line of intimate male friends by allowing him to use Mansfield as his stage. As mentioned, the plan to perform a play takes shape during a dinner-table conversation. Tom, in keeping with his position as regent, takes the initiative throughout these early discussions. Mansfield produces the theatrical impulse itself, as well as importing it from outside. Tom enthusiastically supports the general proposition that a play might be the thing to pass the time:

> the inclination to act was awakened, and in no one more strongly than in him who was master of the house; and who having so much leisure as to make almost any novelty a certain good, had likewise such a degree of lively talents and comic taste, as were exactly adapted to the novelty of acting. (MP, pp. 148–9)

He then insists, against the wishes of both Henry and Maria, that acting can only really take place in a proper theatre. He starts off by emphasising the need for a curtain, which would transform public spaces into more private ones. He is not content, however, until he has transformed the billiard-room into a miniature theatre. He takes the estate carpenter, Christopher Jackson, away from useful business and hires a scene painter from Northampton. The housemaids are used to make the curtain. Tom's scheme to alter the physical character of his father's house also disrupts its social structures, since this scene painter succeeds in making 'five of the under-servants idle and dissatisfied' (MP, p. 206). The image of the regent as a lord of misrule is reinforced by the fact that one of the scenes which is painted is an ale-house. Tom drinks heavily when away from Mansfield and so can be seen to be using his father's absence, together with the cover or curtain provided by the play, to bring at least a version of his pleasures much closer to home.[19]

It is also Tom who eventually ends the bickering over the choice of a play by proposing *Lovers' Vows*. He sketches in how this particular play might suit the individual talents of the aspiring actors, although typically he is only concerned with the male parts. Nevertheless he enters into the subsequent debate over the women's parts with the 'authoritative urgency' (MP, p. 172) that characterises this period of his regency. He insists that Mary takes the part of Amelia, not out of any romantic feelings for her, but because he values her abilities as a comic actress. He is so concerned with getting everything decided quickly that he does not foresee that the casting of Mary as Amelia sets up the problem of what parts his own sisters are to play. The regent, who ought to safeguard the interests of the family, puts the claims of outsiders first.

Henry may have danced with Julia at the ball but he, like Tom, also needs change and novelty. Therefore he selects Maria to play opposite him. It is at this point in the anarchic proceedings that Tom suggests, in a highly theatrical speech, a form of cross-dressing to try to placate Julia:

> We cannot have two Agathas, and we must have one Cottager's Wife; and I am sure I set her [Julia] the example of moderation myself in being satisfied with the old Butler. If the part is trifling she will have more credit in making something of it; and if she is so desperately bent against every thing humorous, let her take Cottager's speeches instead of Cottager's wife's and so change the parts all through; *he* is solemn and pathetic enough I am sure. It could make no difference in the play; and as for Cottager himself, when he has got his wife's speeches, I would undertake him with all my heart. (MP, pp. 158–9)

This piece of casting allows for a transgression of class boundaries. Tom, who has already appropriated the part of an old servant, the

Butler, declares his willingness to take on another working-class character. It also inverts generational distinctions as the young master will have to play two old men. He suggests that Julia should follow the same pattern and agree to play an elderly working-class character. He is not content with just turning class and generational distinctions upside down and so adds potentially more subversive gender ones as well. His scheme is for Julia and himself to play parts which are a mixture of the male and the female. Henry, trying perhaps to get back in Julia's good books, notes that given Tom's 'partiality for Cottager's wife' (MP, p. 159) there may not be much of a part left for her. Tom starts off ignoring the women's parts and then enthusiastically volunteers to play at least a version of one of them. He puts a representation of an ale-house up in his father's billiard-room and offers to perform a drag act in front of it. Some massive timbers would have come crashing down if he had had his way.

Cross-dressing is referred to in *Pride and Prejudice* when Lydia Bennet reports how she and Mrs Forster dressed up one of the officers, significantly named Pratt, 'in women's clothes, on purpose to pass for a lady' (PP, p. 248). Tom signals, albeit briefly, his desire to pass for a woman. The status and reputation of the Regency theatre and its performers will be considered later on, although it is worth mentioning here that *Lovers' Vows* was a play that was cross-dressed on the professional stage. Charlotte Goodall was one of the actresses who took the part of Frederick. Tom opens up the doors of Mansfield not just to the theatre itself, but also to the high society Regency masquerade ball. Sarah Spencer records how two young male aristocrats went to a masquerade 'as two tall young ladies, dressed in the last fashion, with diamonds, spotted muslin, and silver turbans and feathers'. Men from lower social classes who dressed up as women in the molly houses were put in the pillory. Class and generational distinctions were also turned upside-down in masquerade. Mary Berry dressed up, or rather down, as an old peasant woman for a masquerade, while her sister Agnes went as a housemaid. They met a Miss Godfrey there who was dressed as a monk. Tom's regency offers the transgressive pleasures of the masquerade ball.[20]

Tom is different from the other aspiring players in that he does not covet a particular role. He is much more interested in playing a variety of parts and signals this interest even before *Lovers' Vows* has been chosen. All the parts that he ends up rehearsing are relatively minor ones which suggests that, although regent, he nevertheless desires a less responsible social position. He starts off by choosing the part of the Butler, an occupation not entirely unconnected with drinking. This allows him to play the servant to Yates's master. He does not manage to convince the others that his pantomime dame version of Cottager's Wife would solve any problems and so has to settle for playing the part of the Cottager instead. He almost certainly snaps up the trifling part of Countryman as well and, with a bit of editing, is probably able to add the Landlord of the ale-house to his growing collection. He could also have played one of the gamekeepers.

Tom is a marginal character for much of the novel and this may explain why his more central role during the theatrical rehearsals is not given the attention that it deserves. He dominates the initial discussions over the choice of both a venue and a play. His casting of the parts, particularly in the cases of Henry and Maria, has far-reaching and disruptive consequences. Speed, sudden movement and selfishness are, once again, revealed to be the hallmarks of his regency. He threatens to ride off and invite an outsider to take the part of Anhalt before Edmund agrees to play it. He still dashes around the neighbourhood issuing invitations for the performance, despite an earlier promise that the audience would be strictly limited. He is so impatient for the curtain to go up that he speaks his lines much too quickly when rehearsing them. Those who hold out against involvement in the play, such as Julia and Fanny, are either ignored or bullied.

Tom is rapidly marginalised again when the return of Sir Thomas eventually leads to the destruction of the theatre and the end of the regency period. Edmund reports that his brother 'is certainly not at his ease'(MP, p. 211) following the restoration of the old order. Tom stays at Mansfield for some time, perhaps under orders to do so. He then all but disappears from the narrative. Mary indicates that he has left Mansfield when she tells Fanny how pleased she is that Edmund can now be referred to as Mr Bertram, showing that she is still concerned about the fact that Edmund is not the eldest son. Edmund himself becomes concerned about his elder brother's unpredictable movements. His plans to get Fanny a chain so that she can wear her amber cross at the ball are delayed because Tom was not in London when he was supposed to be. This delay makes Fanny more vulnerable to the machinations of the Crawfords and is therefore part of the pattern by which Tom's carelessness, either directly or indirectly, provides openings and opportunities for Mansfield's enemies.

It is only towards the end of Fanny's stay in Portsmouth that more information is provided about Tom's mysterious movements. Fanny receives a letter from Lady Bertram, the contents of which are summarised:

>Tom had gone from London with a party of young men to New-
>market, where a neglected fall, and a good deal of drinking, had
>brought on a fever; and when the party broke up, being unable to
>move, had been left by himself at the house of one of these young
>men, to the comforts of sickness and solitude, and the attendance
>only of servants. Instead of being soon well enough to follow his
>friends, as he had then hoped, his disorder increased considerably,
>and it was not long before he thought so ill of himself, as to be as
>ready as his physician to have a letter dispatched to Mansfield. (MP,
>p. 416)

Tom has obviously absented himself from Mansfield so that he can
continue to drink and gamble in the company of a new set of intimate
male friends. Newmarket offered opportunities to gamble both on and
off the course since William Crockford, who owned one of the leading
gaming clubs in London, had started a similar establishment there.
The lid was partially lifted off the seamier side of Newmarket life in
1812 when Daniel Dawson was tried and eventually convicted for
poisoning a horse. He was executed at the top of Cambridge Castle on
a market day before a large crowd. The case attracted a lot of publicity
and so might have been a reference point for Regency readers.[21]

Tom's selfishness is well-matched by that of his new set of intimate
friends who, calculating the odds that he will probably survive, race off
in search of new pleasures. He wanted to play servants in *Lovers' Vows*
and is now left at their mercy until a physician arrives. His illness is
represented in such a way as to provide insights into almost every other
character except himself. Lady Bertram abandons her semi-recumbent
posture on the sofa as a result of both the news of Tom's condition and
the sight of him when he is eventually brought home to Mansfield. She
still has to be protected from some of the more serious implications of
his illness. Johnson notices the way in which, despite this, she merely
plays at being frightened. Tom's sisters, however, are completely
unaffected by the news and remain in London. Mrs Norris's melodramatic habit of 'heightening danger in order to enhance her own
importance'(MP, p. 422) shows that she too remains unchanged. As
noticed earlier, Mary's responses, despite all her affectations that she is
not interested in the title, are also selfish ones. Sir Thomas is shaken by
his eldest son's collapse, which forces him to begin the slow process of
recognising his almost complete failure as an educationalist. He is still
not much use to Tom as his voice is too loud for the sick-room. It is left
therefore to Edmund to read and talk to his brother and generally to
nurse him back to health. Fanny is more concerned with the effect of
the illness on the inhabitants of Mansfield as a whole than she is with

Tom's particular circumstances. She still hopes that he might recover so that he can start to lead a useful life.

The illness is seen initially, albeit indirectly, in terms of its physical manifestations. Tom's fever gives way to 'some strong hectic symptoms'(MP, p. 419) and his family are 'apprehensive for his lungs'(MP, p. 419). It looks as though he may have consumption. This emphasis on physical symptoms is then gradually replaced by a concern for his moral health. Fanny recognises that the road to recovery will have to be paved with good moral intentions:

> There was not only the debility of recent illness to assist; there was also, as she now learnt, nerves much affected, spirits much depressed to calm and raise; and her own imagination added that there must be a mind to be properly guided. (MP, pp. 419–20)

It is tempting to say that Tom emerges from the sick-room as a new man and this, as will be seen in a moment, is what the resolution itself appears to be saying. Such a conservative message, which supports the rights of eldest sons in particular and the anti-Jacobin position more generally, is at least compromised by the fact that there is no direct representation of this event.

The silence about Tom's return to the family circle may in the end be more significant than the clean bill of health that is eventually briskly written out for him in the resolution:

> He had suffered, and he had learnt to think, two advantages that he had never known before; and the self-reproach arising from the deplorable event in Wimpole Street, to which he felt himself accessory by all the dangerous intimacy of his unjustifiable theatre, made an impression on his mind which, at the age of six-and-twenty, with no want of sense, or good companions, was durable in its happy effects. He became what he ought to be, useful to his father, steady and quiet, and not living merely for himself. (MP, p. 447)

The prodigal son eventually returns and yet no fatted calves are killed for him. The text appears to take pleasure in locking him away in the sick-room for as long as possible. There are, perhaps, elements of a revenge fantasy against an eldest son at work in the descriptions of his illness and long confinement.

It is technically a misreading to claim that Fanny inherits Mansfield Park. She and Edmund eventually move into Mansfield Parsonage. It is, nevertheless, still very common for readers to form the impression that Fanny does indeed end up living at Mansfield Park itself. Even distinguished historicist critics can make this mistake: Edward Said declares that Fanny 'becomes the mistress of Mansfield Park'.[22] Such slips can be put down to a lack of attention. It can, alternatively, be argued that such a text is actually available. Tom's marginalisation is heightened by his confinement. Although he is eventually allowed out of the sick-room, his reformation forms a relatively minor part of the resolution as a whole. There is also a deafening silence on the crucial question of whether the heir to Mansfield will ever produce an heir himself. Questions remain unanswered about his sexuality. The recovery of the eldest son forms part of an orthodox resolution. The fact that it is written about in such a way as to make it instantly forgettable for many readers and critics points in a more subversive direction. Tom's own reformation also quickly pushes to one side, rather than resolves, the problem of how to prevent a businesslike Mansfield from always being in danger of producing Bacchanalia from within. The banishment of the Crawfords does not provide a satisfactory answer to this question.

There is certainly an open critique of Tom's anarchic, Regency lifestyle and yet, as will become apparent later on, this is not the whole story. The restoration of the old order that takes place when Sir Thomas returns from the West Indies is by no means unreservedly endorsed. As will be seen, there are moments when Tom's point of view is selected in order to undermine his father's authority. Regency values are sometimes celebrated while they are being repudiated. This happens not just in relation to the regent of Mansfield, but also with the dandy who comes to dominate the political house during the regency period.

THE DANDY ON PARADE

Henry Crawford shares a few of Tom Bertram's sporting interests. He has enough money to go hunting on a regular basis and his Norfolk estate provides him with good shooting. There is, nevertheless, a crucial difference between these men of pleasure. Tom chooses the racecourse, the gambling table and the ale-house as his particular battlegrounds. Henry uses the drawing-room for his campaigns. Tom's apparent 'indifference' to women poses its own kind of threat to the continuation of Mansfield values, but then so does Henry's interest in their society. His presence in the drawing-room is just as dangerous as Tom's absence from it.

Henry's conversation is repeatedly associated with military metaphors. He makes an 'attack of gallantry and compliment' (MP, p. 181) to try to humour Julia when she does not get a part in the play. He conducts a 'parley of compliment'(MP, p. 157) with Yates over which one of them is going to dress up in the military uniform. His conversation during his pursuit of Fanny is frequently alluded to as a military attack that she tries to repulse. He is particularly dangerous because he can adapt his conversational advances to suit the ebb and flow of the battle. He is at his most lethal when the 'general buz' (MP, p. 253) of conversation provides him with the necessary 'shelter' (MP, p. 253) for making a quick and unexpected advance.

The differences between Henry and Tom can be seen in their attitudes towards card games. Tom, like Scrope Davies and Brummell, is a professional gambler and therefore refuses to play with amateurs like Mrs Norris. Although Henry's voice is the most powerful weapon in his armoury, it is well supported by his skill at cards. He is an expert at Speculation, being 'pre-eminent in all the lively turns, quick resources, and playful impudence that could do honour to the game' (MP, p. 249). He is nevertheless primarily interested in employing these particular skills in order to attack Fanny at the Grants' second dinner party. There is no such thing as safe ground when he is present. Fanny and the patriotic William remain at the card-table after the end of the game. Sir Thomas makes a formal speech to Henry about the evils of clerical pluralism. It is the first time that evening that Fanny appears to be safe from attack. The party is about to break up anyway, so she can be forgiven for relaxing her defences for a moment or two. This however is precisely when the Napoleon of the drawing-room starts another advance:

> William and Fanny were the most detached. They remained together at the otherwise deserted card-table, talking very comfortably and not thinking of the rest, till some of the rest began to think of them. Henry Crawford's chair was the first to be given a direction towards them, and he sat silently observing them for a few minutes; himself in the meanwhile observed by Sir Thomas . . . (MP, p. 256)

Fanny is relatively fortunate on this particular occasion since Henry wants to stage a scene to impress Sir Thomas rather than her. She, like the chair, becomes one of his stage props.

Sudden movement is one of the keys to his success. He can turn conversations quickly, give his chair a rapid change of direction and generally conduct the kind of tactical manoeuvres that immediately alter the terrain of his particular battlefield. The early arrivals at Fanny's ball are confronted by the 'gravity and formality of the first great circle'(MP, p. 279). In other words, everybody had to stand together in the kind of large, formal group that was increasingly seen during the Regency period as being old-fashioned. Henry, who always times his entrances well, arrives a little later and proceeds, with the Grants and Mary, to break up the main group. Fanny is grateful for Henry's tactical skill on this occasion, although she is usually made painfully aware that it is really her enemy rather than her friend.

Tom is a Regency sportsman and Henry is a representation of a Regency dandy. Tanner notices, when dealing with the metropolitan mentality of the Crawfords, that the novel belongs to the age of Beau Brummell and yet he does not go on to explore this context in any detail.[23] This may be because it is difficult to visualise Henry as a dandy. There are only two hints about the kind of clothes that he might have worn, neither of which is conclusive. The evidence for his dandyism is in fact provided by both his mode of address and accompanying gestures, rather than by his dress itself. Some of his off-the-cuff remarks have all the arrogance of Brummell himself. Edmund wonders whether he asked anyone for confirmation that he was in Thornton Lacey, after he has had to leave the hunting field. He replies: 'No, I never inquire. But I *told* a man mending a hedge that it was Thornton Lacey, and he agreed to it' (MP, p. 250). This remark exhibits the seemingly nonchalant minimalism that Hazlitt identified as being one of the defining characteristics of the dandy mode of address. It shows that Henry, like his sister, adopted a haughty attitude towards rural workers. Like Brummell, he fashions his conversation into exquisite little mirrors to reflect his own sense of superiority.

Henry's gestures also reveal his dandyism. There are frequent references to his habit of making elegant bows. This gesture is explicitly referred to as a mocking one after his attempt to impress Fanny by reading from Shakespeare. He acknowledges Edmund's genuine compliments 'with a bow of mock gravity' (MP, p. 336). Sir Thomas bows politely to him at the beginning of the speech against clerical pluralism. He responds with one bow to express his 'acquiescence' (MP, p. 255) and another almost immediately afterwards to indicate his 'thanks' (MP, p. 255). His behaviour is technically correct and yet there is a strong hint that it hovers on the dividing line between social poise and theatrical pose. The second bow mocks the propriety of the first. Henry hovers, like Brummell, on the verge of insolence.

Henry does not have Tom Bertram's natural good looks and presence. Maria and Julia initially consider him to be plain and it is only his 'pleasing address'(MP, p. 77) that persuades them to think otherwise. He may not have a particularly classical body but, like other dandies, does his best to make it appear so through careful cultivation.

Brummell's broken nose did not prevent him from becoming the epitome of shape and proportion. Henry improves himself in much the same way as he claims to be able to improve a landscape: by removing the plain and ordinary in order to emphasise the stylish and stylised.[24] He is remarkably successful at this since almost everybody is captivated by his charm. Sir Thomas declares that he has 'address and conversation pleasing to everybody' (MP, p. 316). Even Mr Rushworth initially forms a good opinion of Henry, indicating that the dandy exhibited himself as much for male as for female admiration.

Henry's mobility within the drawing-room is part of a wider pattern. He is able, like Frank Churchill in *Emma*, to exit from a particular location when it suits him to do so. By contrast, Fanny is totally dependent on the provision of transport to undertake even the short distance between Mansfield Park and Mansfield Parsonage. Henry retreats to Bath after the disruption of the theatricals and then makes an unexpected entrance just in time for the first dinner party at the Parsonage. This is when he decides to make an equally dramatic entrance into Fanny's life. Tom establishes what he thinks are 'intimate' male friendships within the space of ten days and Henry believes that a fortnight is all he needs to get Fanny to change her hostile opinion of him. Churchill's first visit to Highbury lasted a fortnight. Henry is so confident of his ability to win this particular battle that he plans to attack her only on the days when he is not out hunting. He describes this pursuit of Fanny as 'labour' (MP, p. 239), just as he referred to the theatrical rehearsals as 'employment' (MP, p. 236). His only profession, however, is to make professions of his love. He is a professional lover. Bacchanalia is his business.

His first skirmish is not a particularly successful one. He reads the latest naval intelligence, not out of any patriotic concern over the current state of the war with France, but only to find out when William Price might be expected at Mansfield. The theatrical messenger enters too late with his message, since Fanny already knows when William is going to arrive. His next attack is more successful. The fact that he had never bothered to register William's existence, just as he all but denies the presence of the rural hedger, does not prevent him from forming an immediate and intimate friendship with him. William is delighted to be offered the chance of travelling to London with 'such a good humoured agreeable friend' (MP, p. 272) the day after Fanny's ball. Henry issues the invitation unexpectedly on the day of the ball itself by sending round a note 'soon after breakfast' (MP, p. 272). Although he does not state categorically here or elsewhere why he needs to go to London in such an apparent hurry, he lets it be assumed that important business summons him. His lack of employment allows him to play at being employed.

Henry becomes associated with breakfast at Mansfield. Earlier on, when he and Dr Grant call to pay their respects to Sir Thomas on his return from the West Indies, it is 'at rather an early hour' so 'they were ushered into the breakfast-room, where were most of the family' (MP, p. 207). For all his parade of manners, Henry is not quite a gentleman because he disturbs the family before it is socially acceptable to do so. He may, however, be able to get away with this breach of etiquette on this particular occasion because he is leaving for Bath. The breakfast-room was nevertheless a family space which was not supposed to be used for the reception of callers. Mary Mitford was surprised to find, when staying in Northumberland, that this general rule was broken by early morning calls that disturbed the family before breakfast had been completed. Austen herself used the period before breakfast, which happened at nine o'clock at Chawton, for writing.[25]

Henry does not need to make a surprise attack, or dawn raid, on Mansfield the morning after the ball because he is actually invited to breakfast by Sir Thomas before setting off for London with William. His 'business' (MP, p. 282) involves introducing William to his guardian, Admiral Crawford. He then makes sure that the Admiral uses his influence to help the young sailor gain promotion. The text makes no overt criticism of the widespread practice of using family connections to secure preferment, unless the idea that Sir Thomas's influence might help Mr Rushworth to become a member of Parliament is seen as the unacceptable face of patronage. Family influence is, nevertheless, how Edmund is able to establish himself as a clergyman and this is seen as being entirely appropriate. It is just possible, however, that Regency readers might have made a connection between William's promotion and the scandal that was associated with the Duke of York and Mary Ann Clarke in 1809. Austen's sailors, as will be seen more clearly during the reading of *Persuasion*, are usually represented in flattering terms. Admiral Crawford, along with drunken Mr Price, are the exceptions to this rule: 'Admiral Crawford was a man of vicious conduct, who chose, instead of retaining his niece, to bring his mistress under his own roof' (MP, p. 74). His niece is, of course, Mary Crawford, who escapes from the 'trial' (MP, p. 74) of living in this scandalous Regency household to Mansfield Parsonage. It is the way in which the issue of promotion becomes linked with the question of sexual immorality that provides the admittedly very tenuous connection with the Clarke scandal.

William's promotion is confirmed so Henry is now in a position to promote his own claims on Fanny's affection. He catches her off guard as he arrives at Mansfield 'at an earlier hour than common visiting warrants' (MP, p. 302). He is shown straight to the breakfast-room. Lady Bertram characteristically displays no interest in the purpose of this early call and is quite content to leave Fanny alone with him:

> Henry, overjoyed to have her go, bowed, and watched her off, and without losing another moment, turned instantly to Fanny, and taking out some letters said, with a most animated look, 'I must acknowledge myself infinitely obliged to any creature who gives me such an opportunity of seeing you alone . . .' (MP, p. 302)

His bow may not be a mocking one on this occasion, although the correctness of his behaviour in this detail only serves to underline the general impropriety of his call. He is now able to act out the proposal scene that he has planned and scripted so carefully. Fanny is, of course, delighted with the news of William's promotion and momentarily neglects her defences. Henry, as she admits later on, takes her 'wholly by surprise' (MP, p. 349). The Napoleon of the domestic battlefield has at last succeeded in outflanking his most watchful opponent.

Fanny's refusal of the proposal only whets Henry's appetite for the part of the ardent suitor. Johnson suggests that he probably thinks she is acting the part of the elegant female of the conduct books and only playing at being hard to get.[26] He makes another of his early morning raids on Mansfield the next day, although this time Fanny is fortunate enough to catch a glimpse of her enemy advancing: 'She could not but be astonished to see Mr Crawford, as she accidentally did, coming up to the house again, and at an hour as early as the day before' (MP, p. 312). She decides that the best tactic is to withdraw to her room until the danger is over. She is still there when the dandy's powerful ally, Sir Thomas, enters to try to persuade her, through a mixture of concern and threats, to accept the proposal.

Fanny is put under considerable and sustained pressure to make a socially advantageous marriage. Although she is frequently seen as being a weak heroine, this denies the strength and determination that she has to show after Henry's proposal. Even Edmund deserts her because of his infatuation with Mary Crawford:

> and as Edmund perceived, by his [Henry] drawing in a chair, and sitting down close to her, that it was to be a very thorough attack, that looks and undertones were to be well tried, he sank as quietly as possible into a corner, turned his back, and took up a newspaper, very sincerely wishing that dear little Fanny might be persuaded into

explaining away that shake of the head to the satisfaction of her ardent lover; . . . (MP, p. 339)

Edmund takes a more interventionist attitude later on when he tries to talk Fanny into an acceptance. Her continuing refusal becomes not just a rejection of Henry, but also a denial of Sir Thomas's authority. He had made the match by giving a ball for her and by generally encouraging close relationships with the Parsonage. He decides to send her back to Portsmouth in the hope that both social and geographical distance will eventually lend enchantment to her view of Henry. He plays the part of the supposedly rational doctor who knows how to cure an apparently mad woman: 'It was a medicinal project upon his niece's understanding, which he must consider as at present diseased' (MP, p. 363). John Wiltshire suggests that such medical metaphors draw attention to the way in which Sir Thomas, the actor, attempts to disguise his bullying behind a 'mask of kindness'.[27] The plan turns out to be another of his failed experiments.

Fanny is even more vulnerable to Henry's attacks in Portsmouth. It is probably just after breakfast, as she and her sister Susan 'were preparing to remove as usual up stairs' (MP, p. 392), when he first knocks on the door. The correct way of paying such a call, particularly as he had not visited the house before, would have been to have sent a servant from the hotel round with his card and then to have appeared in person later on in the day. This, however, would have meant surrendering the element of surprise. He is still favourably received by Mrs Price in his role as William's patron, although she is bewildered by the fact that he has no business to attend to in Portsmouth that might involve visits to the port-admiral and others.

Henry and Fanny, together with Susan and Mr Price, make a tour of the naval dockyards. Henry stages a scene to show Fanny that he is now a benevolent landowner. He is quite content to use the docks as a background for this scene, almost as if they had been represented by a painter from Northampton. The 'timber' in the yard and the 'seat on board a vessel in the stocks' (MP, p. 396) become his stage props. He transforms a vitally important location in the war against France into a theatrical set in which, ironically, he plays the leading role. This clear juxtaposition between the world of pleasure and the business of war makes explicit the hints that would have been available to some Regency readers when Tom Bertram describes his holiday at Albion Place in Ramsgate. The concept of a total war involving the whole of a population was certainly alien to Regency England. The representation of Henry parading around the docks nevertheless seems to raise the question of whether the war might have been conducted more successfully if England had indeed expected every man to do his duty. Austen knew, and apparently liked, Charles Pasley's *Essay on the Military Policy and Institutions of the British Empire* (1810). Although Pasley argued against introducing the kind of conscription associated with Napoleonic France, he emphasised the need for everybody to feel as if they were engaged in the war effort, even if they did not belong to the armed services.[28]

Many Regency readers would have been aware that the dockyards at Portsmouth were regarded as being one of the great technological achievements of this period. New blocking machinery, designed by Isambard Brunel, had been installed by convict labour between 1804 and 1808. Visitors to Portsmouth, such as Dorothy Jordan and Lady Bessborough, made a point of visiting the docks to watch this new machinery in action. War was one of the major industries of this period and Portsmouth was one of its shock cities. Just as social tourists flocked to Manchester in the 1840s, so they came to marvel at Portsmouth in the Regency period. *Mansfield Park* caters to some extent for this particular kind of tourism, just as *Pride and Prejudice* allows readers to make a more orthodox guided tour of Pemberley.[29]

The second day, or act, of Henry's visit to Portsmouth follows the same pattern as the first. It starts with an early call. He had signified his intention of visiting the Prices again, although he had been careful not to specify a time:

> The Prices were just setting off for church the next day when Mr Crawford appeared again. He came – not to stop – but to join them; he was asked to go with them to the Garrison chapel, which was exactly what he had intended, and they all walked thither together. (MP, p. 400)

Fanny herself may respond favourably to the new note of responsibility in Henry's speeches. Readers are nevertheless reminded constantly of his stagecraft. The Garrison Chapel, another location connected with the war effort, also becomes a backdrop for his parade of affection for Fanny. An early Victorian guide book notes that the walls of the chapel were covered with monuments erected to the memory of those who had died in the Revolutionary and Napoleonic Wars.[30] Henry's footwork is remarkably nimble:

> In chapel they were obliged to divide, but Mr Crawford took care not to be divided from the female branch; and after chapel he still continued with them, and made one in the family party on the ramparts. (MP, p. 400)

The young dandy strolls along the ramparts enjoying the view of 'the ships at Spithead and the island beyond'(MP, p. 401). Regency readers familiar with Portsmouth itself, or with the extensive newspaper coverage about it, would have known that the ships that were used to hold French prisoners-of-war could also be seen from these ramparts. The novel sketches in some of the new developments, such as the reference to the 'stocks', while allowing others to be read into its representations.

Henry prepares the ground for the third act of his play, before he exits from Portsmouth, by telling Fanny that she only has to say the word and he will come down again to escort her back to Mansfield: 'you know the ease, and the pleasure with which this would be done' (MP, p. 402). The choice of words is lethally precise since both 'ease' and 'pleasure' have acquired a particular set of associations as far as he is concerned. The ironic use of other keywords such as 'acting'(MP, p. 397) and 'improvement' (MP, p. 405) also continue to remind readers of his past.

Henry accompanies the Price family back to the door of their house and then pretends 'to be waited for elsewhere' (MP, p. 403). Lack of employment allows him to play at leading a busy life. He has in fact a full three hours to kill before he can sit down to his own dinner at the Crown. The name of the hotel, although a common one, reinforces Condition-of-England contexts. The Crown is also, as will be seen, the name of the inn in Highbury in *Emma*. Henry detains Fanny on the doorstep of her house, after everybody else has gone inside, in order to deliver his final speech. Gentlemen were not expected to make early calls and they were certainly not meant to hold intimate conversations in the street. The most blatant reminder that Fanny may be in danger of deceiving herself about Henry's reformation comes at the end of this farewell scene. He 'pressed her hand, looked at her, and was gone' (MP, p. 404). This is meant to recall the events immediately after Sir Thomas's return from the West Indies. Henry was literally in the act of 'pressing' (MP, p. 192) Maria Bertram's hand to his heart when the news is broken and yet he still lingers a little longer in this pose. Fanny has a good eye at a dandy, although the narrator has a better one.

The third act never takes place since Henry drifts back into his relationship with Maria. Her initial coolness towards him acts as a challenge, just as Fanny's refusal only spurs him on: 'he could not bear to be thrown off by the woman whose smiles had been so wholly at his command' (MP, p. 452). The military metaphor once again keeps alive the question of his patriotism. The resolution appears at first sight to lay most of the blame on Maria for the elopement and subsequent events:

> All that followed was the result of her imprudence; and he went off with her at last, because he could not help it, regretting Fanny, even at the moment, but regretting her infinitely more, when all the bustle of the intrigue was over, and a very few months had taught him, by the force of contrast, to place a yet higher value on the sweetness of her temper, the purity of her mind, and the excellence of her principles. (MP, p. 452)

It is hard to adjust to this new Henry, who apparently loves somebody other than himself and is more sinned against than sinning, because it was still the old Henry who was on parade in Portsmouth.

As will become more apparent, *Lovers' Vows* was a play that belonged to the sentimental school of German literature. The reading of both French and German sentimental writers was often seen in this period as provoking a desire to elope. Lady Juliana in Susan Ferrier's *Marriage* (1818) elopes to Gretna Green with her head full of ideas picked up from the writings of 'the French and German school'. History repeats itself in a general sense when one of her daughters, Lady Adelaide, exchanges 'French and German sentiments' with Lord Lindore before eloping with him. Henry has some French characteristics and both he and Maria act together in a German play. These are some of the influences that threaten the stability of the political house.[31]

It is possible that the resolution allows Henry to become the innocent party as a way of highlighting the social conventions that victimised women rather than men in most representations of scandal. As indicated, Austen's support for Princess Caroline was a response to the operation of such double standards. The resolution returns to this theme:

> That punishment, the public punishment of disgrace, should in just measure attend *his* [Henry's] share of the offence is, we know, not one of the barriers, which society gives to virtue. In this world, the penalty is less equal than could be wished; but without presuming to look forward to a juster appointment hereafter, we may fairly consider a man of sense like Henry Crawford, to be providing for himself no small portion of vexation and regret . . . (MP, pp. 452–3)

Henry is allowed the luxury of being able to punish himself because Regency society condones, and therefore can be said to encourage, male sexual indiscretions and scandals. It is implied, through the use of a religious term like 'hereafter', that this goes against religious teachings. The more secular sense of the passage also carries a potentially subversive message. It holds out no hope that society will change its gendered rules in the future. The countenance is deferential at first and then mocking.

Another way of reading the resolution is to see the special pleading for Henry as being consistent with his representation as a whole. His drawing-room manoeuvres and other theatrical finesses are very minutely catalogued indeed. These details can clearly be used to support anti-Jacobin readings of the novel. A selfish dandy, who occasionally speaks in French, invades Mansfield and then parades about in Portsmouth of all places. There is certainly an argument that he lacks the patriotism of William Price who has 'known every variety of danger, which sea and war together could offer' (MP, p. 245). Readers nevertheless are encouraged to take more interest in Henry's responses to William's patriotic tales than in the stories themselves. Narrative interest and energy are reserved for the dandy rather than for the sailor. Henry's performances can be seen therefore as being celebrated at the same time as they are repudiated. As will become clear, similar contradictions occur in *Emma*. There may be one countenance that recommends openness, but there is also another one that revels in, while it reveals, Frank Churchill's abilities to finesse. Both novels maintain the virtues of following a profession, at the same time as they foreground the idle dandy and responses to him.

AN IMMORAL AUTHOR

There has been a tendency for many influential critics to suggest that Sir Thomas's own anti-theatrical prejudices are being endorsed by the novel itself. Duckworth acknowledges that the head of the political house is fallible, while believing that 'his response on discovering the theater is exemplary'.[32] It will be suggested here that this view, still quite common in more modern criticism, seriously underestimates the complexities that surround theatre and theatricality in the novel. The highly theatrical figure of the dandy is celebrated as well as repudiated and the same kind of double countenance is present in the representation of the theatrical rehearsals themselves. After the general flaws in Sir Thomas's responses have been identified, there will be an account of relationships between the novel and the play. This will be followed by a more detailed consideration of the way in which Bacchanalian opportunities for laughter are available during the descriptions of his businesslike destruction of the theatre.

Sir Thomas sets about removing all visible traces of *Lovers' Vows*, even though it seems likely that he has not read it. He burns 'every unbound copy' that meets 'his eye' (MP, p, 206). He is a firm believer in binding, or restraint, and it is almost enough for him that these untidy play texts are different in appearance from the tightly bound volumes in his library. His practice of judging by appearances means that he is primarily concerned to remove 'every outward memento' (MP, p. 206) of the rehearsals. He leaves it to Edmund to volunteer explanations, rather than requiring him to do so, and is more than happy to postpone a full investigation. He does not play the part of the detective:

> He did not enter into any remonstrance with his other children: he was more willing to believe they felt their error, than to run the risk of investigation. The reproof of an immediate conclusion of every thing, the sweep of every preparation would be sufficient. (MP, p. 203)

He concentrates his attention instead on the state of the floors and the ruin of 'all the coachman's sponges'(MP, p. 206). He dismisses the scene-painter and yet is quite content to sweep from his mind the significance of some of the scenes, such as the ale-house, that had been painted. He is much more concerned about the existence of idleness and dissatisfaction amongst the servants than in his own family. Everyone as well as everything is judged by outward appearances. He singles out the flamboyant, overstated Mr Yates as the villain of the piece and thus fails to detect the dangers that lurk behind the Crawfords' elegant parade of respectability. By placing the blame on a complete outsider, he finds more excuses to postpone his investigation.

Mark Girouard notes that a number of country houses had theatres added to them in this period.[33] Private theatres were in fact often connected with the professional stage. One of the plays that Anne Seymour Damer staged in the private theatre at Strawberry Hill in 1802 had a very brief run at Drury Lane. Lord and Lady Abercom cast professionals, as well as their friends, when they put on their theatricals.[34] The public theatres at watering places like Ramsgate were often hired out for private performances. A dandy who became known as 'Romeo' Coates, whose money came from West Indian plantations, hired out the theatre in Bath in 1810 so that he could stage what was by all accounts an appalling production of *Romeo and Juliet*.[35] Sir Thomas's strict sense of business is offended by the Regency mania for private theatricals.

Maria suffers the most from Sir Thomas's failure to distinguish between the trivial and the serious. By the time that he has finished methodically restoring the floors and replacing the sponges, she has become determined to marry Rushworth in order to spite Henry. It is made reasonably clear that, if her father had taken the trouble to talk to her earlier, then her disastrous, affectionless marriage might have been prevented. This raises further questions about the ethics of her banishment. Sir Thomas is once again revealed to be an actor because he acts as if Maria is doing the right thing in marrying Mr Rushworth, even though he knows that this is unlikely to be the case.

If Sir Thomas had read *Lovers' Vows*, he would almost certainly have disapproved of one of its main messages that forms of social binding ought to be rejected. The play is a free adaptation by Elizabeth Inchbald of August von Kotzebue's *Das Kind Der Liebe*, which can be translated idiomatically as 'The Love Child' or 'The Natural Child'. It was very popular in London between 1798 and 1802, as well as enjoying success at Bath and other watering places. There were at least eleven editions of the text. At a more general level, twenty of Kotzebue's plays were published in England between 1796 and 1801.[36]

Although the moment of *Lovers' Vows* was at the turn of the century, Kotzebue's plays in general were still the subjects of controversy at the beginning of the Regency period. A German correspondent had a letter published in *The Morning Post* on 1 August 1811 protesting about the way in which Kotzebue's reputation for immorality was damaging the perception of all German literature. It acknowledges some of the reasons behind Kotzebue's success: 'combining, with a profound knowledge of the human heart, a glowing and intuitive imagination, and depicting mankind such as it is, and not as it ought to be, his language was easily understood by all nations, and his writings read with interest'. The letter is nevertheless primarily concerned to dissociate German culture from the work of 'one immoral author' whose plays had appeared on the English stage in a 'garbled state'. Butler also produces evidence to show that the controversies that had surrounded Kotzebue at the turn of the century remained topical. Meenahski Mukherjee reaches a similar conclusion through the text itself by noticing how even Mr Rushworth has, or claims to have, some knowledge of the play.[37]

Inchbald made changes to the German version of the play to make it less controversial. She increases its comedy by building up the part of the Butler, played by Tom Bertram, and attempts to tone down some of its alleged immorality by making Amelia less of a predatory character. Some political references are lost, such as the long speech by Count Cassel that describes how he was attacked in Paris at the beginning of the French Revolution. Baron Wildenhaim becomes a slightly more sympathetic character as he does not attempt to buy off his son and is provided with a more fully developed conscience. Some of the more minor changes, such as the cutting of a scene designed to show the hypocrisy of some forms of charity, also weaken the radicalism of the original.[38]

Inchbald's version nevertheless still acquired a reputation for being a dangerous and decadent play, mainly because it retained an emphasis on the need for individuals to be governed by their own feelings. It also reproduces the theme that the poor were more virtuous than the rich. Inchbald, a former actress, was one of the few genuinely professional women writers in this period, who left five thousand pounds at her death. Although she obviously knew how to write for a public that included members of the Tory gentry like Rushworth, her associations with a radical, bohemian circle are also apparent in many of her texts. As Sheridan was another playwright who adapted Kotzebue for the English stage, the plays came to be identified with Whigs as well as with radicals. He was used by the Prince during the Regency Crisis as a go-between. He had transformed *Die Spanier in Peru* into *Pizarro* in 1799. This was the play that was being performed at Covent Garden in 1808 when the theatre burned down.

Those who want to see Sir Thomas's reactions as being 'exemplary' often suggest that the novel shows conservative English sense defeating a radical European sensibility. This kind of debate, which had been particularly intense in the 1790s, was still a familiar one in the Regency period. The Admiral in Lady Caroline Lamb's *Glenarvon* (1816) contrasts English sense with German sensibility when he tries to persuade Calantha to reject her Byronic lover and return to her husband, Lord Avondale:

> he is a d——d fine fellow, with none of your German sentiments, not he; and he will no more put up with these goings on, than I shall; nor shall you pallaver him over: for depend upon it, I will open his eyes, unless from this moment you change your conduct. Yes, my Lady Calantha, you look a little surprised, I see, at hearing good English spoken to you; but I am not one who can talk all that jargon of sensibility, they prate around me here. . . . I am for the King, and old England; and a plague on the Irish marauders and My Lord Glenarvon at the head of them.[39]

The Admiral implicitly accuses German playwrights like Kotzebue of causing rebellions that threatened the security of the political house.

One of the problems with readings of *Mansfield Park* that propose sharp contrasts between sense and sensibility is that, as has been suggested, Sir Thomas's responses to the rehearsals are deeply flawed. Another difficulty is that the novel and the play are sometimes remarkably, and intriguingly, similar to each other. Count Cassel, who was to have been played by Rushworth at Mansfield, has the right social pedigree and yet is represented as being gauche and boorish. He treads on Amelia's toes when they are dancing together and, according to the Baron, his conversation is not at all memorable. He adopts a haughty attitude towards the lower orders. When Frederick, the love child referred to in the title, disrupts a shooting party, the Count demands his punishment: 'what police is here! that a nobleman's amusements should be interrupted by the attack of vagrants' (LV, 3. 2). This is reminiscent of Rushworth's own 'zeal after poachers' (MP, p. 142). The similarities between the part itself and the actor who plays it can be striking: Rushworth is also a heavy-footed bore who has inherited status rather than intelligence. Sir Thomas is nevertheless impressed by his social credentials and so, with some brief reservations, allows Maria to marry him. Baron Wildenhaim, by contrast, eventually lets his daughter, Amelia, make up her own mind about marriage. There are also other differences between Cassel and Rushworth. Cassel boasts about his prowess as a great seducer, whereas Rushworth plays the cuckold.

Kotzebue's attack on a dissolute ruling-class is continued around the representation of Wildenhaim. He is a rake who has seduced, and then cast off, Agatha Friburg. He is, however, also seen as a victim as well as a victimiser. It is claimed that he was unable to marry Agatha because his 'kindred' (LV, 5. 1) objected to her background. The play as a whole recommends dispensing with rigid social conventions, which are enforced by families, in favour of individuals following the inclinations of their own hearts. Once again, the two texts are not necessarily in opposition to each other. Fanny's kindred, particularly, as has been shown, Sir Thomas and Edmund, try to persuade her that a marriage to Henry Crawford would be in everyone's interest. She rejects this advice and listens to her own feelings instead. Maria's marriage pleases her kindred, even though it quickly comes to displease her.

Fanny's ambiguous social position is also paralleled, albeit rather sketchily, in *Lovers' Vows*. The Baron meets Agatha, the daughter of a respectable farmer, in the pre-play world because she has been allowed to take up residence at the castle to complete her education. She hovers between being a servant and a companion to the Baron's mother. Fanny's relationship with Lady Bertram is remarkably similar, particularly before she returns from Portsmouth. Just as Agatha eventually marries the Baron in spite of their social differences, so

Fanny's background does not ultimately become an impediment to her marriage to one of the sons of the house.

The play suggests that the lower classes are more in touch with nature, and therefore with goodness, than their social superiors. This not only explains why the Baron's family are so vicious towards Agatha, but also how she is able to survive such an attack. Other variations are played on this theme. Cottager and Cottager's Wife show that it is only the poor who are capable of true charity. There is nevertheless an important contradiction since Kotzebue, despite his reputation for attacking the ruling class, gives Baron Wildenhaim and Count Cassel more theatrical space than these low-life characters. The novel may not represent cottagers and rural hedgers, but it does deal with the way in which two lower-middle-class children, Fanny and William Price, prove themselves to be superior to most members of the gentry. There is a strong suggestion that a third one, Susan Price, will follow the same pattern. The novel may in fact be more radical in what it is saying about class and mobility than the play.

There are nevertheless fundamental differences between these two texts, which may start to cancel out some of the interesting similarities that tend to be neglected by critics. The play preaches the essentially Rousseauesque doctrine that characters need to rely upon their instinct, intuition and innocence. Jean Jacques Rousseau's *Confessions* (1781) argued the case for yielding unreservedly and heedlessly to the affections of the heart. Kotzebue's autobiography reveals that this was a text that he used to carry around in his pocket.[40] Wollstonecraft shows in *A Vindication of the Rights of Woman* that Rousseau's ideas on female education were in fact restricting rather than liberating. Mary Berry makes a broadly similar point in relation to the supposedly new views on motherhood which Rousseau had promoted and made fashionable. She argues that the plea for mothers to rear and educate their children in an unrestricted manner might itself be restrictive for them: 'Swaddling-clothes and convents were equally abjured, and all the female world professed feelings, which, if they had been acted upon, would have swallowed up every other social duty.'[41] The argument advanced against Rousseau by some women writers in this period was that, despite the rhetoric of freedom, women were being denied social as opposed to domestic duties.

Austen's novel rejects Rousseau by remaining close to mainstream Enlightenment thinking in its insistence that nature, or disposition, needs to be both confined and refined through education. Fanny's character is moulded by the way in which she is disciplined, or schooled, in some of the harsher realities of life because of her ambiguous social position. Her sister Susan also has a good disposition and yet it is made reasonably clear that she too will need to submit herself to the rigours of education in order to perfect it. Eldest sons and daughters like Tom and Maria Bertram, together with those like the Crawfords who achieve their independence early, do not have to suffer and therefore do not learn from experience.[42]

Fanny and Edmund see the real danger of *Lovers' Vows* as lying in the way in which it represents women. They are shocked, more precisely, by the inclusion of an unmarried mother in Agatha and a young woman who makes a bold declaration of love in Amelia. Amelia has some similarities with Lady Julia Glistonbury in Maria Edgeworth's *Vivian* (1812) who, under the influence of a governess associated with Rousseau, believes that she only has to propose to the resident tutor to be accepted. Both Agatha and Amelia, in their different ways, follow or have followed the dictates of their hearts. Although the play wants this to be seen as a radical position particularly in relation to Amelia, it nevertheless produces some very traditional stereotypes. Agatha is a weak creature, or vessel, who needs physical, emotional and financial support. This contradicts the pre-play narrative that has to draw attention to her strength in order to generate the plot. After being rejected by the Baron and his kindred, she earns her living as a teacher and so is able to bring up her child in defiance of social conventions. She occasionally has moments of strength in the play itself, for instance when she throws away the Baron's money, although for the most part she remains confined within the stereotype of the fallen woman. She is a pathetic character, who only becomes whole again when she is re-united with the Baron. The dramatic energy of the play is reserved for his conversion to such a reunion, which provides the ranting and storming that attracted Mr Yates to the part. Agatha does not have to persuade herself into a reconciliation, which provides another example of the way in which the play's sympathies are fundamentally male and aristocratic despite some of the signs to the contrary.

Margaret Kirkham draws attention to the way in which the play's final scene reinforces traditional stereotypes.[43] An illustration of this scene is reproduced at the front of the 1798 edition. Agatha is shown to be literally, as well as figuratively, dependent on the power of men. Anhalt leads her onto the stage and then the Baron takes her in his arms. The stage directions indicate that she is 'supported' by him across the stage until she 'sinks' (LV, 5. 2) into a chair. He kneels before her, as does Frederick when he enters. The fallen woman is placed back on the pedestal.

This reconciliation scene is not, however, foregrounded in the novel, which concentrates instead on the discovery scene between Agatha and Frederick in Act One and the proposal scene between Amelia and Anhalt in Act Three. In terms of the proposed Mansfield production, the emphasis is on the way in which Henry holds Maria and on how Mary Crawford declares her love to Edmund. Both Maria and Mary use the cover, or curtain, of the play to try to free themselves from social restraint. The novel, unlike the play, explores the possibility that such seemingly unrestrained behaviour might ultimately be very conformist. It suggests that the permissive woman is always in danger of acting a part in somebody else's play. Kotzebue's particular play provides the kind of happy ending for the fallen women which was usually denied her in the social script. This appears to be the novel's main objection to it and it is one that is never articulated by Sir Thomas Bertram.

The novel's resolution, as noticed, highlights the way in which society itself punishes women rather than men like Henry Crawford for being involved in scandals. A disturbing example of the gendered nature of such punishments is provided by Mr Price. As a former lieutenant in the Royal Marines, he has obviously worked in an environment where military tortures were used to maintain discipline. When he reads the gossip column announcement of Henry and Maria's elopement, he maintains the need for such tortures to be used in the domestic sphere as well:

> I don't know what Sir Thomas may think of such matters: he may be too much of the courtier and fine gentleman to like his daughter the less. But by G– if she belonged to me, I'd give her the rope's end as long as I could stand over her. (MP, p. 428)

The language (belonged/end/stand) reveals that this is a sadistic sexual fantasy and one which, if it had occurred in a Renaissance play rather than in an Austen novel, would have received more attention than it has done. Although Mr Price goes on to claim that a 'little flogging' (MP, p. 428) would be good for men as well as for women, he is nevertheless clearly more excited by the prospect of having the power to 'stand over' a woman.

Perhaps Maria's eventual banishment to 'another country' (MP, p. 450), in company with Mrs Norris, is merely meant to provide another extreme example of such double standards. The severity of her punishment is used to expose the conventions at the same time as they are reproduced. More specifically, Maria has made the mistake of believing that there will always eventually be a happy ending for the fallen woman. Her punishment is severe because she has confused the conventions of sentimental German drama with those of Regency society. It is, nevertheless, particularly harsh since she is a product of Sir Thomas's educational system. Despite all the talk of his reformation, he merely continues his old policy of providing her with money rather than attention when she is forced to banish herself. Mary Evans reads her fate differently, suggesting that she chooses to exile herself as a way of continuing to humiliate her father.[44] It was, as suggested, his obsession with sponges, floors and unbound texts that helped to force her into the marriage with Rushworth. Kotzebue's Baron, for all his parade of sensibility, is sometimes more sensible than Austen's Baron whose behaviour is far from being exemplary.

CHANGING FACES

Edmund and Fanny adopt ambivalent attitudes towards the proposed production of *Lovers' Vows* and therefore do not provide unproblematic endorsements of English sense. The representation of the theatre in *Mansfield Park* is complicated not just by the fact that this section of the novel records as many points of view as there are characters involved, but also by the way in which some of the individual characters hold contradictory views towards it.[45] Edmund's objections to it take the form of a mixture of high morality and crude economics: 'the innovation, if not wrong as an innovation, will be wrong as an expense' (MP, p. 152). The sheer quantity of his objections tends to detract from the quality of any of them. He then ignores his own advice so that he can join the cast and play opposite Mary Crawford. Instead of acknowledging this to be the real reason for his change of position, he claims that it is his duty to prevent her from having to act opposite a strange young man who would become 'domesticated among us – authorized to come at all hours – and placed suddenly on a footing which must do away all restraints'(MP, p. 175). This would carry more conviction if the cast was indeed limited to members of the family. It nevertheless contains Yates, Henry, Mrs Grant and Mary herself. Edmund unwittingly describes the potential threat posed by Mary while, ironically, seeking to protect her from it.

Edmund's confused objections to the proposed production at Mansfield reveal specific anxieties about the professional Regency theatre. This material context has not received the attention that it deserves, perhaps because of the residual influence of Lionel Trilling's work in which a few generalities about Plato's views on acting were used to contain the novel's debates about theatre within an easily knowable framework for literary critics.[46] Edmund believes that actresses have no reputations to lose and so would not be contaminated when they played the parts of Agatha and Amelia. This underestimates the fact that actresses were beginning to achieve the kind of status and respectability that was denied to them during the Restoration period. *The Lady's Magazine* recorded that Sarah Siddons was 'on a footing of familiar intimacy' with members of the aristocracy. Dorothy Jordan's great rival, Elizabeth Farren, married into the aristocracy, becoming the Countess of Derby in 1797. Jordan herself was, as already indicated, the wife in all but name of the Duke of Clarence.[47]

This respectability was, nevertheless, extremely precarious. Siddons had to ride out a very public scandal in 1809 when Catherine Galindo wrote a pamphlet that accused her of committing adultery with Mr Galindo, whom she had employed at one time as a fencing teacher. There had also been the makings of another scandal earlier on when Thomas Lawrence, the portrait painter, appeared to some to be in love with Siddons as well as with her two daughters.[48] Farren had been the constant companion of the Earl of Derby while his first wife was still alive and married him with what was regarded as indecent haste when he eventually became free. There were accusations at the time of the wedding that she was having a lesbian affair with Anne Seymour Damer.[49] Mary Robinson and Jordan were, according to one way of defining their status, Royal mistresses. There had never been a Mr Jordan. The Regency theatre therefore still retained an ability to shock respectable members of society. Edmund sees actors and actresses as still belonging to a 'trade'(MP, p. 130) and some of his other remarks imply that he regards it as being a particularly dishonourable one. Fanny thinks that a 'woman of modesty'(MP, p. 161) would not be able to play the parts of Amelia and Agatha. Amelia and Anhalt were played by a husband and wife team, the Johnstons, in one of the early productions perhaps as a way of trying to minimise controversy.

One of the ways in which eighteenth-century actresses had tried to counter accusations about their lack of modesty was to insist that they were married, and therefore respectable, even if this was not actually the case. George Anne Bellamy was the 'natural' daughter of an aristocrat, who published her scandalous memoirs in 1785 in order to raise money. She stopped being Miss Bellamy and became Mrs Bellamy early on in her career. This flouting of social conventions paled into insignificance beside the fact that one of her many lovers became known as Mr Bellamy.[50] Actresses wore the trousers, or played the breeches part, on the stage. Peg Woffington and Jordan were both celebrated for their playing of such roles. Opponents of the theatre were worried by the way in which actresses continued to wear the trousers when they were off-stage. Like Woffington, Fanny Abington rose from extreme poverty to a position of some affluence by being an actress. She had married a music teacher and, after their separation, paid him an annuity to stop him from bothering her any more.[51] The theatre could then be the world turned upside down in which men took the name of women and women pensioned off discarded lovers. Mr Siddons was able to play the feminised part of the invalid, while his wife continued to earn the money. One of her letters from Brighton in 1798 pictured him as being 'quite lame absolutely walking on crutches. Something is the matter with his knee but whether Rheumatism or Gout, or what it is heaven knows.'[52]

Actresses were women in public and thus continued to run the risk of being equated with prostitutes. At a more general level, theatres and their environs were still the stages on which the real prostitutes displayed themselves. Henry Darnford in Wollstonecraft's *Maria*, which was published posthumously in 1798, confesses his passion for the women he meets in London's theatre district and thus perhaps provides a warning about the success of any long-term relationship between himself and Maria. Mary Shelley wrote in the 1820s about the impossibility of a 'lone woman' going to the theatre.[53]

The links between the theatres and immorality were one of the grievances of the 'old price' rioters in 1809. The rebuilding of Covent Garden had involved the construction of a tier of private boxes which the rioters alleged would be used solely for immoral purposes. As Marc Baer suggests, these ideologically very complex riots need to be used as a context for *Mansfield Park*.[54] They indicate the way in which there was a melodramatic critique of melodrama in this period and thus show that the idea that the novel may offer a theatrical critique of theatricality has some historical foundation. In addition to the new prices, one of the central grievances of the rioters was the way in which a British theatrical tradition had been buried under foreign influences. These were mainly held to be Italian and French in origin, although the sustained attack on sentimental melodramas can also be seen as one that questioned Kotzebue's reputation and popularity. The choice of *Lovers' Vows* as the play to be rehearsed at Mansfield can therefore be seen as a continuation of a contentious, topical debate.

Like Edmund, Fanny does not adopt a consistent attitude towards the theatre. Her response to the rehearsals hovers between the 'eagerness' (MP, p. 161) and outrage that she had experienced when she read the play itself. She has mixed feelings about the theatre, even before *Lovers' Vows* is chosen:

> Fanny looked on and listened, not unamused to observe the selfishness which, more or less disguised, seemed to govern them all, and wondering how it would end. For her own gratification she could have wished that something might be acted, for she had never seen even half a play, but every thing of higher consequence was against it. (MP, p. 156)

She adopts her familiar position as a spectator and the double negative neatly catches some of her uncertainty. The shock that she receives when she reads through the play, and comes across the parts of Agatha and Amelia, leads to a period of more hostile spectatorship. The aspiring actors try to pressurise her into joining them. Despite all her moral objections to the play, part of her still wants to be involved with it.

She becomes increasingly indifferent to the 'danger' (MP, p. 179) of her position. Although she remains a spectator rather than becoming a player, she now makes her particular talents available to the members of the cast. She listens sympathetically to their individual complaints and takes pleasure from exposing herself to what she knows to be dangerous:

> Fanny believed herself to derive as much innocent enjoyment from the play as any of them; – Henry Crawford acted well, and it was a pleasure to *her* to creep into the theatre, and attend the rehearsal of the first act – in spite of the feelings it excited in some speeches for Maria. – Maria she also thought acted well – too well; – and after the first rehearsal or two, Fanny began to be their only audience, and – sometimes as prompter, sometimes as spectator – was often very useful. (MP, p. 185)

She also helps Mrs Norris with the costumes and tries to get Rushworth to learn his lines. Armstrong suggests that her ambiguous social status is highlighted by the way in which, off-stage, she acts the part of a servant.[55]

Fanny looks forward to the proposal scene with her usual mixture of eagerness and astonishment. She was 'longing and dreading' (MP, p. 187) to see how Mary and Edmund would perform in it in the theatre. She is given a preview of their performance when they rehearse in front of her in the East Room. Her knowledge that the scene will be 'a very suffering exhibition to herself' (MP, p. 190) during the full rehearsal does not prevent her from creeping once again into the theatre. Mrs

Grant's unexpected absence means that she is forced to agree to play the part of Cottager's Wife:

> why had not she gone to her own room, as she had felt to be safest, instead of attending the rehearsal at all? She had known it would irritate and distress her – she had known it her duty to keep away. She was properly punished. (MP, p. 191)

One of the reasons why she is there is because she derives pleasure, as well as pain, from playing the part of a spectator. The rehearsals allow some of the characters to play unrestrained versions of themselves. Mary Crawford, for all her worldliness, is not able to propose marriage to either Tom or Edmund. The play releases her from social obligations and proprieties. Fanny may not have a part until the very last moment and yet the rehearsals still allow her to play a heightened version of herself. She has always been a spectator: watching Mrs Norris and Mrs Rushworth match-making during the impromptu ball and, more importantly, sitting on a bench at Sotherton while other characters make their entrances and exits. Edmund may tell Sir Thomas that only Fanny has been 'consistent' (MP, p. 203) in her opposition to the theatre. This nevertheless underestimates the way in which she has been able to indulge herself as a spectator. As Armstrong puts it, she is 'free to be almost consumed with looking'.[56] Tanner's picture of her as a bright moral beacon amidst the encircling darkness of the rehearsals is one of the many critical responses that is based on taking Edmund's praise for her too literally.[57]

Trilling's lazy gestures towards Plato were gradually replaced by a more historically informed kind of criticism that tried to claim that the novel was endorsing the values of early nineteenth-century Evangelicalism. One of the main problems with this interpretation was that it failed to differentiate clearly enough between a novel that contains characters, such as Edmund and Fanny, who sometimes subscribe to an Evangelical suspicion of the theatre, and an Evangelical novel. Once again, the novel was read backwards to find support for what was taken to be a stable and fixed resolution. Another problem was the way in which dubious speculations about Austen's own life were used to authenticate the reading. She was pictured as moving quickly into a premature middle age in which she emphatically renounced her earlier love of theatre. Michael Williams has shown nevertheless that the letters can be used to question as well as to support this version of the author.[58]

The full rehearsal of the first three acts is about to begin after Fanny has agreed to take part in it. The show is then stopped by Julia, who makes a dramatic entrance with the news that 'My father is come! He is in the hall at the moment' (MP, p.191). This provides the cliffhanger ending to the first volume of the novel. Kotzebue's theatre is upstaged by Austen's theatre. *Mansfield Park* may offer some criticisms of this particular play and yet it is still difficult to follow critics like Butler, Roberts and the many others who suggest the existence of an Evangelical suspicion of theatre. If there is a critique of theatre then, paradoxically, it is a highly theatrical one. The second volume retains the emphasis on melodrama. The actors pause to consider their impending doom: 'It was a terrible pause; and terrible to every ear were the corroborating sounds of opening doors and passing footsteps' (MP, p.192). Tom, Edmund and Maria, accompanied by Julia who eventually had the best theatrical part, exit from the theatre to appear before their father. Rushworth plods along behind them and is followed in turn by a 'trembling' (MP, p.193) Fanny. The Crawfords, who time their retreats as well as their attacks to perfection, slip back to the Parsonage. Yates is left alone in the theatre.

The melodramatic mood is replaced by a comic one for the drawing-room scene. Mrs Norris tries to hide the massive pink satin cloak that was to have been worn by Rushworth. She is cross that she did not have the opportunity to make the dramatic announcement about Sir Thomas's return. The novel may eventually banish her and yet it shares her taste for melodrama. Lady Bertram, who has been half-asleep on the sofa for most of the time during the rehearsals, is provided with a comic line that alerts Sir Thomas to what has been happening in his absence. She claims that 'We have been all alive with acting' (MP, p. 197). Tom steps in immediately with a long speech about field sports to try to prevent his father from asking too many questions.

This highly theatrical comic mood continues as Sir Thomas sets off slowly but surely to cast a loving eye over 'his own dear room' (MP, p. 197). Readers are held in suspense. He reaches the library where his expression, weary but contented, begins to change as in the flickering candlelight he notices some alterations to his beloved bookcases. His confusion increases when he hears an unknown voice ranting away in the adjacent billiard-room. He gingerly opens the connecting door and suddenly finds himself on stage:

> opposed to a ranting young man, who appeared likely to knock him down backwards. At the very moment of Yates perceiving Sir Thomas, and giving perhaps the very best start he had ever given in the whole course of his rehearsals, Tom Bertram entered at the other end of the room; and never had he found greater difficulty in keeping his countenance. His father's looks of solemnity and

amazement on this his first appearance on any stage, and the gradual metamorphosis of the impassioned Baron Wildenhaim into the well-bred and easy Mr Yates, making his bow and apology to Sir Thomas Bertram, was such an exhibition, such a piece of true acting as he would not have lost upon any account. It would be the last – in all probability the last scene on that stage; but he was sure that there could not be a finer. The house would close with the greatest eclat. (MP, p. 198)

Tom's point of view is used to intensify the comedy at Sir Thomas's expense. The anarchic regent is preferred here to more Evangelical characters such as Fanny and Edmund. The scene is a brilliant piece of situation comedy and much better theatre than anything in *Lovers' Vows*, where entrances and exits are often very clumsy and forced. Butler is right to see this as being an 'irresistibly comic moment' and yet, because she is committed to reading the novel in terms of its supposed Evangelicalism and anti-Jacobinism, does in fact resist its implications. Her argument is concerned to make sure that readers do not 'miss the underlying point of the meeting', which is taken to be an anti-Jacobin one of sympathy for Sir Thomas, because they have been allowed to witness it from Tom's point of view. The fact that they may be actively encouraged to miss, albeit briefly, this orthodox point is not given sufficient weight.[59]

The text then changes its face, or countenance, and the scene becomes a criticism rather than a celebration of Regency values. Tom puts on a straight face and reflects upon the error of his ways:

Tom understood his father's thoughts, and heartily wishing he might be always as well disposed to give them but partial expression, began to see more clearly than he had ever done before that there might be some ground of offence – that there might be some reason for the glance his father gave towards the ceiling and the stucco of the room; and that when he inquired with mild gravity after the fate of the billiard table, he was not proceeding beyond a very allowable curiosity. (MP, p. 199)

The values of the old order, together with their reticent articulation, begin to re-assert their authority over the political house. This is the anti-Jacobin message that Butler wants readers to register. It is not, however, the only political statement that is being made in this scene.

Tom's repentance is unconvincing because his subsequent behaviour takes no account whatsoever of his father's thoughts and feelings. More immediately, he and other characters are unable to keep a straight face for very long. Sir Thomas finds 'nothing disagreeable in Mr Rushworth's appearance' (MP, p. 195). His future son-in-law's vehement outbursts against Henry Crawford and the theatre are not treated as significant clues as to what has been happening. The scene ends as farce as Sir Thomas ponderously praises Rushworth's desire for domesticity and claims him to be an ally of 'weight' (MP, p. 201). The on-stage audience is unable to keep its countenance: 'It was impossible for many of the others not to smile' (MP, p. 202).

CONCLUSIONS

Mansfield Park debates a range of topical issues such as female education, romance and landscape improvement. The concentration here, however, has been on the possibility that it also discusses the question of a regency, given both the commonplace connections between estate and state in this period and the fact that it was written during the second Regency Crisis itself. Austen's own intentions have deliberately not been not reconstructed, although her letters show that she was better informed about national politics than is generally recognised. Even if some of the compelling similarities between Tom Bertram and the Prince Regent are rejected for want of supporting evidence, it should still be clear that reading the novel through his eyes opens up new themes such as cross-dressing and masquerade. It has also allowed the idea that the Bacchanalian is not simply and emphatically rejected in favour of the businesslike. The previous analysis of Brummell and dandyism supports the reading of Henry Crawford. Once again, the novel reveals its ability to wear different countenances. Henry is both the hero and the villain. The remarkably detailed dissection of his conversation, movements and manoeuvres shows a fascination for the highly theatrical figure of the dandy who is nevertheless ultimately banished from Mansfield. The banishment of the theatre itself is equally complicated. Sir Thomas doggedly sets about the business of replacing sponges as a way of postponing an investigation into the activities of the regency period. Unlike Kotzebue's Baron, he drives his daughter into a disastrous marriage. Here and elsewhere the play comments on events and characters in the novel. There are thus important similarities between the two texts and, on occasions, it is Austen rather than Kotzebue who adopts the more radical stance. Fanny and Edmund certainly articulate some of the Evangelical objections to the theatre, although they are both shown to hold more contradictory opinions. The novel itself is also intriguingly contradictory. It offers a melodramatic criticism of melodrama and, more generally, a highly theatrical critique of theatricality.

Part IV

The sick society: Leisure and invalidism in the later writings

5 *Emma*: The village and the watering place

INTRODUCTION

This chapter begins by establishing the related themes of invalidism and leisure through a brief consideration of an argument between Mr Woodhouse and Isabella Knightley over healthy holidays. This is followed by a more extended examination of the culture of the watering place that pays particular attention to Weymouth. The conflict between the values of the watering place and those of the village is then explored more specifically around the representation of Mr Perry, the apothecary. His ambiguous social status is set first of all in the debates that surrounded the Apothecaries' Act of 1815. It is then argued that, although there is one text that appears to support Perry and the other rising professionals in the village, this may be in conflict with another one which remains fascinated by the mentality of Frank Churchill, an unemployed young dandy associated not just with Weymouth but also with French attitudes. The next section continues the discussion of rivalries between the watering place and the village by considering the politics of transport and other forms of communication such as letter writing. There is, finally, a summary of the points that have been made about Emma herself.

WHERE HEALTH IS AT STAKE

Emma Woodhouse lives about twenty-one years in the world without so much as a sight of the sea. She finally gets her chance to view it when she and Mr Knightley make a two-week 'tour to the sea-side'(E, p. 464) after their marriage. The choice of this kind of honeymoon does not sit very comfortably with Knightley's well-aired prejudices against watering places. Perhaps this provides a hint that Emma will still get what she wants when married. The name of the particular resort that they intend to visit is not revealed, despite the fact that the relative merits of specific Regency watering places are debated in some detail in the novel.

Mr Woodhouse and his elder daughter, Isabella, are both hypochondriacs who affect to be ruled totally by medical opinion. They start quarrelling while they are waiting for their gruel to be served. Isabella claims that she was only obeying the instructions of her medical practitioner, Mr Wingfield, when she took her family to Southend instead of making her annual pilgrimage at the appointed time to Highbury:

> Mr Wingfield most strenuously recommended it, sir – or we should not have gone. He recommended it for all the children, but particularly for the weakness in little Bella's throat, – both sea air and bathing. (E, p. 123)

Mr Woodhouse has allowed himself to become virtually immobile so that his family and neighbours are forced to dance attendance on him. Isabella's holiday threatens his power as a professional invalid. He attempts to regain it by challenging fashionable medical opinions on the healthy effects of bathing. He declares that he tried it once himself and that it almost killed him. His own medical man, the absent but still omnipresent Mr Perry, is obviously of exactly the same opinion.

Despite Emma's gallant attempts to turn the conversation towards less contentious issues, the two hypochondriacs are determined to prove that their own particular practitioner knows best. Mr Woodhouse changes his ground. Instead of maintaining the position that all bathing is bad for you, he argues that some watering places are infinitely superior to others. Perry was allegedly very surprised to learn that Isabella had 'fixed upon South End' (E, p. 127). If he had been consulted, he would have prescribed Cromer instead:

> You should have gone to Cromer, my dear, if you went any where. – Perry was a week at Cromer once, and he holds it to be the best of all the sea-bathing places. A fine open sea, he says, and very pure air. And, by what I understand, you might have had lodgings there quite away from the sea – a quarter of a mile off – very comfortable. You should have consulted Perry. (E, p. 128)

Cromer might then have been the diplomatic choice for Emma's honeymoon. Although not brought to the surface, there is a class dimension to these arguments that would have been accessible to Regency readers. Southend and the other resorts that could be reached relatively easily by both boat and coach from London had acquired reputations for being overcrowded and therefore not exclusive. A letter in *The Gentleman's Magazine* for July 1812 claims that the attendants at the warm-water baths at Southend 'do not abound in official assiduity'. The service at the post office seems to have been even worse since it was 'under the management of not the most courteous of the human race'.[1] The problem about Southend for this particular visitor was that there was no clearly defined area for people of fashion to call their own. Everybody was forced to mix together. One of the implications therefore of Mr Woodhouse's remarks is that Isabella has lost her sense of social position since leaving Highbury.

Mr Woodhouse is so determined to remind Isabella of his power to command her presence that he brushes aside the perfectly reasonable objection that Cromer may be too far from London for a family trip:

> 'Ah! my dear', as Perry says, 'where health is at stake, nothing else should be considered; and if one is to travel, there is not much to chuse between forty miles and an hundred. – Better not move at all, better stay in London altogether than travel forty miles to get into a worse air. This is just what Perry said. It seemed to him a very ill-judged measure.' (E, p. 128)

Ironically, Mr Woodhouse, who is unable to travel three-quarters of a mile down the road from his own house without getting into a state of high anxiety, still has the power to advise everybody else about their travel arrangements.

Mr Woodhouse makes one of his very rare journeys away from Hartfield when he is persuaded to visit Donwell Abbey for the strawberry-picking party. He remains inside in front of a fire, even though it is a warm day. He is provided with various family collections to amuse him. The narrator does not keep her countenance as easily as Emma does when dealing with this tyrannical invalid:

> Mrs Weston had been showing them all to him, and now he would show them all to Emma; – fortunate in having no other resemblance to a child, than in a total want of taste for what he saw, for he was slow, constant, and methodical. (E, pp. 356–7)

His childishness is also combined with the ponderousness of premature old age. Both these qualities are in play during the successful attempt to put Isabella back in her place.

Isabella herself is also represented as a slow child who lacks powers of discrimination:

> Mrs John Knightley was a pretty, elegant little woman, of gentle, quiet manners, and a disposition remarkably amiable and affectionate; wrapt up in her family; a devoted wife, a doating mother,

and so tenderly attached to her father and sister that, but for these higher ties, a warmer love might have seemed impossible. She could never see a fault in any of them. She was not a woman of strong understanding or any quickness; and with this resemblance of her father, she inherited also much of his constitution; was delicate in her own health, over-careful of that of her children, had many fears and many nerves . . . (E, p. 116)

She is the kind of delicate child-woman or perpetual baby, praised for her fragile mind and body by the writers of conduct manuals, whose existence angered rationalists like Mary Hays and Wollstonecraft. Her father believes that 'Young ladies are delicate plants' (E, p. 295). She is determined never to be well and is, like Lady Sondes, apparently never entirely free from 'little nervous head-aches and palpitations' (E, p. 125). A pallid languor, sometimes self-consciously cultivated through the application of leeches to draw the blood, was regarded as enhancing beauty in this period. Mr Woodhouse is unable to persuade Isabella and her children to extend their stay. His 'lamentations over the destiny of poor Isabella' are undermined by a particularly caustic reminder that his daughter has in fact achieved what society regards as her true and perhaps only destiny:

> – which poor Isabella, passing her life with those she doated on, full of their merits, blind to their faults, and always innocently busy, might have been a model of right feminine happiness. (E, p. 158)

The narrator is, once again, unable to keep her countenance.

The topical debate over the relative merits of Southend and Cromer, and the medical men who recommend them to patients, is brought abruptly to an end by Isabella's husband, John Knightley. He is a lawyer by profession and believes that doctors should be treated as servants rather than as masters. He transforms Mr Perry from the fount of all wisdom into a mere tradesman who sells drugs and ought therefore not to presume to tell his betters how to run their lives. One of Mr Woodhouse's ponderous opening sallies against Isabella is to claim that her husband is 'very far from looking well' (E, p. 126). John Knightley nevertheless has no intention of allowing his own health to become another bone of contention between these feuding hypochondriacs:

> 'My dear Isabella', – exclaimed he hastily – 'pray do not concern yourself about my looks. Be satisfied with doctoring and coddling yourself and the children, and let me look as I chuse.' (E, p. 126)

He associates the need for 'doctoring' with women and children and therefore implies that he considers it to be a sign of weakness. Later on, when he brings his eldest children to stay at Hartfield, he gives Emma specific instructions not to 'physic' (E, p. 310) them. Perhaps his hostility towards Perry has its roots in a belief that doctors are tradesmen, who prey upon those he holds to be particularly gullible.

Emma declares, very sensibly, that the happiness of her nephews 'must preclude false indulgence and physic' (E, p. 310). Most critics have noted that she is an exceptionally powerful heroine although some, as Claudia Johnson has shown, have felt the need to assert their own power by re-positioning her as a child who has to be scolded for her faults.[2] One of the ways in which her power is represented is through her health. Butler draws attention to her 'healthy, vigorous, almost aggressive' presence.[3] Emma is unlike both her father and her sister 'for she hardly knew what indisposition was' (E, pp. 332–3). She is 'always well' (E, p. 409) and is, according to Mrs Weston, 'the complete picture of grown-up health' (E, p. 68). As will become more apparent, her physical strength and power are highlighted by the presence in Highbury of sick women such as Harriet Smith and Jane Fairfax.

THE IDLEST HAUNTS OF THE KINGDOM

The specific debates about Mr Perry's social status will be set in a more detailed historical context after a general consideration of relationships between the village and the watering place. Weymouth is probably the last resort that Emma and Mr Knightley would consider visiting on their honeymoon. Frank Churchill and Jane Fairfax meet for the first time in London. It is nevertheless at Weymouth that their relationship develops to such an extent that they enter into a secret engagement. Jane is there because her guardian, Colonel Campbell, has been told that warm-water baths might cure his deafness. Although Frank likes to represent himself as the victim of his aunt's invalidism, it does not prevent him from following Jane to Weymouth.

Isabella and Colonel Campbell go to watering places in search of medical cures. According to Mr Knightley, young men like Frank are attracted to such places in the hope that they might provide cures for boredom. He refuses to accept that Frank is unable to free himself from his aunt, Mrs Churchill, in order to visit Highbury:

He cannot want money – he cannot want leisure. We know, on the contrary, that he has so much of both, that he is glad to get rid of them at the idlest haunts in the kingdom. We hear of him for ever at some watering-place or other. A little while ago, he was at Weymouth. This proves that he can leave the Churchills. (E, p. 163)

Mrs Churchill is certainly like Mr Woodhouse in the way in which she uses real and imaginary illnesses to maintain her power. It is she rather than her husband who governs Enscombe, the family seat. When Frank eventually gets to Highbury, he is summoned back to Enscombe because she claims that she is unable to manage without him. She too appears to be very dependent on medical opinion. She is eventually persuaded to move first to London and then to Richmond because she 'had been recommended to the medical skill of an eminent person there'(E, pp. 314–15). Her death is the occasion for some particularly savage remarks on the culture of invalidism:

> Mrs Churchill, after being disliked at least twenty-five years, was now spoken of with compassionate allowances. In one point she was fully justified. She had never been admitted before to be seriously ill. The event acquitted her of all the fancifulness, and all the selfishness of imaginary complaints. (E, p. 379)

The last sentence obviously means the opposite of what it appears to say and thus provides another example of the way in which the text sneers at imaginary invalids. John Wiltshire notes that Mrs Churchill is in fact killed by a different disease, or disorder, from those that had allegedly plagued her throughout her life. This reinforces the idea of her as a hypochondriac. A more important part of Wiltshire's reading, which in this instance shows the influence of Gilbert and Gubar, is the suggestion that she functions as Mr Woodhouse's dark double. In other words, the tyrannical power of the invalid is clearly exposed in relation to her so that readers are tempted to see parallels with Mr Woodhouse's treatment of Emma even though these are not made visible in the text itself. Like other attempts to locate camouflaged meanings, this one does not pay sufficient attention to what is in fact visible in the text. There are moments, such as in the argument over watering places, when Mr Woodhouse's desire for power is quite apparent.[4]

Seaside resorts and spa towns were in the business of providing pleasure for idle young men like Tom Bertram, John Yates and Frank Churchill. Yet they also fulfilled other functions. Besides pandering to the whims of real and imaginary invalids, they provided marriage markets. Mr Elton goes to Bath when he is in want of a wife. It is not clear where Colonel Campbell's daughter, Miss Campbell, first meets her husband, Mr Dixon. It is possible that this takes place in Weymouth itself. Dixon certainly brings a portfolio of drawings of his estate at Baly-Craig in Ireland to Weymouth, perhaps with the intention of using them to help him demonstrate his eligibility. He is described by Frank Churchill as being engaged and on the point of marriage to Miss Campbell during their stay in Weymouth. He is nevertheless a shadowy character who offers opportunities for those with imagination, like Frank and Emma, to fashion him into almost any shape that they please. Frank's story, supported by Jane, is that it was the gallant Dixon rather than he himself who rescued her from a boating accident. Emma invents the more scandalous, and therefore more specifically Regency, story that Dixon is Jane's secret lover. Frank helps to promote it when he eventually arrives in Highbury. Dixon's own story may be the more prosaic one of an Anglo-Irish Regency landowner who goes to a watering place to find a wife.

Miss Campbell and Mr Dixon have no reason to keep their engagement a secret. She has a modest amount of money and he has the park gates, together with the drawings to prove it. Frank and Jane decide to keep their own engagement a secret on the grounds that the proud Mrs Churchill would not countenance it. Jane's father was killed in action, possibly at the beginning of the French Revolutionary Wars. She is brought up by Colonel Campbell after her mother's death, although she has always been destined to become a governess. Perhaps she would never have been accepted as a future mistress of Enscombe. Perhaps Frank, like the Prince of Wales and other Regency figures, is attracted by the idea of a secret relationship and allows the predicted wrath of Mrs Churchill to sanction it.

Mr Knightley's inference that Weymouth is to be classed amongst the 'idlest haunts of the kingdom' shows that his emotions are quite capable of impairing his judgement. For, unlike Brighton, Weymouth had a reputation for being somewhat staid and starched. George III paid the first of many visits in 1789, after he had partially recovered from the illness that caused the first Regency Crisis. Fanny Burney, who accompanied the Royal party, felt that 'Nothing but the sea at Weymouth affords any life or spirit'.[5] The King's continued patronage was gratefully acknowledged by the town through the erection of a large statue of him in 1809.

Members of the Royal Family attended the assembly rooms on a regular basis. Abigail Gawthern records in her diary for 1805 how a silk cord was used to divide the ballroom into a space for those people to whom the Royal Family had already been formally introduced and another one for those who had not had this privilege. Those who were excluded from the King's immediate presence were nevertheless apparently able to eavesdrop discreetly on his conversations, at least when the German band was not playing the national anthem too loudly.[6] Elizabeth Ham's autobiography adds some more details about this attempt to preserve exclusivity. She describes how the Royal Family

> were met in the Lobby by the Master of Ceremonies, Mr Rodber, with a candle in each hand, who walked backward before them, up the stairs and into the Ball-room, where all those who had the *entrée* were standing within the cord . . . It generally took from three quarters to an hour to make this short transit. The cord was then removed, but the door was always left open where their Majesties and their invited guests were taking their tea.[7]

It will be argued later on that the debates in *Emma* about how exclusive to make the ball at the Crown can be related to the customs and practices of Regency watering places.

Besides welcoming important guests, a master of ceremonies had to make sure that too many undesirables did not gain entrance. Gentlemen had to leave their swords at the door and both gentlemen and ladies were forbidden to dance in coloured gloves at Weymouth.[8] The particular threat posed by Frank Churchill to the worlds of both the village and the watering place is that he is a disruptive character who nevertheless enjoys access to the most exclusive places. The danger is difficult to detect because, figuratively at least, he wears his coloured gloves underneath his white ones. He is, like Henry Crawford, the potential enemy within the rural gentry.

Mr Knightley's intense scrutiny and surveillance eventually lead him to suspect that Frank has formed a secret engagement with Jane. His conviction is nevertheless not a solid one and appears to be unsettled by Frank's performance at Box Hill. Despite mistakes and blunders, Frank's raffish coloured gloves are not completely exposed by Knightley or any other member of the Highbury community. He wins the great game, even though it is at the expense of Jane's health and happiness. Although readers are often told by the kind of critics who enjoy re-positioning Emma that they have to side with Knightley in his quest for stable meanings and openness, this underestimates the other positions that are available to them. R.W. Chapman, Robert Liddell and others have seen *Emma* as being a detective story, a view which has subsequently been elaborated upon by well-known writers of this genre such as P.D. James.[9] The crime is a Regency secret engagement rather than a murder. Some readers may well identify themselves with the position of the detective, even though he narrowly misses solving the crime. Others may nevertheless retain some admiration for the criminal, who achieves the seemingly impossible task of keeping a secret in Highbury.

When Frank eventually arrives in Highbury, he tries to transform it into at least a version of a watering place. He converts the Crown Inn into an assembly room with himself as master of ceremonies. The name itself, although a common one, nevertheless encourages Condition-of-England interpretations particularly as the inn is used by the local magistrates for regular discussions of parish business. Besides being the place where the gentlemen and 'half-gentlemen'(E, p. 209) of the village meet to play cards, it is also the seat of government. It has seen better days and the ballroom, an extension to the original premises, is no longer used as such. Frank's passion for dancing probably means that he is behind the suggestion to round off the dinner party at the Coles with two dances. Like Tom Bertram and the Regent himself, he is associated with the disruptive movement of furniture.

Frank then flirts with the possibility of holding a less spontaneous dance at either Randalls or Hartfield. Emma sensibly argues that both houses are too small and that the event would be unpleasantly crowded. She, like the lady patronesses at the exclusive Almack's Ballroom in London in this period, is in favour of the silken cords of discrimination that were used at Weymouth. Given that he has secrets to hide, Frank may well see safety in crowds. He returns nevertheless to an idea of reviving the tradition of holding dances at the Crown. If he is unable to transform private houses into public spaces, then he might as well start with a public house. The idea for the dance first comes to him when he is being shown around Highbury soon after his much-heralded arrival. Emma is concerned that such an event would mean that the greater and lesser families would have to mingle together on terms of rough equality, as happened at Southend and the less exclusive Regency watering places. Frank tries to brush aside such objections:

> he was still unwilling to admit that the inconvenience of such a mixture would be anything, or that there would be the smallest difficulty in every body's returning into their proper place the next morning . . . his indifference to a confusion of rank, bordered too much on inelegance of mind. (E, p. 210)

These are Emma's thoughts, although, having assembled the case against Frank, she then enters some special pleas for him.

The dance has to be cancelled when Frank is summoned back to Enscombe by Mrs Churchill. It eventually takes place during one of his later flying visits. It is characterised by a series of confusions. Emma believes that she has been accorded the special privilege of checking the arrangements before everything begins, only to discover that several other opinions have to be solicited. Mr and Mrs Elton forget to send their carriage to collect Jane Fairfax and her aunt, Miss Bates. There is some confusion about the exact purpose of the dance. Emma believes that it is being given in her honour, whereas Mrs Elton is convinced that she is the queen of the ball. Frank eventually turns his complete attention to Emma and yet it is clear to her that some of it is still missing. New characters, such as Dr and Mrs Hughes, are mentioned only to fade quickly into the background again. Mr Elton appears to want to dance and then refuses to partner Emma's friend, Harriet Smith, who is eventually rescued from her confusion and humiliation by Mr Knightley. This sets in train further confusions, which begin to manifest themselves after the ball as Harriet imagines that Knightley is in love with her. It would be very easy to argue that the chaotic events at the Crown merely confirm the strength of Knightley's case against Frank Churchill and watering places. The problem with such a reading is that the novel itself celebrates confusion and secrecy in the very act of exposing and condemning them. It is as fascinated with the mind and machinations of the criminal as it is with those of the detective.

Frank is a disruptive figure who nevertheless has easy access to exclusive places. This, as has been argued in relation to Brummell, is one of the definitions of the dandy. Frank's dandyism is even more apparent than that of Henry Crawford or John Yates. There is, for instance, a little more information about his clothes. The initial inspection of the Crown Inn is followed by a trip to Mrs Ford's shop. Frank suggests popping in there so that he can avoid, albeit briefly, being questioned by Emma about his relationship with Jane Fairfax in Weymouth. He decides to buy a pair of gloves and so inspects 'the sleek, well-tied parcels of "Men's Beavers" and "York Tan". . .' (E, p. 211). The implication is that he is as sleek and well-tied as these parcels. Douglas Jefferson is wrong to assert that the novel does not raise the question of whether Frank 'dressed with a certain amount of Regency foppery'.[10]

Frank then surprises everybody by disappearing up to London, apparently just to have his hair cut. His dandyism is revealed not just by the action itself, but also by the way in which he justifies it. He responds to Emma's mild criticism with the kind of elegant, polished one-liner that was cultivated by both Brummell and Henry Crawford: 'I have no pleasure in seeing my friends, unless I can believe myself fit to be seen' (E, p. 230). As James Thompson suggests, characters clothe

hemselves in words and Frank's rhetorical costume is that of the
dandy.[11] He is also like Crawford in that he never loses an opportunity
:o execute an elegant bow. Gesture becomes another form of clothing.
He and Emma discuss at their very first meeting whether Mrs Weston,
who has recently married his father, ought to know that he thinks of her
as a 'pretty young woman':

> 'I hope I should know better', he replied; 'No, depend upon it, (with
> a gallant bow), that in addressing Mrs Weston I should understand
> whom I might praise without any danger of being thought extrava-
> gant in my terms.' (E, p. 204)

His somewhat cryptic meaning, perhaps another feature of his dandyism, is that it would be perfectly proper for him to describe Emma as a
'pretty young woman' to Mrs Weston. The flourish of the compliment
is itself complemented by the gallantry of his bow. The text contains
five other references to his habit of making graceful bows.

Watering places were amongst the favoured refuges for French
émigrés during the Revolutionary and Napoleonic Wars. Mr Knightley
believes that Frank's lifestyle is that of a French aristocrat rather than
one appropriate for an English gentleman:

> No, Emma, your amiable young man can be amiable only in French,
> not in English. He may be very 'aimable', have very good manners,
> and be very agreeable; but he can have no English delicacy towards
> the feelings of other people: nothing really amiable about him. (E,
> p. 166)

The implication of Knightley's argument is that the decadent behaviour of Frank and his kind might trigger off a revolution in England,
just as the selfishness of the French ruling-class helped to precipitate
revolution across the Channel. Although *Emma* was first published
just after the end of the Napoleonic Wars, debates between the relative
merits of English and French values were still highly topical and
political. Critics have certainly not overlooked this theme. Ward
Hellstrom's work on the text's alleged Francophobia has been developed by Butler, Roberts and the others who present Austen as an
anti-Jacobin. The problem with their work is that they see these
debates between English and French values as being remarkably one-
sided. It is argued here, in contrast, that the text is more open,
genuinely dialogic and unresolved than these critics are willing to
concede.[12]

Knightley displays his own Francophobia before Frank arrives in
Highbury. It is Francophobia in a double sense: dislike of the country

as well as jealousy of a man called Frank. The detective has scrutinised
the evidence, such as Frank's letters, and has made his own deductions.
They turn out to be remarkably perceptive ones, which makes his
ultimate failure to expose the crime all the more surprising. Frank's
conversation, like that of both Henry and Mary Crawford, is sprinkled
with French words and phrases. He affects, for Emma's benefit, to be
displeased with the way in which Jane Fairfax has arranged her hair for
the dinner party at the Coles:

> but really Miss Fairfax has done her hair in so odd a way – so very
> odd a way – that I cannot keep my eyes from her. I never saw any
> thing so outrée! – Those curls! – This must be a fancy of her own. I
> see nobody else looking like her! – I must go and ask her whether it
> is an Irish fashion. (E, p. 231)

The reference to 'Irish fashion' is meant to reinforce Emma's scandalous suspicions that sensible Mr Dixon is really Jane's secret lover.

The strawberry-picking party at Donwell Abbey continues the
political debate about the differences between English and French
values, embodied respectively by the village and the watering place.
Mrs Elton, who as indicated is associated with Bath, plays the queen of
the ball at the Crown and is now determined to play the part of Marie-
Antoinette at Donwell. Hellstrom did not extend his thesis about
Francophobia to include women characters. Mrs Elton's plans for the
party resemble the French Queen's passion for elaborate, ornate
pastoral games at Little Trianon. Mr Knightley politely tries to prevent
her highly theatrical imagination from running riot. He refuses her
request to be allowed 'carte-blanche'(E, p. 350) as far as invitations are
concerned. He pours cold water over her ideas for an open-air 'gipsy
party':

> My idea of the simple and the natural will be to have the table spread
> in the dining-room. The nature and simplicity of gentlemen and
> ladies, with their servants and furniture, I think is best observed by
> meals within doors. When you are tired of eating strawberries in the
> garden, there shall be cold meat in the house. (E, p. 351).

The promotional materials for both spa towns and seaside resorts such
as Ramsgate usually contained descriptions of delightful picnic spots in
the vicinity. Mrs Elton is restrained, although not completely prevented, from transforming Donwell Abbey into just such a spot.

Frank is a very late arrival at this party, apparently because Mrs
Churchill had 'a nervous seizure, which had lasted some hours' (E, p.
358). He does not mention that he has also been detained by a chance

meeting with Jane Fairfax. Emma, playing the part of mistress of Donwell to perfection, attempts to make the irritable young man feel more at home in a setting that has already been explicitly praised for its Englishness. He cools down a little while eating a 'very comfortable meal' (E, p. 359) and then returns to watch Emma and the tasteless Mr Woodhouse plod through the collection of views. The pictures of Switzerland provoke him to renounce his own Englishness in favour of a more cosmopolitan identity:

> 'As soon as my aunt gets well, I shall go abroad', said he. 'I shall never be easy till I have seen some of these places. You will have my sketches, some time or other, to look at – or my tour to read – or my poem. I shall do something to expose myself.' (E, p. 359)

Emma dampens these restless aspirations in much the same way as Mr Knightley tries to restrain Mrs Elton from playing Marie-Antoinette. Frank nevertheless continues, perhaps playing the part of Lord Byron, to complain that he is 'sick of England' (E, p. 359). He continues playing this part on Box Hill the next day. For Mr Knightley, if not quite for Emma, it is Frank's cosmopolitan, salon values which are in real danger of producing sickness in England itself. These values have been acquired at watering places which, in Mr Knightley's view, produce as much sickness as they cure. It is a sickness which, specifically associated with French manners and morals, he sees as threatening to destroy the English village. He is clearly articulating a form of Francophobia in his responses to both Mrs Elton and Frank. It is less clear that the text itself consistently endorses the same position.

SETTING UP HIS CARRIAGE

The social status of Mr Perry 'the apothecary' (E, p. 50) is, as suggested, ambiguous. He may be Mr Woodhouse's friend and yet John Knightley treats him as a lowly tradesman who ought to know his place. This debate is necessarily an important one in a text that explores and exposes the culture of invalidism. It is also a highly topical one since the precise status of the apothecary was a matter that reached the parliamentary agenda between 1812 and 1815. The Apothecaries' Act was finally passed in July 1815. *Emma* was written between January 1814 and March 1815.

As mentioned earlier, Jane Austen spent some time in London just before the publication of *Emma* helping to nurse her brother Henry through a serious illness. This was how she came into contact with Charles Haden, who was one of the physicians called in to attend her brother. He set in motion the train of events, already described, that led to the dedication of this novel to the Prince Regent. Austen's letters indicate that she derived a great deal of personal pleasure from his reasonably regular presence at the dinner-table. She admired both his manners and conversation. She therefore affected to be shocked that Cassandra should mistake her cultivated friend for a mere apothecary:

> But you seem to be under a mistake as to Mr. H – You call him an Apothecary; he is no Apothecary, he has never been an Apothecary, there is not an Apothecary in this Neighbourhood – the only inconvenience of the situation perhaps, but so it is – we have not a medical Man within reach – he is a Haden, nothing but a Haden, a sort of wonderful nondescript creature on two legs, something between a Man & an Angel – but without the least spice of an Apothecary. (L, pp. 439–40)

The reference to 'spice' hints very heavily at the apothecary's associations with drugs and trade. Cassandra's mistake was an understandable one since an earlier letter from London had mentioned the existence of an apothecary named Haydon, who had been in charge of bleeding Henry Austen.

Haden himself was a physician and therefore a member of the most exclusive part of the medical profession. The vast majority of the members of the Royal College of Physicians had been educated at either Oxford or Cambridge. The fact that neither of these universities, unlike some of the more enlightened Scottish and Dutch ones, offered intensive, specialist training in medicine was considered to be unimportant, since the physician was supposed to be a gentlemanly, classically literate scholar with broad horizons rather than narrow skills. As John Mullan notes, medical writings during the long eighteenth century were accessible to the general reader.[13] The physician's task was to deduce, or detect, the causes of internal diseases and then recommend an appropriate course of treatment. His expertise lay in the mental agility he brought to a case rather than in any manual or technical dexterity. Essentially, he made a diagnosis based on the information that he was able to extract about a patient's lifestyle. This might involve carrying out basic tests, although the main method was still to conduct an interview. One of the physicians treating George III during the first Regency Crisis based his whole reading of the case on the fact that on one occasion, immediately prior to his collapse, the King had been allowed to wear wet stockings for too long. Once a physician had made his diagnosis, he prescribed a course of treatment and left it to the apothecaries to dispense the appropriate drugs.[14]

Medical operations, particularly to cure external complaints, usually had to be placed in the hands of the surgeon rather than left in the minds of physicians. Surgeons formed their own Royal College in 1800, although they had only emancipated themselves from their traditional associations with barbers and therefore with trade in 1745. Austen was moved to Winchester during her final illness so that she could be attended by Giles King Lyford, who was the Surgeon-in-Ordinary at the County Hospital. It was felt that the local apothecary at Alton could no longer be expected to cope with such a serious illness. The Lyfords were a prominent medical family in Hampshire. Giles Lyford's uncle, John Lyford, attended the Austen family when they lived at Steventon. Charles Lyford was a surgeon who practised at Basingstoke and was the member of the family referred to in Austen's famous letter to her niece, Anna, about the craft of fiction:

> I have also scratched out the Introduction between Lord P & his Brother, & Mr. Griffin. A Country Surgeon (dont tell Mr. C. Lyford) would not be introduced to Men of their rank. (L, p. 394)

A broadly similar point is made in one of Austen's unfinished novels, *The Watsons*. Sam Watson is a surgeon and therefore not regarded as a particularly eligible suitor by Mary Edwards's parents. Charles Haden was a physician with contacts at court and so was able to mix with the members of the aristocracy. The Lyfords, like Mr Griffin, had a lower professional status and so could not always expect such a privilege.

Apothecaries were ranked below surgeons in the medical hierarchy, although this tripartite division was in fact only strictly adhered to in London. They did not enjoy the privileges of belonging to a royal college, being members instead of the Worshipful Society of Apothecaries. They could, in other words, join the equivalent of a trading company. They had originally been members of the Company of Grocers. The regulations governing their status were nevertheless frequently at variance with the position that they actually achieved in the medical market place. They had become increasingly successful at dispensing their own advice and drugs, as well as making up prescriptions for physicians and surgeons, since the beginning of the eighteenth century. They were starting to fulfil many of the functions that were to become associated with the general medical practitioner, who did not officially come into existence until 1858. The evidence suggests that in practice the boundaries between the three main branches of the medical profession were often very flexible. Many apothecaries also practised as surgeons and were known as 'mixed practitioners'.

Despite this flexibility, the apothecary was always in danger of having a case taken out of his hands by the more senior branches of the medical profession. When Marianne is ill in *Sense and Sensibility*, Elinor thinks quite seriously about the need to replace Mr Harris, the local apothecary, with somebody who could offer more specialised advice. Caroline Bingley and Mrs Hurst reveal their snobbery in *Pride and Prejudice* by declaring that the country apothecary, Mr Jones, is not fit to treat Jane Bennet, even though she is only suffering from a heavy cold. They recommend instead sending 'an express to town for one of the most eminent physicians' (PP, p. 86). Jones nevertheless is called in to treat Jane and, as he just happens to arrive at Netherfield at the same time as Mrs Bennet does, is very firmly of the opinion that the patient should not be moved.

The apothecaries started a campaign in 1812 to try to register the fact that they had established themselves during the previous century as practitioners whose skills went beyond dispensing drugs. Indeed, they wanted to protect themselves against competition from those whom they felt were mere druggists, as well as to persuade the physicians and surgeons to recognise the need for even more flexibility. Druggists and other irregulars had started to flood the market place at the turn of the eighteenth century. A survey conducted in Lincolnshire in 1804 revealed that qualified medical men were outnumbered nine to one by the irregulars.[15] *The Medical and Physical Journal* summarised the apothecaries' case in 1812:

> the practice of the Apothecary has passed, or is passing, to no small extent, into the hands of a description of men unknown in former times; who, being ignorant of the elements of medical science, exercise the trade, to the injury of the regular Apothecary, to the hazard always of the public, in some instances to the direct, and in many to the indirect, destruction of human life. (18, p. 405)

Rumours circulated that some physicians were actually employing the irregulars to make up their prescriptions. The case that was made against the apothecaries by their competitors was that they charged too much for their products. This was such a familiar accusation during the eighteenth century that Adam Smith felt the need to contest it in *The Wealth of Nations* (1776).

The apothecaries' campaign began as a defensive move to protest against the way in which the government had imposed indirect taxes on glass bottles in order to raise additional revenue for the conduct of the war. It nevertheless developed into a more assertive pressure group campaign designed to improve status. Members of the College of

Physicians and others with vested interests, such as the druggists, lobbied successfully against the first bill which was brought before Parliament in 1813. The Act that was eventually passed in 1815 had to contain amendments designed to appease these various interest groups. It did not interfere with the commercial activities of the druggists and satisfied the physicians by reinforcing, rather than re- moving, the links between apothecaries and trade. They still had to qualify by serving an apprenticeship and were still controlled by a company rather than by a college. The difference was that the com- pany's powers were more clearly defined, as well as becoming more national in their remit. Local forms of registration were increasingly seen as being anachronistic. This codification of practice, which re- moved some of the ambiguities that had been allowed to develop between the various branches of the medical profession, meant that apothecaries were probably even more dependent on the physicians than had been the case in most parts of the country. They could, for instance, be prosecuted and fined for refusing to make up any physi- cian's prescription. What had begun as an attempt to improve social status was turned into a measure that re-imposed many of the restric- tions from which the apothecaries wished to emancipate themselves. As far as readings of *Emma* are concerned, the complicated passage and provisions of the act itself are not as important as the fact that the precise status of the apothecary was being debated in Parliament and elsewhere while it was being written. These debates would have been familiar to most Regency readers.[16]

Before returning to the representation of Mr Perry, something of the apothecary's ambiguous social position can be seen in the hostility that was directed towards John Keats's poetry. Keats became an apprentice to Thomas Hammond in 1811 and then went to Guy's Hospital in 1815 to complete his training. Astley Cooper was one of the surgeons who taught him. He passed his exams the following summer and, although he continued his hospital job as a dresser for some time after this, eventually abandoned his medical career. A dresser accom- panied a surgeon on his rounds, as well as being present when operations were performed in front of a gallery of students in what was quite literally an operating theatre. Keats's decision to leave medicine was, according to John Gibson Lockhart's infamous review in *Black- wood's Magazine*, a great mistake. He urges Keats to use his medical skills to cure himself of the infection of poetry and then return to his true social position behind the shop counter: 'It is a better and a wiser thing to be a starved apothecary than a starved poet; so back to the shop Mr John, back to plasters, pills, and ointment boxes! &c.'

Lockhart's snobbish treatment of the apothecary, who is named as a servant might be, has some similarities with John Knightley's refusal to become involved with Perry, even as a topic of conversation. It is a more overstated version of Austen's own defence of Charles Haden from the charge of being a mere apothecary.[17]

The scene in *Emma* which, when set in the context of Regency medical history, acquires the kind of political topicality that has not been noticed even by those who have written on Austen and medicine such as J.R. Watson and Wiltshire, is the one where Frank Churchill very nearly gives his secret away. He catches sight of the apothecary riding by on his horse and asks what has become of 'Mr Perry's plan of setting up his carriage' (E, p. 341). He claims that his intelligence comes from one of Mrs Weston's letters, although it becomes clear that he must have received it during his secret correspondence with Jane Fairfax. The debates in Parliament and elsewhere about the status of the apothecary hinged on whether he was to be a tradesman on a horse, or a professional man who used a carriage for daytime visits. Although nothing has come of Mr Perry's, or more precisely Mrs Perry's, plan of setting up a carriage, Mr Weston is confident that it is only a matter of time before such a change in status is achieved.

Perry's friendship with Mr Woodhouse is not allowed to produce a confusion of ranks. The apothecary may call on little Emma four times a day when she has measles, but this does not entitle him to be invited to dinner. He is, however, permitted to call after it. He belongs to the second 'set' (E, p. 89) of Highbury society which includes the Coles and the Coxes. He invites the Eltons to dinner but does not receive social invitations to visit Hartfield, Donwell Abbey and Randalls. The poorer members of this second 'set' such as Miss Bates experience some difficulties in reconciling his fees with his friendship. She meets him in the street and gets some free advice about the wholesome qualities of baked apples. Her lack of money means that she has to think carefully about home visits:

> If Jane does not get well soon, we will call in Mr Perry. The expense shall not be thought of; and though he is so liberal, and so fond of Jane that I dare say he would not mean to charge anything for attendance, we could not suffer it to be so, you know. He has a wife and family to maintain, and is not to be giving away his time. (E, p. 175)

Her remarks suggest that Perry himself might experience problems negotiating the boundaries between fees and friendship. A more cynical interpretation would be that, in the absence of a carriage to advertise his professional credentials, the goodwill of the talkative Miss Bates is to be encouraged.

Perry is a socially mobile Regency character on the threshold of setting up his carriage. He is also a physically mobile character in a village-like community which is suspicious of movement. This represents one of his attractions as far as Mr Woodhouse is concerned. He is able to relay pieces of gossip that he has already gathered, such as the fact that Mr Cole never touches 'malt liquor' (E, p. 221). He performs the function of a local newspaper or, as Wiltshire puts it, he is a 'relay-station of gossip'.[18] He is also employed to gather new information:

> His good friend Perry too, whom he had spoken to on the subject, did not at present recollect any thing of the riddle kind; but he had desired Perry to be upon the watch, and as he went about so much, something, he thought, might come from that quarter. (E, p. 96)

Mr Woodhouse is not alone in relying upon the mobile Perry for a sense of what is happening in the neighbourhood. It is the apothecary who relays the news to one of the teachers at Mrs Goddard's boarding school, and therefore to the community as a whole, that Mr Elton has been sighted making a mysterious trip to London. Apothecaries are also associated with gossip in Austen's earlier writings. It is Mr Donovan who breaks the news to Mrs Jennings about the secret engagement between Edward Ferrars and Lucy Steele in *Sense and Sensibility*. Mrs Philips finds out that Jane Bennet has left Netherfield from Mr Jones's boy in *Pride and Prejudice*.

Perry owes his growing status and respect as much to his diplomatic as to his medical skills. He is polite enough to agree with Mr Woodhouse that wedding cake should only be eaten in small quantities, even though his own children are seen eating large quantities of it. As noted, he tells Miss Bates exactly what she wants to hear about the medicinal properties of baked apples. Although Mr Woodhouse obviously sends for him on the most trivial matters, the other residents of Highbury prefer to try their own remedies before involving themselves in the expense of a visit. Mrs Goddard offers an important contrast to the 'model of right feminine happiness' represented by Isabella.[19] She is independent, practical and in favour of forms of physical education:

> Mrs Goddard's school was in high repute – and very deservedly; for Highbury was reckoned a particularly healthy spot: she had an ample house and garden, gave the children plenty of wholesome food, let them run about a great deal in the summer, and in winter dressed their chilblains with her own hands. (E, p. 52)

Emma has every faith in her 'experience and care' (E, p. 131). Mrs Goddard only sends for Perry to treat another one of the sickly Harriet Smith's sore throats after both she and Emma have attempted to cure it with their own remedies. Harriet's frailty emphasises Emma's own physical strength.

John Knightley's version of Perry as a mere druggist is not supported by the one diagnosis of his that is given in any detail. He is summoned to attend Jane Fairfax after she has terminated her engagement to Frank Churchill. He then calls at Hartfield to attend to one of Mr Woodhouse's imaginary complaints and, in his role as a provider of news, gives Emma a shorthand diagnosis of Jane's illness:

> He thought that she had undertaken more than she was equal to, and that she felt it so herself, though she would not own it. Her spirits seemed overcome. Her present home, he could not but observe, was unfavourable to a nervous disorder: – confined always to one room; – he could have wished it otherwise – and her good aunt, though his very old friend, he must acknowledge to be not the best companion for an invalid of that description. Her care and attention could not be questioned; they were, in fact, only too great. He was very much feared that Miss Fairfax derived more evil than good from them. (E, p. 381)

The diagnosis, even though it is reduced to reported speech, nevertheless reveals something of Perry's diplomatic manner. He blames Miss Bates for aggravating Jane's illness and yet does so in such a way as to avoid giving any offence. It is his ability to make what seem to be perfectly legitimate connections between illness and environment that mark him out as a medical practitioner rather than a druggist selling spices behind a shop counter. The medical man who is called in to treat Lady Aurora Granville in Fanny Burney's *The Wanderer* (1814) also writes out, at a much more comic level, a social rather than a purely medicinal prescription. He advises his patient to avoid 'hot rooms, dancing, company, and talking'.[20]

Perry is granted a voice as his diagnosis is given and yet he is also denied one because it is rendered briefly in reported speech. Attitudes towards him are ultimately more significant than his own opinions. The text can certainly be seen as recommending the benefits of following a profession as opposed to the pursuit of pleasure. Mr Knightley takes a professional, scientific interest in agriculture and encourages his tenants such as Robert Martin to do the same. Most of his capital is invested in improvements to his estate. Frank Churchill, by contrast, has no profession and is therefore able to idle his time away at watering places. The text nevertheless pays much more attention to Frank than it does to an aspiring professional like Perry. Perry is in the background riding by on his horse, while Frank is in the foreground wondering when the apothecary will be able to set up his carriage. Perry calls after dinner and his conversation with Mr Woodhouse is regarded as being unimportant. Frank's conversation and behaviour at dinner parties and other social events are meticulously recorded. His secret engagement matters much more than any of the apothecary's professional engagements.

Although Knightley makes a strong case for professional values and the work ethic as part of his plea for Englishness, the text itself appears to take a more contradictory position. It does not ignore the village characters like Perry and Martin, who stand on the brink of professional status. They are nevertheless they are kept in the margins so that there can be a more detailed study of the mentality of a young Regency dandy who forms a secret engagement at a watering place. As suggested, a similar contradiction occurs in *Mansfield Park*. There is one text, or countenance, that looks favourably upon those like Sir Thomas Bertram and William Price who uphold a professional work ethic and another one that remains fascinated by the mentality of a young dandy like Henry Crawford. It will be argued later on that some of the same problems surround the representation of professionalism in *Persuasion*. Austen's young dandies may be criticised, but they are never in fact dispossessed and forced to work in the professions for a living. This, however, is exactly what happens to Lord Glenthorn in Edgeworth's *Ennui*. His claim to his title, and the lifestyle that goes with it, is revealed to be fraudulent so he starts climbing the lower rungs of the legal profession, admittedly with the help of patronage. This is represented as being the best thing that could have happened to him. Austen's Regency novels, by contrast, are reluctant to carry their undoubted commitment to professionalism quite so far.

THE ROAD AND THE POST OFFICE

Highbury is not on a main coaching route, so Mr Elton's trunk has to be taken in a butcher's cart 'to where the coaches past' (E, p. 199) when he leaves for Bath. The 'letter-boy on an obstinate mule' (E, p. 241), whom Emma imagines as part of the street scene that she is constructing while looking out of the window at Ford's, would have been employed to carry letters to and from the main road. The relative seclusion of Highbury means that connections between mobility and power are particularly apparent. Mr Elton is the 'adoration of all the teachers and great girls in the school' (E, p. 160). Harriet Smith tells Emma what happened once when he was sighted walking past in company with Mr Cole:

> The two Abbotts and I ran into the front room and peeped through the blind when we heard he was going by, and Miss Nash came and scolded us away, and staid to look through herself; however, she called me back presently, and let me look too, which was very good-natured. And how beautiful we thought he looked! (E, p. 101)

The women crowd around the window to gaze at a male figure on the public highway. Their desires and longings can be admitted amongst themselves, but have to be suppressed in the village world as a whole.

Although Mr Elton only sets up his carriage after his marriage, he is nevertheless still a highly mobile character before then. It is very easy for him to slip up to London on his horse to have Emma's picture of Harriet framed in Bond Street. As noted, it is while he is making this journey that he meets Perry on the road which leads to gossip about the romantic nature of his expedition being put into circulation. He is able to please himself and travel to Bath when he is in want of a wife. Mr Knightley decides to leave Highbury after the Box Hill expedition and is able to ride up to London immediately.

Female characters, by contrast, often have to wait, just like Mr Elton's trunk, until the necessary travel arrangements have been made for them. According to Miss Bates, Jane Fairfax is unable to fix the time of her arrival in Highbury because her movements are dependent upon those of Colonel Campbell:

> Yes, Friday or Saturday; she cannot say which because Colonel Campbell will be wanting the carriage himself one of these days. So very good of them to send her the whole way! But they always do, you know. (E, p. 172)

She continues to be almost totally dependent on others for movement. She is conveyed to and from the dinner party at the Coles in Mr Knightley's carriage. She is brought regularly to the vicarage in the Eltons' new carriage. The Eltons also assume responsibility for taking her to the ball at the Crown. She has to fight hard to assert her right to walk about Highbury on her own. As will be seen in more detail later on, she is closely examined by John Knightley about her walks to the post office. She has to persuade Emma that she is perfectly capable of walking back to Highbury from Donwell Abbey on her own. Emma offers her the use of either a servant or a carriage. The news that she has been 'wandering about the meadows, at some distance from

Highbury' (E, p. 382) reaches Emma, and presumably others, very quickly. Jane's movements are monitored and discussed in ways that are very different from the gossip that surrounds Mr Elton's trip to London. His right to be on the road is not questioned. She is subjected to a different kind of surveillance.

Emma herself is not nearly so dependent as Jane is on the charity of others for movement. Mr Woodhouse's carefully cultivated inertia means that she is able to command the carriage. She takes Harriet in it to pay a very brief visit to the Martins. She and Harriet also travel together to both the ball at the Crown and Box Hill. She makes a belated gesture of friendship towards Jane after she has heard Perry's diplomatic diagnosis:

> she ordered the carriage, and drove to Mrs Bates's in the hope that Jane would be induced to join her – but it would not do; – Miss Bates came to the carriage door, all gratitude, and agreeing with her most earnestly in thinking an airing might be of the greatest service – and every thing that message could do was tried – but all in vain. (E, pp. 381–2)

Emma does not bother to consult her father about this trip.

Emma is, potentially, the most mobile of Austen's heroines because of her father's invalidism. Yet she has never made the seven-mile journey to Box Hill before, not to mention never having seen the sea. Her control over travel arrangements does not always extend to those rare moments when her father is persuaded to leave Hartfield. His comfort and safety become 'the first object' (E, p. 148) when there is a slight fall of snow during the dinner party at Randalls. There is a blunder in the travel arrangements because everyone is fussing around the fussy old man and Emma finds herself alone in a carriage with Mr Elton. He has fortified himself with drink and proceeds to make 'violent love to her' (E, p. 148). Her ordeal is prolonged by the fact that her father's carriage, which is travelling in front, has slowed right down to walking pace. She eventually arrives back at Hartfield, after Mr Elton has been dropped off at the vicarage, and is greeted by her father:

> There she was welcomed, with the utmost delight, by her father, who had been trembling for the dangers of a solitary drive from Vicarage-lane – turning a corner which he could never bear to think of – and in strange hands – a mere common coachman – no James. (E, p. 151)

Mr Woodhouse's total inadequacy as a father is revealed by the way in which he imagines his daughter to have been in more danger during the last, rather than the first, part of the journey.

Emma may be powerful and yet even she is momentarily revealed to be in danger when travelling on the public highway. Assaults on women in this period were committed in the home and the workplace as well as on the road. Wollstonecraft's *Maria* highlights this fact both through Jemima's narrative of the way in which she was sexually abused by an employer and by the discovery that Maria's husband has had a sexual relationship with one of his servants. It was nevertheless the attacks on women who were travelling that tended to come to the attention of the public. This conveniently buried the fact that the crime could be much closer to home, as well as reinforcing the notion that women should not travel alone.

Although it happened before the Regency period, the much-publicised case of the alleged rape of Catherine Wade by John Motherill in Brighton in 1786 is one that could be read alongside Mr Elton's verbal assault on Emma. Elton recognises an opportunity to make his own kind of 'violent love' to Emma when she, like Catherine Wade, was not chaperoned and on the road.[21] Another case concerns the activities of the 'monster', who stalked fashionable London streets in 1790 attacking women often in broad daylight. He was a slasher who used a long knife to cut clothing as well as the body. One of his victims, Anne Porter, received a nine-inch-long wound that was four inches deep in places. The attacks were usually accompanied by a torrent of verbal abuse. It seems that he was motivated by a belief that women should not be allowed to walk the streets either on their own or in groups.[22] There are, of course, differences between such cases and the comedy of errors that surrounds Emma's journey with Mr Elton. It would nevertheless be a mistake to ignore some of the broader similarities.

Mrs Elton may affect to lead a confined life and yet she, like Emma, appears able to have control of the carriage most of the time. This allows her to patronise Jane Fairfax in a similar fashion to the way in which Emma establishes an unequal friendship with Harriet Smith. She nevertheless plays the part of a confined woman when she imagines her entrance at the strawberry-picking party:

> The thing would be for us all to come on donkies. Jane, Miss Bates, and me – and my caro sposo walking by. I really must talk to him about purchasing a donkey. In a country life I conceive it to be sort of necessary; for let a woman have ever so many resources, it is not possible for her to be always shut up at home; – and very long walks,

you know – in summer there is dust, and in winter there is dirt. (E, p. 351)

A donkey, sometimes with a cart, was often the only form of transport that women in the country could call their own, as Diana Sperling's contemporary Regency watercolours of gentry life illustrate.[23] Austen herself planned to get well by going for donkey rides during her final illness, as has been seen. Despite all the affectations to the contrary, Mrs Elton sees donkies as being disposable stage props in the pastoral play in which she is to perform the part of Marie-Antoinette. She has in fact some control over travel arrangements which is why she is able to become a serious rival to Emma.

Some Regency women were able cover great distances. As a professional actress, Dorothy Jordan sometimes had to travel over a hundred miles a day between engagements, getting up at five in the morning and travelling until ten at night. Sarah Siddons undertook a particularly strenuous theatrical tour of Ireland in 1802/3. Then there were those who might be described as professional travellers, such as Lady Hester Stanhope who journeyed to and then around the Lebanon in order to find environments in which she could indulge her passions for leadership and cross-dressing. Anne Lister, who also cultivated a masculine look, travelled widely throughout continental Europe before dying of fever in Georgia in 1840.[24] These women and a few others were, however, exceptions to the general rule that lack of access to transport led to confinement.

Mr Knightley takes pains to assure Mrs Elton that the road between Highbury and Donwell is neither dusty nor dirty and therefore perfectly safe. Roads are nevertheless represented elsewhere as being potentially dangerous places for women. Harriet Smith and Miss Bickerton are half a mile outside Highbury on the Richmond Road when they encounter a group of gypsies. Miss Bickerton bolts, while Harriet freezes. Their actions are seen as provoking the gypsies: 'How the trampers might have behaved, had the young ladies been more courageous, must be doubtful; but such an invitation for attack could not be resisted' (E, p. 350). Harriet is eventually rescued in the nick of time by Frank Churchill who just happens to be walking along the Richmond Road. He takes her back to Hartfield where, like a good sentimental heroine, she faints. The incident can be read as an extended literary parody. Julia Prewitt Brown suggests how it might be related to previous events when she makes a distinction between Knightley's heroic rescue of Harriet at the Ball and Frank's mock-heroic rescue of her here.[25] It can also be seen as offering some support for Mrs Elton's view that women were not always able to escape from confinement by taking walks. One of the more practical reasons why Emma cultivates Harriet's friendship in the first place is because she needs a 'walking companion'(E, p. 56), which indicates that she is aware of the dangers of walking around Highbury on her own. Anne Lister was a member of the Yorkshire gentry whose diaries record not only her lesbian relationships, but also the occasions on which she was molested by men while out walking alone. She writes on 11 January 1820 about how a young, well-dressed man had without any warning 'suddenly attempted to put his hands up my things behind'.[26]

Ellen Weeton, a Regency governess, was considered earlier on as a letter writer. Her experiences as a traveller reveal some of the restrictions imposed on Regency women, while at the same time showing how they could at times be transcended. She decided not to tell her family and friends that she had taken employment with the Pedders at Dove's Nest just in case things went wrong, as this might damage her future prospects as a governess. The fact that she was seen leaving with a gentleman in a chaise caused everybody to believe that she was involved in an elopement. This was the only possible explanation as to why a young woman should be on the road with an apparent stranger. Weeton eventually left Dove's Nest in 1811 and took another post with the Armitages near Huddersfield in Yorkshire at the time of the Luddite disturbances there. While she was between these situations, she travelled by herself to the Isle of Man where she passed the time taking long solitary walks. Although she was conscious that this was a potentially dangerous recreation, her fears were not realised.

Her marriage in 1814 put an abrupt stop to her walking tours. She describes her husband as a monster who, after a brief honeymoon period, used all of his power to try to drive her from the house. She was physically beaten, denied money, starved of food and locked out of the house. When she broke one of the windows to get back in, she was prosecuted as well as threatened with being confined in a lunatic asylum. Her room was set on fire on one of the rare occasions when she left the house. A separation was agreed in 1822 on condition that she gave up almost all rights as far as her daughter was concerned. She moved out and the husband's mistress quickly took her place. It is a story that would not have been out of place in Wollstonecraft's *Maria*.

She began walking again after the end of her marriage, not least so that she could pay surprise visits to her daughter's school. Both before and after her trip to London in 1824 she regularly walked distances of up to twenty miles in a day. She meticulously recorded these distances in her letters and journals as a way of making a general statement about her independence. She travelled to London on the outside of the mail coach, which was particularly hazardous during the overnight part of the journey as passengers had to stay awake or else risk being thrown off into the road. She discovered, like other Regency passengers, that it was difficult to judge the exact amount of brandy that was needed to keep her warm without sending her to sleep. Her eleven-week stay was mainly devoted to visiting tourist attractions, although she also went to employment agencies on behalf of friends. Jane Fairfax shocks as well as bewilders Mrs Elton with her attack on these agencies which were primarily concerned with recruiting governesses: 'There are places in town, offices, where inquiry would soon produce something – Offices for the sale – not quite of human flesh – but of human intellect' (E, p. 300). Weeton calculated with precision and triumph that she had walked a total of five hundred and thirty-eight miles during her stay. She added an extra three-quarters of a mile for good measure.

Her return journey was an unpleasant one. Heritage reproductions foreground the mail coach along with other forms of horse-drawn transport as a symbol of an elegant, leisured world that has been lost. This particular journey, however, developed into a struggle for survival for the Regency woman who had dared to travel alone. Her inside seat was taken from her by one of a party of Irishmen after the coach had been changed at Birmingham. The guard tried to reclaim it for her but, after a violent struggle which she thought might actually overturn the new coach, gave up the attempt. She therefore had to spend the overnight part of the journey on the outside:

> I rode the rest of the night on a very dangerous outside seat behind, backwards. We were four upon it, and it was too short by much for the number; but every seat was equally crowded. It was very necessary to keep my eyes open, for the least drowsiness, and I should have dropped headlong. The man on my left kept a constant motion with his head upon my shoulder, up and down, the night through, . . . the brim of his hat endangering my eyes. The iron rail bruised me sadly, I was so jammed against it.[27]

Weeton eventually recovered her original seat in the morning, although there were still some more unpleasant incidents to be endured before she reached Liverpool. Two years later she undertook a solitary walking tour of Wales and climbed Snowdon without a guide. Although it is clear that she herself found ways of evading the restrictions that were placed on women's movement in this period, her exceptional experiences nevertheless also highlight the general pattern. She was treated as a nuisance on the Liverpool coach and regarded as an eccentric on most of her walking tours.

To return to *Emma* itself, Frank affects to have his movements severely curtailed by Mrs Churchill and yet he is a highly mobile character. In the incident with the gypsies, he makes a melodramatic entrance first to rescue Harriet and then when he appears with her on his arm at Hartfield. The gypsies take themselves off in a hurry because they do not fancy appearing before Mr Knightley and the other magistrates. Frank is also in a hurry to be off and so makes a dramatic exit after he has explained why he just happened to be walking down the road in the first place. He had ordered his horses to meet him outside Highbury so that he could pay a last-minute call on Jane Fairfax. This is achieved under the pretence of needing to return a pair of scissors and wanting a walk. It is a story that may not have convinced the detective, or magistrate, if he had been allowed to consider it in detail.

Frank's entrances and exits are unpredictable, usually because that is the way in which he decides to stage them. He eventually arrives in Highbury earlier than expected, which pleases Emma:

> He had reached Randalls the evening before. She was pleased with the eagerness to arrive which had made him alter his plan, travel earlier, later, and quicker, that he might gain half a day. (E, p. 203)

This pleasant surprise is nevertheless followed three days later by one of Frank's unpredictable exits. He orders the chaise from the Crown and drives to London. Because Highbury is off the main coaching route, the Crown does not bother to keep a large stable of horses: 'a couple of post-horses were kept, more for the convenience of the neighbourhood than for any run on the road' (E, p. 209). Frank wants to transform the Crown into a smart coaching inn as well as a fashionable assembly room. He hires the chaise again to escape from Highbury after the Box Hill expedition, even though he is not under instructions to return that night to Richmond. It is the ostler at the Crown who puts this piece of gossip into circulation, adding that Frank was 'going a good pace, and driving very steady' (E, p. 376). Frank is able to choose whether he walks or has a 'run on the road'. He is also able to decide when, as well as how, he will travel. The 'neighbourhood' becomes a stage on which he makes surprising entrances and dramatic exits. The same opportunities are not available to women, even powerful ones like Emma. The sheer weight of the detail about travel arrangements in *Emma*, together with the way in which much of it highlights relationships between mobility and power, needs to be seen as an important part of a political argument about the positioning of women. The same is also true of Austen's other Regency novels.

Jane Fairfax encounters John Knightley and his two sons when she is setting off for the post office in the rain. As mentioned earlier, the receiver of a letter was usually expected to collect it and pay for it. During the Napoleonic Wars people who lived away from the main coaching routes might walk to the post office for news of battles and national politics, as details were often displayed there. John Knightley feels that it is entirely appropriate for him to ask Jane to explain her movements when they meet later on the same day for dinner at Hartfield. She has her explanation ready: 'It is my daily errand. I always fetch the letters when I am here. It saves trouble, and is a something to get me out. A walk before breakfast does me good' (E, p. 293). Readers may doubt that this particular walk does her good, since they know that she hardly ever eats any breakfast after it. She and John Knightley then engage in stilted small talk about the differences between public and private correspondence which, given her secret correspondence with Frank, is acutely embarrassing for her.

John Knightley may be polite towards Jane, whom he regards as an old friend. He is nevertheless a lawyer whose conversation retains the air of a cross-examination. As Wiltshire notes, Jane's ambiguous social position means that she can be treated with an aggressive form of kindness.[28] Her new patroness, Mrs Elton, is neither formal nor polite. She wants to display to everyone, but perhaps particularly to Emma, that Jane's movements are now subject to her control. Jane is being given an unpleasant foretaste of what life as a governess might be like:

> there must be some arrangement made, there must indeed. I shall speak to Mr E. The man who fetches our letters every morning (one of our men, I forget his name) shall inquire for your's too and bring them to you. That will obviate all difficulties you know; and from *us* I really think, my dear Jane, you can have no scruple to accept such an accommodation. (E, p. 296)

Jane then makes two unsuccessful attempts to tell her new patroness that she is determined to carry on collecting the letters.

It is at this point that Jane, perhaps flustered by the way in which the small talk has started to run very deep, delivers her eulogy on the post office as an institution. It is out of character, and thus a potential clue, as she is normally associated with reserve:

> 'The post-office is a wonderful establishment! said she. – 'The regularity and dispatch of it! If one thinks of all that it has to do, and all that it does so well, it is really astonishing! . . . So seldom that any negligence or blunder appears! So seldom that a letter, among the thousands that are constantly passing about the kingdom, is

even carried wrong – and not one in a million, I suppose, actually lost! And when one considers the variety of hands, and of bad hands too, that are to be deciphered, it increases the wonder!' (E, p. 296)

John Knightley tempers this uncharacteristic enthusiasm by reminding her that the post office is not some philanthropic concern, but a business which has to be efficient. The problem that Regency readers may have experienced with this part of the conversation was that the post office was notorious for its inefficiency, as well as resented for its high charges. In addition to the grievances already mentioned during the discussion of Austen's letters, there were wide-scale abuses of the franking privilege. This was originally restricted to members of Parliament and those of equivalent status, but was extended to a much wider male group during the Revolutionary and Napoleonic Wars. Ingenious ways were found to evade charges by those who still had to pay them. It was cheaper to send newspapers than letters so messages were often written on them instead. Austen herself occasionally waited for friends to carry and deliver letters rather than trusting them to the post office. Jane's praise for an unpopular institution may have alerted Regency readers to the fact that she is not telling the whole truth about other matters. She praises 'regularity' and yet is using the post office to conduct an irregular, or secret, correspondence with Frank Churchill. Letters are apparently hardly ever 'carried wrong', even those between people who are carrying on wrongly. The reference to 'bad hands' only serves to reinforce the script that begins to emerge when the speech itself is seen as a blundering attempt to cover up the blunder of insisting a little too much on the need to collect letters from the post office. Mary Favret puts it nicely when she shows that Jane runs the risk of 'exposure to more than the elements' in her trips to the post office.[29]

Different readers will let themselves into the secret of the secret engagement at different points, although most of them should be aware of it before Mr Knightley's suspicions are fully aroused. They may have their suspicions straightaway if they know about Regency England, given the fact that watering places were closely associated with secret relationships in this period. They may have to wait until the coincidence of Frank's trip to London and the arrival of Jane's piano stretches credibility. Frank tries to cover his tracks by making sure that the piano is accompanied by Irish melodies in order to perpetuate the fiction that Mr Dixon may be the secret lover, but perhaps he is not careful enough. As Mary Lascelles and Butler have both noted, some of the clues are cleverly planted in Miss Bates's speeches where they are not likely to be read attentively.[30] Jane's flustered praise for the post office is one of the many clues that are available to readers. The text plays an intricate game with its readers by planting genuine clues, as well as producing red herrings such as Dixon. This means that readers are ultimately placed in a contradictory position. They are encouraged to play the game and then have to listen to Mr Knightley moralising about the need to banish forms of play in favour of openness. The text itself is pleasurable because it is closed, secretive and playful. It then starts to wear a different countenance and begins to deny its own pleasures.

Jane and Frank's correspondence appears to be concerned with Highbury gossip rather than with grand passion. This at least is the impression that is given by the one glimpse that readers are given of it which, as noted, concerns Mr Perry and his plans for a carriage. The correspondence may not be that exceptional in its subject matter, although it is unusual in that it is intended for their eyes only. Other letters have a much wider circulation. Emma may only be exaggerating a little when she claims that every letter that Jane sends to her aunt 'is read forty times over' (E, p. 110). Frank's letters are accorded a similar status at Randalls. Everyone except Mr Knightley agrees that he wrote a good letter to Mrs Weston on the occasion of her marriage to his father. Even Mr Woodhouse was roused from his inertia to have a look at it:

> 'it was an exceeding good, pretty letter, and gave Mr and Mrs Weston a great deal of pleasure. I remember it was written from Weymouth, and dated Sept. 28th – and began, "My dear Madam", but I forget how it went on; and it was signed "F.C. Weston Churchill". – I remember that perfectly.' (E, p. 119)

Mr Woodhouse is methodical enough to remember the beginning and end of the letter, but his lack of discrimination means that he has no sense of its contents. The reader does not know at this stage whether the precise date is a clue of any significance.

Mr Knightley is less favourably disposed towards 'pretty' letters which he considers to have been written in 'woman's writing'(E, p. 297). Other members of the village community continue to regard Frank's letters as a welcome source for conversation. If Mr Perry's gossip fulfils some of the functions of a local newspaper, Frank's letters can be seen as playing the part of a national newspaper. Mr Weston brings one of them with him when he arrives late at the dinner party at Hartfield. He makes little distinction between his 'public news' (E, p. 303) and intelligence about Frank. Emma and Mrs Weston both read the letter which announces that Frank will be coming to Highbury again in a fortnight. He writes later to postpone his entrance. Mr

Weston then uses the arrival of the letter as an excuse to try to impress Mrs Elton with his son. He finds, in a scene that contains some highly theatrical comic writing, that Mrs Elton's obsessions are every bit as strong as his own. The exchange anticipates the neurotic world of *Sanditon* in which, with the exception of the heroine, all the main characters can only talk relentlessly about themselves and their own concerns.

Although letters from outsiders like Jane and Frank are the most highly prized ones within the community, communications from other characters are also there for discussion. Emma offers advice to Harriet on the written proposal that she receives from Robert Martin which disrupts Mr Knightley's own match-making activities. Mr Elton writes 'a long, civil, ceremonious note' to inform Mr Woodhouse that he is going to Bath. It pointedly makes no mention of Emma. Mr Woodhouse is shown once again to be unable to read letters which have a bearing on the happiness of his daughter. Instead of being concerned about the snub to Emma, he merely uses the note as an excuse to talk about his own concerns:

> Her father was quite taken up with the surprize of so sudden a journey, and his fears that Mr Elton might never get safely to the end of it, and saw nothing extraordinary in his language. It was a very useful note, for it supplied them with fresh matter for thought and conversation during the rest of their lonely evening. Mr Woodhouse talked over his alarms, and Emma was in spirits to persuade them away with all her usual promptitude. (E, pp. 158–9)

Emma has, of course, already undertaken a surprising journey with Mr Elton and she was thankful to 'get safely to the end of it'. She nevertheless keeps her countenance in order to humour her father. Mr Elton continues to supply fresh conversational matter when he arrives at Bath. He writes to Mr Cole and he in turn passes on the news to Miss Bates. She also gets the news of Mr Elton's engagement from a letter to Mr Cole. She is determined that this particular engagement at a watering place will not remain a secret for very long as far as other members of the village community are concerned. The news she has is a valuable commodity that needs to be marketed as soon as possible in order to confirm, albeit briefly, her own importance. Although Mr Knightley brings the same news from the same source to Hartfield, he is scooped by the breathless Miss Bates when he tries to deliver it. He may affect to despise gossip as well as match-making and yet he is prepared to indulge in both. Emma's plans for Harriet spoil his own schemes. This is not to deny his status as hero but, rather, to notice that there are some occasions when he is shown to be hypocritical.

Mr Knightley eventually has his suspicions about the secret engagement confirmed in a letter from Mr Weston while he is in London. He immediately rides sixteen miles through the rain and makes an unexpected entrance at Hartfield. Love brings out at least a hint of the Frank Churchill in him. It is appropriate that letters should play such a crucial part in the resolution to a text which has been so concerned with them and what they can reveal about both their writers and readers. Frank's long letter to explain the secret engagement, which is brought into the open by Mrs Churchill's death rather than by Knightley's surveillance, arrives later than anticipated. Mrs Weston sends it to Emma to supplement the explanations that have already been given to her.

This letter reveals amongst other things that, even if the post office was really 'a wonderful establishment', those who used it could still make some elementary blunders. Frank and Jane quarrel when they meet unexpectedly on their respective ways to and from the strawberry-picking party. He wants to seize the opportunity to walk with her, although she maintains that they must do nothing to jeopardise their secret. This at least is the story contained in the letter. It is nevertheless written by somebody who, like Emma herself, has a habit of preferring fiction to fact. Jane is offended by Frank's Byronic conduct at Box Hill and writes to him breaking off the engagement. His reply does not get posted in the confusion surrounding Mrs Churchill's death. It is only when he receives all his letters back from Jane two days later that he realises his mistake. He therefore has to make yet another flying visit to Highbury to try to retrieve the situation. The lovers were able to maintain their secret for so long because post offices helped them to keep in touch. This is why Jane commits the blunder of describing them as wonderful establishments, even though the historical evidence tells a story of high charges and attempts at evasion.

Emma is reasonably satisfied with Frank's explanations, although Mr Knightley is much more hostile towards them. His views on the appropriate conventions for what was known as the familiar letter are similar to those expressed by the eighteenth-century writer Robert Dodsley:

> A letter should wear an honest, cheerful Countenance, like one who truly esteems, and is glad to see his Friend; and not like a Fop admiring his own Dress and seemingly pleased with nothing but himself.[31]

Knightley's more critical reading of the letter is often held to contain the message of the novel. Butler endorses his position by declaring quite categorically that 'the theme of the novel is scepticism about the qualities that make up the inner life – intuition, imagination, original insight'.[32] His reading of the letter can be seen alternatively as merely re-stating a problem that has been running throughout the novel rather than in any way resolving it. He comments on the earlier part of the letter:

> Very bad – though it might have been worse. – Playing a most dangerous game . . . Fancying you to have fathomed his secret. Natural enough! – his own mind full of intrigue, that he should suspect it in others. Mystery; Finesse – how they pervert the understanding! My Emma, does not every thing serve to prove more and more the beauty of truth and sincerity in all our dealings with each other? (E, p. 430)

Mystery, finesse and secrecy are all represented as being part of a 'dangerous game'. They are opposed by a desire for openness and sincerity. *Emma* nevertheless plays some dangerous games with its readers. It engages them in the mystery of a secret engagement. It reveals, bit by bit, the intrigues and finesses that are required to sustain the relationship. It then allows the failed detective to have the last word. It tries to keep its countenance and ends up condemning parts of itself.

Tony Tanner is more attuned to the text's contradictions than those critics who see it as carrying a relatively unproblematic anti-Jacobin, or Francophobic, message. He argues that the arrival of Frank Churchill 'means a novelty, a mystery, an uncertainty – in a word, a novel'.[33] This allows for the possibility that it is the Regency watering place with its French associations, rather than the village, that produces a pleasurable text that is then unsatisfactorily denied. Tanner's sense of a profoundly contradictory novel in which meanings and messages may not be fixed even by the resolution itself is shared by other critics. Patricia Meyer Spacks notices what she describes as the 'double pattern' of the novel which allows gossip and speculation to be seen as enabling for a heroine, at the same time as they are condemned.[34] Joseph Litvak locates a broadly similar duality around the relationship between Emma and Knightley. He suggests that they each offer competing and equally compelling definitions of the self.[35]

CONCLUSIONS

As the selection of themes here has sometimes led to the relative marginalisation of Emma herself, it is important to end by summarising and also elaborating upon some of the points that have been made about her. Most critics have drawn attention to her power. Some of them celebrate it, whereas others see it as being much more threatening. It has been suggested here that one of the ways in which Emma gains this power is by being determined to be well. Her robust health is highlighted through the contrasts provided by the presence of weak and sickly women such as Isabella Knightley, Harriet Smith and Jane Fairfax. She believes, unlike her sister, that children do not need to be dosed continually with medicine in order to be healthy.

Her relationship with her father is a complex and contradictory one. At one level, her power is enhanced by his imaginary invalidism. She is able to organise the household as well as control the use of the carriage. Mr Elton's proposal on the trip back from Randalls, and, it could be added, the return journey from Box Hill when she is in tears, nevertheless show that there are still times when she, like other Regency women, is at her most vulnerable when travelling. The flickering, sneering and insolent commentary on Mr Woodhouse, which critics tend to miss, comes from the narrator rather than from Emma herself. She is concerned to prevent him from making spiteful remarks to Isabella and, more generally, to soothe away some of his more absurd anxieties. His invalidism denies her power, as well as giving it to her, in the sense that she too has to dance attendance on him. The complexities of the relationship are re-stated rather than resolved in the ending. After her wedding and honeymoon at an unnamed watering place, Emma remains at Hartfield so that her father will not be left on his own. Mr Knightley leaves Donwell Abbey to move in with his wife. This arrangement can be seen as allowing Emma to retain some of her independence since she carries on living in the house in which she grew up. Her husband comes to her. It can also be seen as being the result of the way in which she is still dependent on the whims of a tyrannical invalid.

Although the ending itself is open to different interpretations, it is reasonably clear that Emma's relative immobility earlier on is the product of her father's carefully cultivated inertia. She has not seen the sea, or been to Box Hill, when the novel opens. She is certainly mobile within the village world of Highbury and yet is, for a Regency heiress of her class who has some control over travel arrangements, still remarkably sheltered from the wider world. This helps to explain why, initially at least, the watering place and its characters hold such a fascination for her and therefore for readers as well. She starts to write her own novel about it when she invents the scandalous story that Mr Dixon is really Jane Fairfax's secret lover. Johnson, who writes well about the fictions within the fiction, notices that some of Emma's other stories are also about sexual scandals such as the possibility that Mrs Churchill may have given birth to several 'natural' children.[36]

Emma's sense of the necessity for rigid hierarchies within the village leads her to formulate some objections to Frank Churchill's plans for the ball. These are nevertheless quickly put aside because she craves the novelty that can be imported into the village from the watering place. Her special regard for Frank does not survive his departure at the end of his first visit to Highbury. The dandy from Weymouth increasingly comes to be seen by Emma as a suitable partner for Harriet Smith. He is still a very necessary character for her novel even though he is now in danger of becoming inseparable from his bow, or seeming to be superficial.

Emma is not the only character in Austen's novel who needs to create fictions about those associated with watering places in order to escape from the boredom of the village. Mrs Weston not only imagines a match between Emma and Frank, but also fancies that there may be a relationship between Jane Fairfax and Mr Knightley. Miss Bates's horizons would be even more restricted if she did not have opportunities to gossip about the arrivals of both Jane and Mrs Elton. As Tanner implies, Frank's own arrival provides the occasion for the kinds of story-telling that the village world, left to itself, has difficulty in producing. Emma has nevertheless had the opportunity to speculate about Harriet Smith's parentage. She follows the plot of fashionable novels such as Anna Maria Porter's *Lake of Killarney* (1804) and imagines that Harriet is nobly born. Highbury is capable of providing some of the materials for a novel. The mystery may be resolved with the revelation that Harriet's father is in fact no more than a respectable tradesman but, until this point, she remains a character who has secrets to be fathomed. It is, however, mainly the characters who are associated with watering places who provide the novelty for the novels that are written by both Emma and Austen herself. The Regency watering place, with its scandals, secrets and mysteries, is celebrated before it is condemned.

6   *Persuasion*: The war and the peace

INTRODUCTION

This chapter begins by situating the representation of Sir Walter Elliot in the contexts that have already been established in relation to the Prince Regent, Beau Brummell and dandyism. It then reads the textual debates about the role of the navy in war and peace alongside some of the available historical evidence. This is followed by a consideration of Anne Elliot's practicality and rationality at both Uppercross and Lyme, which continues the discussion of invalidism and watering places started in the last chapter. The final section deals with the chapters that are set in Bath and looks in particular at the social status of the midwife in Regency England in order to historicise the representation of Nurse Rooke. Although there are some references throughout to literary history, the emphasis is once again on showing the meanings that become available when an Austen text is read alongside a wider social history. This is not to deny the importance of other approaches that are primarily concerned with identifying literary allusions and echoes.[1] The argument is that there are also important topical allusions as well as more purely literary ones.

A DRESSY MAN FOR HIS TIME OF LIFE

Persuasion debates the question of who will, and who deserves to, win the peace after the ending of the Napoleonic Wars. Sir Walter Elliot is just two years older than the Prince Regent. He would, nevertheless, probably insist that he looked at least ten years younger. His estate, or state, is Kellynch Hall in Somersetshire. *Persuasion*, like *Mansfield Park*, is both a romance and a Condition-of-England novel that deals with the inheritance of estate. One of the differences is that Sir Walter, unlike Sir Thomas Bertram, does not have a son to succeed him. His estate, like that of Mr Bennet in *Pride and Prejudice*, is not able to be inherited by women. He therefore nominates his nephew, William Elliot, to be his heir. The ending of the novel is ambiguous and open-ended. Perhaps William Elliot will eventually inherit both the title and the estate, even though he has forfeited any moral rights to be the ruler of Kellynch. Alternatively, Admiral and Mrs Croft, who rent the estate, may take up a more permanent form of residence there.

Financial extravagance forces Sir Walter to rent his ancestral seat to the Crofts, while he decamps to Bath. It is clear that it passes into both better and safer hands. *Mansfield Park* suggests that Fanny Price, despite being a poor female relation, is the best character to inherit the estate even though she is unable to do so. *Persuasion* also casts doubt on the benefits to be derived from male lines of descent. Anne Elliot may not even be Sir Walter's eldest daughter and yet she demonstrates throughout the novel that she possesses exactly the right qualities to ensure both the survival and prosperity of Kellynch. The question of female rule for the state itself was, it will be remembered, raised during the Regency Crisis in an attempt to prevent the Prince of Wales from gaining control of his father's political house. The issue remained topical since Princess Charlotte was the heir to the throne until her death following the birth of a stillborn child in 1817.

Sir Walter is an ageing dandy who spends a lot of time admiring his face and figure in large looking-glasses. The family portraits watch him watching himself. He also passes the time by endlessly re-reading the entry on his family in a book about the baronetage. He sees his family history as being unique and therefore fascinating. Readers are informed that it is in fact a very familiar story, told 'in the usual terms' (P, p. 35), of a relatively obscure family eventually being rewarded for loyal rather than outstanding political services. It is possible that the title was purchased because it was granted at the accession of Charles II when honours were openly on sale. Sir Walter nevertheless only sees what he wants to see in both the mirror and the book. He takes up his pen to make sure that the entry is as precise as possible. He inserts the exact date of his wife's death as well as details about the marriage of his youngest daughter. He also feels it necessary to record the name of his 'Heir presumptive'(P, p. 36).

The original entry offers a version of history which marginalises women. Their presence requires explanation, whereas a godlike Sir Walter just appears at the beginning:

> Walter Elliot, born March 1, 1760, married, July 15, 1784, Elizabeth, daughter of James Stevenson, Esq., of South Park, in the county of Gloucester; by which lady (who died 1800) he has issue

Elizabeth, born June 1, 1785; Anne, born August 9, 1787; a still-born son, Nov 5, 1789; Mary, born Nov 20, 1791. (P, p. 35)

Women enter the 'handsome duodecimo pages' (P, p. 36) of this official version of history at birth, marriage and death. Their identity is dependent upon their male connections. James Stevenson's daughter becomes Sir Walter Elliot's wife. Her children become his 'issue'. He is somebody, or something, while she is nobody, or nothing. Elizabeth has some consequence in this history because she is the eldest daughter. Mary is accorded a second mention in the up-dated entry as a result of her marriage. Nothing appears to have happened to Anne since she was born, or rather had the privilege of becoming Sir Walter's 'issue'. A similar form of marginalisation occurs in the obituary notices of the period in which widows are frequently described as being the relics of their former husbands.

Sir Walter believes that Anne will never marry and will therefore always remain the most marginal living figure in the family history. She has become a listener because her opinions are not taken seriously. Her marginality is also signalled by her name which has never been a popular one in this particular dynasty. Sir Walter's indecision meant that he never actually forbade her to marry Captain Wentworth when she was nineteen:

> Sir Walter, on being applied to, without actually withholding his consent, or saying it should never be, gave it all the negative of great astonishment, great coldness, great silence, and a professed resolution of doing nothing for his daughter. He thought it a very degrading alliance; . . . (P, p. 55)

He gives his opinion of a bad husband in much the same way as Brummell pronounced on the subject of bad knees: looks and gestures are more important than words. He nevertheless allowed Lady Russell to persuade Anne against the marriage. He still considers that the name of Wentworth would pollute the pages of his precious family history. He describes Captain Wentworth's brother as being a 'nobody' (P, p. 52) because he is not connected to any great family. One of the main ironies that is allowed to emerge out of such pronouncements on family and history is that Sir Walter himself may be a nobody who has nothing better to do than to remind himself of a not very illustrious past. Tanner draws attention to the intricate wordplay that takes place throughout the novel around definitions of somebody and nobody.[2] Sir Walter's version of history, for all its parade of facts and dates, is challenged more directly later on in the novel. As will be seen, the man with the pen in his hand is shown to be remarkably gullible about his

'Heir presumptive' by women who rely on gossip rather than on what are taken to be more solid facts. The true family history is constructed by Anne with help from Mrs Smith and Nurse Rooke.

Sir Walter and Elizabeth believe that they are entitled to live in the same style as their supposedly illustrious ancestors. They are unable to economise as this would represent a great betrayal of the glorious past. Elizabeth only goes through the motions of identifying areas where savings could be made. Perhaps they could stop giving money to unnecessary charities and postpone having new furniture in the drawing-room. There is no suggestion in her mind that the annual visit to London ought to be cancelled, although there may be a saving if they do not buy a present for Anne while they are there. Anne's present becomes another unnecessary charity. Anne's own stringent proposals for economy never see the light of day since Lady Russell's more modest ones cause such offence:

> What! Every comfort of life knocked off! Journeys, London, ser-
> vants, horses, table – contractions and restrictions every where. To
> live no longer with the decencies even of a private gentleman! (P, p.
> 44)

Sir Walter therefore allows himself to be persuaded to rent his house and move to Bath. As noted, the Prince of Wales retired to another watering place, Brighton, in an equally vain attempt to try to control his debts.

Sir Walter's departure is not mourned by his tenants. Although he rehearses the part of the benevolent landowner in front of one of his many mirrors, the estate workers have to be persuaded to turn up to watch his final bow. Like the Prince at Portsmouth, he becomes his bow. There is nothing else. Anne's credentials for inheriting the estate are demonstrated by the way in which she takes her own leave. She catalogues the pictures and makes the necessary arrangements for the garden. She explains to her sister Mary that she went to 'almost every house in the parish' because she was told that the inhabitants 'wished it'(P, p. 66). The Crofts establish their own credentials to govern the estate by continuing Anne's charitable work as well as, more generally, her unostentatious style of management. She

> felt the parish to be so sure of a good example, and the poor of the
> best attention and relief, that however sorry and ashamed for the
> necessity of the removal, she could not but in conscience feel that
> they were gone who deserved not to stay, and that Kellynch Hall had
> passed into better hands than its owners. (P, p. 141)

Anne appears to reject the hereditary principle in favour of a system in which merit and distinction are rewarded.

It is doubtful whether Sir Walter saves much money by going to Bath. He rents an expensive house with two drawing-rooms in Camden Place. It is stuffed with 'mirrors and china'(P, p. 224). He has nothing to do and so is able to devote his time to cruising up and down the streets in search of confirmation that no man or woman is better looking than him. He lounges in shop windows and vainly waits for even a 'tolerable face' (P, p. 155) to pass by. He promenades in company with Colonel Wallis and registers the way in which everyone gazes admiringly at such a handsome couple. Kirkham puts it nicely when she suggests that he behaves like 'a smart society woman of uncertain age'.[3] Although he is obsessed by all aspects of appearance, he seems to be particularly concerned about complexion. He is a self-appointed expert on make-up. He believes that Lady Russell needs to wear more rouge if she wants to receive morning callers with the blinds open. While taking a haughty attitude to the culture of advertisements, he nevertheless sings the praises of Gowland's Lotion. He wishes that Elizabeth's companion, Mrs Clay, did not have freckles. Brummell washed and scourged his own body, although he did not use much perfume or make-up. The Regent, by contrast, used both in very liberal quantities.

Sir Walter dislikes sailors because, both socially and physically, they are nobodies. The profession plays havoc with a man's complexion. Anne gives her father a brief description of Croft's distinguished career: he fought at the Battle of Trafalgar (1805) and was stationed in the East Indies. Sir Walter is more interested in complexion than courage: 'Then I take it for granted', observed Sir Walter, 'that his face is about as orange as the cuffs and capes of my livery' (P, p. 51). The wordplay makes Sir Walter appear unpatriotic as well as ridiculous. Trafalgar is the name of the cape near to which the great naval battle was fought. A battle sometimes retained the word cape in its name, as for instance it does in the Battle of Cape Saint Vincent (1797). Admiral Croft spent the war years fighting, or cuffing, the enemy at various capes. Sir Walter spent them admiring the 'cuffs and capes' of his livery. There are other examples of this kind of wordplay. Sir Walter notices the wreckage of personal appearance in others, whereas the naval officers inhabit a world in which ships are wrecked and lives are lost. Readers are left in little doubt that those who won the war ought to win the peace. The ambiguity surrounds the question of whether this will in fact be the case. Sir Walter is, however, pleasantly surprised by Croft's appearance when they first meet. The complexion passes muster and Sir Walter declares that, if his valet could arrange the Admiral's hair, then he would have no objections to being seen in public with him. It is the highest compliment that he can pay somebody.

Sir Walter's patronising attitude towards Croft contrasts sharply with the way in which he fawns upon anyone who possesses an hereditary title. He ingratiates himself back into favour with his cousin, Lady Dalrymple, simply because of her rank and her smart address in Bath. Anne has no desire for such an acquaintance:

> Had Lady Dalrymple and her daughter even been very agreeable, she would still have been ashamed of the agitation they created, but they were nothing. There was no superiority of manner, accomplishment, or understanding. (P, p. 162)

Anne is quite prepared to reverse the categories that are held to be so sacred in Sir Walter's beloved 'book of books' (P, p. 38). Those who appear in its handsome pages may be 'nothing', just as those who do not may be something. Nevertheless, Sir Walter is delighted to be seen in Lady Dalrymple's company, making the most of his theatrical entrance with the rest of her party for a concert at the Octagon Room in Bath. Captain Wentworth also attends the concert and engages Anne in conversation before it, while Sir Walter and Elizabeth pose ostentatiously in front of a fire-place. Sir Walter acknowledges Wentworth's presence by returning his bow, although does not consider it necessary to talk to him. He is merely 'a bowing acquaintance' (P, p. 169), whereas Lady Dalrymple belongs to a more exclusive circle. Sir Walter becomes more impressed with Wentworth, however, when he has a chance to study, or quizz him, and his complexion 'repeatedly by daylight' (P, p. 250). This broad satire on the ageing dandy who is obsessed by appearance has some similarities with the way in which Leigh Hunt, Cobbett, Hone and others represented the Regent.

Sir Walter originally courted his 'Heir presumptive' with a view to persuading him to marry Elizabeth. This does not happen since William Elliot makes an opportunistic marriage for money:

> Sir Walter had resented it. As the head of the house, he felt that he ought to have been consulted, especially after taking the young man so publicly by the hand: 'For they must have been seen together', he observed, 'once at Tattersal's, and twice in the lobby of the House of Commons.' (P, p. 39)

Tattersalls, situated at Hyde Park Corner in London, was the leading establishment for buying and selling horses, as well as for placing bets on them. The Prince of Wales's racehorses were sold here the year after the scandal at Newmarket that forced him to quit the turf. It was also regarded as a fashionable place to be seen. The fact that Sir Walter can only think of the House of Commons as a similar venue, or stage, may continue the argument about his lack of patriotism. He believes that the privilege of being seen in such a public place with somebody as handsome as him could only be repaid by marrying his daughter. Brummell also regarded his public approval of a person as the making of them. When he was asked why he had not repaid a loan, he claimed that he had just done so when he was standing in the window of his club and wished his creditor a good morning. When he was accused of leading a young aristocrat astray, he argued that nothing could be further from the truth since they had been seen together walking arm-in-arm. This meant that the aristocrat would now be accepted within high society. This provides another example of the way in which dandyism playfully reversed roles: the nobody plays the part of the somebody whose public approval is crucial.

Sir Walter's resentment at the way in which his own public approval of his heir is treated turns out to be short-lived. Although he considers William Elliot to be 'under hung' (P, p. 154), he is easily placated by his excuses and pleasing manners. He judges by appearances and his heir appears to be perfectly sincere when he arrives in Bath with a view to ending the family quarrel. William Elliot seems to be worthy of his place of honour in this particular family's Bible. Readers are provided with clues to suggest that there is something suspicious about him. Like Henry Crawford, he calls at unusual hours. He lacks openness and is also remarkably skilful at finessing himself into the right seat. Anne notices some of these things and, with help from Mrs Smith and Nurse Rooke, is able to challenge the way in which 'the head of the house' both reads and writes the history of his family.

Elizabeth and, to a lesser extent, Mary have inherited Sir Walter's concern for rank and consequence. Elizabeth became mistress of Kellynch at the age of sixteen at her mother's death. Sir Walter claims that he never married again in case Elizabeth felt displaced. It is revealed, however, that the old dandy put in for being a widower again only to meet with 'one or two private disappointments in very unreasonable applications' (P, p. 37). Perhaps there were differences of opinion about make-up or cabbage. Elizabeth is therefore able to reign at Kellynch unchallenged:

> For thirteen years had she been doing the honours, and laying down the domestic law at home, and leading the way to the chaise-and-

four, and walking immediately after Lady Russell out of all the drawing-rooms and dining-rooms in the country. (P, p. 38)

She is like Emma Woodhouse with none of the playfulness, wit or imagination. She chooses to make Mrs Clay rather than Anne her companion so that her superiority will remain unquestioned. Mary is also concerned with rank. She fights an absurd battle with her mother-in-law, Mrs Musgrove, about which one of them should take precedence, or have consequence, at Uppercross. She also adopts a haughty attitude to neighbours like the Hayters.

Anne feels that her father and eldest sister do not deserve to stay at Kellynch. The estate passes into 'better hands' when they remove themselves to Bath. Her radicalism is supported by the way in which Sir Walter's obsessions with appearances are ridiculed. This critique is open and sustained rather than self-consciously covered up. The head of the estate, or state, cares more for complexions and capes than he does about the great issues of war and peace. He is hopelessly in debt but is much more concerned with the arrangement of hair than with the fact that the war may have had a profound effect on social arrangements. There are clear echoes and reminders throughout of the world of the Regent and Brummell.

Anne's radicalism nevertheless involves contradictions. Admiral Croft has, after all, been fighting at Trafalgar and elsewhere to preserve the hereditary principle. The peace of 1815 saw the restoration of what was described as legitimate authority, with a repetition of the banquets that were held in Portsmouth and elsewhere for visiting heads of state in 1814. The text therefore seems to be aware of the ways in which the defence of legitimacy can produce a critique of it. Those who are defending Sir Walter's rights to do nothing are also establishing their own credentials by doing something. Mary Poovey makes a similar point when she notices that the qualities of Wentworth which Lady Russell distrusts are the very ones which help to win the war and therefore safeguard her own social position.[4]

Another way of exploring the text's contradictions is to suggest that satire may ultimately be a form of flattery. Sir Walter's absurdities particularly in the earlier chapters produce some of the best comic writing which often involves intricate, but nevertheless open and accessible, wordplay. Although he has become marginalised by the time the action moves to Bath, he is by no means discarded entirely as a source for humour. The argument that post-war society can manage perfectly well without such ageing dandies is possibly compromised by the way in which he remains a necessary comic character in a satirical novel about this society. As has been argued at some length in relation to *Mansfield Park*, Austen's Regency novels find ways of celebrating highly theatrical characters in the act of repudiating them.

FINE NAVAL FERVOUR

Admiral and Mrs Croft maintain Anne's charitable work when they move into Kellynch Hall. They make a number of changes to the house itself. The Admiral removes 'some of the large looking-glasses from my dressing-room' (P, p. 143). He prefers functional to ostentatious objects and so is quite happy to manage with a 'little shaving glass' (P, p. 143). He is also concerned to establish more flexible relationships between upstairs and downstairs and so decides to keep umbrellas by one of the doors instead of in the butler's pantry. Sir Walter presumably had to send a liveried servant to collect an umbrella every time he needed one to prevent drops of rain from spoiling the arrangement of his hair or the hue of his complexion. The Crofts also repair a laundry door that does not open properly. This was probably in a part of the house that Sir Walter felt it was beneath his dignity to visit. The estate, and by implication the state, is a more functional, informal place under the rule of the Crofts.

As indicated, Sir Walter is a remarkably indecisive character which is another trait that he shares with the Prince Regent. He remains silent on the subject of Anne's original relationship with Wentworth. He has to be manipulated by his lawyer, Mr Shepherd, into the decision to rent Kellynch. He and Elizabeth agonise about the best way to approach Lady Dalrymple. The Crofts, by contrast, are brisk and decisive. They do not take long to make up their minds about Kellynch. Mr Shepherd reveals that it was Mrs Croft who took charge of the business arrangements:

> And a very well-spoken, genteel, shrewd lady, she seemed to be . . . asked more questions about the house, and terms, and taxes, than the Admiral himself, and seemed more conversant with business . . . (P, p. 52)

Anne imagines later on that the couple run their lives in much the same way as they drive their gig: the Admiral may hold the reins, but Mrs Croft's interventions prevent him from having accidents. Sir Walter and two of his daughters inhabit a world in which questions about individual precedence and preference are vital. The Crofts inhabit a world in which partnership is important.

Mrs Croft accompanied her husband on most of his voyages during the Napoleonic Wars. She is dismissive of Wentworth's claim that he does not like women on board his ships:

> But I hate to hear you talking so, like a fine gentleman, and as if women were all fine ladies, instead of rational creatures. We none of us expect to be in smooth water all our days. (P, p. 94)

She goes on to declare that the only time that she was in danger of slipping into the culture of invalidism and imaginary illnesses, and thus into the dominant model of right feminine happiness, was when she had to spend a winter alone at Deal:

> I lived in perpetual fright at that time, and had all manner of imaginary complaints from not knowing what to do with myself, or when I should hear from him next; but as long as we could be together, nothing ever ailed me, and I never met with the smallest inconvenience. (P, p. 95)

Boredom and leisure produce her invalidism.

It is Wentworth who is maintaining the traditional, or Admiralty, view in this exchange. Captains were expected to obtain written permission to carry women on board when they were at sea. This meant that they were supposed to clear a ship of all the women who had been living there while it was in port. Most captains were reluctant to grant shore leave in case their men deserted. It thus became the custom for prostitutes, and wives if it was a home port, to be rowed out to a ship. Thomas Rowlandson's drawing, 'Scene off Spithead', represents this custom.[5] It is difficult to estimate how many women remained on the lower decks after a ship put to sea since, given the Admiralty regulations, they could not usually appear in the muster lists. The evidence nevertheless suggests that a limited number of women could still be found on the lower decks of some ships even after they had left port. Christina White asked for a pension because she had performed the roles of dresser and nurse both during and after the Battle of Aboukir Bay in 1798.[6] Some members of a ship's crew were expected to travel with their wives. The gunner's wife, for instance, usually had the task of looking after the cabin-boys. The position of such women was a potentially dangerous one. Members of the crew of the *Hermione* mutinied in 1797 while sailing in the Caribbean. They killed the captain and most of the other figures of authority including the boatswain. The boatswain's wife, who may have been the only woman on board, was taken by the mutineers to the Spanish Main before being released.[7]

There are also a few cases of women who dressed themselves as men. Their presence might suggest that the Admiralty regulations were often enforced quite rigidly. The most notorious example was probably Mary Anne Talbot whose autobiography was published in 1809, shortly after her death. She was, like George Anne Bellamy, the 'natural daughter', or lovechild, of an aristocratic father. After the death of her mother, she was brought up by a guardian who appears to have sold her to a Captain Bowen, whom she accompanied to the West Indies disguised as a boy soldier. It was after Bowen's death and her return to Europe that she served in the navy, first as a powder-monkey and then as a cabin-boy. She also spent time being treated in the naval hospital at Portsmouth. Her later career included a short period in London as an actress in an unlicensed theatre playing female parts. The autobiography is thus another text which shows that Regency theatres could still be associated by their enemies with what were taken to be dangerous and disreputable people. The fact that the earlier part of Talbot's life reads like a script by Kotzebue might have re-enforced such prejudices.[8]

There is plenty of evidence in Austen's letters and the other important historical sources that commission(ed) officers were sometimes accompanied by wives or other women. Although difficult to generalise, the pattern appears to be that women did not accompany officers on a regular basis. They were present on what were seen to be special trips. Naval ships were expected to carry important passengers, who might well be the wives and families of officers or diplomats posted overseas. The debate between Mrs Croft and Wentworth is in fact triggered off when Admiral Croft mentions that Wentworth arrived in Lisbon just too late 'to give a passage to Lady Mary Grierson and her daughters'(P, p. 93). Lady Hester Stanhope and her party travelled in 1810 by naval frigates on the earlier stages of their journey to the Lebanon. Although Emma Lady Hamilton disliked sailing, she accompanied Admiral Lord Nelson in 1800 on a journey to Malta.[9] The Admiralty regulations were nevertheless quite specific that women should only be on board operational ships in exceptional circumstances. That this was not always the case proves that Nelson was not the only sailor who turned a blind eye to some orders and regulations. Mrs Croft argues the need for changes to such regulations. Her partnership with her husband is not so much an accurate account of life on the quarter-deck during the Napoleonic Wars, as a potentially radical proposal about how it ought to be organised in the future.

Sir Walter's obsessions with precedence rule out the possibility of most forms of male friendship. He nevertheless consents to be seen promenading with Colonel Wallis, even though his hair is a little too sandy. Wallis is hardly a true friend since he turns out to be part of William Elliot's conspiracy against the family. French writers from Barbey D'Aurevilly onwards have always been particularly intrigued by the paradox that the dandy was forced to be a very sociable person, while also having to remain an essentially isolated one. The insider is also the ultimate outsider. Sir Walter may lack Brummell's wit and yet there is a sense in which he too thrives on the public rituals of high society while appearing to stand aloof from them. The naval officers, in contrast to the dandy, inhabit a world which values comradeship or partnership. Captain Benwick is at sea when Fanny Harville, whom he plans to marry, dies. Wentworth takes it upon himself not just to break the news to Benwick, but also to stay with him for a week while he recovers from it. Captain and Mrs Harville then make a home for Benwick at Lyme. There is a hint of rivalries between officers when Croft mentions that Admiral Brand and his brother 'played me a pitiful trick once – got away some of my best men' (P, p. 180). The overall impression that is conveyed of naval life is nevertheless one of comradeship and common purpose.

The book that gives the roll call of the nation's baronets becomes Sir Walter's Bible. Its place is taken by the navy lists for all those who display 'fine naval fervour'(P, p. 178). These are not actually named, although the reference is probably to publications such as *The Naval Chronicle*, *Pepys's List of the Royal Navy* and *Steel's Original and Correct List of the Royal Navy*. Anne studies them, together with the newspapers, in order to keep in touch with Wentworth's career after she has been persuaded to end her relationship with him. This is why she is able to provide the information that Admiral Croft had fought off Cape Trafalgar. The appearance of Wentworth at Uppercross, where Anne stays with Mary after she leaves Kellynch, leads Henrietta and Louisa Musgrove to acquire a belated interest in the navy. They now acquire a smattering of naval history to add to their other accomplishments and charms, much to Anne's suppressed annoyance:

> she found the Miss Musgroves just fetching the navy list – (their own navy list, the first that had ever been at Uppercross) – and sitting down together to pore over it, with the professed view of finding out the ships which Captain Wentworth had commanded. (P, p. 89)

The Miss Musgroves therefore already know the answers to the charming questions that they ask.

Like Willam Price, Wentworth is only too happy to entertain the family circle with dashing tales of narrow escapes and prize-money:

after taking privateers enough to be very entertaining, I had the good luck, in my passage home the next autumn, to fall in with the very French frigate I wanted. I brought her into Plymouth; and here was another instance of luck. We had not been six hours in the Sound, when a gale came on, which lasted four days and nights, and which would have done for poor old *Asp*, in half the time, our touch with the Great Nation not having much improved our condition. Four-and-twenty hours later, and I should only have been a gallant Captain Wentworth, in a small paragraph at one corner of the newspapers; and being lost in only a sloop, nobody would have thought about me. (P, p. 90)

Prize-money attracted both officers and crews to the navy. It came in different shapes and sizes. If an enemy ship was sunk, then all the members of the victorious ship received a reward. This was known as 'Head and Gun' money because the size of the reward was calculated either according to the numbers of men on the enemy vessel, or else according to the number of guns that were being carried. Officers and their men did not get rich from this kind of prize-money. They were luckier if they actually captured an enemy ship, since the Admiralty was often prepared to buy it from them. As the condition of the *Asp* itself suggests, there was always a demand for new ships. The best payouts for those of Wentworth's rank came if the captured ship was carrying a valuable cargo. Unlike 'Head and Gun' money, this kind of prize-money was divided up in such a way that officers received more than the men. Under a revised set of regulations which became effective in 1808, a captain was entitled to claim a quarter of the prize-money. His entitlement became higher if he were sailing under what were known as Admiralty Orders because then there was no admiral of his station to demand a cut. Captains received three-eighths of the prize-money under such circumstances. It is indeed 'good luck' that Wentworth spots the French frigate on his way back to Plymouth because he would have been sailing under Admiralty Orders. Such details would have been well-known to many Regency readers.

There were often problems involved in claiming prize-money. The prize agents made their money by trying to invest the proceeds from a particular ship for as long as possible. Delays were therefore built into the system. Nelson and others employed their own agents to make sure that they were not cheated through the indolence of office. Nelson spent some time just before Trafalgar trying to make sure that his crew got their money for the capture of a French merchant ship called the *Marie Therese* the year before. He drew the Admiralty's attention to the way in which both officers and crew felt the 'hardship of being so kept out of their money'. This appears to be an example of what Frank Austen described as Nelson's 'happy talent' for trying to make all those under his command feel as if they were included in any enterprise.[10] The problem here, however, was that the *Marie Therese* had been seized by those members of the crew who were sailing another captured vessel back to port. They were therefore technically aboard a ship that was not commissioned, which meant that all the proceeds went directly to the Admiralty.

The regulations were exceptionally complicated so that those without Nelson's influence often had extreme difficulty in claiming their just rewards. Mary Anne Talbot was arrested for losing her temper while trying to claim prize-money. Thomas de Quincey records how one of the first things that he was asked to do after he had been offered hospitality during his rambles around Wales was to write a letter on behalf of a former sailor to claim overdue prize-money.[11]

Besides getting prize-money, officers could also increase their salaries by carrying valuable freight either for the government itself or else for merchants. Although there were several attempts to clamp down on these practices during the Napoleonic Wars, they were still regarded by captains as a legitimate source of income. William Robinson, also known as Jack Nastyface, records in his autobiography of life on the lower decks during the Napoleonic Wars that officers made money as well by smuggling home valuable items that they had captured.[12] Wentworth makes 'five-and-twenty thousand pounds'(P, p. 250) out of the war, at the same time as Sir Walter is running badly into debt. In addition to having the luck to take a frigate while he was sailing under Admiralty Orders, he was also fortunate to have been stationed in the West Indies as this was regarded as the happiest of hunting grounds for prize-money.

Wentworth's adventure stories ignore some of the harsher realities of naval service and therefore offer a romanticised view of it. They do not deal with the widespread anxieties over homosexual practices which have already been discussed here. Sailors were about four times as likely to die either of disease, or in an accident, than they were to be killed in action. Naval surgeons usually had fewer paper qualifications than those who practised on land, which led to debates about their professional status at the end of the war. Nelson, himself a walking testimonial to the skill of the surgeons, was worried that the best ones were always in danger of leaving.[13] Elaborate precautions were taken to prevent sailors from deserting since many of them had been pressed into service. One way of trying to avoid the clutches of the press-gang was to dress as a woman. A passport, or ticket-of-leave, was required to get off a ship even if it was in the home port. Jack Nastyface, who was carrying a passport, recalls how he was stopped at Alton by a party of soldiers lying in wait to claim the £5 bounty that was given for the capture of any deserter.[14]

Captains had to be conscious of the possibility of mutiny, which provided the justification for harsh punishments. As noted earlier, the radical opposition to the Regent often focused upon the question of the way in which the armed services were allowed to torture enlisted men. Burdett, Cobbett and others were therefore quick to seize upon the case of a sailor named Jeffery. He had been flogged for stealing from the ship's supplies of rum and beer. When he committed the same offence again, his captain marooned him on an uninhabited island in the West Indies with few supplies. He was eventually rescued, against all the odds, by a passing ship.[15] Although floggings and other severe punishments were meant to prevent mutiny, there was always a chance that they might provoke it. There were plenty of other flash-points. Food and clothing were supplied by contractors who were concerned with their own profit margins. Short measures of food was one of the principal grievances in the great mutinies of 1797 at Spithead and the Nore.

Maria Edgeworth's *Manoeuvring* (1809) goes further than *Persuasion* by representing a world of court martials and mutinies. There is a mutiny on board the *Dreadnought* while it is stationed in the West Indies. This has been provoked by the negligence of the captain who is both an epicure and a dandy. The ship itself can also be seen as the ship-of-state which was shortly, as has been shown, to have a dandy at its helm. Order is eventually restored when the crew realise their dependency upon the skill and integrity of Captain Walsingham. He, like Wentworth, is a professional who is able to improve his social status through the acquisition of prize-money. His openness is contrasted with the deceits and self-deceits practised by the old gentry as represented in terms of the male characters by Sir John Hunter.[16]

Persuasion's version of the navy at war may be a glamorous one. It is nevertheless severe with those who indulge in what is seen as being a hypocritical attitude towards heroism. The Musgroves had a son called Richard who was sent to sea as a midshipman, eventually ending up under Wentworth's command. Mrs Musgrove is desperate to be allowed the comfort of believing that he did not die in vain:

> The real circumstances of this pathetic piece of family history were, that the Musgroves had had the ill fortune of a very troublesome, hopeless son; and the good fortune to lose him before he reached his twentieth year; that he had been sent to sea, because he was stupid

and unmanageable on shore; that he had been very little cared for at any time by his family, though quite as much as he deserved; seldom heard of, and scarcely at all regretted, when the intelligence of his death abroad had worked its way to Uppercross, two years before. (P, p. 76)

Mrs Musgrove, like Sir Walter, is unable to see any blemishes in her 'family history'. She wants to believe that her 'stupid and unmanageable' son might have been a future Nelson if he had not been cut off in his prime. There is little sympathy for her and her low, theatrical voice and none for Richard. A fragment from one of his illiterate letters, written on the orders of Wentworth, is quoted. Its only merit lies in the fact that it is not a begging letter.

Mrs Musgrove's attempt to play the grieving mother of one of the nation's fallen heroes continues to be mocked very openly. Wentworth does his duty, after putting on a straight face, and joins her and Anne on a sofa. Anne is in her familiar position as listener:

they were divided only by Mrs Musgrove. It was no insignificant barrier indeed. Mrs Musgrove was of a comfortable substantial size, infinitely more fitted by nature to express good cheer and good humour than tenderness and sentiment; and while the agitations of Anne's slender form and pensive face may be considered as very completely screened, Captain Wentworth should be allowed some credit for the self-command with which he attended to her large fat sighings over the destiny of a son whom alive nobody cared for. (P, p. 92)

This abusive outburst is followed by an unsuccessful attempt by the narrator to keep countenance through the claim that the large Mrs Musgrove ought, in theory, to be just as entitled to show grief as anybody else. Her sentimental patriotism is still seen as the last refuge of an inadequate mother, despite the existence of what Marvin Mudrick has termed the 'bland apology'[17] that is offered almost immediately afterwards.

Many critics have been troubled by this moment, arguing, quite correctly, that there is a discrepancy between the cruel representation here and the more sympathetic ones encountered elsewhere of Mrs Musgrove's old-fashioned virtues. They often go on to argue that Austen would have toned down this scene if illness and then death had not prevented her from editing the manuscript. Even Kirkham, who is more alert than most to the possibility that Austen's novels can carry open rather than submerged or camouflaged critiques of prevailing orthodoxies, takes this view. She argues more particularly that Austen's obsession with the comic possibilities of the name Richard/Dick got the better of her on this occasion.[18]

It has been suggested here, in contrast, that this rapid alternation between vicious mockery and more socially acceptable statements runs throughout Austen's writings and should not therefore be regarded as a momentary lapse when it occurs once again in *Persuasion*. Although this movement may be at its clearest in the letters, it is also a distinctive feature of the Regency novels. Tom Bertram, and therefore readers, are allowed to laugh at Sir Thomas during his discovery of the theatre before another 'bland apology' is given. Isabella Knightley and Mr Woodhouse are treated scornfully, as well as more tolerantly. Mrs Musgrove is sneered at in a scene that hovers 'on the verge of insolence' before there is an attempt to keep 'within some curious mean', to return to Woolf's remarks on dandyism which also help to define more generally a Regency style of writing. The narrator loses her countenance and then attempts to recover it.

The ability to keep a straight face is indeed one of the themes of the scene itself. As noted, Wentworth has to compose himself before taking a seat on the sofa. James Thompson, who writes perceptively on the language of gesture in Austen's novels, notices the way in which Anne attempts to read Wentworth's face at this particular point.[19] She detects a 'momentary' and 'transient' (P, p. 92) look that tells her that in reality Wentworth had very little time for poor Dick Musgrove. He keeps a straight face but with some difficulty. The narrator is in the more powerful position of being able to lose her own countenance completely.

The action of the novel begins in the summer of 1814. The naval officers provide an important contrast to the values that Sir Walter holds so dear. Croft makes Kellynch a less ostentatious and more functional environment. Both he and Mrs Croft are capable of taking quick, practical decisions. The Crofts and Wentworth prize partnership and comradeship. The navy is represented as a profession in which a man may rise in the world, provided he has a certain amount of luck. Although the profession is glamorised, there is nevertheless a strong suggestion that it should not exclude women as much as it does. The attempt to create heroes out of such unpromising material as Richard Musgrove is treated scornfully. Sir Walter's book preaches predestination. Destinies are determined at birth and a nobody is unable to become a somebody. The navy lists hold out the promise of a more open society by registering the way in which a Wentworth or a Walsingham are able to write their own histories.

NO ONE SO PROPER, SO CAPABLE AS ANNE

Anne's sister Mary is an imaginary invalid who has little control over her children. If the local butcher is reported as saying that there is a bad sore throat in the area, then she is convinced that it is only a matter of time before she catches it. She spends a lot of time on 'the faded sofa of the pretty little drawing-room'(P, p. 64) at Uppercross Cottage because her husband, Charles Musgrove, devotes most of his own time to field sports. He too is an eldest son who is able to follow the profession of pleasure. Their relationship, based as it is on long periods of separation, is the norm from which the Crofts, with their view of marriage as partnership, are departing. It has some similarities to the relationship of Mary's parents in Wollstonecraft's *Mary: A Fiction* (1788), as well as to that of the Melvilles in Mary Hays's *Letters and Essays, Moral and Miscellaneous* (1793).[20] The Middletons in *Sense and Sensibility* are another couple who are divided by field sports. When Anne arrives at Uppercross, Mary claims to 'be so ill that she can hardly speak' (P, p. 64). She nevertheless recovers relatively quickly as a result of Anne's tactful conversation. Her invalidism is also the product of a combination of boredom and leisure, as well as possibly being a forlorn attempt to attract her husband's attention.

Anne is prevented from meeting Wentworth for the first time since their engagement was called off because one of Mary's unruly children dislocates his collar bone. She immediately assumes control, just as she does later after Louisa Musgrove's famous accident on the Cobb at Lyme:

> It was an afternoon of distress, and Anne had everything to do at once – the apothecary to send for – the father to have pursued and informed – the mother to support and keep from hysterics – the servants to control – the youngest child to banish, and the poor suffering one to attend and soothe; . . . (P, p. 79)

Anne calmly and collectedly stands in for the hysterical mother. Mr Robinson, the apothecary, puts back the dislocated collar bone and checks to see whether other bones are broken. He comes back the next day and leaves 'directions' (P, p. 82) about how the patient is to be treated. He, like Mr Perry in *Emma*, is a medical practitioner rather than a mere druggist. It is left to Anne to follow his instructions since Mary, as soon as she has been brought back from the verge of hysterics, decides that she ought to go out to dinner. She justifies herself by claiming that Anne is exactly the right person to look after the child because she does not have to contend with 'mother's feelings'(P, p. 82).

It is fortunate for Mary that she is not required to describe such feelings.

Charles and Mary Musgrove are members of the party that is made up to go to Lyme. As the only married couple in the party, they ought to have been in charge of it. The other members are Anne, Wentworth, Henrietta and Louisa Musgrove. Wentworth is able to combine the pleasure of the trip itself with visiting his old comrades, Harville and Benwick. Lyme was a fishing village which, like Brighton, Weymouth, Ramsgate and many other resorts, had adapted itself to cater for the increasing demand for healthy holidays. Harriette Wilson describes Lyme as 'a sort of Brighton in miniature, all bustle and confusion'.[21] As noted, Austen herself stayed here in 1804 and affected to play the part of the sick woman. Lyme was not, however, just a seaside resort. It provided an important link in the cattle trade between the Channel Islands and England during the Napoleonic Wars. The Select Committee that investigated the state of the Cobb in 1818, finding it to have foundations of shingle rather than rock, might not have done so had the port lost all of its primary economic functions.[22]

As many medical practitioners recommended bathing in cold water, the season was not necessarily confined to the summer months. Austen's vivacious cousin, Eliza de Feuillide, described her visit to Margate with her sickly son in a letter to another member of the family dated 7 January 1791:

> I had fixed on going to London the end of this month but to shew you how much I am attached to my *maternal duties*, on being told by one of the faculty whose skill I have much opinion of that one month's bathing at this time of year was more efficacious than six at any other & that consequently my little boy would receive the utmost benefit from my prolonging my stay here beyond the time proposed, like a most *exemplary parent* I resolved on foregoing the *fascinating delights* of the great city for one month longer, & consequently have determined on not visiting the metropolis till the 28th of Febry. Was not this heroic?[23]

Eliza's playful, mocking tone is similar to that employed in some of Austen's own letters. The local medical practitioner, if reported correctly, was given to making extravagant claims in order to try to keep the resort full throughout the year. The party from Uppercross visit Lyme in November when it could still have been open for business, although it is clear that its particular season is already over. The attractions of the resort and its neighbourhood are praised in the style of a guidebook:

the Cobb itself, its old wonders and new improvements, with the very beautiful line of cliffs stretching out to the east of the town, are what the stranger's eye will seek; and a very strange stranger it must be, who does not see charms in the immediate environs of Lyme, to make him wish to know it better. (P, p. 117)

Lyme is represented, initially at least, as being a less dangerous resort than Weymouth is in both *Mansfield Park* and *Emma*.

There are nevertheless still some important similarities between what happens in Lyme and what is reported as having taken place in Weymouth in *Emma*. A stranger's eye gazes admiringly at Anne while she is walking up the steps from the beach. Wentworth watches him watching her. She is flattered. The stranger turns out to be the devious dandy, William Elliot, so this watering place is shown to have at least the potential for producing a dangerous liaison based on lack of knowledge. Butler claims that Elliot's entry at this point is the result of 'unusually clumsy stage management' on Austen's part.[24] This ignores the fact that dandies are frequently associated with watering places in Austen's novels, as well as in other Regency texts. It is an association which provides alert readers with important clues.

Danger of another sort is associated with Lyme as well as with Weymouth. Jane Fairfax apparently nearly falls out of a boat into the sea. Louisa Musgrove mistimes her playful, childlike series of jumps down the steps of the Cobb when she attempts them for the second time and knocks herself out. The accident allows Anne to demonstrate, once again, that she is able to keep her head while all about her are losing, or hitting, theirs. Mary becomes hysterical and Henrietta faints. Charles Musgrove, who ought to be in charge of the party, starts to cry. Anne not only takes command of these civilians, but also issues orders to the naval officers. She orders Benwick to look after Wentworth, who is acting melodramatically because he thinks that he has caused the accident. She then orders Benwick to go and find a surgeon as quickly as possible. The text is quite open here about the strengths of female government. Anne is in complete control of the situation until the arrival of Harville, who orders Louisa to be taken to his house instead of to the hotel, which was Anne's original plan.

The surgeon declares that there is no real cause for alarm or hysterics:

The surgeon was with them almost before it had seemed possible. They were sick with horror while he examined; but he was not hopeless. The head had received a severe contusion, but he had seen greater injuries recovered from; he was by no means hopeless; he spoke cheerfully. (P, p. 132)

Lyme, like most other watering places, has a greater range of medical practitioners than a country village like Uppercross. Henrietta had argued earlier on that Dr Shirley, the vicar of Uppercross, ought to retire to Lyme because he would receive much better medical attention there. Her motives may be self-interested, since she wants Shirley to vacate the vicarage, but her information is accurate.

Mr Robinson and the surgeon at Lyme are represented, albeit briefly, as being good professionals who are cool, quick and decisive in a crisis. Although they do not merit the same attention that is given to Mr Perry in *Emma*, they can be seen nevertheless as displaying some of his soothing qualities. *Persuasion* differs from *Emma*, however, by placing a much greater emphasis on the role of the woman as healer and nurse. It expands the relatively brief references to Mrs Goddard's practical medical skills and Emma's common sense into a major theme.

Anne remains in Louisa's room after the surgeon has departed. Although Wentworth's proposal that she should be allowed to stay behind to continue nursing the patient is eminently sensible, it is nevertheless successfully opposed by Mary who sees it as a threat to her own consequence. As Anne has no control over her own movements, she is forced to accept the travel arrangements that are made for her and return to Uppercross. Louisa is nevertheless cared for by other women after the surgeon has made his quick diagnosis and departed. Mrs Harville and her nursery-maid both have the necessary experience: 'Mrs Harville was a very experienced nurse; and her nursery-maid, who had lived with her long, and gone about with her every where, was just such another'(P. p. 132). These nurses are eventually joined by another when Sarah, the old nursery-maid at Uppercross, is sent to Lyme. Anne does not initiate this proposal, but is instrumental in seeing it put into effect. The presence of such an experienced team of women to look after Louisa means that Mary is able to have a holiday.

Mary is an imaginary invalid who lies on a faded sofa and claims to be too ill to speak. She is more interested in her own health than that of her children. Any crisis is likely to produce an hysterical response from her. This model of the woman as invalid is contrasted with one that shows her to be practical, resourceful and capable of coping with illness. The juxtaposition is topical not just because it engages in important general debates about the education and aspirations of women associated particularly with the writings of Wollstonecraft, Hays and the Enlightenment Feminists, but also because it raises more specific questions about women and medicine at a time when all branches of the medical profession were becoming increasingly male-dominated. It is a theme that is developed in more detail around the representation of Nurse Rooke in the chapters that are set in Bath.

CALL IT GOSSIP IF YOU WILL

Sir Walter and Elizabeth are not entirely displeased when Anne is brought to Bath by Lady Russell. They will now have even numbers for dinner and an opportunity to get somebody else to admire the decor at Camden Place. They also hope that Anne will tell them how much they have been missed by the afflicted tenantry and cottagers at Kellynch, although she is too truthful to pay such a compliment. Her arrival does not lead to any change in Mrs Clay's status as Elizabeth's live-in companion. Elizabeth is quick to reassure her freckled friend that Anne 'is nothing to me, compared with you' (P, p. 158).

Anne has two mysteries to solve when she is in Bath. The first concerns Wentworth's movements and motivations. She has to solve this mainly on her own. The second concerns the sincerity of William Elliot. This time her own suspicions are confirmed by a network of female friends. Anne's sister Mary gives her the news that Louisa Musgrove is going to marry Benwick rather than Wentworth. She retires to her room to try to make sense of such a surprising event, given that there was a moment in Lyme when it looked as though Benwick wanted to have a relationship with her. The sick woman, Louisa, has appealed to Benwick's latent sentimentality. Admiral Croft then helps Anne to piece together Wentworth's movements after the expedition to Lyme by telling her that he has been staying for a long time with his brother. Croft, however, is not quite as well informed as he pretends to be. He thinks that Mrs Croft ought to write to Wentworth to persuade him to come to Bath so that he can find a suitable wife. The Crofts are match-making for Anne. Their schemes turn out to be unnecessary because Wentworth suddenly and unexpectedly appears in Bath before any letter gets written.

Anne notices Wentworth when her party is stuck in a shop taking shelter from the rain. Discussions are under way about the best means of conveying the various members back to the safety of Camden Place. As at Lyme, Anne has to allow arrangements to be made for her, this time by William Elliot. The severe restrictions on her movement are in marked contrast to Wentworth's ability to please himself:

> It was fixed, accordingly, that Mrs Clay should be of the party in the carriage; and they had just reached this point, when Anne, as she sat

near the window, descried, most decidedly and distinctly, Captain Wentworth walking down the street. (P, p. 185)

There is no overt comment about the gendered nature of transport and movement. The scene is graphic enough nevertheless: Anne has to wait in the shop like a commodity while arrangements are made for her, and Wentworth is unexpectedly walking in the street outside. Once again, the text about the positioning of women seems to be more of an open than a camouflaged one.

The mystery continues. Anne does not know how long Wentworth intends to stay in Bath. She sees him the next day while she is out with Lady Russell. He is, once again, walking in the streets. There are no clues about where he is going. It is not clear whether he has seen them. Anne thinks that there is a good chance that he will be present at the concert in the Octagon Room, although she does not know for certain. She turns out to be right and so is able to begin the conversations that make her realise that he is in love with her and therefore jealous of William Elliot. She remains in suspense, however, about whether he will accept Elizabeth's invitation to the party at Camden Place. She is put out of her pleasurable misery by his written declaration of love and the explanations that he furnishes her with as they walk around Bath together. He is no longer the mysterious figure who appears unexpectedly outside the shop window. He walks with her along the streets passing the shop windows.

Anne is more socially mobile than the rest of her family and so does not remain confined within their narrow circle, or set, of acquaintances. She pays a call on her old governess and this in turn leads her to visit Mrs Smith, an old schoolfriend. Mrs Smith is now a poor widow who has taken cheap lodgings close to the hot baths because she is crippled with rheumatic fever. Her condition has not been improved by the fact that she caught a cold on her journey to Bath. Mary Musgrove has the leisure to lie on the sofa and imagine that she is ill. Mrs Smith's illness, by contrast, is in her body rather than her mind. She tries to bear it with fortitude and is helped to do so by her nurse. She is determined to be well and therefore to win her own kind of peace. Nurse Rooke is a sister of Mrs Smith's landlady. Her conversation as well as her medical skills help to maintain the invalid's morale:

Call it gossip if you will; but when Nurse Rooke has half an hour's leisure to bestow on me, she is sure to have something to relate that is entertaining and profitable, something that makes one know one's species better. One likes to hear what is going on, to be *au fait* as to the newest modes of being trifling and silly. To me, who live so much alone, her conversation I assure you is a treat. (P, p. 168)

The apothecary at Uppercross and the surgeon at Lyme make brief entrances and then leave their patients to the care of largely unpaid female nurses. Nurse Rooke can be seen as a more complete medical practitioner than these medical men in that she takes the time to treat the person as well as the illness. Besides brightening up Mrs Smith's life with her gossip, she does her best to get her patient some money. She encourages Mrs Smith to knit as well as to make things with her hands, which is obviously a constructive attempt to treat rheumatism, and then sells the products to her richer clients. She is a skilled entrepreneur who 'thoroughly understands when to speak' (P, p. 182) to these clients.

Nurse Rooke is a nurse by profession who also acts as a midwife. She is the midwife to Mrs Wallis, the wife of the sandy-haired Colonel Wallis. It is while she is performing these duties that William Elliot's devious plans are revealed to her. She is able therefore to become a midwife to the truth. Medical men became more active in both birth and death during the course of the long eighteenth century. The old practice of giving over, or refusing to carry on treating an incurable patient, was gradually replaced by the belief that such patients ought, at the very least, to be given pain-killing drugs. Austen's own surgeon, Giles King Lyford, continued to try to treat her almost to the end. He must have administered a powerful drug to her on the evening of 18 July 1817 since it appears to have lasted for over nine hours. Cassandra records in a letter to Fanny Knight that Lyford gave her sister 'something to give her ease' (L, p. 515). It was possibly opium.

Birth was the other event which gradually came to be under the control of medical men. The practice in the early eighteenth century was for surgeons, or other practitioners, to be sent for only in emergencies. A normal birth was supervised by either female midwives, or else by knowledgeable female members of the extended family. The advent of what became known as the man-midwife was due to several causes. Apothecaries and surgeons were keen to find ways of expanding their practices. The availability of forceps from the 1730s may have encouraged a belief that it was better to be attended at childbirth by somebody who claimed to be qualified to use them. As men-midwives became associated with more than just emergencies, so some of them started to campaign against interventionist techniques. One of the most successful practitioners, William Hunter, was against the use of forceps. Despite the prestige of Hunter and others, the man-midwife nevertheless often inhabited an ambiguous social position. His popularity was sometimes associated in pamphlets and elsewhere with the provision of sexual as well as medical services.[25]

Female midwives were denied the kind of training that was available for them in continental Europe and were therefore increasingly vulnerable in a medical market place where qualifications came to matter more and more. The apothecaries started campaigning in 1812 to try to get their changing status officially recognised. As noted, the representation of Mr Perry in *Emma* can be read in the context of this campaign. It also provides a context for the representation of Nurse Rooke since one of the demands made by the apothecaries was that there ought to be some form of regulation and basic training for both male and female midwives. The Apothecaries' Act of 1815 contained no such provisions, which meant that many midwives, particularly female ones, remained on the lowest rungs of the profession. The positive representation of Nurse Rooke's range of skills, together with the more general emphasis that is placed on the experience of Mrs Harville and others, ought therefore to be seen as a contribution to a topical debate. She is a very different kind of character from the criminalised midwives who appear in novels by Daniel Defoe, Dickens and many others. This demonised figure with her close associations with prostitution, baby farming and drink also haunts popular Regency and Victorian underworld journalism. Just as Mrs Croft's experiences are used to suggest improvements in the naval profession, so Nurse Rooke's skills carry the suggestion that the medical profession is also in need of reform. Wiltshire's very illuminating study of Austen's representations of the body notices both the presence and marginality of female nurses in *Persuasion*, without quite being able to historicise the point.[26]

Gilbert and Gubar also see Nurse Rooke as a positive character, even though they too do not explore material historical contexts in any detail. They suggest that she subversively exposes the sickness within high society itself and therefore provides a representation within the text of a writer who is also committed to such exposures.[27] This does not pay enough attention to some of the complications that surround the representation. When Anne arrives one time at Westgate Buildings, the door is held open for her. She observes 'no one in particular' (P, p. 204). It is only later that Mrs Smith reveals that it was Nurse Rooke who was holding the door: 'It was my friend Mrs Rooke – Nurse Rooke; who, by the bye had a great curiosity to see you, and was delighted to be in the way to let you in' (P, p. 204). Mrs Smith may be reduced to poverty and yet her credentials as distressed gentry mean that she is not kept hovering silently and deferentially on the doorstep, or threshold, of representation. Nurse Rooke is, at one and the same time, a positive character and 'no one in particular'. She is something and nothing. The novel has a great deal of subversive fun at the expense of Sir Walter's obsessions with precedence and yet it can also subscribe to a version of them. Sir Walter would never dream of calling on anybody called Smith. The novel challenges Sir Walter's snobbery at the same time as it too draws back, perhaps with regret, from actually calling on somebody called Rooke. This double movement supports Fullbrook's point about the way in which Austen's texts can sometimes speak in the voice that they also mock.

Most Regency readers would have brought to this text, which was published posthumously in 1818, memories of the death of Princess Charlotte the year before. Her 'confinement' was supervised by Sir Richard Croft, who was the most fashionable man-midwife of the day. He prescribed a course of treatment that was designed to lower the 'animal spirits' of his patient. This meant regular bleeding together with a diet of gruel. He changed his tactics when Charlotte, after an exceptionally long period of labour, gave birth to a stillborn boy. He then ordered that she should be given both brandy and wine as a way of stimulating her. Wollstonecraft was also plied with wine just before her death after the birth of the child who became Mary Shelley. Although Percy Shelley self-consciously and somewhat insensitively (given the similarities just mentioned) refused to mourn the death of Charlotte, his voice was that of the exiled gentry radical who prided himself on being born for opposition without worrying too much about the process of birth itself. Others saw Charlotte as being preferable to the Regent, who rather predictably only arrived on the scene after she had died. The death of the heir to the throne obviously received extensive coverage in the newspapers and elsewhere. There was further coverage when, at the beginning of 1819, Croft shot himself when faced with a delivery that looked as though it might follow the same tragic pattern as Charlotte's death. All of these events took place after *Persuasion* had been written, although it is quite possible that it was first read in the light of them. The status, role and gender of the midwife were topical issues throughout the early years of the nineteenth century, although perhaps particularly so in 1817/19.[28]

Sir Walter's precise, factual version of history is concerned to establish direct lines of descent. He himself is directly descended from the first baronet. He is concerned to show that William Elliot, although not his son, is nevertheless capable of keeping the title within the family. He takes up his pen and describes his heir as being 'great-grandson of the second Sir Walter' (P, p. 36). A very different version of history emerges from Mrs Smith's unfashionable lodgings in

Westgate Buildings partly as a result of Nurse Rooke's revelations. Mrs Smith's narrative is circular rather than linear. Some of her information reaches her by an indirect route: 'it does not come to me in quite so direct a line as that; it takes a bend or two, but nothing of consequence' (P. p. 211). Although the story uses written evidence in the form of letters, these are less important than what is referred to as 'authentic oral testimony' (P, p. 210). Call it gossip if you will. Gossip and gossipers had little authority within society as a whole. *The Medical and Physical Journal* reassured its readers in 1812 that society was better now that female gossips were losing their powerful position in relation to childbirth: 'The influence of nurses and gossips in the management of infants, was much greater forty or fifty years ago, than it is at present.'[29] It has already been shown how Austen-Leigh removed what he considered to be unnecessary digressions and indirections from some of Austen's own letters. The privileging of gossip, and more particularly the gossip of a midwife, within *Persuasion* can therefore be seen as a potentially radical strategy.[30]

The gossip, initially and perhaps inevitably, turns out to be unreliable since it suggests that Anne is actually on the point of becoming engaged to William Elliot. Many critics have difficulties with the fact that Mrs Smith, believing an engagement to be the case, does not warn Anne but rather schemes in order to be able to have some influence through Anne over Elliot. Gilbert and Gubar suggest that, despite her marginalisation, she still embodies the moral sickness of the high society world that she used to inhabit. Duckworth finds her a cynical character, although he also argues that she is another example of the poverty-stricken woman who haunts all of Austen's novels. Susan Morgan shows that her narrative style is not necessarily gossipy, but depends upon some of the stock features of gothic.[31] Surprisingly little attention has been paid to the possibility that Mrs Smith, who reads as well as listens to stories about 'silver-fork' life in Bath, might be one version of the Regency reader-in-the-text. The difficulties that critics have experienced over her characterisation and function are part of a wider problem that they often have with the ending of the novel. Butler sees its main weakness as being the way in which the villain, William Elliot, only has a shadowy existence during the Bath chapters.[32] Such reservations about this particular ending have some validity, even though they are motivated by the more suspect general assumption that resolutions can and must resolve conflicts.

Mr Knightley plays the part of the detective in *Emma* and, as noted, just fails to solve the mystery of Frank Churchill. The female detectives in *Persuasion*, Nurse Rooke and Mrs Smith, are more successful.

William Elliot had been a fairweather friend of Mrs Smith's husband. She is able to reveal to Anne that his family motto is in reality 'to do the best for himself' (P, p. 208). He encouraged Mr Smith to spend money that was not there and then refused to help the widowed Mrs Smith to try to recover what remained of her husband's estate. It is, however, Nurse Rooke who provides the vital piece of information about the plot that is being hatched to ensnare Anne:

> she it was who told me you were to marry Mr Elliot. She had had it from Mrs Wallis herself, which did not seem bad authority. She sat an hour with me on Monday evening, and gave me the whole history. (P. p. 205)

William Elliot's original scorn for the title has been replaced by a desperate desire to succeed to it. Perhaps it provides the only pleasure that he has not already tasted in his dissolute life. The problem, as outlined to him by Colonel Wallis, is that Sir Walter may decide to turn a blind eye to Mrs Clay's freckles and marry her. The heir presumptive therefore has to act quickly. He must marry Anne and have issue by her. He may need to make sure that the marriage settlement includes a clause that restrains Sir Walter from marrying Mrs Clay. The female detectives, or gossips, eventually provide Anne with the proof that she needs to confirm her own suspicions that William Elliot's attentions may not have been honourable and open.

William Elliot has to face the ruin of his schemes when Anne announces her engagement to Wentworth:

> The news of his cousin Anne's engagement burst on Mr Elliot most unexpectedly. It deranged his best plan of domestic happiness, his best hope of keeping Sir Walter single by the watchfulness which a son-in-law's rights would have given. (P, p. 252)

He is nonetheless able to pluck a kind of victory from the jaws of defeat. He appears to persuade Mrs Clay to detach herself from Sir Walter and to live with him in London. There is a possibility that she in turn will persuade him to make her 'the wife of Sir William' (P, p. 252). Kellynch, and by extension England, may be inherited by this pair of cunning schemers.

Mrs Clay is another shadowy character who figures prominently in the ending. She is the daughter of Mr Shepherd, the lawyer, who becomes, as has been mentioned, Elizabeth's companion and thus increases Anne's marginalisation within the family. She has left an 'unprosperous marriage'(P. p. 46) and has two children. She ingratiates herself through the art of pleasing others and yet behind this particular mask she is obviously plotting how best to please herself.

Although she does not have the social position of Austen's Lady Susan, she is like her in the sense that behind a sweet and often simpering countenance she dreams of power. She is also like her in that she is forced to make a quick swop of partners at the end.

Although there is some justification for the critical commentaries on the uneven nature of the ending, it is also true that too many critics still expect Austen's final chapters to conclude arguments. The resolution of *Persuasion* is nevertheless open-ended because it offers both an optimistic and pessimistic answer to the question of who will win the peace. The optimistic one suggests that Anne's marriage to Wentworth will eventually produce a very different kind of house from that presided over by Sir Walter. Another variation might be that the Crofts will eventually purchase Kellynch itself. The pessimistic ending suggests that there may be very little change. Perhaps, as David Spring suggests, Sir Walter will clear his debts and return to the family seat.[33] Perhaps William Elliot and Mrs Clay will eventually inherit it from him. The future of Kellynch is every bit as uncertain as that of Mansfield Park.

Wentworth purchases rather than inherits his estate. It is his reward for years of patriotic service. He does not, however, settle down to lead the indolent, spendthrift life of a private gentleman but continues in his profession. All the signs are that the marriage will be based on partnership. It does not exclude female friendships since both Lady Russell and Mrs Smith are welcome visitors. Nurse Rooke nevertheless is excluded, which provides a more general reminder that the social mobility within the novel is not as great as it sometimes promises to be. Anne does not marry a character like Captain Benwick who is living in reduced circumstances, or go to live in cramped surroundings such as those inhabited by the Harvilles. Wentworth certainly belongs to the same professional world as these other sailors and yet he is also an acceptable husband because, despite Sir Walter's pompous pronouncements to the contrary, he actually starts off in the ranks of the lesser gentry. The new household, despite these reservations, can be seen as an open one. The future of the old estate is left unclear in the same way as questions are allowed to remain about what might happen to Mansfield Park. Kellynch under the rule of William Walter Elliot would also be an open estate since it would accommodate Mrs Clay and her connections. It is also implied, however, that one dandy would merely succeed another and that the style of government would stay the same. The optimistic ending recommends that those who won the war deserve to win the peace. The pessimistic one wonders whether the estate, and thus the state, will ever change.

7 *Sanditon*: The madhouse and the greenhouse

INTRODUCTION

This final chapter begins by showing how Austen's representation of the development of Sanditon as a Regency watering place raises Condition-of-England themes. It then explores in more detail the satire on the culture of invalidism. The conclusion takes the form of a reading of one of the completed versions of Austen's text by a modern writer. It is argued that this particular text seeks to suppress Austen's specifically Regency themes and styles.

A DESERTED VILLAGE

Austen began writing *Sanditon* at the end of January 1817. Her deteriorating health forced her to abandon her most stinging satire on the culture of invalidism towards the end of March when she had almost completed the twelfth chapter. She died four months later. Protest movements against the Regent and his ministers became more visible in the immediate post-war period. There were food riots in East Anglia and elsewhere, as well as violent political demonstrations at Spa Fields in London. The re-emergence of radicalism allowed Cobbett's *Political Register* to increase its circulation. Roberts notices that a number of Austen's characters express fears about the working classes.[1] At a more general level, *Sanditon* represents the highly precarious nature of post-war society.

There are bound to be disagreements about just how unedited the surviving text remains. Some critics see it as a first draft that would probably have changed its countenance quite considerably before publication. Others argue that it is a good first draft which had already been edited in the process of writing. The state of the manuscript itself lends some support to the second view.[2] The other main area of disagreement is over whether the novel as it stands suggests new directions or familiar themes. The heroine, twenty-two-year-old Charlotte Heywood, appears to be both more detached and knowing than previous ones. She quizzes the crazy world of Sanditon with an 'amused curiosity' (S, p. 173). Although she is irritated by its obsessive characters, she usually manages to keep her 'countenance' (S, p. 189).

The heroine may have some different characteristics, but the text itself is thematically closer to Austen's other Regency novels than is often acknowledged. They all explore the culture of invalidism, the commercialisation of leisure and, more generally, the Condition-of-England. Duckworth is in danger of underestimating such continuities when he claims that this is the first time Austen represents a 'thoroughly Regency world'. Oliver MacDonagh, who offers a perceptive account of Regency mentalities, also tends to distance *Sanditon* too much from the earlier writings.³ Despite these reservations, it needs to be emphasised that both these critics have a precise sense of the history of this particular period. They do not therefore write about *Sanditon*, as others have done, as if it were a Victorian novel.

The inhabitants of a country village such as Uppercross in *Persuasion* relied on the services of the local apothecary, whereas those at a resort like Lyme could employ a surgeon. The quality of medical provision at a watering place helped to attract visitors there during the season. It also influenced those who were considering retiring to one. This is why Mr Parker decides that it is worth his while to make a detour on his way back to Sanditon to try to persuade a surgeon to accompany him to the new resort. He has seen an advertisement in the newspapers announcing the 'dissolution of a partnership in the medical line' (S, p. 157). A hurried departure from London in a hired carriage means that he does not have time to read the advertisement carefully and so ends up in the wrong place. More precisely, he leaves the turnpike road and tries to take the carriage up an unsuitable country lane. It overturns and he finds himself in what he considers to be immediate need of a surgeon because he has twisted his ankle.

The promoter of Sanditon inhabits a Regency world that is characterised not just by confused activity, but also by the way in which everyone and everything can be merchandised through advertising. Parker is rescued by Mr Heywood, a farmer who is working alongside his men in the hayfield. Didactic contrasts are immediately established between these two characters and their worlds. Parker is associated with movement and it becomes more apparent that the lack of profession common for an eldest son of his class allows him to devote his restless energy to the commercialisation of leisure. Heywood is a much more stationary figure who rarely moves away from Willingden where he works to produce essential commodities. They also have contrasting attitudes towards medicine. Heywood believes that, even if there were a surgeon in the neighbourhood, it would be unnecessary to call him out for a such relatively minor injury as a twisted ankle. He preaches instead the virtues of medical self-help or empiricism:

> We are always well stocked . . . with all the common remedies for sprains and bruises – and I will answer for the pleasure it will give my wife and daughters to be of service to you and this lady in every way in their power. (S, p. 158)

This continues the debate in *Persuasion*, and to a lesser extent that of *Emma*, about whether medical men ought to be allowed to colonise all aspects of health care.

Parker stays at Willingden much longer than is really necessary and so displays signs of the hypochondria that is, as will be seen, much more rampant in some of the other members of his family. He likes being nursed. Ironically, he passes his time away from Sanditon advertising the benefits of being there:

> The finest, purest sea breeze on the coast – acknowledged to be so – excellent bathing – fine hard sand – deep water ten yards from the shore – no mud – no weeds – no slimey rocks – Never was there a place more palpably designed by nature for the resort of the invalid – the very spot which thousands seemed in need of. (S, pp. 159–60)

His hurried speeches are stuffed with the promotional slogans of the guide book. The search for a medical man seems to overturn his argument that Sanditon's air and sea will cure all known diseases. As far as he is concerned, however, the resort's medicinal advantages are complemented by its size. It is small and therefore potentially exclusive, unlike neighbouring places such as Brighton, Worthing and Eastbourne. Size is nevertheless a problem. Although everyone has heard of the 'large, overgrown places' (S, p. 159), very few know about the existence of Sanditon which is why it is already in danger of becoming a deserted village.

Parker returns to Sanditon with Charlotte Heywood and readers come to some extent to see the place and its neurotic inhabitants, or inmates, through her quizzical eyes. Lady Denham, another of Austen's powerful widows, is Parker's partner in the enterprise of transforming the obscure fishing village into an exclusive watering place. She has already proved her credentials as a speculator by playing the marriage market remarkably successfully. She starts out with money (thirty thousand pounds) and then gains an estate when she marries an elderly invalid when she is 'about thirty' (S, p. 135). He dies as expected and she eventually decides to put in for being a widow again by marrying Sir Harry Denham. She thus acquires a title but makes sure that her new husband and his family are unable to get their hands on any of her money before he dies. She tells Charlotte that she has never been 'over-reached' (S, p. 186) in any financial or legal transaction. She invests some of her fortune in building houses which can be rented to visitors during the holiday season. Although she has proved herself to be a shrewd speculator, she lacks Parker's breathless zeal for Sanditon. She believes that visitors would in fact be much better off staying at home but, if they are going to come, then she might as well try to make some money out of them as quickly as possible.

Although Lady Denham is seventy, she is still one of the most active characters in a text that is crawling with imaginary invalids. She believes that both she and Sanditon can survive perfectly well without a surgeon:

> I am very sorry you met with your accident, but upon my word you deserved it – Going after a doctor! – Why, what should we do with a doctor here? It would be only encouraging our servants and the poor to fancy themselves ill, if there was a doctor at hand. – Oh! pray, let us have none of that tribe at Sanditon. (S, p. 181)

Just as John Knightley claims in *Emma* that medical men prey upon gullible women like Isabella, so Lady Denham dogmatically asserts that they would feed off the anxieties of the poorer members of the community. Her own hostility is conditioned by self-interest. She can get more work out of servants if they are not encouraged to consider the possibility that they may ever get ill. She also has more opportunities to sell her celebrated asses' milk if other remedies are not easily available. Wiltshire notes that asses' milk was prescribed for those who had tuberculosis.[4] Lady Denham believes that medical men charge too much money for doing too little. The doctor whom she confidently alleges actually killed Sir Harry wanted 'Ten fees, one after another' (S, p. 181).

The topography of Sanditon is revealed as Mr and Mrs Parker, together with Charlotte, drive through it on their return from Willingden. The old village lies in a hollow behind the cliffs and is thus protected from storms. The Parkers originally lived on the outskirts of this village but decided to rent out the house that had been in their family for at least two or three generations. As Duckworth suggests, they, like Mr Rushworth, have probably been influenced by fashionable landscape theories that scorned low-lying buildings.[5] They have moved to a new house perched on top of the cliff with no protection from storms because the trees are newly planted. The safety of the old house is contrasted with the precarious position of the new one. Parker claims that he is now able to appreciate the picturesque qualities of storms. His views are similar to those of Edmund Bartell, who tried to market Cromer on the strength of the grandeur of its storms and shipwrecks.[6]

If Sanditon stands for England, then this move may symbolise a change from the security of an old order to the shifting sands of Regency society. This allows critics like Duckworth and Butler to see the text as endorsing the conservative ideas of place and estate associated with Burke. Such a reading is certainly available, even though it underplays the way in which it is the watering place that produces the energy and focus of the unfinished narrative. As suggested in relation to *Emma*, relationships between the watering place and the village are often much more complex than is suggested by those who see Austen as an anti-Jacobin writer.

Perhaps Parker bears some resemblance to the Prince Regent himself since he too abandons the security of an old house in favour of building his own equivalent of an eccentric pavilion, or folly, by the sea on the Sussex coast. Such Condition-of-England readings are encouraged by the title itself. Tanner identifies the way in which it foregrounds 'a Sandy-town, a town built on sand' and thus, in turn, highlights the broader question of social foundations.[7] There is also some more specifically Regency wordplay wrapped up in this name which Tanner overlooks. The ton, sometimes extended to the *bon ton*, was a term that was very widely used for describing either high society or fashionable people. It is incorporated into the name of the Beau Brummell figure, John Russelton, in Edward Bulwer Lytton's *Pelham* (1828). It is also used by Edmund Bertram during his debates with Mary Crawford on the social role of the clergyman: 'A clergyman cannot be high in state or fashion. He must not head mobs or set the ton in dress' (MP, p. 120). These two examples of unbecoming clerical conduct can be regarded as random and disconnected. If taken together, however, they show that Edmund is drawing attention to links between dandyism and radicalism. The Regency wordplay in the title suggests that fashionable society is built on shifting sands. Another implication is that the ton, for all its claims to be glittering and multi-coloured, is in fact dull and monotonous in appearance. Brighton becomes Sanditon.

Unlike Willingden, the old village of Sanditon is no longer a productive, working community. The village cobbler now sells 'Blue shoes, and nankin boots' (S, p. 172) and the old farmhouse has been converted into lodgings for accomplished ladies. Charlotte hears the sound of a harp as they drive through the village. Mary Crawford was unable to find a cart to convey her harp to Mansfield Parsonage during harvesting even for ready money. It is implied that the only use for farm vehicles in post-war Sanditon is fetching and carrying harps. Although Parker himself is not personally involved in these developments, he welcomes them enthusiastically as encouraging signs of progress and civilisation.

Parker and Lady Denham are principally concerned with developing the new village on the cliffs. They also encourage others to participate in their speculation. Lady Denham grants her nephew, Sir Edward Denham, a strip of waste ground so that he can run up a 'tasteful little cottage ornee' (S, p. 167) on it that can be rented to visitors. The Royal Lodge at Windsor was perhaps the best known example of the 'cottage ornee' style in this period. Parker's new residence is called Trafalgar House. Although he was pleased with the name when he first chose it, he is now worried that it might not be as fashionable and therefore as marketable as one that referred to Waterloo. He hopes nevertheless that, if business gets better, then Trafalgar House will soon be joined by Waterloo Crescent. The war is only relevant to him if it helps him to fight the more important battle of promoting and advertising Sanditon. A fashionable name might give him 'command' (S, p. 169) of more visitors. The Duke of Clarence stayed at Nelson's Crescent in Ramsgate in 1811 when he was trying to captivate an heiress. Eliza Spurrett found lodgings at No. 6, Plains of Waterloo, when she visited the resort in 1839.[8]

Cobbett indicates that other watering places also liked to associate themselves with famous victories. The new spa of Cheltenham boasted of a Waterloo House, much to his disgust during his second visit in 1826. The Duke of Wellington had stayed in Cheltenham in 1816 to open the new assembly rooms. Cobbett suggests that the only people who really benefited from the existence of Cheltenham and similar resorts were the medical men :

a place, to which East India plunderers, West India floggers, English tax-gorgers, together with gluttons, drunkards, and debauchees of all descriptions, *female* as well as male, resort, at the suggestion of silently laughing quacks, in the hope of getting rid of the bodily consequences of their manifold sins and iniquities. When I enter a place like this, I always feel disposed to squeeze up my nose with my fingers. It is nonsense, to be sure; but I conceit that every two-legged creature, that I see coming near me, is about to cover me with the poisonous proceeds of its impurities.[9]

The East India Company had built a terrace in Cheltenham for its retired employees. Although it had in fact lost its monopoly status in 1813, it was still seen by Cobbett as part of the closed world of 'old corruption'. He draws attention once again to the way in which members of Regency high society only maintained their position by flogging into submission those whom they regarded as being their inferiors. He goes on to represent Cheltenham as being a grotesque marriage market with young men chasing after rich old women and young women in hot pursuit of rotten old men.

Cheltenham's expansion was promoted by the way in which it was able to associate itself with the Royal Family, as well as with national heroes such as Wellington. George III visited the spa in 1788, just before the medical collapse that led to the first Regency Crisis. Fanny Burney, who accompanied the Royal party there, describes it as being 'almost all one street, extremely long, clean, and well-paved'.[10] Eliza de Feuillide offered a similar description when she visited the spa in 1797. Dorothy Jordan, who had been playing at the theatre during the King's visit, commented in 1810 on the rapid growth of the resort since then: 'There has been four hundred houses built within two years, and whole streets and squares new laid out. It is thought that in a few years it will rival Bath.'[11] When Jordan was playing Cheltenham again the following year, she received a message from the Duke of Clarence indicating that their relationship was over. The next year Byron, Scrope Davies and Lady Oxford were in residence.

Austen and her sister visited the spa in the early summer of 1816. She scanned the newspapers when Cassandra returned there later on the same year and came up with the information that the Duchess of Orleans had been drinking water from the same pump as she had done. Watering places had always been popular places for residence or resort by French émigrés during the Napoleonic Wars. The development of Cheltenham was a commercial success at a time when many other spa promotions failed.[12] Johanna Schopenhauer's travel diaries reveal the way in which the successful spas were associated with particular diseases. After commenting on the bored behaviour of the visitors, she notes that Cheltenham catered especially for those with 'skin ailments, scurvy and such complaints'.[13]

Sanditon is new but already decaying. Besides Trafalgar House, it has millinery shops, a library, a hotel and a billiard room. It also contains a terrace of houses that are, like almost everything else, available for rent. Parker is concerned that there are still too many signs in the windows advertising vacancies and not enough Sir Walter Elliots and Beau Brummells looking out of these windows to see if there were any other tolerable faces. It is the new village of Sanditon which is in real danger of becoming the deserted one. The librarian, Mrs Whitby, has plenty of time to read her own books. Her daughter passes the time by admiring herself in the mirror. Trade is extremely slack. Parker instructs his wife to buy more garden produce than she needs from some market gardeners just to keep them in business for a little longer. Economically, Sanditon is already sliding down the cliff.

This is a consumer society with everything except consumers. Lydia Bennets, just looking to indulge a consuming passion for a bonnet, a cucumber or a new officer, are conspicuous by their absence. The residents easily outnumber the visitors. It is like one of Brummell's parties in Caen at which only the host is actually present. Parker anxiously looks through the subscription list at the library on his return to Sanditon to see whether the situation has improved. Last season the old village was only visited by a single family: 'one family of children who came from London for sea air after whooping cough, and whose mother would not let them be nearer the shore for fear of their tumbling in' (S, p. 172). The presence of such names as Miss Scroggs and Mr Richard Pratt on the subscription list, although a numerical improvement on the partial captivation of this Isabella Knightley figure, is nevertheless not what he had in mind for an exclusive resort like Sanditon. As in the letters, names provide an opportunity for broad comedy. Lady Denham shrewdly observes that the very few people who eventually find their way to Sanditon, perhaps by accident, do not bring enough money into the resort to justify financial investments in it.

Parker is therefore reduced to transforming everyone and everything into a commodity to try to rescue the brand new, but already deserted, resort. He declares to both his wife Mary and Charlotte that the presence of his dandified brother, Sidney, may help to attract other visitors. The dandy, himself a commodity, becomes the commodity that might just save Sanditon:

> I wish we may get him to Sanditon. I should like to have you acquainted with him. – And it would be a fine thing for the place! – Such a young man as Sidney, with his neat equipage and fashionable air, – you and I Mary, know what effect it might have: many a respectable family, many a careful mother, many a pretty daughter, might it secure us, to the prejudice of Eastbourne and Hastings. (S, p. 171)

Parker appears to be clutching desperately at straws since Sidney is reported as taking a cynical attitude towards the exclusive pleasures of

Sanditon. He claims that his brother ought to have converted the old family house into a hospital, which suggests that he does not have the same faith in the healing properties of the sea air. He makes a very brief appearance at the end of the text on his way to meet two friends. Although he arrives unexpectedly, he was probably spotted by his brother who anxiously scans the horizon hoping to catch sight of any carriage or chaise. Perhaps business was due to pick up after his arrival in this brand new, but decaying, holiday village. Any visitors at all were a monstrous scarce commodity.

OUR OWN WRETCHED CONSTITUTIONS

Sidney is not the only member of the Parker family who is enlisted to promote the attractions of Sanditon. Miss Diana Parker's extended network of gossip appears initially to have succeeded in persuading two parties to spend the season at the resort. Accompanied by her brother and sister, she dashes to Sanditon to make all the arrangements for one of these parties. She makes a bustling entrance even though she casts herself as a chronic invalid. An earlier letter from her to Parker reeks of invalidism. She claims that an attack of 'spasmodic bile' means that she is 'hardly able to crawl from my bed to the sofa' (S, p. 175). She responds to the news of Parker's twisted ankle by recalling the occasion when she rubbed the ankle of a coachman who had a similar injury 'for six hours without intermission'(S, p. 175). Wiltshire is clearly right to hear the tone of the 'hypochondriac's hyperbole' in Diana's letter.[14] Mr Heywood's sensible approach to minor injuries has no place in this particular family.

Although Diana and Mr Woodhouse have some things in common, such as a fear that sea-bathing might kill them, they are nevertheless different kinds of imaginary invalid. Mr Woodhouse believes that his practitioner can do no wrong, whereas Diana shares Lady Denham's suspicion of this 'tribe':

> But pray never run into peril again, in looking for an apothecary on our account, for had you the most experienced man in his line settled at Sanditon, it would be no recommendation to us. We have entirely done with the whole medical tribe. We have consulted physician after physician in vain, till we are quite convinced that they can do nothing for us and that we must trust to our own knowledge of our own wretched constitutions for any relief. (S, p. 175)

Diana also shares Lady Denham's habit of making emphatic overstatements. Despite her complete rejection of the tribe, she nevertheless offers to tap into her network of gossip to find a medical man if this is what her brother really wants. Here and in the account of the coachman's ankle, the letter draws attention to a restless energy that ironically can only find a socially acceptable outlet through invalidism. The text is certainly comic in the way in which it casts Diana as an immobile character only to allow her later on to make a bustling, 'nimble' (S, p. 192) entrance. She turns out to be quick, decisive and animated. Comedy is the countenance that is worn to make a more serious point about the culture of invalidism.

A broadly similar representation occurs in Ferrier's *Marriage*. Lady Juliana demands that a surgeon is sent for to treat one of her dogs shortly after her arrival at Glenfern. Grizzy Douglas nevertheless proudly announces that she and her two sisters, who are also unmarried, are the 'doctors here'.[15] There is a comic text that jokes about her various self-help remedies. A more serious text begins to emerge, however, after the introduction of the London-based medical practitioner, Dr Redgill, who is totally preoccupied with eating and drinking. It becomes clear that, with all her eccentricities, Grizzy is in fact a much better doctor than him.

As some reservations were raised earlier on about Gilbert and Gubar's approach, it is important to acknowledge here that this reading of the figure of the 'mad' woman doctor is influenced by their work. The various operations that Diana Parker carries out on her sister Susan exhibit, as will become apparent, a dangerous kind of madness. This has, however, been produced by a society that refuses even to acknowledge that she and Grizzy Douglas may have professional skills. This too is a dangerous kind of madness. The exclusion of women from the higher levels of medical practice is highlighted by the life of Dr James Miranda Barry. She dressed as a boy so that she could study medicine at Edinburgh in 1809 before going on to complete her training in London. Dressed as a man, she went on to hold senior positions in hospitals in the British colonies.[16]

Diana advises Susan to have her blood drawn by 'six leeches a day for ten days' (S, p. 175) in order to cure a common headache. Leeches, as is revealed later on, usually took three hours to do their business. The treatment itself was not in fact that unusual. Fanny Knight, Austen's niece, used leeches to try to cure headaches.[17] What is unusual, however, is the excessive nature of Diana's doctoring. When this treatment proves to be unsuccessful, the sisters diagnose that the problem may be to do with the gums rather than the head. Susan promptly has three teeth removed. Parker sees such behaviour as normal, probably because it corresponds at an admittedly extreme level to models of right feminine happiness. He praises his angelic sisters for being able to spare thoughts for others despite all their sufferings.

It is left to Charlotte and Mary Parker to register the fact that this behaviour is really abnormal, thus alerting readers to the more serious script about female invalidism. Charlotte immediately registers the ironies that have escaped Parker's notice: 'I am astonished at the cheerful style of the letter, considering the state in which both sisters appear to be' (S, p. 176). She considers some of the remedies to be extreme. Mary Parker is harshly represented as being a weak woman herself who was 'terrified' (S, p. 156) by the carriage accident and, more generally, unable to control her husband's crazy enthusiasms. Even she considers that the sisters are capable of taking their obsession with medicine 'too far sometimes' (S, p. 177). Both she and Charlotte make serious points here, although the way in which they understate them adds to the comedy of the scene.

The Parker sisters are professional patients whose patience with the male-dominated medical profession has been exhausted. Whereas Mr Woodhouse remains indolent, they are active in the sense that they are forever experimenting with new cures. These cures are usually much more destructive than the symptoms:

> Some natural delicacy of constitution in fact, with an unfortunate turn for medicine, especially quack medicine, had given them an early tendency at various times, to various disorders; – the rest of their sufferings was from fancy, the love of distinction and the love of the wonderful. – They had charitable hearts and many amiable feelings – but a spirit of restless activity, and the glory of doing more than anybody else, had their share in every exertion of benevolence – and there was vanity in all they did, as well as in all they endured. (S, p. 198)

They are prepared to endure leeches, brutal dentistry and quack medicines because such cures make them more interesting. A pallid, languid, whispering female body commands more attention and respect than a healthy one in this society. Bleeding was used systematically in lunatic asylums such as Bethlem Hospital as a way of rendering violent male and female inmates more docile.[18] Medical treatment also transforms Susan Parker into an exceptionally docile body.

Lady Denham is able to enter into business speculations because of the way in which she has successfully played the marriage market. Diana does not have such financial independence and is therefore like Mrs Norris in *Mansfield Park* in that there is no productive outlet for her energies. Mrs Norris also plays the part of a medical practitioner. She is involved in 'doctoring' (MP, p. 205) a coachman for rheumatism and tries to bribe the gardener at Sotherton with a 'charm' (MP, p. 131) to cure his grandson. She pounces on the jellies that were left over after Fanny's ball, before going home to 'nurse a sick maid' (MP, p. 288).

Invalidism is one of the right destinies for women of marginal status like the Parker sisters and they play their different parts to the full. Diana is also allowed by society to channel some of her energy into charitable activities. Once again, her excess threatens to undermine from within the narrow role that has been prescribed for her. Instead of being content to administer charity on a local scale, her schemes encompass Worcestershire, Burton-on-Trent and York. As W. R. Martin notes, she makes 'the whole of England her parish'.[19]

The joke about Diana's energetic entrance is repeated as far as her brother, Arthur, is concerned. Charlotte expects him to be 'very puny' (S, p. 199) on the evidence presented in Diana's letter. He nevertheless turns out to be as heavily-built as the Prince Regent: 'as tall as his brother and a great deal stouter – broadmade and lusty – and with no other look of an invalid, than a sodden complexion' (S, p. 199). There is more than a hint that he uses invalidism as a convenient screen for alcoholism. He tells Charlotte that, as biliousness is the only complaint from which he is not suffering, there is no need for him to stop drinking wine:

> The more wine I drink(in moderation) the better I am. – I am always best of an evening. – If you had seen me today before dinner, you would have thought me a very poor creature. (S, p. 201)

Charlotte is tempted to say that invalidism is being used as a mask but decides to keep her own 'countenance' (S, p. 201). She is determined to be well and so preaches the virtues of fresh air and physical exercise. Tanner comments that Arthur's diagnosis is 'an unforgettable proposition which would not be out of place in *Alice through the Looking Glass*'.[20] Arthur, who is revealed to be 'heavy in eye as well as figure' (S, p. 200), seems incapable of moderation. He claims that he is drinking very weak cocoa, although the ever-watchful Charlotte notices that it is as strong as possible. Although he shares Mr Woodhouse's taste for fires on warm days, which is probably why Susan gets her headaches, he differs from him in that invalidism is used so that appetites can be indulged with impunity. Diana claims that he has a habit of eating and drinking too much. This, rather than leeches and quack remedies, is his medicine:

> Mr Arthur Parker's enjoyments in invalidism were very different from his sisters' – by no means so spiritualised – A good deal of earthly dross hung about him. Charlotte could not but suspect him of adopting that line of life, principally for the indulgence of an indolent temper – and to be determined on having no disorders but such as called for warm rooms and good nourishment. (S, p. 203)

Tom Bertram becomes an invalid because he drinks too much, whereas Arthur Parker uses invalidism as a cover for indulgence. He has gone into retirement at the age of twenty-one, his only acknowledged profession being the toasting of bread, and so can devote his time to secret pleasures. Like the other members of his family, he is totally obsessed with self. He is a voluptuary who likes nothing better than talking about his digestion.

Cobbett was relieved to leave Cheltenham after his first visit to it in 1821 because he saw it as 'the resort of the lame and the lazy, the gormandising and guzzling, the bilious and the nervous'.[21] Sanditon aspires to cater for just such types, if only they would pay it a visit. Diana, Arthur and Susan Parker descend on the resort in order to make preparations for one of the two parties that have been lured there. The Parkers outnumber the visitors. They may continue to do so since it is revealed that the two parties are in fact the same one. Diana's lines of communication have become hopelessly entangled. Gossip helps to resolve problems in *Persuasion*, whereas here it creates them.

A Miss Lambe, a sickly West Indian heiress, arrives in the custody of Mrs Griffiths who runs a seminary for young ladies. She is something of a lamb to the slaughter since Lady Denham immediately spots opportunities to marry off her nephew, Sir Edward, as well as to sell some asses' milk to the invalid. Lady Denham wants Sir Edward to marry an heiress so that she is not obliged to leave him any money. The narrative breaks off too soon after this point for there to be any clue as to whether she might have had her wishes granted. It is revealed, however, that she was unable to sell any of her self-help medicinal remedies since Mrs Griffiths had to use the prescriptions that had been written out by 'an experienced physician' (S, p. 207). Mrs Griffiths nevertheless makes an exception to this rule 'in favour of some tonic pills, which a cousin of her own had property in'(S, p. 207). There is then in the margins of the text another woman who is not subservient to medical men.

Charlotte thinks, but is careful not to say, that Diana Parker's sudden arrival in Sanditon to engage a house for a party that she does not know is an example of 'Activity run mad' (S, p. 196). Everyone talks and talks about their own concerns, never listening to anybody else. Cobbett held his nose to guard against the moral stench of Cheltenham. Stray visitors to Sanditon probably needed to block their ears to stop having to listen to the neurotic din. The talk runs mad because it has lost connection with a grotesque reality. Diana Parker talks about herself, and is praised, as a ministering angel, when it is clear that her advanced neurosis puts both herself and others in considerable danger. Sanditon gets so few visitors as it is a secluded asylum that caters for inmates who have quite literally become their own obsessions. John Lauber describes it very aptly as a kingdom of folly in which the private languages of many of the characters are 'mutually unintelligible'.[22]

As Tanner shows, the text does not ignore the specifically economic debates of the immediate post-war period on the causes of inflation. It is primarily concerned, however, with the way in which this new society allows individual characters to inflate themselves and their concerns. Obsessional characters certainly populate Austen's earlier Regency writings. Wiltshire sees Diana Parker as a more benevolent version of Mrs Norris.[23] As indicated, Highbury carries anticipations of Sanditon in its representations of characters like Mrs Elton and Mr Weston, who can only talk incessantly about themselves. A variation on the same theme is played in *Persuasion*. Sir Walter Elliot may not be much of a talker and yet he places his elegant body at the centre of every scene to the exclusion of others. *Sanditon* may differ from these earlier writings by allowing obsession to become its main obsession.

Sanditon can be seen as the world turned upside down. Young men retire to cultivate invalidism and claim that wine is the best medicine. It is regarded as normal to have three teeth removed to cure a common headache. Houses are rapidly built only to stand empty. Commodities are displayed even though there are no consumers to buy them. The commercial activity of Parker and his partners, itself the product of inactivity, only succeeds in producing more inactivity in the shape of a deserted new village.

Imaginary invalids, together with those like Parker and Lady Denham who aspire to cater for them, are not the only inmates of the Sanditon asylum. Sir Edward Denham is confined there because he has become obsessed with the idea that he is a dangerous seducer of women. While some of the other inmates imagine themselves to be weak, although only in order to gain power, he exhibits the more classical will to power of the insane which could easily have been translated into a fantasy that he was really Napoleon or Beau Brummell. He opts instead for the belief that he is the direct descendant of some of the well-known literary rakes such as Samuel Richardson's Lovelace, even though he has none of Henry Crawford's qualifications for the part.[24]

Charlotte is momentarily deceived into thinking that she is dealing with somebody who does not suffer from such delusions of grandeur when she first meets him. He enters rooms with some style and his conversation is superficially pleasing. He also has the additional advantage of being titled. This favourable first impression is quickly rejected when she has a chance to hear more of his jumbled, nonsensical monologues about literature, which are stuffed with long words and misquotations. His preferences are for male authors who write passionately about passion. He likes to read about how strong heroes 'obtain' heroines against all the odds:

> Such are the works which I peruse with delight, and I hope I may say, with amelioration. They hold forth the most splendid portraitures of high conceptions, unbounded views, illimitable ardour, indomptible decision – and even when the event is plainly antiprosperous to the high-toned machinations of the prime character, the potent, pervading hero of the story, it leaves us full of generous emotions for him; – our hearts are paralyzed–. (S, p. 190)

This is another example of rhetorical activity run mad. The rhetoric is as empty as the village. It is also dangerous because it provides the justification for Sir Edward's attempts to seduce the powerless Clara Brereton. Charlotte calmly responds to this torrent of words by telling the great seducer that their taste in novels is not the same.

ANOTHER LADY

Different tastes in novels also emerge very clearly when twentieth-century attempts to rewrite Austen's novels are considered. Her completed texts are often rewritten in accordance with the conventions of the Regency reproduction and heritage industries. There is, unfortunately, no room to consider such examples as the way in which the world of Mansfield Park has been represented through the eyes of both Susan Price and Maria Rushworth or how Highbury has been imagined from Jane Fairfax's point of view. Unfinished texts such as *The Watsons* and *Sanditon* itself obviously provide modern writers with more freedom to develop plot lines and introduce new characters.[25]

The writers of modern versions of Austen put into practice what has been a common reaction to her work by some literary critics. As noted during the discussion of *Persuasion*, critics who are unsettled by the representation of Mrs Musgrove's 'fat sighings' sometimes assert that Austen would have toned down this scene if she had been able to revise the manuscript. Those who are unprepared for the satire in *Sanditon* have claimed that it too would have been revised for publication. Such reassurances do not take sufficient note of the fact that some of the revisions that Austen did make to the manuscript built up the excessive nature of characters such as Diana Parker. The modern novelists who are attracted by Austen's plots and characters usually follow this kind of criticism by suppressing the specifically Regency themes and styles of the originals.

Alice Cobbett's 1932 version of *Sanditon* uses Austen's characters and locations, although it does not reproduce her completed chapters.[26] It develops into a swashbuckling adventure story in which Sir Edward, who is in league with the local smugglers, tries to ship Clara Brereton away from Sanditon. His plans are foiled by Charlotte working in association with Countess Westborough. One of the merits of the text is that the Countess is modelled on powerful Regency women such as Lady Hester Stanhope and Lady Bessborough. Instead of nothing happening in Sanditon and its neighbourhood, they become locations for pleasurable activities such as a picnic and a fête as well as the backdrop for the adventure story itself. The world of Regency smugglers is nevertheless given little of the gothic menace that haunts Daphne du Maurier's *Jamaica Inn* (1936).

Another completed version of *Sanditon*, sub-titled *A Novel by Jane Austen and Another Lady*, was published in 1975. This, it will be remembered, was the year of the bicentenary of Austen's birth during which nostalgic images of her circulated almost unchecked despite the existence of important historical studies by Butler, Duckworth and others. The other lady uses Austen's chapters before continuing the story in her own words. Like Alice Cobbett, she is concerned to represent Sanditon as a pleasant location rather than allowing it to remain a disturbing and unsettling one.

The other lady provides a short 'Apology' at the end of the volume. The general popularity of Austen's novels is seen primarily in terms of their nostalgic appeal: 'Ever increasing numbers, seeking to escape the shoddy values and cheap garishness of our own age are turning to the past to catch glimpses of life in what appear to be far more leisured times' (AL, pp. 326–7). The other lady is untroubled by the possibility that the deserted, half-built new village of Sanditon might be a representation of the shoddiness of the new Regency world. She sees the novels, by contrast, as mirroring an 'age of elegance' that has been irretrievably lost:

> In rereading Jane Austen, we are able to experience something of that age of elegance which too often eludes us in the twentieth century. We are unrepentant about this form of escapism and turn to her six novels for relaxation on plane journeys, in family crises and after the sheer physical exhaustion of our own servantless world. (AL, p. 327)

The reader of Austen is being positioned in class terms as somebody who ought to be able to employ a lot of domestic servants, if only they did not have the impertinence to demand too much money. The passage also shows how the novels are distanced and detached from conflict and crisis. The fact that *Sanditon* itself, to take just one example, shows the extended family as a site of conflict in its treatment of the struggle over who will eventually get their hands on Lady Denham's money is conveniently ignored. James Thompson makes a broadly similar point when he argues that extended families in Austen's novels are not represented 'as a haven in a heartless world, but rather as something suffocating'.[27]

The 'Apology' is in fact surprisingly unapologetic, or 'unrepentant', in the way in which it proposes that Austen's novels can only be read nostalgically rather than historically. It is also confident in its assertions about both Austen's romance plots and the way in which she, as a miniaturist, must have copied a particular location. Sanditon is apparently really Sidmouth. The tone in fact only becomes apologetic at the very end when the question of the unfinished *Sanditon*'s style is considered:

> Her language, her integrity and her painstaking methods of work – that terrifyingly accurate and meticulous technique – combine to give us the same sense of serenity and assurance in the six novels in which she brought her world to life and made it real for us. None of these things can be faithfully copied. (AL, p. 329)

The idea that the style of Austen's *Sanditon* can be described as serene is a particularly extraordinary one. The text provides a stage for three different voices, none of which is defined by its 'serenity'. First of all, there are the domineering voices of the obsessive, neurotic characters such as Mr Parker, Diana Parker, Lady Denham and Sir Edward. Then there is the amused, quizzical voice of Charlotte herself which although, as noted earlier, may sometimes be calm and sensible is also capable of expressing some irritation. Finally, there is the sharp, caustic voice of a satiric narrator which delights in exposing the ways in which personal vanity masks itself.

The other lady turns out to be very like Austen's own obsessive characters. Parker continues to believe that Sanditon is paradise on earth even though nobody else wants to go there. His sister Diana still insists that she has been instrumental in getting two families to visit the resort despite the conclusive revelation to the contrary. They remain unrepentant even when the evidence stares them in the face. The other lady is obsessed with promoting the cultural myth that Austen could only have written serenely about romantic relationships which are set in a leisured, elegant world free from domestic and political conflicts. She therefore has no trouble in finding these things in *Sanditon*.

The finished version of *Sanditon* could not completely abandon themes such as invalidism and yet it has to gentle them in order to produce a serene text. The imaginary invalids become relatively minor characters in order to make room for the two romance plots: one involving Charlotte and Sidney Parker and the other dealing with Clara Brereton and a new character called Henry Brudenall. A comic script still continues, for instance when Susan Parker is stung on the nose by a bee, but it is divorced from the more serious consideration of models of right feminine happiness. The invalids become quaint eccentrics rather than dangerous neurotics. Arthur is partially transformed into an active naturalist who eventually marries Miss Lambe.

The text leaves the confines of the asylum as the romance plots allow for a series of pleasurable activities. Charlotte and Clara go bathing. They and their future husbands visit Sir Edward's cottage. They then all walk around the older parts of the fishing village. Although the younger characters dominate this middle section of the completed novel, the visit to the tea rooms, the expedition to Brinshore and the Sanditon Ball provide opportunities for the more obsessive characters to reappear. The resort is transformed from a place where nothing actually happens, despite all the mad activity to promote activity, into one which is capable of providing pleasant holidays and therefore escapism for readers.

Charlotte retains some of her strength, although she becomes 'tongue-tied with embarrassment' (AL, p. 248) and 'flustered into silence' (AL, p. 265) in the presence of the unpredictable Sidney. He dominates her thoughts in the same way as his mysterious movements become, more generally, the novel's main focus of attention. Austen's own heroines may sometimes lose their voice when confronted by romance but never as early, or for so long, as happens to Charlotte here. She also disconcertingly follows Harriet Smith at one point by developing a sentimental attachment to what appear to be the useless relics of her relationship with Sidney.

Austen's version breaks off just as Charlotte and Mary Parker have called at Sanditon House and are waiting for Lady Denham to make an entrance. As noted, Mary voiced the understated opinion that her sisters-in-law sometimes went too far with their self-help medical remedies. She is nevertheless represented more generally as being a weak woman who is 'terrified' by the carriage accident and unable to provide a rational counterpoint to her husband's crazy enthusiasms. There was some talk immediately before this particular visit to Sanditon House of getting her to ask Lady Denham to provide charity for a local family that had fallen on hard times in this deserted village. She is greatly relieved when she is no longer required to perform this task as she does not have Diana Parker's boundless energy for charitable enterprises.

The difference between the two texts can be seen by looking briefly at the way in which Mary, cast now as a modern representation of the Regency country lady, becomes a much more positive character in the completed version. She acquires the status of a second heroine. Although she is too polite or 'sweet-tempered' (AL, p. 83) to say openly that Lady Denham's behaviour is rude, she is quite firm in the way in which she tries to turn topics of conversation. She is always keen to get off the subject of romantic relationships, particularly if it is being discussed in a worldly, gossipy way.

Mary is shown as being contented within the domestic sphere. She keeps 'a very good table' (AL, p. 85), silently aided by poorly paid servants who never get ill. Delicacies served up on this table include saddle of mutton, well-filled corner dishes, roast duckling and cranberry custard. Such details are Austenesque in the sense that they are based on references in the novels, for instance Mr Weston carves a saddle of mutton at Randalls. The way in which they are lovingly foregrounded as simple signs of an elegance that is to be admired nevertheless runs counter to the wider messages of the novels, having more in common with modern heritage films and television programmes.

Mary manages her husband in the same way that she organises her table. When the facetious Sidney sends him a *Guide to Watering Places* that extols the pleasures of Brinshore, she quietly suggests that he ought to write something for it about Sanditon instead of relying upon his conversational powers: 'But perhaps it would be no bad idea to arrange for a mention of Sanditon in such a book . . . Surely many people we cannot know of must consult a library or buy this book before deciding on a seaside holiday' (AL, p. 198). Her husband, after a lot of bluster, eventually compiles the entry that saves Sanditon. He rushes to the new greenhouse to show it to her believing that it will relieve her boredom. She has another enthusiasm, however, that is almost equal to his missionary desire to promote Sanditon:

> Though lacking her husband's general enthusiasm, Mrs. Parker had developed a quiet fanaticism of her own in becoming a dedicated gardener. She grew all her own flowering plants from seed, experimented with new varieties, and was rarely content to hand anything over to the gardener till it became too large for her to house or for him to damage by treatment. (AL, p. 202)

Parker does not realise that his wife has converted the greenhouse into a room of her own. Mary Parker, the Regency country lady, is allowed to acquire some of the omniscient qualities of Ruth Wilcox in E.M. Forster's *Howards End* (1913). A better comparison is with Edith Holden whose *The Country Diary of an Edwardian Lady* became a surprise, or underground, bestseller when it was published in 1977. This text, which was compiled in 1906, attracted the same kind of nostalgic and pastoral longings that attached themselves so firmly to the figure of Austen two years earlier during the bicentennial celebrations.[28]

Mary is once again in the greenhouse when she gently offers Charlotte some words of wisdom about Sidney's seemingly unknowable behaviour:

> But usually, you know, there is a very good reason for everything Sidney does. He may joke and pretend he moves about for his own amusement, but it is seldom really the case. I myself am quite sure that this time his business has something to do with Mr. Brudenall which he wants none of us to guess. (AL, p. 253)

She turns out to be absolutely right, which confirms earlier impressions that despite a studied vagueness she is the only character who has a detached but secure sense of the way in which the romance plots are developing. This vagueness is part of her serenity. Her advice to Charlotte is offered when it seems as though the relationship with Sidney is going smoothly. She becomes very supportive when it appears from gossip and rumour that Sidney may have been playing Charlotte false. She tells her husband that even 'the most sensible girls can be misled by attentions as marked as these seem to have been. Oh, I am sure Sidney means no ill, but it is really bad of him to behave in this thoughtless way' (AL, p. 260). She is proved in the end to have a sounder judgement than the gossips of Sanditon, who include her husband. Her detachment from gossip is shown again when the engagement is announced between Arthur Parker and Miss Lambe. While nearly everybody else attributes purely mercenary motives to Arthur, she unobtrusively seeks to promote the relationship by quietly befriending Miss Lambe: 'She sought her frequent company, kindly offered her assistance in all her plans, and was pleased as her husband to feel that they could soon number near relations as near neighbours'(AL, p. 276). This unobtrusive kindness is also part of her serenity.

The other lady has transformed Mary into another lady. Austen's own harsh representation of Mary's weaknesses is replaced by an emphasis on quiet strength and serenity. At one level, it is always very rewarding to be given opportunities to read any text from the point of view of a seemingly marginal character. A broadly similar strategy has indeed been employed earlier on here in relation to male characters such as Tom Bertram and Mr Perry. The reminders that are constantly provided in rewritten versions of Austen of the need to read sometimes through the eyes of Maria Rushworth, Susan Price, Jane Fairfax and those of other apparently marginalised female characters are very important ones. As argued, the modern cultural activities that take place around Austen are relevant because they can open up as well as close down meanings.

The potentially productive manoeuvre of developing the character of Mary Parker is nevertheless constrained by an obsessive desire to reproduce heritage images of both Austen and Regency England. Mary is seen by the other lady as being similar to Austen. The unfinished text of *Sanditon*, however, keeps a very different countenance: quizzical, irritable and satirical. The other lady is searching for elegance in a servantless world and finds it in Mary's table. This is like turning Isabella Knightley, another weak woman, into the heroine of *Emma*. Yet the unfinished text appears to have arrived at much more unsettling conclusions about relationships between elegance and madness. It sees the crazy world that exists on both sides of the elegant Regency looking-glass. The finished text can only see tables and mirrors as elegant period objects to be coveted. Sanditon therefore becomes a mildly eccentric, but nevertheless pleasurable, location rather than a claustrophobic asylum. The other lady's literal attempts to equate it with Sidmouth miss the more important point that, in Austen's version, it is an anticipation of Brummell's imaginary parties in Caen. She is concerned, however, to allow her genteel readers to potter quietly about in the greenhouse rather than allowing them to remain in the madhouse. Sanditon is allowed to become as full of servants, visitors and action as it is empty of topical debates about the Condition-of-England and the culture of invalidism. Regency England becomes a timeless, mythological place called Austenshire. Austen herself becomes another lady: serene and detached rather than satirical and topical.

Appendix:
The plot of *Lovers' Vows*

The full text of the play is reprinted at the end of Chapman's edition of *Mansfield Park*. I offer this summary of it for the benefit of those students who may still have problems gaining access to it.

The play is set in rural Germany. It opens with Agatha Friburg being thrown out of the inn by the Landlord because she can no longer afford to pay her bills. He takes pleasure in telling her that she will now have to beg for her food. Two potential alms-givers take no notice of her. She begs heaven to take care of her son and his father, believing that she is close to death. A country girl takes pity on her, offering to bring back money after produce has been sold at market.

At this point Frederick enters 'dressed in a German soldier's uniform' with 'a knapsack on his shoulders' (LV, 1.1). He notices Agatha lying in the road in front of the inn and gives her what little money he has. She recognises him as the son who went off to war five years before. He orders some wine for her, which is sold to him at an inflated price by the knavish Landlord. Mother and son start to tell each other what has happened since they were last together. Frederick declares his intention of leaving the army, claiming that he is only hindered from doing so because he is unable to produce his birth certificate. He has returned home to collect it. Agatha has to tell him that he is a 'natural son' (LV, 1.1). After moments of uncertainty, she begins to recount the circumstances of his birth, detailing how she had been 'intoxicated by the fervent caresses of a young, inexperienced, capricious man, and did not recover from the delirium till it was too late' (LV, 1.1). Frederick becomes very agitated during the telling of this story and, in tears, urges his mother to finish it as quickly as possible. She concludes by indicating how she was eventually be-friended by the local clergyman and how she was able subsequently to earn her living as a teacher. She reveals that her seducer, whom she names as Baron Wildenhaim, married a 'woman of virtue – of noble birth and immense fortune' (LV, 1.1) after he had discarded her. When all these painful revelations are over, she presses Frederick to her breast. He makes an unsuccessful attempt to secure a bed for her at the inn and then knocks on the door of a cottage. The cottager and his wife offer to take in the sick woman with little prompting.

Act Two begins inside the cottage with Agatha 'reclining on a wooden bench' (LV, 2.1). Although the cottagers are naturally charitable, they have neither food nor money. Frederick resolves to go into the highways and byways to seek assistance. After he has departed 'in haste and confusion' (LV, 2.1), the cottagers reveal that the Baron has recently returned to the castle following the death of his wife. They gossip good-naturedly about his previous relationship with Agatha, who faints during the course of this embarrassing dialogue.

The action then moves to the castle. The Baron is irritated that Count Cassel has not yet emerged from his bedroom. He wonders whether he really wants such 'an ape for a son-in-law' (LV, 2.2). He questions his daughter Amelia about her feelings for Cassel when she enters. She claims that she has dreamt of Anhalt, the chaplain, rather than of Cassel. Despite his own misgivings, the Baron claims that Cassel must be regarded as a worthy suitor because he is 'rich, and of great consequence' (LV, 2.2). Amelia is more consistent, declaring that she loves to laugh at the Count. Her father decides to ask Anhalt to explain her duty to her.

Cassel finally enters while the Baron and Amelia are still at breakfast. He immediately starts paying extravagant compliments to Amelia which she tries to laugh off. He prides himself as being a man of the world, 'I am an epitome of the world' (LV, 2.2), who prefers sophisticated intrigues and seductions to falling in love. His costume and stage props both emphasise a decadent foppishness. He has, for instance, an elegant gun with a mother-of-pearl butt. When asked whether he can shoot, it is time once again to play the part of the great seducer: 'That I have never tried – except, with my eyes, at a fine woman' (LV, 2.2). Before the shooting party sets out, the Baron has a private interview with Anhalt. He places the chaplain in a difficult position by asking him not just to reform the Count, but also to try to persuade Amelia to make a socially advantageous marriage.

Act Three opens in a field in front of the castle. Frederick is counting out the very meagre sum of money that he has been able to raise for his mother through begging. The appearance of gamekeepers and others tells him that a nobleman must be in the vicinity. The Baron enters with the gundogs. He is followed eventually by the breathless Count, who acts very haughtily when Frederick deferentially asks for alms. The Baron is more sympathetic and provides money, while declaring that a soldier really ought to be with his regiment. Frederick nevertheless asks for more money and draws his sword in order to threaten the Baron. He is arrested by the gamekeepers and taken back as a prisoner to the castle. Although the Baron refused to be intimidated by the demands of a soldier with a drawn sword, he nevertheless gives orders that Frederick's mother should be found and provided with money.

The next scene is the one where Amelia declares her love for Anhalt. He attempts to follow the Baron's instructions and advise her about matrimony. He pictures a perfect marriage and then a less satisfactory one: 'when convenience, and fair appearance joined to folly and ill-humour, forge the fetters of matrimony, they gall with their weight the married pair' (LV, 3.2). He continues to talk about marriage whereas she wants to talk about love and more particularly her love for him. She suggests a reversal of the teacher–pupil relationship by offering to teach him about women. He attempts yet again to steer the subject back to marriage: 'The subject I came to you upon was marriage'(LV, 3.2). Amelia takes this as a proposal, which she immediately accepts. Anhalt's defences are eventually overcome. He admits his own love for her at the same time as pointing out that 'your birth and fortune make our union impossible' (LV, 3.2).

The Butler enters with the news that the Baron has been attacked while out hunting. He insists on reading out a poem on the subject. When Amelia sees Frederick being dragged off to the tower, she is immediately struck by the honesty of his countenance. This is why she pleads his case with her father and then decides to take food up to the tower. It is she who unknowingly lets slip the information that the man he has attacked is none other than his own father. He reacts to this disclosure with violent emotion. Anhalt is the next visitor to the tower. He suggests that Frederick pleads for forgiveness and their conversation fills in the missing pieces of the family jig-saw as far as the prisoner is concerned.

Amelia starts trying to explain to the Baron why she is unable to marry Cassel. She dislikes the way in which he is continually bragging about his conquests. If even half of what he has said is true, then 'a hundred female hearts will at least be broken' (LV, 4.2) when they marry. He has also discovered via the Butler that he has seduced and then abandoned a 'poor young creature' (LV, 4.2). The Butler confirms the story. When Cassel saunters in he is accused by the Baron of being engaged to another woman while he is courting Amelia. He refuses to take the situation seriously: 'To only *one* other woman?'

(LV, 4.2). As far as he is concerned, to make vows of love only to one woman is 'an absolute slight upon the rest of the sex' (LV, 4.2). His nonchalant remarks that all men are equally guilty clearly fluster the Baron, who is also the father of a love-child.

Amelia and her father continue the discussion over whether she ought to marry Cassel. She confides in him about her proposal scene with Anhalt, declaring how she had maintained that 'birth and fortune were such old-fashioned things' (LV, 4.2). She is on her knees begging her father to allow her to marry Anhalt when the chaplain himself enters to entreat that the 'poor soldier' (LV, 4.2) be given a hearing. The Baron and Frederick are eventually brought face-to-face again. Instead of using his mother's illness as the excuse for his conduct, Frederick chooses to blame his father's cruelty. After a generalised description of his unhappy childhood, he names the Baron as his father. He goes on to attack him for his sinful conduct: 'In this house did you rob my mother of her honour; and in this house I am a sacrifice for the crime' (LV, 4.2). Anhalt enters to save the Baron from further attack and Frederick exits. While Anhalt himself rushes off to find Agatha, the Baron storms and frets about the stage trying to come to terms with the way in which his past has suddenly caught up with him.

The final act opens back at the cottage. Agatha is agitated by the fact that Frederick has not returned, even though the Baron's money has already been delivered to her. When Anhalt enters, she has an opportunity to tell her story. She has a moment of anger when she throws down the purse of money: ' He despised my heart – I despise his gold – He has trampled on me – I trample on his representative' (LV, 5.1). She nevertheless tends to accept Anhalt's explanations of the Baron's conduct. These are that he succumbed to family pressure, was called away to war and was then influenced by 'worldly friends' (LV, 5.1) to marry the daughter of a nobleman. Agatha claims that she will 'forget my claims as a woman, if the Baron will atone to the mother' (LV, 5.1).

Meanwhile, back at the castle, the Baron and Frederick are in the middle of a man-to-man conversation about war. The harmony between them is nevertheless extremely precarious and is quickly disrupted when the Baron reveals his plan to let Frederick live as his son in the castle but to find somewhere more discreet for Agatha. He is bluntly told that mother and son will not be parted in this way. After Frederick's angry exit Anhalt enters. He too urges his master to marry Agatha: 'she brings a dower greater than any princess can bestow – peace to your conscience' (LV, 5.2). The Baron, after pacing restlessly up and down, eventually agrees to marry her. His prejudices on the side of ancestry give way completely when he gives his blessing to the marriage between Amelia and Anhalt. All that remains is for Agatha, her future now decided by the male characters, to make her appearance at the castle for the final reconciliation scene.

Afterword
Austenmania

Jane Austen and Representations of Regency England was first published in hardback towards the end of 1994. As other writers of academic books will appreciate, this meant that the manuscript had to be submitted a year earlier. There have been many important studies of Austen since 1993, as well as a new edition of her letters. There have also been some significant publications on the cultural history of Regency England. To take just one example, shortly after the publication of the hardback edition of this book the Jane Austen Society of North America held a conference in New Orleans entitled 'Jane Austen and the Three Rs: Rebellion, Revolution and the Regency'.

Many of the papers covered themes that I had written about such as perceptions of the Prince Regent, ideas of empire and constructions of masculine identities. It might just have been possible to have persuaded my publishers to let me include some references to a limited amount of new material in the paperback edition. I decided, however, not even to attempt this for two main reasons. First, the sheer volume of critical and editorial work on Austen would have made it extremely difficult to have fixed any realistic limits at all. Second, although I have certainly read studies since 1993 that would have allowed me either to have elaborated upon or to have qualified some of my individual points, particularly on medical history, I have not found anything that has forced me to revise any of my central arguments. Indeed, I would argue that the reverse has been the case and that a significant number of recent studies could have been used to support not just these arguments themselves but also, more generally, the historical approach that I take towards Austen. When I read through the proceedings of the New Orleans conference in the 1994 issue of *Persuasions*, I had a strong sense that, prompted by previous studies whose influence I have acknowledged, I had written about issues that were now becoming increasingly important to other Austen scholars as well. As indicated, this was not an isolated experience.

I have nevertheless decided to make one exception to this general rule of not revising the text of the hardback edition. I mentioned very much in passing in the first chapter the possibility that there was going to be another television adaptation of *Pride and Prejudice*, which might replace the one that I was about to discuss. This reference was made in the context of both a general argument that established Austen's remarkable topicality within contemporary British culture, as well as a more particular one that showed how her writings were often completely distanced and detached from debates about sex and sexualities. I quoted the *Sun*'s mock–shock reaction to the rumour that this new adaptation might contain scenes that involved nudity.

The six-part adaptation of *Pride and Prejudice* by Andrew Davies was eventually bought up by the BBC and, beginning on 24 September 1995, screened on Sunday nights with a repeat the following Saturday. There followed a period of what was variously called 'Austenmania', 'Austenfever', 'Austenitis' and, perhaps the most frequently used description of all, 'Darcymania'. Some commentators with longish memories claimed that there had been nothing quite like it since the Beatlemania of the 1960s.

The viewing figures for this adaptation, rising to over ten million for the last episode, were the highest that there has ever been for a classic serial, or what the *Radio Times* preferred to call a 'costume classic'. When the video priced at just under £20 was released in advance of the final episode, it sold 12,000 copies in just two days and 50,000 within the week. Many viewers were obviously desperate to find out for themselves as quickly as possible how the romance was going to end. Publications such as *The Times* and the *Radio Times*, which spoilt the suspense for other viewers by revealing in advance the two-weddings-and-no-funerals ending, were taken to task for doing so by some of their readers. The day before the final episode was screened the *Independent* declared that 'lovelorn women and adoring marketing men are murmuring just one name: Darcy'. Nearly 100,000 copies of the video had been sold by the end of October and the BBC had to abandon other projects in order to reissue it in time for the Christmas market; 20,000 copies of the BBC book, *The Making of Pride and Prejudice*, had been sold by the end of October and by December it was top of the non-fiction bestseller list. Costume classics are an expensive form of television to produce with each episode costing around £1 million. Even so, the Austen industry is clearly a very profitable one at the moment, both at home and abroad. The adaptation has already been televised in America, in three parts, and sold to various European countries.

Austen's novel itself started climbing both the hardback and paperback bestseller lists for fiction. According to some estimates, paperback sales were somewhere in the region of 25,000 copies a week. There was a significant increase in visitors to Austen's house in Chawton, as well as to the four National Trust properties that were used as locations in the adaptation.

The truly phenomenal success of this adaptation probably provides the most important, but by no means the only, example of 'Austenmania'. The *Irish Times* noticed the existence of two other adaptations of Austen novels in an article about the unstoppable 'Austen revival' on 9 October 1995: *Persuasion* and Amy Heckerling's teen movie, *Clueless*, set in Beverly Hills but drawing on the plot of *Emma*. *Persuasion*, which has won awards, was first shown on Easter Sunday and then repeated on Christmas day. These slots show the way in which Austen is treated almost like royalty by television. This film version, similar in some respects to the adaptation of *Northanger Abbey* that I discussed in my first chapter, was given a short run at a London cinema after Christmas. It has also been shown in America. Additional manifestations of 'Austenmania' include the predictable storm that followed Terry Castle's review of the new edition of Austen's letters in the August issue of the *London Review of Books*, which was headlined 'Was Jane Austen Gay?' Newspapers quickly rounded up many of the usual suspects to comment on Castle's suggestion that Austen may have had a sexual relationship with her sister.

My first chapter shows that there is in fact nothing new about 'Austenmania' and thus helps to provide the necessary historical context for these very recent events. It still has to be said, however, that the popularity of this particular adaptation of *Pride and Prejudice* has transformed Austen into an even more newsworthy, or topical, figure than she has ever been. It is quite possible that this already extremely intense level of interest in her life and works will actually increase. The film version of *Sense and Sensibility*, nominated for awards in America, will have been released in Britain by the time this book is published in paperback. The book about the film, *Sense and Sensibility: The Screenplay and Diaries*, is already available. It seems quite likely that there will be adaptations of *Emma* on both BBC and ITV in the near future. There will also be a film of this novel, shot in Dorset and reported to have cost around £5 million. What has been described as the 'Austen avalanche' is on its way. If this book is reprinted, I shall probably have to write an afterword to the afterword.

Considerable newspaper coverage was devoted to the 'tumultuous', 'terrific', 'heaving', 'bursting' and 'bounteous' bosoms that were displayed in this adaptation of *Pride and Prejudice*. One of the first laws of heritage television is that ratings soar if necklines plunge. The costume classic has to have a super-abundance of what became known as 'the period bosom'. The fact that a small company in Portsmouth that manufactured corsets was advertising for a few extra staff would not normally be considered national news. Yet it was reported by some national newspapers as an example of how 'Austenmania' was helping to promote a resurgence of interest in old-fashioned undergarments. There was an article in the *Daily Express* on 19 October 1995 entitled 'Pride in Your Cleavage', which offered readers in search of a 'classic cleavage' the chance to win a bustier and matching briefs designed by Berlei. This company, which apparently had a rush on their bone corsets, promised in some of its promotional material that its garments would produce 'an authentic *Pride and Prejudice* cleavage'. The *Sunday Express* published an article called 'Sense and Sensuality' on 29 October 1995 which contrasted the elegant, 'sensually alluring' costumes worn in the television adaptation with the 'scrawny' look allegedly favoured by modern designers. Here and elsewhere, the soft elegance of heritage versions of Austen's world is contrasted with what are taken to be the harsher realities of the present. Many other newspapers and magazines discussed at length what the *Daily Telegraph* described on 24 October 1995 as 'the bonnet and bosoms boom'. According to the *Sunday Times* on 15 October 1995, 'the sound of squealing bosoms being squeezed into period costume has been deafening'.

Male costume and the male body also figured prominently in the gossip that circulated ceaselessly around the adaptation. It was confidentially claimed by *The Times* on 20 November 1995 that a million women, no more and no less, wanted to unbutton the damp white shirt that was worn by Colin Firth when he played Mr Darcy. It was auctioned for charity and fetched £500. What the *Sun* described on 1 November 1995 as Darcy's 'straining breeches with the trapdoor front' may well have fetched considerably more had they too gone under the hammer. Mr Darcy's trousers attracted even more attention than Elizabeth Bennet's frocks and cleavage. The *Guardian* had noted on 2 October 1995 that in the earlier episodes 'the soldiers' trousers were all-too-obviously filled with the joys of Spring'. These trousers were, apparently, specially made for this production since the ones that had originally been hired were too stretchy and thus not revealing enough. The gaze of the *Guardian*'s television reviewer fell more

irectly on Mr Darcy's nether regions in an article on 23 October
995, which claimed that 'no one could live in trousers like that
vithout the tension finally getting to them'. Mr Darcy's trousers still
igured very prominently in the mind's eye of those who had to write
rticles recording the high points of the year. According to *The Times*
in 26 December 1995, they were without any doubt at all the outfit
if the year:

> Nothing came close to Colin Firth and those trousers. . . . The sight
> of Firth wearing button flap, full-front breeches sent women every-
> where into fainting fits. The Regency dandy's preference for a snug
> fit added to the garment's charm.

The *Independent* declared on the same day that Firth was its man of
he year because he was a 'sex symbol to outshine all Hollywood's
iunkiest'. Those trousers were speaking for, as well as to, England.
Clint Eastwood they ain't.

Firth was reported in the press to have had a brief but passionate
iffair on location with Jennifer Ehle, the actress who played Elizabeth
3ennet. This prompted Imogen Edward-Jones to warn readers of the
Evening Standard on 16 October 1995 never ever to 'lay a luvvie',
iince according to her thespians were notoriously fickle in their affec-
ions. Perhaps the 'hot gossip' about this affair helps to explain why
he scenes between Darcy and Elizabeth attracted so much interest.
Peter McKay had already suggested to readers of the *Standard* on 10
October 1995 that, although the dialogue spoken by Darcy and
Elizabeth implies sexual innocence by modern standards, their on-
screen presence and chemistry emphatically contradicted this.

A letter to the *Radio Times* for the 18–24 November 1995 issue
claimed that 'Colin Firth is the sexiest person on the screen . . . The
scenes with Jennifer Ehle are truly erotic, and they hardly touch each
other.' Incidentally, another letter in the same issue pointed out that
classic cleavages could be, and were, created by the line of a dress
without the aid of wonderbras and bustiers. This was also the issue
that carried what was described as 'the very first *Radio Times* pin-up'.
A full-page portrait showed Firth, attired in Regency evening dress,
striking a smouldering, glowering pose with a suitably stormy sky in
the background. His trousers are not, however, as much in evidence
in this up-market piece of Regency raunch as they were on the
television screen since the pin-up is decorously, or perhaps mischie-
vously, cut off just below the waist.

Descriptions of Firth in the newspapers included 'national heart-
throb', 'dreamboat', 'dashing', 'dishy' and 'drop-dead gorgeous'.

Although most journalists agreed that he, together with his wet shirt and snug trousers, was indeed the latest flame, opinion was quite sharply divided as to whether he was a new man or an old one. Some detected signs of newness in his tormented vulnerability, whereas Lynda Lee-Potter told readers of the *Daily Mail* on 1 November 1995 in no uncertain terms that he was simply 'an unsmiling, brooding domineering chauvinist' straight out of old-style popular romance fiction. As will be clear, the mainstream press was not interested in considering the possibility that Darcy might have an appeal for men as well as for women.

The journalists who bombarded us with endless stories about bosoms like balconies and tension-filled trousers were carrying on the 'carry on' game that had been started by members of the production team, who described *Pride and Prejudice* as a novel about sex as well as one about money. I gave a brief indication of the rules of this game in my first chapter when discussing the cartoon in the *Sunday Telegraph* about the 'extremely chaste' Jane Austen sex shop. The idea is to tease everybody by taking a national icon like Austen, who is thought to remain silent about sex, and then go straightaway to the other extreme and declare that her novels are in fact completely saturated with 'it'. This proposition is then gleefully seized on by those who smell the literary equivalent of Royal sex scandal, much to the oh-so predictable annoyance of those pundits who promote a very different version of Austen.

Although this particular debate about sex is often both too polarised and predictable to be of much real interest, the current 'Austenmania' has produced some important reflections on other aspects of Austen's life and work. Claire Tomalin, writing in the *Independent on Sunday* on 21 October 1995, drew attention to Austen's tragedy: just when her writings were beginning to promise the economic independence that she was struggling towards she was struck down by a fatal illness Tomalin has recently published an excellent biography of Dorothy Jordan and is currently working on one on Austen herself. Another biography of Austen, by David Nokes, is due to be published soon. A.S. Byatt, writing in the *Daily Telegraph* on 30 October 1995, told her readers that heritage versions of Austen's world should not be allowed to disguise the fact that the lack of privacy for women in Regency households would have driven modern women 'demented'. Nicci Gerrard previewed the serial for the *Observer* on 10 September 1995 in an article intriguingly entitled 'Mistress of the Scalpel'. This had no time whatsoever for the 'received biography'. Gerrard followed Gilbert and Gubar's work and suggested, by contrast, that Austen's very early and very late writings are characterised by a 'pitilessness' that is 'uncamouflaged'. She also argued that the novels that come in between, particularly of course *Pride and Prejudice*, display an authorial 'ice and sarcasm', together with the 'feeling of a nasty and small-minded world closing in'. She followed, as I have done, D.W. Harding's remarkably perceptive essay on 'Regulated Hatred', published in 1940, and noticed the way in which Austen represents forms of social and domestic surveillance. Although the great debate was supposed to be about Austen and sex, Gerrard and others realised that the real issue at stake was the need to insist that Austen wrote about Regency society and its ills much more directly and openly than we have often been conditioned to believe. I was just as pleased to find confirmations of my thesis in these newspaper articles as I was when reading through conference proceedings and other academic publications. This current outbreak of 'Austenmania', despite some of its 'silly season' characteristics, has shown that it is at least possible for there to be an informed public debate about Austen and her work.

Anything and everything about Austen was considered to be newsworthy. She was discussed not just in the media and fashion pages of the national press, but also made regular appearances in financial reports, medical briefings, sports coverage and elsewhere. The story of her brief engagement to Harris Bigg Wither, which I looked at in my first chapter, was dug out, dusted down and run again in an allegedly exclusive article in the *Mail on Sunday* on 29 October 1995. The legal complexities of the entail on the Longbourn estate were keenly debated. Austen cropped up in an article in the *Observer* on private banks on 19 November 1995: 'You've seen the TV series; you've bought the video. But what about the bank account?' Austen's banker, still in business, was given a plug. I noticed briefly in the first chapter how Austen's association, however tenuous, with a particular house could be turned into a major selling point. The property page of the *Daily Mail* on 20 October 1995 told readers who 'wish to feel nearer to Jane Austen' about yet another golden opportunity to buy into her world and its supposed values.

The coverage given to Mr Darcy far exceeded that accorded to Elizabeth Bennet. The BBC book, *The Making of Pride and Prejudice*, has a chapter-length interview with Colin Firth rather than with Jennifer Ehle. Many newspapers devoted themselves almost exclusively to the question of why Darcy had caught the imagination of the viewing public. Rosemary Carpenter, writing for the women's page in the *Daily Express* on 26 October 1995, posed a series of gushing questions for her readers in an article entitled 'Why do we all adore

Darcy?' One of the answers that is suggested is that the 'subtle hint of passion' conveyed by Darcy is much more erotic than raw sex. Even so, Mr Darcy's cult status still had its puzzling aspects. Firth was clearly not tall enough for the part and was sometimes filmed with a tilted camera to give an illusion of greater stature. The actors who played Wickham and Colonel Fitzwilliam did not appear to be so deficient in the height department. The make-up team apparently had to work overtime on Firth's hair, sideboards and eyelashes to make sure that he was dark enough for the part. He reportedly wore mascara around his eyes, whereas the actresses were forbidden to use it in order to create a natural look.

The *Daily Express* continued to tremble away about Darcy. It reported in some detail on 30 October 1995 on the lives of four men whose only claim to fame was that they too were called Darcy. Once again, there are a string of breathless questions. Would these men turn out to be 'classic English gentlemen, cool and reserved on the outside, but with a delicious simmering centre of repressed emotion?' The four very ordinary blokes who were eventually 'tracked down' by the *Daily Express* stood no chance at all of living up to such great expectations. Fantasy collided painfully with reality.

Andrew Davies explained to readers of the *Daily Mail* on 31 October 1995 why he had taken the decision to build up Darcy's character:

> I wanted to show, or at least hint, from an early stage, that there's a lot more to Darcy than meets the eye. Also I wanted to remind the audience that he, like the other young people in the story, is a real human being, with a physical and mental life, who likes to ride his horse at a full gallop and subjects himself to a gruelling workout with his fencing master when he's trying to overcome his emotional turmoil.

The adaptation opens with Darcy and Bingley galloping around the countryside in search of, not a wife, but a house. They are spotted by Elizabeth who is out for the first of her many walks. We see Darcy, accompanied by both Bingley and Mr Hurst, enjoying a day's shooting at Netherfield, as well as walking slowly back to the house afterwards. He and Bingley go shooting again later on, just before the scene in which he very bluntly advises his friend to 'go to it' and propose to Jane Bennet. The adaptation also finds room for short scenes between Darcy and Wickham. Darcy enters a college room to find a scantily-clothed woman climbing all over Wickham. He arrives in Ramsgate in the nick of time to prevent his sister from eloping with Wickham.

We see him at the shotgun wedding between Lydia Bennet and Wickham, as well as making the financial arrangements for it with the Gardiners.

In addition to these scenes which explore Darcy's relationships with other men, we encounter him on his own. He has a bath, helped by a servant, and then watches Elizabeth playing in the garden with one of his dogs. We see him walking moodily back to Rosings after Elizabeth has rejected his proposal. He then spends all night writing her a letter. We see him riding back to Pemberley on his own and going for a swim. He walks around the house with his two dogs, after Elizabeth has spent the evening there, thinking about her. We see him leave the next day to call on her at her hotel. When Elizabeth breaks to him the news of Lydia's scandalous elopement, we see him back at Pemberley spending a miserable evening. He then sets off for London with the coachman shouting at and whipping the horses. This melodramatic narrative created by Davies is cut into Austen's one that deals with Elizabeth's return to Longbourn. We are shown Darcy arriving in London, slaking his thirst after the long journey. This is followed by a sequence in which he descends into the underworld to hunt down Wickham and Lydia.

We are certainly shown a whole lot more of Darcy than meets our eye in Austen's novel, and then some more. This compromises one romance plot which emphasises the mystery that often surrounds his manners, movements and motives. Elizabeth either has to piece these together from the scraps of information that are available to her and the other women, or else learn to wait more patiently for explanations. This romance plot teaches its female readers how to read as accurately as possible small signs and muffled clues. As indicated in my first chapter, parts of this plot were present in the 1980 adaptation in spite of all of the heritage carriages-and-candles bricolage. Although Davies's decision to give viewers some access to Darcy's point of view weakens this particular romance plot, it emphasises another equally important one. We see Darcy's torture and torment, and thus the way in which romance empowers Elizabeth. According to Colin Firth, Darcy is pursuing Elizabeth and yet trying to reject her at the same time. The 'workout' in the fencing club is an important scene in this romance plot. Darcy fences with the professional, attracting admiring gazes from some of the young gents who are lounging around. After the bout has finished he says 'I shall conquer this, I shall', meaning the romance that has begun to take over his life. At one level, he has every incentive to do just this when faced with the prospect of the mother-in-law from hell. This adaptation is good at making the

Bennets, together with their relations like Mr Collins, extremely embarrassing at social occasions like the Netherfield ball. Yet Darcy's manly thoughts and pursuits do not provide an adequate defence against the power of romance. Elizabeth wins the romantic fencing bout based on verbal parries and thrusts, looks and glances. She has power, albeit perhaps only briefly during this courtship phase, over one of the most powerful men in England. Despite all his strenuous efforts, Darcy is ultimately unable to conquer some of his perfectly rational objections to the marriage. 'Darcymania' clearly marginalises Elizabeth and yet, paradoxically perhaps, it also highlights aspects of her strength.

As suggested in my first chapter, heritage television will always have a problem with the representation of Elizabeth Bennet regardless of whether Darcy is foregrounded or not. The 'bonnet and bosoms boom' means that she must be in danger of just becoming the kind of 'elegant female' that she despises. This adaptation, shot on film rather than videotape and making much more, and much better, use of outdoor locations than the previous one, finds ways of conveying her energy and unconventionality. It also, as just suggested, shows how romance empowers her. The exchange of looks with Darcy in the later episodes is very effective. Jennifer Ehle delivers some of her more spirited lines, for instance in response to Darcy's letter and in her interview with Lady Catherine De Bourgh, particularly well. There is still a strong sense, however, that Austen's Elizabeth Bennet and heritage television's Elizabeth Bennet will always be very different characters.

I think that the inter-related categories of nostalgia, heritage tourism and Englishness, which I considered in the first chapter, are also the appropriate ones for discussions of this adaptation. As to be expected, the BBC book about the serial makes much ado about its historical accuracy and authenticity. This did not prevent some eagled-eyed viewers from noticing that a billiard table and fishing reels were out of period. The *Radio Times* also tried to do its bit to vouch for the painstaking historical research that underpinned the adaptation. The issue for 30 September to 6 October carried an article significantly entitled 'Lifting the Skirts on Pride and Prejudice' which discussed Regency costumes, locations and dance routines. All this talk about lifted skirts and unbuttoned shirts carried on the nudge-and-wink sexual innuendo that the makers of the adaptation had encouraged from the very start. The most interesting fact to emerge from this article was that the period dance floor had to be coated with a modern fizzy drink, and then left to dry, so that the poor luvvies could keep their feet. This was a cola classic, as well as a costume one.

The following week there was an article in the *Radio Times* called 'You are Invited to a *Pride and Prejudice* Dinner Party', in which the chef, Colin Capon, who cooked the meals shown in the adaptation revealed some of the mysteries of his art. Three reasonably detailed recipes were provided. After you have watched the serial, bought the video, opened the bank account, read the newspapers, perhaps even purchased the house and maybe thought about reading the novel, you can then amaze your foodie friends by cooking 'the' meal. You should of course only invite those with authentic cleavages or tight trousers. If you decide on chicken, you had better explain straightaway that chickens were always served with their heads and legs on, and were usually well past their prime by the time that they actually hit the table. I could not in fact spot its head, but the chicken that makes several appearances during supper at the Netherfield ball very definitely still had feet. As in the 1980 adaptation, there are too many scenes in this one as well which show the gentry ploughing their way through large breakfasts and dinners. Breakfast was served four times during the first episode, twice at Longbourn and twice at Netherfield.

Although this adaptation prided itself on the depth of its historical research, there is also a sense in which it did not draw so much attention to its artefacts, through close-ups or the use of action-props, as happened in the 1980 one. Some of the reasons for this have already been suggested. As many of the quotations that I have used here indicate, this was first and foremost a costume drama or classic. There are certainly some fussy domestic interiors and yet, as noted, there are also scenes that are shot out-of-doors. This is an adaptation in which gardens are almost as important as homes. A surprising amount of the action takes place on the drive at Longbourn as family members and visitors come and go. Perhaps, also, heritage television has just become more confident about itself: instead of insisting that viewers inspect every single object in the Regency museum, there is more of an understated feel to the way in which these objects are displayed. They are present and allegedly correct, but are not allowed dominate scenes.

This confidence may also manifest itself in the number of over-the-top-and-beyond performances: Alison Steadman as Mrs Bennet, Julia Sawalha as Lydia Bennet and Barbara Leigh-Hunt as Lady Catherine de Bourgh. At one level, this is a very conventional, decorous piece of heritage television. It is difficult to see why there has been so much of a frenzy about it. It merely aims to recreate the experience of what the *Sunday Telegraph* described on 1 October 1995 as 'a lovely day out in some National Trust property'.

At another level, however, this adaptation at times seems to be more knowing, self-conscious and mischievous in its reproduction of the conventions for heritage television. It is less obviously restrained by them than was the case with the 1980 serialisation. There is a jokey campness in the script and therefore in some of the performances based on it. The display of historical objects may be understated at times and yet, as suggested, there is an overstated, camp emphasis on the 'period bosom' and the period breeches. It would not have taken a great deal of editing to have transformed some of the scenes into a much more explicit parody of men-in-tight-trousers costume dramas. This is heritage television that knows that it is heritage television and can sometimes draw attention to itself as such. This in turn means that viewers have some opportunities themselves to be equally frivolous about what had previously been served up in a much more serious and reverential manner.

As I hope that some of the quotations from newspapers used here will have suggested, 'Darcymania' was often a very tongue-in-cheek game. Some of the journalists who trembled and swooned over this rather stocky Darcy affected not to notice the dyed hair and the mascara around the eyes, while at the same time being all too aware that his appearance was very carefully cultivated indeed. Alternatively, perhaps Darcy's 'feminised' appearance was part of his appeal even though this was not debated in the mainstream press. He was certainly dressed up in the various uniforms of the Regency dandy and yet never really came across as being one. This may be because the production team chose to emphasise instead a more sultry Byronic look. These two looks are certainly not mutually exclusive. Byron himself was friends with most of the leading dandies and was quite happy to confess to having had at least a tinge of dandyism in his youth. Yet the scenes in which Darcy fences, goes for a swim and walks around his house with his dogs draw on memories of Byron rather than ones of Brummell. The scenes in which he reveals his struggle and torment also show him to be closer to the Romantic hero than to the Regency dandy. He is dressed for one part and yet is sometimes playing another one. I am looking forward to seeing whether this year's conference of the Jane Austen Society of North America on 'Jane Austen and her Men' will be able to shed more light on Darcy's recent popularity than I have been able to do here.

The 1995 *Pride and Prejudice* and its spin-offs were clearly well marketed, although this is not a sufficient explanation for 'Austenmania'. Many heritage products are hyped, only to die a very quick death in the marketplace. An adaptation of Austen will always deliver a reasonably large audience for the reasons that I discussed in the first chapter. Yet this still leaves the question of why this particular one at this particular time should have been so successful. Although I have tried to make some suggestions in this afterword along the lines that some licence was given for a respected cultural figure or icon to be treated more frivolously, the real answer may be that it is very difficult, especially so close to the event, to ascertain why some texts succeed and others fail.

I wrote in passing in one of my footnotes that 'the 1990s have seen the monarchy increasingly associated once again with a number of sexual scandals, some of which have at least a Regency flavour'. Although the Regency period has always been topical, there has been a very marked increase of interest since I wrote this book in women like Dorothy Jordan and Princess (later Queen) Caroline, who were dumped by male members of the Royal Family. We, like Regency readers, seem to be enthralled by gossip about the lives of our current Prince of Wales, his brothers and the women both in and out of their lives. Interest in the Regency period has been revived as an essentially Victorian construction of the monarchy has started to crumble away. The important question, which I do not have space to address here, is whether there are connections between this particular Regency revival and heritage 'Austenmania'. I think that there may be since the romance plots in this adaptation are set against elopements, a shotgun wedding and unhappy marriages. Yet I would still want to argue that 'Austenmania' generally distances us from the history of the Regency period while, at the same time, still having the capacity to bring us occasionally much closer to it.

Notes

1 REWRITING THE REGENCY

1 Sarah Tytler, *Jane Austen and Her Works* (Cassell, Petter Galpin & Co., London, 1880), p. 11. For brief details of Tytler's literary life see V. Blain *et al.* (eds), *The Feminist Companion to Literature in English: Women Writers from the Middle Ages to the Present* (Batsford, London, 1990), p. 1104.

2 Tytler, *Jane Austen and Her Works*, p. 201 and p. 16.

3 Patricia Meyer Spacks, 'Female Resources: Epistles, Plot and Power', Elizabeth C. Goldsmith (ed.), *Writing the Female Voice: Essays on Epistolary Literature* (Northwestern University Press, Boston, 1989), pp. 63–75.

4 Margaret Kirkham, 'The Austen-Leighs and Jane Austen. . .', Janet Todd (ed.), *Jane Austen: New Perspectives* (Holmes & Meier Publishers, Inc., New York, 1983), pp. 29–38. This probably remains the most valuable collection of essays on Austen. See also Margaret Kirkham, *Jane Austen: Feminism and Fiction* (Harvester Press, Brighton, 1983), ch. 8.

5 Jan Fergus, *Jane Austen: A Literary Life* (Macmillan, Basingstoke, 1991), esp. ch. 1. I deal with some of the women who wrote to attract charity in a forthcoming essay, 'Poor Relations: Writing in the Working Class', David Pirie (ed.), *The Penguin History of English Literature: Romanticism* (Penguin, London, forthcoming). For the literary market place and the woman writer before Austen see, amongst others, Cheryl Turner, *Living by the Pen: Women Writers in the Eighteenth Century* (Routledge, London, 1992).

6 Deborah Kaplan, 'The Disappearance of the Woman Writer: Jane Austen and Her Biographers', *Prose Studies*, 7, 1984, pp. 124–47, p. 136. On the theme of the disappearance of the woman writer, Austen-Leigh borrowed with acknowledgement a lot of his material, including the remarks about quizzing, from a manuscript written in 1867 by his sister Caroline Austen which was only published much later, *My Aunt Jane Austen: A Memoir* (Spottiswoode, Ballantyne & Co., London and Colchester, 1952).

7 'Style and Miss Austen', *Macmillan's Magazine*, 51, 1884, pp. 84–91, p. 85.

8 As quoted in Countess of Ilchester and Lord Stavordale (eds), *The Life and Letters of Lady Sarah Lennox 1745–1826* . . . (John Murray, London, 1901), 2, 2, p. 292. Lady Lennox later became Lady Napier.

9 See earlier chapters of Ian Hamilton, *Keepers of the Flame: Literary Estates and the Rise of Biography* (Hutchinson, London, 1992), for more details.

10 Constance Hill, *Jane Austen: Her Homes and Haunts* . . . (John Lane, London, 1923 edn; 1st pub. 1901). For the inventions of Englishness in this

period see Robert Colls and Philip Dodd (eds), *Englishness: Politics and Culture 1880–1920* (Croom Helm, Beckenham, 1986) and relevant chapters in Martin J. Wiener, *English Culture and the Decline of the Industrial Spirit 1850–1980* (Cambridge University Press, Cambridge, 1981). The Austen industry was stimulated by the heightened nostalgia for country life that developed around the turn of the century.

11 G.E. Mitton, *Jane Austen and Her Times* (Methuen & Co., London, 1905), p. 9. One of the later books to make the same claims is Mary Augusta Austen-Leigh, *Personal Aspects of Jane Austen* (John Murray, London, 1920), p. 59. For reception in general in this period see B.C. Southam (ed.), *Jane Austen: The Critical Heritage: Volume Two: 1870–1940* (Routledge & Kegan Paul, London, 1987). The first volume deals with the period before 1870.

12 Marilyn Butler, *Jane Austen and the War of Ideas* (Clarendon Press, Oxford, 1987 edn; 1st pub. 1975). This edition contains a useful Introduction, pp. ix–xlvi, that reviews Austen criticism between 1975 and *c.* 1987. For reasons of space I have had to overlook some of the other academic publications in 1975 such as D.D. Devlin, *Jane Austen and Education* (Macmillan, London, 1975). There were also collections of essays associated with the bicentennial: John Halperin (ed.), *Jane Austen: Bicentenary Essays* (Cambridge University Press, Cambridge, 1975) and Juliet McMaster (ed.), *Jane Austen's Achievement: Papers Delivered at the Jane Austen Bicentennial Conference at the University of Alberta 1975* (Macmillan, London, 1976). The December issue of *Nineteenth Century Fiction* was devoted to articles about Austen.

13 Alistair Duckworth, *The Improvement of the Estate: A Study of Jane Austen's Novels* (The Johns Hopkins University Press, Baltimore, MD 1971).

14 Raymond Williams, *The Country and the City* (Chatto & Windus, London, 1973), ch. 11.

15 *Illustrated London News*, 263, December 1975, pp. 53–5. Texts that have had to be excluded for reasons of space include BBC TV, 'Celebrating Jane Austen', transmitted on 18 December 1975 and reviewed by many national newspapers the following day. It included sequences shot in both Bath and Cheltenham.

16 Patrick Wright, *On Living in an Old Country: The National Past in Contemporary Britain* (Verso, London, 1991), p. 107.

17 For an example of this coverage see *Daily Telegraph*, 9 September 1989.

18 David Rhydderch, *Jane Austen: Her Life and Art* (Jonathan Cape, London, 1932), p. 208 and p. 116. He also distances the novels from their society whenever possible. Other books from this period that reproduce the Austen-Leigh version include G. Linklater Thomson, *Jane Austen: A Survey* (Horace Marshall & Son, London, 1929), although it has the merit of an interesting discussion of dramatic techniques in Austen's novels.

19 Lord David Cecil, *A Portrait of Jane Austen* (Penguin, Harmondsworth, 1986), p. 67.

20 For an example of a Cartland text that develops this theme see *The Disgraceful Duke* (Corgi, London, 1976).

21 I have not seen this series and am basing my brief remarks about it on the accompanying book, John Burke, *Prince Regent* (Fontana/Collins,

London, 1979). See also Harry Edgington, *Prince Regent: The Scandalous Private Life of George IV* (Hamlyn Paperbacks, Feltham, 1979).

22 Although it deals with a different historical period, see Sheila Jeffreys, *The Spinster and Her Enemies: Feminism and Sexuality 1880–1930* (Pandora, London, 1985), for the ways in which spinster can be used as a term of abuse rather than of affection.

23 In addition to *Persuasions*, which has carried some important feminist and historicist criticism, the North American Society has been associated with Joan Mason Hurley's play, *Our Particular Jane: A Piece of Theatre Based on the Life, Letters and Literature of Jane Austen* (A Room of One's Own Press, Victoria, British Columbia, 1975). This at least raised questions about gender that were usually lost in the English bicentennial celebrations. For a more sympathetic view of the English Society than I offer see Graham Handley, *Criticism in Focus: Jane Austen* (Bristol Classical Press, Bristol, 1992), pp. 6–9.

24 Patrick Wright, *On Living in an Old Country*, esp. 'The vagueness of Deep England', pp. 81–7 and p. 109 for the significance of 'green' in nostalgic texts.

25 Park Honan, *Jane Austen: Her Life* (Weidenfeld & Nicolson, London, 1987), p. 334.

26 Accounts of the classic serial in this period include Paul Kerr, ' Classic Serials – to be Continued', *Screen*, 23, 1982, pp. 6–19. Although this contains some good historical material, it makes the mistake of assuming that such programmes merely reproduced a Leavisite canon or great tradition. Accounts of filmic adaptations include Cairns Craig, 'Rooms Without a View', *Sight and Sound*, 1(ns.), 2, 1991, pp. 10–3. In addition to Wright's lively account, my thinking about writers and their heritage representations has been much influenced by Peter Widdowson, *Hardy in History: A Study in Literary Sociology* (Routledge, London, 1989).

27 For two good recent collections of essays that explore relationships between film/television and the political culture of the 1980s see Lester Friedman (ed.), *Fires Were Started: British Cinema and Thatcherism* (University of Minnesota Press, Minneapolis, 1993) and John Corner and Sylvia Harvey (eds), *Enterprise and Heritage: Crosscurrents of National Culture* (Routledge, London, 1991), esp. Tania Wollen, 'Over Our Shoulders: Nostalgic Screen Fictions for the 1980s', pp. 179–93. Some of the essays in both collections expand upon points made by Mike Poole, 'Englishness for Export', *Time Out*, 7 April 1980. I have not had room to consider the ways in which individual viewers can go against the grain and convert a classic serial into, say, a soap opera or a situation comedy. Much of the best recent academic work on television has concerned itself with audiences. For more details see David Morley, *Television, Audiences and Cultural Studies* (Routledge, London, 1992).

28 See Robert Giddings *et al.* (eds), *Screening the Novel: The Theory and Practice of Literary Dramatization* (Macmillan, Basingstoke, 1990), p. 168, for the way in which viewers inspect the detail of military uniforms. This uneven collection deals extensively with the 1987 BBC TV version of *Vanity Fair*, another Regency reproduction that could have been considered here.

29 Robert Hewison, *The Heritage Industry* (Methuen, London, 1987), p. 29.

For an example of the kind of coaching prints that are used to create the look of classic serials see N.C. Selway, *The Regency Road: The Coaching Prints of James Pollard* (Faber & Faber, London, 1957). For an example of a more general collection of prints see Reay Tannahill, *Regency England: The Great Age of the Colour Print* (The Folio Society, London, 1964).

30 For Gainsborough's use of costumes see Sue Harper, 'Art Direction and Costume Design', Sue Aspinall and Robert Murphy (eds), *Gainsborough Melodrama* (BFI, London, 1983), pp. 40–52, which suggests a more complicated relationship between past and present than I have had time to imply.

31 Andrew Higson, 'Re-presenting the National Past: Nostalgia and Pastiche in the Heritage Film', Lester Friedman (ed.), *Fires Were Started*, pp. 109–29. The theatre does not as a rule share this obsession with 'heritage space', allowing modern dramatists to provide more challenging representations of early nineteenth-century culture. Examples include Caryl Churchill, *Soft Cops*, first performed at the Barbican Pit on 2 January 1984, and Howard Brenton, *Bloody Poetry*, first performed at the Haymarket, Leicester on 1 October 1984.

32 Susan Watkins, *Jane Austen's Town and Country Style* (Thames & Hudson, London, 1990), p.84. This distasteful book relies far too heavily in parts on a much better one, Penelope Byrde, *A Frivolous Distinction: Fashion and Needlework in the Works of Jane Austen* (Bath City Council, 1981). Earlier examples of coffee-table books include Marghanita Laski, *Jane Austen and Her World* (Thames & Hudson, London, 1969).

33 Nigel Nicolson, *The World of Jane Austen* (Weidenfeld & Nicolson, London, 1991), pp. 169–70. For a more sensible account of Austen and buildings see Nikolaus Pevsner, 'The Architectural Setting of Jane Austen's Novels', *Journal of the Warburg and Courtauld Institutes*, 31, 1968, pp. 402–22.

34 Maggie Lane, *Jane Austen's England* (Robert Hale, London, 1986), p. 150. Georgian building is one of the subjects discussed in Don Cruikshank and Neil Burton, *Life in the Georgian City* (Viking, London, 1990).

35 Joanna Richardson, *The Regency* (Collins, London, 1973), p. 77. For a more recent and detailed celebration of Regency craftsmanship see Stephen Parissen, *Regency Style* (Phaidon, London, 1992).

36 *Pride and Prejudice: Jane Austen* (Macmillan Students' Edition, Basingstoke, 1982), illustration no. 2. Manydown also appeared in a number of the bicentennial texts, e.g. Marion Morrison, 'Jane Austen and Her Gardens', *Country Life*, 158, December 1975, pp. 1701–2.

37 Masterpiece Theatre began in the 1970–71 season as a result of the previous success of *The Forsyte Saga* on American television. See various volumes edited by Larry James Gianakos as well as Alistair Cook, *Masterpieces: A Decade of Classics on Television* (Bodley Head, London, 1982) for details of programmes transmitted. See Spencer Golub, 'Spies in the House of Quality', Peter Reynolds (ed.), *Novel Images: Literature in Performance* (Routledge, London, 1993), pp. 139–56, for the American reception of *Brideshead Revisited*.

38 For a discussion of Austen's class see, amongst others, Terry Lovell, 'Jane Austen and Gentry Society', *Literature, Society and the Sociology of Literature: Proceedings of the Conference Held at the University of Essex July 1976* (University of Essex, 1977), pp. 118–32.

39 Ian Ousby, *The Englishman's England: Taste, Travel and the Rise of Tourism* (Cambridge University Press, Cambridge, 1990). For two important accounts of the wider cultural contexts for these developments see Neil McKendrick *et al.*, *The Birth of a Consumer Society: The Commercialisation of Eighteenth-Century England* (Europa, London, 1982) and Roy Porter, *English Society in the Eighteenth Century* (Penguin, Harmondsworth, 1992 edn).

40 *Novels by Miss Austen, Complete in Five Volumes* (Richard Bentley, London, 1833), 5, 1, p. xv. For silver-fork writings see Alison Adburgham, *Silver Fork Society: Fashionable Life and Literature from 1814 to 1840* (Constable, London, 1983) and Carol L. Bernstein, *The Celebration of Scandal: Toward the Sublime in Victorian Urban Fiction* (The Pennsylvania State University Press, University Park, 1991), ch. 3.

41 Monica Lauritzen, *Jane Austen's Emma on Television: A Study of a BBC Classic Serial* (Acta Universitatis Gothoburgensis, Göteborg, 1981), pp. 114–15. The edition of the novel that was published to coincide with the serial, *Emma* (Panther, London, 1972), reproduces a number of Austen-Leigh's assumptions about his aunt in its editorial matter.

42 Weldon dramatised some of the themes of *Letters to Alice on First Reading Jane Austen* (Coronet, London, 1984) in a television programme entitled 'England's Jane', first transmitted in the Channel Four *J'Accuse* series and repeated on cable television, TLC: The Learning Channel, 2 January 1993. This contains useful commentary on the growth of the Austen industry by both Marilyn Butler and John Lucas, author of *England and Englishness: Ideas of Nationhood in English Poetry 1688–1900* (The Hogarth Press, London, 1990). Weldon's position is more complex. She acknowledges her associations with the Austen industry through the adaptation of *Pride and Prejudice* and yet uses some of the letters to call its assumptions into question. She still believes nevertheless that Austen hardly ever wrote about political themes, defined both narrowly and more generally, and thus reproduces important parts of the Austen-Leigh version while offering a critique of it.

2 THE LETTERS: KEEPING AND LOSING HER COUNTENANCE

1 Details from Introduction, Jo Modert (ed.), *Jane Austen's Manuscript Letters in Facsimile: Reproductions of Every Known Extant Letter, Fragment and Autograph Copy* ... (Southern Illinois University Press, Carbondale and Edwardsville, 1990). For the more conventional view of Cassandra's editing see, amongst others, Helen Ashton and Katharine Davies, *I Had a Sister: A Study of Mary Lamb, Dorothy Wordsworth, Caroline Herschel, Cassandra Austen* (Lovat Dickson, London, 1937).

2 R.W. Chapman (ed.), with an Introduction by Marilyn Butler, *Jane Austen: Selected Letters 1796–1817* (Oxford University Press, Oxford, 1985), p. xxvii. The letters are given the 'heritage' treatment in a more recent selected edition that is lavishly illustrated, Penelope Hughes-Hallett (ed.), *Jane Austen: 'My Dear Cassandra'* (Collins and Brown, London, 1990).

3 Warren Roberts, *Jane Austen and the French Revolution* (Macmillan, London, 1979), p. 114. He deals extensively with a letter from 1805 that

refers to an invasion scare, pp. 80–7, which provides another example of the topicality of the letters as a whole.

4 Joseph Kestner, 'The *Letters* of Jane Austen: The Writer as Emetteur/Récepteur', *Papers in Language and Literature*, 14, 1978, pp. 249–68, p. 259 and James Thompson, *Between Self and World: The Novels of Jane Austen* (The Pennsylvania State University Press, University Park, 1988), p. 123. Other studies of the letters include Frank Bradbrook, 'The Letters of Jane Austen', *Cambridge Journal*, 7, 1953–54, pp. 259–76 and Suzanne Juhasz, 'Bonnets and Balls: Reading Jane Austen's Letters', *Centennial Review*, 31, 1987, pp. 84–104, which considers the ways in which Jane creates bonds of intimacy with Cassandra. On this theme see also Park Honan, *Jane Austen: Her Life* (Weidenfeld & Nicolson, London, 1987), p. 124. For a neglected account that uses the letters to argue against Austen-Leigh's version of his aunt see Kathleen Freeman, *T'Other Miss Austen* (Macdonald, London, 1956). For studies that provide useful contexts even though they do not deal with Austen's letters themselves see Ruth Perry, *Women, Letters and the Novel* (AMS Press, Inc., New York, 1980) and Judy Simon, *Diaries and Journals of Literary Women from Fanny Burney to Virginia Woolf* (Macmillan, Basingstoke, 1990).

5 For further details see A. Aspinall (ed.), *Mrs Jordan and Her Family: Being the Unpublished Correspondence of Mrs Jordan and the Duke of Clarence* . . . (Arthur Barker, London, 1951), p. 115 and p. 127. Biographies of Jordan include Brian Fothergill, *Mrs Jordan: Portrait of an Actress* (Faber & Faber, London, 1965).

6 Betty T. Bennett (ed.), *The Letters of Mary Wollstonecraft Shelley* (The Johns Hopkins University Press, Baltimore, MD, 1980/3/8), 3, 1, p. 495.

7 D.W. Harding, 'Regulated Hatred: An Aspect of the Work of Jane Austen', *Scrutiny*, 8, 1940, pp. 346–62.

8 A. Aspinall (ed.), *Letters of the Princess Charlotte 1811–1817* (Home & Van Thal, London, 1949), esp. many of the earlier letters.

9 Mary A. Favret, *Romantic Correspondence: Women, Politics and the Fiction of Letters* (Cambridge University Press, Cambridge, 1993). I regret only being able to read this important study after much of my own work had been completed.

10 R. Brimley Johnson (ed.), *The Letters of Lady Louisa Stuart* (Bodley Head, London, 1926), p. 155. This edition contains an interesting letter on the Cato Street Conspiracy of 1820, pp. 177–82, and a definition of quizzing, pp. 199–201.

11 Oswald G. Knapp (ed.), *The Intimate Letters of Hester Piozzi and Penelope Pennington 1788–1822* (Bodley Head, London, 1914), p. 234. She is sometimes better known as Hester Thrale.

12 J.A. Doyle (ed.), *Memoir and Correspondence of Susan Ferrier 1782–1854* (Everleigh, Nash & Grayson, London, 1929), p. 66.

13 Countess of Ilchester and Lord Stavordale (eds), *The Life and Letters of Lady Sarah Lennox, 1745–1826* . . ., (John Murray, London, 1901), 2, 2, p. 50.

14 Hon. Mrs Hugh Wyndham (ed.), *Correspondence of Sarah Spencer, Lady Lyttleton, 1787–1870* (John Murray, London, 1912), p. 25. Spencer's earlier letters before her marriage are particularly interesting and deserve to be more accessible.

15 Historical accounts that deal with the Post Office in this period include: Brian Austen, *English Provincial Posts 1633–1840: A Study Based on Kent Examples* (Phillimore, London, 1978); M.J. Daunton, *The Royal Mail: The Post Office since 1840* (Athlone Press, London, 1985); G.F. Dendy Marshall, *The British Post Office from its Beginnings to the End of 1925* (Oxford University Press, Oxford, 1926); Keith Ellis, *The Post Office in the Eighteenth Century: A Study in Administrative History* (Oxford University Press, London, 1958); and Howard Robinson, *The British Post Office: A History* (Princeton University Press, Princeton, NJ, 1948).

16 Ellen Weeton, *Miss Weeton's Journal of a Governess* (David & Charles Reprints, Newton Abbot, 1969), 2, 1, p. 50. Although it deals with a later period, Mary Poovey writes well on the ambiguous social status of the governess, 'The Anathematized Race: The Governess and *Jane Eyre*', *Uneven Developments: The Ideological Work of Gender in Mid-Victorian England* (Virago, London, 1989). Ch. 2, Joseph Litvak, *Caught in the Act: Theatricality in the Nineteenth-Century English Novel* (University of California Press, Berkeley, 1992), considers the governess's role in *Jane Eyre* as a theatrical one.

17 Weeton, *Journal*, I, p. 237.

18 Weeton, *Journal*, I, pp. 299–300.

19 *Mrs Jordan and Her Family*, pp. 188–9.

20 James Fordyce, *Sermons to Young Women in Two Volumes* (A. Miller and T. Cadell, London, 1766), 2, 1, p. 59 and p. 103. Alison G. Sulloway, *Jane Austen and the Province of Womanhood* (University of Pennsylvania Press, Philadelphia, 1989), esp. ch. 1, deals well with the contradictions contained in conduct manuals.

21 John Gregory, *A Father's Legacy to His Daughters* (John Colles, Dublin, 1774), p. 14.

22 Castilia Countess Granville (ed.), *Lord Granville Leveson Gower (First Earl Granville) Private Correspondence 1781–1821* (John Murray, London, 1961), 2, 2, p. 352. For a gushing but also rather coy biography of Lady Bessborough see Ethel Colburn Mayne, *A Regency Chapter: Lady Bessborough and Her Friendships* (Macmillan, London, 1939).

23 Ruth Richardson, *Death, Dissection and the Destitute* (Penguin, Harmondsworth, 1989), pp. 61–2 and pp. 66–8. This is one of the best recent accounts of early nineteenth-century social history which clearly challenges ideas of it as an age of elegance.

24 Sulloway, *The Province of Womanhood*, p. 103.

25 *Correspondence of Sarah Spencer*, p. 37.

26 *Leveson Gower . . . Private Correspondence*, 2, p. 409.

27 James Thompson, *Between Self and World*, p. 28. Sulloway, *The Province of Womanhood*, p. 20, also sees the letters as revealing Austen's impoverished rather than elegant background.

28 *Correspondence of Sarah Spencer*, pp. 39–40.

29 Lady Theresa Lewis (ed.), *Extracts of the Journals and Correspondence of Miss Berry from the Year 1783 to 1852* (Longmans, Green & Co., London, 1865), 3, 2, p. 471.

30 H. W. Garrod, 'Jane Austen: A Depreciation', *Essays by Divers Hands* (Royal Society of Literature, London, 1928), pp. 21–40.

31 E. M. Forster, *Abinger Harvest* (Edward Arnold, London, 1936), p. 156.

32 *Life and Letters of Lady Sarah Lennox*, 2, p. 249.
33 Joan Jacobs Brumberg, *Fasting Girls: The Emergence of Anorexia Nervosa as a Modern Disease* (Harvard University Press, Cambridge, MA, 1988), p. 56. The pamphlet literature includes: *An Account of the Extraordinary Abstinence of Ann Moor, of Tutbury, Staffordshire . . .* (R. Richards, Uttoxeter, 1809); *A Faithful Relation of Ann Moore . . .* (G. Wilkins, Derby, 1810) and *An Examination of the Imposture of Ann Moore, Called the Fasting Woman of Tutbury . . .* (Underwood and Black, London, 1813). See also *Medical and Physical Journal*, 19, 1813, pp. 111–12.
34 John Halperin, *The Life of Jane Austen* (Harvester Press, Brighton, 1984), pp. 62–3, 144–50, 229–30 and 256–7 for more details. One of the merits of the biography is that it is aware of the problematic nature of Austen's resolutions.
35 For Wollstonecraft's critique of conduct literature see Miriam Kramnick (ed.), *Wollstonecraft: Vindication of the Rights of Woman* (Penguin, Harmondsworth, 1978), esp. pp. 191–201. Austen's *Pride and Prejudice* also contains a critique of Fordyce's *Sermons*. Mr Collins tries to read from it, only to be interrupted by Lydia Bennet's gossip. He is the personification of Fordyce during the proposal scene with Elizabeth.
36 One of the most important recent studies of the cult of the dying/dead woman is Elizabeth Bronfen, *Over Her Dead Body: Death, Femininity and the Aesthetic* (Manchester University Press, Manchester, 1992), which I am very grateful to have had the opportunity of reading before it was published. There is a brief, but nevertheless well-informed, survey of sickness and death in Meenahski Mukherjee, *Jane Austen* (Macmillan, Basingstoke, 1991), pp. 6–10. Chs 2, 6 and 7 of Janet Todd, *Gender, Art and Death* (Polity Press, Cambridge, 1993), are also relevant.
37 *Life and Letters of Lady Sarah Lennox*, 2, p. 52.

3 THE PRINCE, THE DANDY AND THE CRISIS

1 For more details of the first Regency Crisis see John W. Derry, *The Regency Crisis and the Whigs 1788–9* (Cambridge University Press, Cambridge, 1963).
2 Ida Macalpine and Richard Hunter argue the case for porphyria, *George III and the Mad-Business* (Pimlico, London, 1991; 1st pub. 1969). See also Charles Chenevix Trench, *The Royal Malady* (Longman, London, 1964). Alan Bennett's play, *The Madness of George III*, first performed at the National Theatre on 28 November 1991, offers a representation of Willis's methods. Roy Porter, *A Social History of Madness: Stories of the Insane* (Weidenfeld & Nicolson, 1989), esp. ch. 3, is essential reading on ideas of madness in this period, as is one of his earlier books, *Mind-Forg'd Manacles: A History of Madness in England from the Restoration to the Regency* (Athlone Press, London, 1987). Other studies include Andrew T. Scull, *The Most Solitary of Afflictions: Madness and Society in Britain 1700–1990* (Yale University Press, New Haven, CT, 1993).
3 Nowell C. Smith (ed.), *Selected Letters of Sidney Smith* (Oxford University Press, Oxford, 1981), p. 59. He noticed that the Regent, usually only too happy to confide in almost anyone, became very reserved during the early phases of the Regency.

4 Castilia Countess Granville (ed), *Lord Granville Leveson Gower (First Earl Granville) Private Correspondence 1781–1821* (John Murray, London, 1961), 2, pp. 374–5.
5 *Hansard*, 18, p. 324, from a speech delivered on 20 December 1810.
6 Spencer Perceval Papers, Cambridge University Library Manuscripts, Add. 8713, 10, f.20. See also f.15 and f.18 for similar statements. Owen Hedley's biography, *Queen Charlotte* (John Murray, London, 1975), is not an illuminating one.
7 A. Aspinall (ed.), *Letters of the Princess Charlotte 1811–1817* (Home & Van Thal, London, 1949), p. 23. Similar views are expressed in an earlier letter, p. 21.
8 A. Aspinall (ed.), *Mrs. Jordan and Her Family* (Arthur Barker, London, 1951), p. 190.
9 As quoted in The Duke of Buckingham and Chandos, *Memoirs of the Court of England during the Regency 1811–1820 . . .* (Hurst and Blackett, London, 1856), 2, 1, p. 373. For more details about Horner see his *Memoirs: with Selections from His Correspondence* (Chambers, Edinburgh, 1849).
10 Hon. Mrs. Hugh Wyndham (ed.), *Correspondence of Sarah Spencer, Lady Lyttleton, 1787–1870* (John Murray, London, 1912), pp. 103–4. Although the Prince became particularly associated with his extravagant residences, Linda Colley is right to emphasise that his father was also involved in an extensive building programme, 'The Apotheosis of George III: Loyalty, Royalty and the British Nation 1760–1820', *Past and Present*, 1984, pp. 94–129.
11 Wilfred S. Dowden (ed.), *The Letters of Thomas Moore* (Clarendon Press, Oxford, 1964), 2, 1, pp. 152–3.
12 A.D. Harvey, *Britain in the Early Nineteenth Century* (Batsford, London, 1978), p. 286. The earlier chapters of his *Collision of Empires: Britain in Three World Wars* (Hambledon, London, 1992) deal with the impact of the Napoleonic wars on Regency society.
13 *Hansard*, 15, p. 191, from a speech delivered on 26 January 1810.
14 For a full study of the expedition see Gordon C. Bond, *The Grand Expedition: The British Invasion of Holland in 1809* (University of Georgia Press, Athens, 1979). Michael Roberts, *The Whig Party 1807–1812* (Frank Cass, London, 1965), is one of the books that considers the impact of the expedition on domestic politics. For divisions amongst the Whigs on this and other issues see also E.A. Smith, *Lord Grey 1764- 1845* (Clarendon Press, Oxford, 1990).
15 See Christopher D. Hall, *British Strategy in the Napoleonic War 1803–15* (Manchester University Press, Manchester, 1992) for an overview of military history and, amongst others, Carola Oman, *Sir John Moore* (Hodder & Stoughton, London, 1953) for specific details on the Corunna campaign.
16 *Correspondence of Sarah Spencer*, p. 77.
17 As quoted in E.P. Thompson, *The Making of the English Working Class* (Penguin, Harmondsworth, 1968), p. 605. Other accounts of Luddism include: F.O. Darvall, *Popular Disturbances and Public Order in Regency England: Being an Account of the Luddite and other Disorders in England during the Years 1811–1817 . . .* (Oxford University Press, Oxford, 1934); J. Dinwiddy, 'Luddism and Politics in the Northern Counties', *Social History*,

4, 1979, pp. 33–63; and Malcolm I. Thomis, *The Luddites: Machine Breaking in Regency England* (David & Charles, Newton Abbot, 1970). As I discuss cross-dressing later on, it is worth mentioning that Thomis refers, p. 22, to a crowd in Stockport that was led by two men dressed as women.

18 Home Office Papers, HO/40/1, f.11, from a letter dated 16 April 1812. I deal in some detail with carnivalesque forms of popular protest in the second part of my *English Literature in History 1780–1830: Pastoral and Politics* (Hutchinson, London, 1983).

19 As quoted by E.P. Thompson, *The Making of the English Working Class*, p. 658.

20 *Report of Proceeding under Commissions of Oyer & Terminer and Gaol Delivery for the County of York, Held at the Castle of York* . . . (Luke Hansard & Sons, London, 1813), p. 2 and p. 73.

21 The full trial is printed in Thomas Jones Howell (ed.), *A Complete Collection of State Trials and Proceedings for High Treason and other Crimes and Misdemeanors* . . . (T.C. Hansard, London, 1823), 31, pp. 335–68. It was the proprietor, James Perry, who was tried.

22 Drakard's trial is also printed in *State Trials*, 31, pp. 495–544. See J.R. Dinwiddy, 'The Early Nineteenth-Century Campaign Against Flogging in the Army', *English Historical Review*, 1982, 97, pp. 308–31 for a useful study of the background to these trials.

23 *Cobbett's Weekly Political Register*, 1 July 1809, col. 993. Michel Foucault, *Discipline and Punish: The Birth of the Prison* (Penguin, Harmondsworth, 1977), trans. Alan Sheridan, suggests that spectators did not always collude in public punishments. I discuss Foucault's ideas in some detail in my *Christopher Marlowe* (Macmillan, Basingstoke, 1992). For the culture of crime and punishment more generally see Peter Linebaugh, *The London Hanged: Crime and Civil Society in the Eighteenth Century* (Penguin, Harmondsworth, 1993) and Philip Rawlings, *Drunks, Whores and Idle Apprentices: Criminal Biographies of the Eighteenth Century* (Routledge, London, 1992).

24 For brief accounts of Robinson's literary career see Alice Browne, *The Eighteenth-Century Feminist Mind* (Harvester Press, Brighton, 1987), p. 168 and Janet Todd, *The Sign of Angellica: Women, Writing and Fiction 1660–1800* (Virago, London, 1989), p. 223. There is also a good entry by Margaret Maison in Janet Todd (ed.), *Dictionary of British Women Writers* (Routledge, London, 1991), pp. 575–8. Robinson's autobiography, which was published posthumously in 1801, *Memoirs of the Late Mrs. Robinson by Herself* (Cobden-Sanderson, London, 1930 edn), breaks off just before her relationship with the Prince began in earnest. She is the heroine of Jean Plaidy, *Perdita's Prince* (Robert Hale, London, 1969).

25 Chifney published an autobiography, *Genius Genuine by Samuel Chifney of Newmarket* (Skury, Berwick Street, 1804), expensively priced at five pounds, to vindicate both himself and the Prince.

26 As quoted in W.H. Wilkins, *Mrs Fitzherbert and George IV* (Longmans, Green & Co., London, 1905), 2, 1, p. 137. For more details about Fitzherbert see Shane Leslie, *Mrs Fitzherbert: A Life Chiefly from Unpublished Sources* (Burns Oates, London, 1939). I found Christopher Hibbert's biography of the Prince, *George IV* (Penguin, Harmondsworth, 1976), invaluable. See also Alan Palmer, *The Life and Times of George IV*

(Weidenfeld & Nicolson, London, 1972). The process by which the monarchy largely distanced itself from scandal in the Victorian period is discussed by David Cannadine, 'The Context, Performance and Meaning of Ritual: The British Monarchy and the "Invention of Tradition"', Eric Hobsbawm and Terence Ranger (eds), *The Invention of Tradition* (Cambridge University Press, Cambridge, 1983), pp. 101–64. The 1990s have seen the monarchy increasingly associated once again with a number of sexual scandals, some of which have at least a Regency flavour.

27　*Leveson Gower . . . Private Correspondence*, 2, p. 349.

28　Lord Stavordale (ed.), Henry Richard Vassall, Third Lord Holland, *Further Memoirs of the Whig Party 1807–1821 . . .* (John Murray, London, 1905), p.27. There is an erratic biography of Clarke by Paul Berry, *By Royal Appointment: A Biography of Mary Ann Clarke Mistress of the Duke of York* (Femina Books, London, 1970). She needs to be taken more seriously as a writer.

29　For more details about the Vere Street affair see Rictor Norton, *Mother Clap's Molly House: The Gay Subculture in England 1700–1830* (GMP, London, 1992), ch. 12. An earlier study that deals with homosexuality in this period, Jeffrey Weeks, *Sex, Politics and Society: The Regulation of Sexuality since 1800* (Longman, London, 1981), stresses the heightening of anxieties about it during the war. This is also the subject of a number of articles such as Arthur N. Gilbert, 'Sexual Deviance and Disaster during the Napoleonic Wars', *Albion*, 9, 1977, pp. 98–113 and A.D. Harvey, 'Prosecutions for Sodomy in England at the Beginning of the Nineteenth Century', *Historical Journal*, 21, 1978, pp. 939–48. Austen alludes to homosexual practices at the end of 'The History of England' in a 'Sharade', or riddle, about James I's relationship with his favourite, or pet, Robert Carr. The King is described as 'of that amiable disposition which inclines to Freindships, & in such points was possessed of a keener penetration in Discovering Merit than many other people'. The riddle of the carpet is: 'My first is what my second was to King James the Ist, and you tread on my whole' (MW, pp. 147–8).

30　As quoted by Park Honan, *Jane Austen: Her Life* (Weidenfeld & Nicolson, London, 1987), p. 160.

31　I deal with the various investigations into Caroline's 'private' life as well as her trial in 1820 in *English Literature in History 1780–1830*, pp. 178–86. There is a more sustained reading of some of the implications of the trial by Anna Clark, 'Queen Caroline and the Sexual Politics of Popular Culture in London: 1820', *Representations*, 31, 1990, pp. 47–68.

32　*The Annual Register*, 1814, Chronicle, p. 46. See pp. 46–55 for further details of the festivities.

33　*History of the Regency and Reign of King George IV* (Cobbett, London, 1830–34), 2, 1, ch. 5., para. 281. Given Cobbett's personal dislike of the Regent, his writing in these two volumes is surprisingly flat. There are jibes at the animalistic pursuit of pleasure and yet the satire is never fully developed.

34　Thomas Cross, *The Autobiography of a Stage Coachman* (Kegan Paul, Trench, Trubner & Co., London, 1904), 2, 1, p. 167. This provides some support for the argument developed later on that war was an industry and Portsmouth one of its shock cities. Cross had served as a midshipman in the navy, although his account of his experiences is not a particularly revealing one.

35 For more details about Manchester at this time see John Bohstedt, *Riots and Community Politics in England and Wales 1790–1810* (Harvard University Press, Cambridge, MA, 1983), ch. 3.

36 D.B. Wyndham Lewis (trans.), *The Anatomy of Dandyism, with some Observations on Beau Brummell; Translated from the French of Barbey D'Aurevilly* (Peter Davies, London, 1928; 1st pub. 1845), p. 10.

37 J.B. Priestley, *The Prince of Pleasure and His Regency 1811–20* (Sphere, London, 1971), p. 47.

38 Ellen Moers, *The Dandy: From Brummell to Beerbohm* (University of Nebraska Press, Lincoln, 1978), which remains the best study of Regency dandyism. The 1954 MGM film *Beau Brummell* smooths over these contradictions by allowing its hero, played by Stewart Granger, to embody democratic principles in a much more obvious way. It also imposes classical Hollywood conventions on the enigma of his sexuality by allowing his relationship with Lady Patricia, played by Elizabeth Taylor, to hold the centre of the stage. His decline and fall are gentled. He dies in Calais of what appears to be a very mild form of consumption after he has been reconciled with the Prince Regent. The film is nevertheless quite perceptive in the connections it makes between dandyism and gambling.

39 W.E. Henley and R.L. Stevenson, *Beau Austin* (R.R. Clark, Edinburgh, 1884), p. 4.

40 Virginia Woolf, *Beau Brummell* (Rimington & Hooper, New York, 1930), p. 4.

41 Captain Jesse, *The Life of Beau Brummell* (privately printed for Subscribers, London, ND; 1st pub. 1844), 2, 2, pp. 57–8. Jesse only met Brummell at Caen in 1830 and is generally regarded as being more accurate on this part of his life. D'Aurevilly was interested in capturing as elegantly and succinctly as possible the essence of dandyism and accused Jesse, with justification, of padding out his volumes. For a modern biography see Hubert Cole, *Beau Brummell* (Granada, London, 1977). There are large numbers of later nineteenth-century writers who include the almost obligatory anecdotes about Brummell in their memoirs. See for examples Captain Gronow, *The Reminiscences and Recollections of Captain Gronow . . .* (R.S. Surtees Society, Frome, 1984; 1st pub. 1860) and William Pitt Lennox, *Fashion Then and Now . . .* (Chapman and Hall, London, 1978), 2. Twentieth-century studies include: Kathleen Campbell, *Beau Brummell: A Biographical Study* (Hammond, Hammond & Co., London, 1948); E. Beresford Chancellor, *Life in Regency and Early Victorian Times: An Account of the Days of Brummell and D'Orsay* (Batsford, London, 1927); Françoise Coblence, *Le Dandysme, Obligation D'Incertitude* (Presses Universitaires de France, Paris, 1988); Willard Connely, *The Reign of Beau Brummell* (Cassell, London, 1940); Carlo Maria Franzero, *The Life and Times of Beau Brummell* (Alvin Redman, London, 1958); James Laver, *Dandies* (Weidenfeld & Nicolson, London, 1968); Roger Boutet de Monvel, *Beau Brummell and His Times with a Chapter on Dress and the Dandies by Mary Craven* (Everleigh Nash, London, 1908); Lewis Melville, *The Beaux of the Regency* (Hutchinson, London, 1908) and *Beau Brummell: His Life and Letters* (Hutchinson, London, 1924); Richard Pine, *The Dandy and the Herald: Manners, Mind and Morals from Brummell to Durrell* (Macmillan,

Basingstoke, 1988) and Keith B. Poole, *The Two Beaux* (EP Publishing, Wakefield, 1976). Brummell is also discussed in ch. 4. of Donald A. Low, *That Sunny Dome: A Portrait of Regency England* (Dent, London, 1977), a book that deserves to be much better known because it also attempts a short reading of Austen as a Regency writer. A great many books on style contain passing references to Brummell. See for example Mark Booth, *Camp* (Quartet, London, 1983), p. 20. Although I follow Moers in distinguishing the dandies of the Regency from those of later periods, I still found Regenia Gagnier, *Idylls of the Marketplace: Oscar Wilde and the Victorian Public* (Scolar Press, Aldershot, 1987), particularly useful. As far as Austen criticism is concerned, my argument is that those who have written on the male characters have not researched masculine identities in this period in enough detail. See for examples Jane Miller, *Women Writing About Men* (Virago, London, 1986) and Judith Wilt, 'Jane Austen's Men: Inside/Outside "the Mystery"', Janet Todd (ed.), *Men by Women* (Holmes & Meier Publishers, Inc., New York, 1981), pp. 59–76.

42 Jesse, *The Life of Beau Brummell*, 2, p. 60.

43 The Regency underworld is the subject of another good book by Donald A. Low, *Thieves' Kitchen: The Regency Underworld* (J.M. Dent & Sons, London, 1982). I deal with underworld themes in 'Pierce Egan and the Representation of London', Philip W. Martin and Robin Jarvis (eds), *Reviewing Romanticism* (Macmillan, Basingstoke, 1992), pp. 154–69. See also J.C. Reid, *Bucks and Bruisers: Pierce Egan and Regency England* (Routledge & Kegan Paul, London, 1971).

44 For more details on Heyer see Helen Hughes, *The Historical Romance* (Routledge, London, 1993) and Jane Aiken Hodge, *The Private World of Georgette Heyer* (Pan, London, 1985).

45 As quoted in Lewis Melville, *Brighton: Its History, Its Follies and Its Fashions* (Chapman and Hall, London, 1909), p. 73.

46 'Brummelliana', Jon Cook (ed.), *William Hazlitt: Selected Writings* (Oxford University Press, Oxford, 1991), pp. 158–62, p. 158.

47 Jesse, *The Life of Beau Brummell*, 1, p. 280.

48 For an example of how one hostess responded to Brummell's unpredictable movements see Hon. F. Leveson Gower (ed.), *Letters of Harriet Countess Granville 1810–1845* (Longmans, Green & Co., London, 1894), 2, 1, p. 40.

49 *Harriette Wilson's Memoirs of Herself and Others* (Peter Davies, London, 1930), p. 41. For biographical details see Angela Thirkell, *The Fortunes of Harriette: The Surprising Career of Harriette Wilson* (Hamish Hamilton, London, 1936). The *Memoirs*, a scandalous bestseller when first published in 1825, deserve more attention as a literary text.

50 Peter Quennell (ed.), *The Journal of Thomas Moore 1818–1841* (Batsford, London, 1964), p. 232. The entry is dated 1 July 1837.

51 Harriet Raikes (ed.), *Private Correspondence of Thomas Raikes with the Duke of Wellington and other Distinguished Contemporaries* (Richard Bentley, London, 1861), p. 86.

52 Jesse, *The Life of Beau Brummell*, 2, pp. 243–4

53 T.A.J. Burnett, *The Rise and Fall of a Regency Dandy: The Life and Times of Scrope Berdmore Davies* (Oxford University Press, Oxford, 1983), p. 150. Although I disagree with Burnett's reading of Austen, I found his study of dandyism compelling.

54 Kate Fullbrook, 'Jane Austen and the Comic Negative', Sue Roe (ed.), *Women Reading Women's Writing* (Harvester Press, Brighton, 1987), pp. 39–57, p. 41.

4 *MANSFIELD PARK*: THE REGENCY CRISIS AND THE THEATRE

1 J. Steven Watson, *The Reign of George III 1760–1815* (Clarendon Press, Oxford, 1960), p. 549.

2 Q.D. Leavis, 'A Critical Theory of Jane Austen's Writings: Lady Susan into *Mansfield Park*', *Scrutiny*, 10, 1941–42, pp. 114–42 and 272–94. These are preceded by 'A Critical Theory of Jane Austen's Writings', pp. 61–87.

3 Mary Evans, *Jane Austen and the State* (Tavistock Publications, London, 1987). Evans, a sociologist, writes perceptively about the family as institution and how it perpetuates itself through the transference of property. Austen's marginality is seen as producing her radical moral stance on the family, property and related issues. The account nevertheless is marred by occasional confusions between the Regency and Victorian periods.

4 Miriam Kramnick (ed.), *Wollstonecraft: Vindication of the Rights of Woman* (Penguin, Harmondsworth, 1978), p. 244.

5 Edgell Rickword (ed.), *Radical Squibs & Loyal Ripostes: Satirical Pamphlets of the Regency Period 1819–1821 . . .* (Adams & Dart, Bath, 1971), p. 47. For more details on Hone see Olivia Smith, *The Politics of Language 1791–1819* (Clarendon Press, Oxford, 1984) and my forthcoming essay, 'Poor Relations: Writing in the Working Class'.

6 Julia Prewitt Brown, *Jane Austen's Novels: Social Change and Literary Form* (Harvard University Press, Cambridge, MA, 1979), p. 84.

7 R.W. Chapman (ed.), *The Novels of Jane Austen* (Oxford University Press, Oxford, 1934), 5, 3, pp. 553–6 and Avrom Fleishman, *A Reading of Mansfield Park: An Essay in Critical Synthesis* (University of Minnesota Press, Minneapolis, 1967), pp. 91–2.

8 Colonisation is discussed in Moira Ferguson, 'Mansfield Park: Slavery, Colonialism and Gender', *The Oxford Literary Review*, 13, 1991, pp. 118–39 and less academically in Selma James, *The Ladies and the Mammies* (Falling Wall Press, Bristol, 1983). My note 22 deals with Edward Said's views. Monk Lewis's account of the West Indies might interest those wishing to do more work on this topic. See Mona Wilson (ed.), *M.G. Lewis: Journal of a West Indian Proprietor 1815–17* (George Routledge & Sons, London, 1929).

9 Warren Roberts, *Jane Austen and the French Revolution* (Macmillan, London, 1979), esp. pp. 97–100.

10 Raymond Williams, *The Country and the City* (Chatto & Windus, London, 1973), p. 114. Williams's basic thesis that Austen only represents one class does not register the wide social distance between the aristocratic Mr Yates and the lower-middle-class Price family. He is also being too simplistic when he places Austen and Cobbett on different sides of the park railings. Without wishing to minimise obvious differences, there are also certain similarities in their satires on the Regent and watering places. Williams's interest in economic and social structures is shared by R.S. Neale, 'Zapp Zapped: Property and Alienation in *Mansfield Park*', *Writing Marxist*

History: British Society, Economy and Culture since 1700 (Basil Blackwell, Oxford, 1985), pp. 87–108.

11 Claudia Johnson, *Jane Austen: Women, Politics and the Novel* (University of Chicago Press, Chicago, 1989), which also contains an excellent study of *Emma*. Austen's endings are also discussed in theoretical rather than historical terms in D.A. Miller, *Narrative and Its Discontents: Problems of Closure in the Traditional Novel* (Princeton University Press, Princeton, NJ, 1981), chs 1 and 2. See also Angela Leighton, 'Sense and Silences: Reading Jane Austen again', in Janet Todd (ed.) *Jane Austen: New Perspectives* (Holmes & Meier Publishers Inc., New York, 1983), pp.128–42, for a very good account of problems caused by the ending of *Sense and Sensibility*.

12 Sandra M. Gilbert and Susan Gubar, *The Madwoman in the Attic: The Woman Writer and the Nineteenth-Century Literary Imagination* (Yale University Press, New Haven, CT, 1979). I ought to have made it clearer that this contains one of the pioneering accounts of the significance of the Juvenilia.

13 In addition to the works already cited see Jane Spencer, *The Rise of the Woman Novelist from Aphra Behn to Jane Austen* (Basil Blackwell, Oxford, 1986) and Dale Spender, *Mothers of the Novel: 100 Good Women Writers Before Jane Austen* (Pandora, London, 1986).

14 W.A. Craik, *Jane Austen: The Six Novels* (Methuen, London, 1965), p. 103; Tony Tanner, *Jane Austen* (Macmillan, Basingstoke, 1986), pp. 164–5 and D.D. Devlin, *Jane Austen and Education* (Macmillan, London, 1975), p. 93.

15 Emily J. Climenson (ed.), *Passages from the Diaries of Mrs. Philip Lybbe Powys of Hardwick House, Oxon., AD 1756 to 1808* (Longmans, Green & Co., London, 1899), p. 347. The expansion of Margate is discussed by John Whyman, 'A Hanoverian Watering Place: Margate before the Railway', Alan Everitt (ed.), *Perspectives in English Urban History* (Macmillan, Basingstoke, 1973), pp. 138–60. I have also consulted a number of Regency guidebooks. For a wider perspective see John K. Walton, *The English Seaside Resort 1750–1914: A Social History* (Leicester University Press, Leicester, 1983).

16 Marylea Meyershon, 'What Fanny Knew: A Quiet Auditor of the Whole', Todd (ed.), *New Perspectives*, pp. 224–30.

17 Johnson, *Women, Politics and the Novel*, pp. 224–30.

18 Isobel Armstrong, *Jane Austen: Mansfield Park* (Penguin, Harmondsworth, 1988), which provides students with the best introduction to the novel.

19 As stated in the Introduction, I am not concerned with pointing out each and every time my readings differ from those offered by the Austen industry, choosing instead to relate them to debates in literary criticism and social history. Nevertheless I want to make an exception to this rule here. Peggy Hickman declares that Austen 'lived in an age when there was much heavy drinking, but in all her major novels except *Sense and Sensibility* there is no hint of this', 'Food and Drink', J. David Grey (ed.), *The Jane Austen Handbook* (Athlone Press, London, 1986), pp. 160–4, p. 162. This is clearly wishful thinking, as Tom's eventual illness illustrates, and provides yet another example of the continuing attempt to distance Austen from the Regency period.

20 Hon. Mrs. Hugh Wyndham (ed.), *Correspondence of Sarah Spencer, Lady Lyttleton, 1787–1870* (John Murray, London, 1912), p. 14, and Lady

Theresa Lewis (ed.), *Extracts of the Journals and Correspondence of Miss Berry from the Year 1783 to 1852* (Longmans, Green & Co., London, 1865), 3, 2, p. 381. See Terry Castle, *Masquerade and Civilisation: The Carnivalesque in Eighteenth-Century Culture and Fiction* (Methuen, London, 1986), for an interesting account of representations and functions of masquerade. Ruth Bernard Yeazell, 'The Boundaries of Mansfield Park', *Representations*, 7, 1984, pp. 133–52, p. 138, notices another potential example of a form of cross-dressing during Tom's regency when Fanny has to read the part of Anhalt in rehearsal with Mary Crawford. The main purpose of her study is to provide an anthropological reading of the novel.

21 Crockford's rags-to-riches story is the subject of Henry Blyth, *Hell and Hazard: or William Crockford versus the Gentlemen of England* (Weidenfeld & Nicolson, London, 1969). See R.C. Lyle, *Royal Newmarket* (Putnam, London, 1945) for general details about the development of Newmarket. For Dawson's first trial see *The Extraordinary Trial of Daniel Dawson . . . on Friday, March 12 on an Indictment Charging him with Poisoning the Eagle Colt . . .* (Robert Rogers, Newmarket, 1812). One of his accomplices, Cecil Bishop, had trained as an apothecary and was able to supply the white arsenic used. As the ambiguous social status of the apothecary is one of the main themes of my chapter on *Emma*, it is worth emphasising here that while some like Mr Perry were close to professional status others like Bishop remained in the criminal underworld. There is an account of the case in J.L. Rayner and G.T. Crook (eds), *The Complete Newgate Calendar* (Navarre Society, London, 1926), 5, 4, pp. 180–3, which confirms that it received a lot of publicity at the time. A surprising number of Austen critics are confused about the location for Tom's illness. Tanner, *Jane Austen*, p. 148, suggests it took place in London and is not alone in doing this.

22 Edward W. Said, 'Jane Austen and Empire', Terry Eagleton (ed.), *Raymond Williams: Critical Perspectives* (Northern University Press, Boston, 1989), pp. 150–64, p. 154 (the essay has also appeared elsewhere). As argued, Said's mistake about the ending is both interesting and understandable. My own totally unscientific readership surveys with both university and school students indicate that on average between 65% and 70% of those taking part in any survey claim in response to an invitation to describe the ending of the novel in their own words that Fanny becomes the mistress of Mansfield. It could also be argued that Said's confusion between Lydia Bennet and Maria Rushworth is not entirely without some foundation. My main criticism is that he deals with J.S. Mill's views on India without exploring the richer possibilities that are offered by the trial of Warren Hastings (1788–95) given the connections between the Austen family and Hastings. Although he deals with the 'Black Jacobins' and the economic structure of Antigua in the early nineteenth century, by choosing to discuss Mill at greater length he too is in danger of reproducing a Victorian Austen.

23 Tanner, *Jane Austen*, pp. 149–50.

24 For more details see Alistair Duckworth, *The Improvement of the Estate: A study of Jane Austen's Novels* (The Johns Hopkins University Press, Baltimore, MD, 1971), ch.4

25 As quoted in G.E. Mitton, *Jane Austen and Her Times* (Methuen & Co., London, 1905), p. 162.

26 Johnson, *Women, Politics and the Novel*, p. 106.

27 John Wiltshire, *Jane Austen and the Body* (Cambridge University Press, Cambridge, 1992), p. 101.

28 I have used the second edition: Sir Charles William Pasley, *Essay on the Military Policy and Institutions of the British Empire* (Edmund Lloyd, London, 1811). For Austen's views on it, see *Letters*, p. 292, p. 294 and p. 304.

29 For the technological revolution in the dockyards see Roger Morriss, *The Royal Dockyards during the Revolutionary and Napoleonic Wars* (Leicester University Press, Leicester, 1983). For further details on Portsmouth see **A.**Temple Patterson, *Portsmouth: A History* (Moonraker Press, Bradford-on-Avon, 1976). For Jordan's visit in 1812 see A. Aspinall (ed.) *Mrs. Jordan and Her Family* (Arthur Barker, London, 1951), pp. 240–1, which is also interesting about the behaviour of the theatre audience.

30 See *Finden's Views of the Ports, Harbours & Watering Places of Great Britain Continued by W.H. Bartlett* (Geo. Virtue, London, 1839), p. 102, for more details. This account also indicates that the areas adjacent to the dockyards were heavily industrialised, by the standards of the time, containing foundries, mills and workshops.

31 Susan Ferrier, *Marriage* (Oxford University Press, Oxford, 1986), p. 153 and p. 432. For a good reading of the novel, relating it to Wollstonecraft's work, see Anne K. Mellor, *Romanticism and Gender* (Routledge, London, 1993), pp. 49–52. She also writes well on Austen, whom she sees as dealing with the failures of patriarchy in a less open way than occurs in Wollstonecraft. Her reading is broadly similar to the ones advanced by Claudia Johnson and Alison Sulloway which have both influenced my own work.

32 Duckworth, *The Improvement of the Estate*, p. 57.

33 Mark Girouard, *Life in the English Country House: A Social and Architectural History* (Yale University Press, New Haven, CT, 1978), p. 236.

34 Percy Noble, *Anne Seymour Damer, A Woman of Art and Fashion 1748–1828* (Kegan Paul, Trench, Trubner & Co., London, 1908), pp. 166–73 and Lewis Melville, *The Berry Papers being the Correspondence hitherto unpublished of Mary and Angus Berry (1763–1852)* (Bodley Head, London, 1914), p. 224.

35 For more details see Lewis Melville, *The Beaux of the Regency* (Hutchinson, London, 1908), 2, pp. 127–35.

36 For details on Inchbald's career see Roger Manvell, *Elizabeth Inchbald, England's Principal Woman Dramatist and Independent Woman of Letters in Eighteenth-Century London: A Biographical Study* (University Press of America, Lanham, 1987). In addition to some of the critics cited earlier in connection with women and writing, her prose works are discussed at some length by Gary Kelly, *The English Jacobin Novel 1780–1805* (Clarendon Press, Oxford, 1976), pp. 64–113.

37 Marilyn Butler, *Jane Austen and the War of Ideas* (Clarendon Press, Oxford, 1987 edn; 1st pub. 1975), pp. 92–3, and Meenahski Mukherjee, *Jane Austen* (Macmillan, Basingstoke, 1991), p. 106.

38 These changes are discussed in Inchbald's Preface, LV, pp. 3–6. There is a more literal translation by Anne Plumptre, *The Natural Son; A Play, in Five Acts, by Augustus von Kotzebue . . . Being the Original of LOVERS' VOWS, now Performing with Universal Applause at the Theatre Royal, Covent Garden: Translated from the German by Anne Plumtre who has Prefixed a*

Preface explaining the Alterations in the Representation (H. Fitzpatrick, Dublin, 1798). For the Preface see pp. v–xi.

39 Lady Caroline Lamb, *Glenarvon* (Scholars' Facsimiles and Reprints, New York, 1972), 3, 2, p. 382. Frances Wilson is currently editing a more accessible edition for Everyman.

40 See *Autobiography: A Collection of the Most Instructive and Amusing Lives ever Published, Written by the Parties Themselves* (Hunt and Clarke, London, 1827–33), 34, 10, p. 114. Books in English on Kotzebue include L.F. Thompson, *Kotzebue: A Survey of His Progress in France and England . . .* (Librairie Ancienne Honoré Champion, Paris, 1928) and G. Sinko, *Sheridan and Kotzebue: A Comparative Essay* (Travaux de la Société des Sciences et des Lettres de Wroclaw, Wroclaw, 1949). Studies that concentrate on the Mansfield rehearsals include Syndy McMillan Conger, 'Reading *Lovers' Vows*: Jane Austen's Reflections on English Sense and German Sensibility', *Studies in Philology*, 1, 1985, pp. 92–113, and Joseph Litvak, *Caught in the Act: Theatricality in the Nineteenth-Century Novel* (University of California Press, Berkeley, 1992), ch. 1. Litvak's reading is particularly good.

41 Mary Berry, *A Comparative View of the Social Life of England and France from the Restoration of Charles the Second to the French Revolution* (Longman *et al.*, London, 1828), p. 404. I do not know of a modern edition of this text, which deserves a wider audience.

42 For a more detailed account of these themes see Devlin, *Jane Austen and Education*, ch. 4.

43 Margaret Kirkham, 'Feminist Irony and the Priceless Heroine of *Mansfield Park*', Todd (ed.), *New Perspectives*, pp. 231–46, esp. pp. 245–6. Kirkham's *Feminism and Fiction* deals extensively with Kotzebue, whose influence she sees as being an important feature of *Emma* as well as of *Mansfield Park*.

44 Evans, *Jane Austen and the State*, p. 25.

45 For a general account of the use of multiple point of view see Roselle Taylor, *The Narrative Technique of Jane Austen: A Study in the Use of Point of View* (University of Texas at Austin, unpub. Ph.D., 1975), pp. 113–39.

46 Lionel Trilling, *The Opposing Self: Nine Essays in Criticism* (Harcourt Brace Jovanovich, New York, 1978 edn), pp. 181–204, which has been reprinted in various editions of the novel. He also thinks that Sir Thomas is the only one of Austen's fathers to be held up for admiration. There are still a few modern critics who strive, remarkably unsuccessfully, to emulate his seemingly detached urbanity. See for example Roger Gard, *Jane Austen's Novels: The Art of Clarity* (Yale University Press, New Haven, CT, 1992).

47 As quoted in Dorothy Margaret Stuart, *Regency Roundabout* (Macmillan, London, 1943), p. 74. For Farren's career see Suzanne Bloxam, *Walpole's Queen of Comedy: Elizabeth Farren Countess of Derby* (Suzanne Bloxam, Ashford, 1988).

48 The pamphlet is entitled *Mrs. Galindo's Letter to Mrs. Siddons: Being a Circumstantial Detail of Mrs. Siddons's Life for the Last Seven Years; with Several of Her Letters* (M. Jones, Newgate Street, 1809). Roger Manvell thinks that it was broadly speaking accurate, *Sarah Siddons: Portrait of an Actress* (Heinemann, London, 1970), p. 268. Some of the letters between Siddons and Mr Galindo appear to have been written in code. Another well-publicised scandal involving an actress took place in 1813 when Charlotte

Goodall, who had played the part of Frederick in *Lovers' Vows*, was foun◦ guilty of 'criminal conversation' or adultery.

49 For more details see Rictor Norton, *Mother Clap's Molly House: The Ga◦ Subculture in England 1700–1830* (GMP, London, 1992), p. 235.

50 For more details see *An Apology for the Life of George Anne Bellamy Lat◦ of Covent-Garden Theatre Written by Herself* (Moncrieffe *et al.*, Dublin 1785), 3, and *Memoirs of George Anne Bellamy, Including All He◦ Intrigues; with Genuine Anecdotes of All of Her Public and Privat◦ Connections* (J. Walker, London, 1785). There is also a modern biograph◦ by Cyril Hughes Hartmann, *Enchanting Bellamy* (Heinemann, London 1956). The *Apology* is another text that ought to be reprinted.

51 For Woffington's career see Janet Dunbar, *Peg Woffington and Her Worl◦* (Heinemann, London, 1968). For Abington's see *The Life of Mrs. Abingto◦ (Formerly Miss Barton) Celebrated Comic Actress . . . by the Editor of th◦ 'Life of Quin'* (Reader, London, 1888).

52 Sarah Siddons's Correspondence with Mrs Pennington, Cambridg◦ University Library Manuscripts, Add. 6445, f5.

53 Betty T. Bennett (ed.), *The Letters of Mary Wollstonecraft Shelley*, (Th◦ Johns Hopkins University Press, Baltimore, MD, 1980/3/8) 1, p. 462. Fo◦ the social history of the actress see Elizabeth Howe, *The First Englis◦ Actresses: Women and Drama 1660–1700* (Cambridge University Press Cambridge, 1992) and earlier chapters of Sandra Richards, *The Rise of th◦ English Actress* (Macmillan, Basingstoke, 1993). Although it deals with th◦ Victorian period, Tracey C. Davis, *Actresses as Working Women: Thei◦ Social Identity in Victorian Culture* (Routledge, London, 1991), is particu◦ larly good at exploring why connections were made between the actress an◦ the prostitute. She also deals with the profession as a whole rather than con◦ centrating on 'stars' as I have done.

54 Marc Baer, *Theatre and Disorder in Late Georgian London* (Clarendo◦ Press, Oxford, 1992), pp. 252–3 for remarks on Austen. The book as ◦ whole, which builds on the work done on riots and disorder in the eigh◦ teenth century by John Brewer and others, opens up many other possibilitie◦ for Austen criticism.

55 Armstrong, *Mansfield Park*, p. 61. Fanny's role as a servant is also notice◦ in, amongst others, Bernard J. Paris, *Character and Conflict in Jan◦ Austen's Novels: A Psychological Approach* (Wayne State University Press Detroit, IL, 1978), p. 47.

56 Armstrong, *Mansfield Park*, p. 60. Fanny's spectatorship is also discusse◦ by Nina Auerbach, 'Jane Austen's Dangerous Charm: Feeling as One Ough◦ about Fanny Price', Todd (ed.), *New Perspectives*, pp. 208–21, and by Tod◦ herself, *Women's Friendship in Literature* (Columbia University Press, New York, 1980) where she is described as a 'voyeur of moral slips', p. 258 Butler, *The War of Ideas*, p. 230, sees her as a 'detached bystander'.

57 Tanner, *Jane Austen*, p. 166.

58 Michael Williams, *Jane Austen: Six Novels and Their Methods* (Macmillan Basingstoke, 1986), pp. 92–7. He is taking issue with the views expresse◦ by Peter Garside and Elizabeth McDonald, 'Evangelicalism and *Mansfiel◦ Park*', *Trivium*, 10, 1975, pp. 34–49, which was an attempt to find historica◦ evidence to support Trilling's views about Austen's anti-theatrical preju◦ dices. This argument is also challenged by David Monaghan, '*Mansfiel◦*

Park and Evangelicalism: A Reassessment', *Nineteenth Century Fiction*, 33, 1978, pp. 215–30.

59 Butler, *The War of Ideas*, p. 235. She also underplays the melodramatic ending of the first volume by suggesting that a two- rather than three-volume structure would have been more appropriate for the novel's educational themes. See also her 'Disregarded Designs: Jane Austen's Sense of a Volume', David Monaghan (ed.), *Jane Austen in a Social Context* (Macmillan, Basingstoke, 1981), pp. 49–65.

5 *EMMA*: THE VILLAGE AND THE WATERING PLACE

1 *Gentleman's Magazine*, 82, 1812, pp. 18–19. See Dorothy Margaret Stuart, *Regency Roundabout*, (Macmillan, London, 1943), pp. 66–7, for brief discussion of letter. See Edmund Bartell, *Cromer, Considered as a Watering Place; with Observations on the Picturesque Scenery in its Neighbourhood* (J. Taylor, London, 1806), for an idea of Cromer's more exclusive nature.

2 Claudia Johnson, *Jane Austen: Women, Politics and the Novel* (University of Chicago Press, Chicago, 1989), pp. 122–4.

3 Marilyn Butler, *Jane Austen and the War of Ideas* (Clarendon Press, Oxford, 1987 edn; 1st pub. 1975), p. 251.

4 John Wiltshire, *Jane Austen and the Body* (Cambridge University Press, Cambridge, 1992), pp. 123–4. This is an important study that is particularly good on both *Emma* and *Sanditon*. An earlier study of medical themes, J.R. Watson, 'Mr Perry's Patients: A View of *Emma*', *Essays in Criticism*, 20, 1970, pp. 334–43, lacks any sort of contextualisation. Toby A. Olshin, 'Jane Austen: A Romantic, Systematic or Realistic Approach to Medicine?', *Studies in Eighteenth-Century Culture*, 10, 1981, pp. 313–26, makes some use of contexts offered by the cult of sensibility.

5 Charlotte Barnett (ed.), *Diary and Letters of Madame D'Arblay* (Swan Sonneschein & Co., London, 1893), 4, 1, p. 191.

6 See Adrian Henstock (ed.), *The Diary of Abigail Gawthern of Nottingham 1751–1810* (Thoroton Society, Nottingham, 1980), p. 117. This entry is quoted in a very useful collection of travel writings, Robin Gard (ed.), *The Observant Traveller: Diaries of Travel in England, Wales and Scotland in County Record Offices in England and Wales* (H.M.S.O., London, 1989), p.24. I regret not having the space to deal with the *Diary* when considering Austen's letters.

7 Eric Gillett (ed.), *Elizabeth Ham by Herself 1783–1820* (Faber & Faber, 1945), p. 45. This is another text that could have been considered in relation to Austen's letters.

8 Details from *The Weymouth Guide: Exhibiting the Ancient and Present State of Weymouth and Melcombe Regis . . .* (P. Delamotte, Weymouth, ND; 1st pub. 1785). Other guide books include J.S. Buckingham, *A Summer Trip to Weymouth and Dorchester Including an Excursion to Portland . . .* (B. Benson, Weymouth, 1842).

9 For more details see R.W. Chapman, *Jane Austen: Facts and Problems* (Clarendon Press, Oxford, 1948), p. 52 and Robert Liddell, *The Novels of Jane Austen* (Longman, London, 1963), p. 94.

10 Douglas Jefferson, *Jane Austen's Emma: A Landmark in English Fiction* (Sussex University Press, London, 1977), p. 81.

11 James Thompson, *Between Self and World: The Novels of Jane Austen* (The Pennsylvania State University Press, University Park, 1988), esp. pp. 19–43. He has also published a good article on clothing that anticipates some of the themes of the book, 'Jane Austen's Clothing: Things, Property and Materialism in Her Novels', *Studies in Eighteenth-Century Culture*, 13 1984, pp. 217–31.

12 Ward Hellstrom, 'Francophobia in *Emma*', *Studies in English Literature*, 5 1965, pp. 606–17. On the institutionalisation of Francophobia in the 1790s and later see E.P. Thompson, *The Making of the English Working Class* (Penguin, Harmondsworth, 1968); Stella Cottrell, 'The Devil on Two Sticks: Franco-phobia in 1803', Raphael Samuel (ed.), *Patriotism: The Making and Unmaking of the British National Identity* (Routledge, London 1989), 3, 1, *History and Politics*, pp. 259–74 and Gerald Newman, *The Rise of English Nationalism: A Cultural History 1740–1830* (Weidenfeld & Nicolson, London, 1987), esp. ch.8. See also Linda Colley, 'Whose Nation? Class and National Consciousness in Britain 1750–1830', *Past and Present* 53, 1986, pp. 97–117.

13 John Mullan, *Sentiment and Sociability: The Language of Feeling in the Eighteenth Century* (Clarendon Press, Oxford, 1988), p. 205.

14 It is difficult to generalise about the structures for medical provision in this period because of the regional variations. The accounts I have consulted include: Irvine Loudon, *Medical Care and the General Practitioner 1750–1850* (Clarendon Press, Oxford, 1986); Noel and Jose Parry, *The Rise of the Medical Profession* (Croom Helm, Beckenham, 1976); Roy and Dorothy Porter, *In Sickness and in Health: The British Experience 1650–1850* (Fourth Estate, London, 1988) and *Patient's Progress: Doctors and Doctoring in Eighteenth-Century England* (Polity Press, Cambridge, 1989); Roy Porter (ed.), *The Popularisation of Medicine 1650–1850* (Routledge, London, 1992); Ivan Waddington, *The Medical Profession in the Industrial Revolution* (Gill & Macmillan, Dublin, 1984). I found Loudon's *Medical Care* and the Porters' *Patient's Progress* particularly useful. I have also consulted a number of biographies, for example V. Mary Crosse, *A Surgeon in the Early Nineteenth Century: The Life and Times of John Green Crosse* (E. & S. Livingstone, Edinburgh, 1968).

15 See Ornella Moscucci, *The Science of Woman: Gynaecology and Gender in England 1800–1929* (Cambridge University Press, Cambridge, 1990), p. 61

16 For the background to, as well as the passage and provisions of the Act, see S.E.F. Holloway, 'The Apothecaries' Act, 1815: A Reinterpretation. Part 1: The Origins of the Act' and 'The Apothecaries' Act, 1815: A Reinterpretation. Part 2: The Consequences of the Act', *Medical History*, 10, 1966, pp. 107–29 and pp. 221–36. See also Loudon, *Medical Care*, chs 7 and 8. For the detail of the Act itself see *The London Medical Repository*, 4, 1815, pp. 152–64.

17 As quoted in G.M. Matthews (ed.), *Keats: The Critical Heritage* (Routledge & Kegan Paul, London, 1971), pp. 109–10. For Keats's medical career see Sir William Hale-White, *Keats as Doctor and Patient* (Oxford University Press, Oxford, 1938), Maurice Buxton Forman (ed.), *John Keats: Anatomical and Physiological Note Book* (Oxford University Press, Oxford, 1934) and Walter A. Wells, *A Doctor's Life of John Keats* (Vantage Press, New York, 1959). For a brief description of the work of a dresser see Reverend Charles

Lett Feltoe (ed.), *Memorials of John Flint South* (John Murray, London, 1884), p. 26. This also draws attention to the elevated position of the physicians after the passing of the Apothecaries' Act, pp. 63–4.

8 Wiltshire, *Jane Austen and the Body*, p. 111.

9 Mrs Goddard is discussed as one of the many impoverished women in the text by Mary-Elizabeth Fowkes Tobin, 'Aiding Impoverished Gentlewomen: Power and Class in *Emma*', *Criticism*, 30, 1988, pp. 413–30. Tobin suggests in a good, historically-informed reading that Emma ought to patronise these impoverished women and that by not doing so she threatens the stability and coherence of the gentry as a class.

10 Fanny Burney, *The Wanderer or Female Difficulties* (Oxford University Press, Oxford, 1991), p. 115.

11 For more details on the Motherill-Wade case see Anna Clark, *Women's Silence, Men's Violence: Sexual Assault in England 1770–1845* (Pandora, London, 1987), p. 34. Her essay, 'The Politics of Seduction in English Popular Culture 1748–1848', Jean Radford (ed.), *The Progress of Romance: The Politics of Popular Fiction* (Routledge & Kegan Paul, London, 1986), pp. 47–70, is also recommended for the sexual politics of this period.

22 See J.L. Rayner and G.T. Crook (eds), *The Complete Newgate Calendar* (Navarre Society, London, 1926), 5, 4, pp. 180–3, for more details.

23 *Mrs. Hurst Dancing & Other Scenes from Regency Life 1812–1823; Watercolours by Diana Sperling; Text by Gordon Mingay* (Victor Gollancz, London, 1981).

24 There are currently two editions of Lister's voluminous diaries available, both edited by Helena Whitbread: *I Know My Own Heart: The Diaries of Anne Lister 1791–1840* (Virago, London, 1988) and *No Priest But Love: The Journals of Anne Lister from 1824 to 1826* (Smith Settle, Otley, 1992). See also Muriel M. Green (ed.), *Miss Lister of Shibden Hall: Selected Letters 1800–1840* (The Book Guild, Sussex, 1992). Lister should have more prominence in discussions of early nineteenth-century women writers, particularly now that Whitbread's second volume has been published.

25 Julia Prewitt Brown, *Jane Austen's Novels: Social Change and Literary Form* (Harvard University Press, Cambridge, MA, 1979), p. 105.

26 Lister, *I Know My Own Heart*, p. 113.

27 Ellen Weeton, *Miss Weeton's Journal of a Governess* (David & Charles Reprints, Newton Abbot, 1969), 2, pp. 316–17.

28 Wiltshire, *Jane Austen and the Body*, p. 116

29 Mary A. Favret, *Romantic Correspondence: Women, Politics and the Fiction of Letters*, (Cambridge University Press, Cambridge, 1993), p. 159.

30 Mary Lascelles, *Jane Austen and Her Art* (Oxford University Press, Oxford, 1939), pp. 175–8 and Butler, *The War of Ideas*, p. 271.

31 As quoted in Bruce Redford, *The Converse of the Pen: Acts of Intimacy in the Eighteenth-Century Familiar Letter* (University of Chicago Press, Chicago, 1986), p. 4. See David Aers, 'Community and Morality: Toward Reading Jane Austen', Aers *et al.* (eds), *Romanticism and Ideology: Studies in English Writing 1765–1830* (Routledge & Kegan Paul, London, 1981), pp. 118–36, for an account that asserts the need to read Knightley, and those critics who support him, in class terms.

32 Butler, *The War of Ideas*, pp. 273–4.

33 Tony Tanner, *Jane Austen* (Macmillan, Basingstoke, 1986), p. 201.

34 Patricia Meyer Spacks, *Gossip* (Alfred A. Knopf, New York, 1985), p. 261
    Her reading of the role of gossip in *Emma* is challenged in an uneven arti
    cle by Casey Finch and Peter Bowen, 'The Tittle-Tattle of Highbury: Gossip
    and Free Indirect Style in *Emma*', *Representations*, 31, 1990, pp. 1–18.
35 Joseph Litvak, 'Reading Characters: Self, Society and Text in *Emma*'
    Publications of the Modern Language Association of America, 100, 1985
    pp. 763–73.
36 Johnson, *Women, Politics and the Novel*, p. 135.

6 *PERSUASION*: THE WAR AND THE PEACE

1 For interesting examples of literary detective work see Jocelyn Harris
    'Anne Elliot, The Wife of Bath and Other Friends', Janet Todd (ed.), *Jane
    Austen: New Perspectives* (Holmes & Meier Publishers, Inc., New York
    1983), pp. 273–92 and her book, *Jane Austen's Art of Memory* (Cambridge
    University Press, Cambridge, 1989).
2 Tony Tanner, *Jane Austen* (Macmillan, Basingstoke, 1986), esp. pp. 217–20
3 Margaret Kirkham, *Jane Austen: Feminism and Fiction* (Harvester Press
    Brighton, 1983), p. 149.
4 Mary Poovey, *The Proper Lady and the Woman Writer: Ideology as Style in
    the Works of Mary Wollstonecraft, Mary Shelley and Jane Austen*
    (University of Chicago Press, Chicago, 1984), p. 228. This also contains an
    interesting account of contradictions in Wollstonecraft's work.
5 Robert R. Wark (ed.), *Drawings by Thomas Rowlandson in the Huntingdon
    Collection* (Huntingdon Library, San Marino, 1975), plate no. 137.
6 See Christopher Lloyd *et al.* (eds), *Medicine and the Navy 1200–1900* (E.
    & S. Livingstone, Edinburgh, 1961), p. 147. Ch. 12, 'Nelson and the
    Surgeons', is good on the status of the naval surgeon.
7 See Jonathan Neale, *The Cutlass and the Lash: Mutiny and Discipline in
    Nelson's Navy* (Pluto Press, London, 1980), pp. 1–5. Other books on naval
    history that I have consulted include: Richard Glover, *Britain at Bay:
    Defence Against Bonaparte 1803–14* (Allen & Unwin, London, 1973);
    Michael Lewis, *A Social History of the Navy 1793–1815* (Allen & Unwin,
    London, 1960); C.J. Marcus, *A Naval History of England: The Age of
    Nelson* (Allen & Unwin, London, 1971); Dudley Pope, *Life in Nelson's
    Navy* (Allen & Unwin, London, 1981); and N.A.M. Rodger, *The Wooden
    World: An Anatomy of the Georgian Navy* (Collins, London, 1986).
8 Details from *Life and Surprising Adventures of Mary Anne Talbot in the
    Name of John Taylor A Natural Daughter of the Late Earl Talbot ...
    Related by Herself* (R.S. Kisby, London, 1809). I have used a version
    reprinted in Menie Muriel Dowie (ed.), *Women Adventurers ...* (T. Fisher
    Unwin, London, 1893), pp. 139–96. Other examples of cross-dressing in the
    services include Sarah Penelope Stanley, the female trooper, who is dis-
    cussed briefly in *The Newgate Calendar* and elsewhere, and Nadezhda
    Durova. For Durova see Mary Fleming Zirin (ed.), Nadezhda Durova, *The
    Cavalry Maiden: Journals of a Female Russian Officer in the Napoleonic
    Wars* (Paladin, London, 1990).
9 See Joan Haslip, *Lady Hester Stanhope* (Penguin, London, 1945), chs 9–11
    and Flora Fraser, *Beloved Emma: The Life of Emma Lady Hamilton* (Guild
    Publishing, London, 1986), ch. 15. For a more detailed although still partial

account of Stanhope see C.L. Meryon, *Memoirs of the Lady Hester Stanhope, as Related in Conversations with her Physician* (Henry Colburn, London, 1845), 3.

9 Frank Austen as quoted in J.H. and E.C. Hubback, *Jane Austen's Sailor Brothers* (John Lane, London, 1906), p. 156. The Nelson cult is discussed in Park Honan, *Jane Austen: Her Life* (Weidenfeld & Nicolson, London, 1987), pp. 162–5. Some critics have suggested that the way in which Wentworth openly flirts with both the Musgrove girls in the presence of Anne alludes to Nelson's promiscuity, although I decided not to deal with this aspect of the text's potential topicality. For Nelson's negotiations over the *Marie Therese* see *The Dispatches and Letters of Vice Admiral Lord Viscount Nelson* (Henry Colburn, London, 1856), 7, 6, pp. 40–1 and 7, p. 1, p. 15 and p. 21. Prize-money cases and judgements can be consulted in all their complexity in E.S. Roscoe(ed.), *Reports of Prize Cases Determined in the High Court of Admiralty, Before the Lords Commissioners of Appeals in Prize Causes . . . from 1745 to 1859* (Stevens & Sons, London, 1905), 2.

1 For Talbot's experiences see Dowie, *Women Adventurers*, p. 171. For De Quincey's see *Confessions of an English Opium-Eater and Other Writings* (Oxford University Press, Oxford, 1985), p. 14. De Quincey did not encounter the kind of hostility that Weeton experienced during his walking tour of Wales.

2 Jack Nastyface, *Memoirs of a Seaman* (Wayland Publishers, London, 1973), pp. 127–8. 1st pub. in 1836 under the title of *Nautical Economy*.

3 For an example of his concern see *Dispatches and Letters*, 6, p. 41.

4 *Memoirs of a Seaman*, p. 69.

5 For more details see, amongst others, *Political Register*, 17 March 1810.

6 *Manoeuvring*, like *Ennui* and *Vivian* which have been referred to earlier here, belongs to a series of novels, *Tales of Fashionable Life* (R. Hunter, London, 1818–24), 6, 3. I would have liked to have been able to devote more attention to them, as well as to deal with Edgeworth's letters. For some of her letters, see Christina Colvin (ed.), *Letters from England 1813–1844, by Maria Edgeworth* (Clarendon Press, Oxford, 1971). Marilyn Butler, *Maria Edgeworth: A Literary Biography* (Clarendon Press, Oxford, 1972), remains an important study.

7 Marvin Mudrick, *Jane Austen: Irony as Defense and Discovery* (Princeton University Press, Princeton, NJ, 1953), p. 212.

8 Kirkham, *Feminism and Fiction*, p. 153

9 James Thompson, *Between Self and World: The Novels of Jane Austen* (The Pennsylvania State University Press, University Park, 1988), p. 100.

0 For a brief account of Hays's career see Jane Spencer's entry in Janet Todd (ed.), *Dictionary of British Women Writers* (Routledge, London, 1991), pp. 320–1.

1 *Harriette Wilson's Memoirs of Herself and Others* (Peter Davies, London, 1930), p. 463.

2 See *Report from the Select Committee Appointed to Inquire into the Repair of the Cobb at Lyme Regis*, 1818 (432), 3, pp. 367–70.

3 R.A. Austen-Leigh (ed.), *Austen Papers 1704–1856* (Spottiswoode, Ballantyne & Co., London, 1942), p. 139. The letter is to her cousin Philadelphia Walter. The physician whose instructions she was following was the very eminent Sir William Farquhar.

24 Marilyn Butler, *Jane Austen and the War of Ideas* (Clarendon Press, Oxford 1987 edn; 1st pub. 1975), p. 208.

25 My main source is Jean Donnison, *Midwives and Medical Men: A History of Inter-Professional Rivalries and Women's Rights* (Heinemann, London 1977). Other accounts include Barbara Ehrenreich and Deirdre English *Witches, Midwives & Nurses: A History of Women Healers* (Writers' and Readers' Publishing Cooperative, London, 1976). Their approach is dis cussed in Margaret Connor Versluyen, 'Old Wives Tales? Women Healers i English History', Celia Davies (ed.), *Rewriting Nursing History* (Croom Helm, Beckenham, 1980), pp. 175–99. Roy Porter deals with the dubiou reputation of the man-midwife, 'A Touch of Danger: The Man-Midwife a Sexual Predator', G.S. Rousseau and Roy Porter (eds), *Sexual Underworld of the Enlightenment* (University of North Carolina Press, Chapel Hil 1988), pp. 206–32. In addition to the modern work that has been done b Porter and others on William Hunter, I have also consulted some of th material on William Smellie such as R.W. Johnstone, *William Smellie: Th Master of British Midwifery* (E. & S. Livingstone, Edinburgh, 1952). Ther is a useful anthology of literary representations of childbirth, Madelain Riley, *Brought to Bed* (Dent, London, 1968). Representation of childbirth i one of the themes that is treated in a more scholarly way in Robert A Erickson, *Mother Midnight: Birth, Sex and Fate in Eighteenth-Centur Fiction* (AMS Press, New York, 1986). I was intending to make some use o Ernest Gray (ed.), *Man-Midwife: The Further Experiences of Joh Knyveton, M.D., Late Surgeon in the British Fleet, During the Years 1763–1809* (Robert Hale, London, 1946), until warned that it was a forger by Adrian Wilson, a specialist in the history of medicine. In retrospect, i quoted so well that it had to be dubious but it certainly had me fooled.

26 John Wiltshire, *Jane Austen and the Body* (Cambridge University Press Cambridge, 1992), pp. 166–7.

27 Sandra M. Gilbert and Susan Gubar, *The Madwoman in the Attic: Th Woman Writer and the Nineteenth-Century Literary Imagination* (Yale University Press, New Haven, CT, 1979), p. 182.

28 See Christopher Hibbert, *George IV* (Penguin, Harmondsworth, 1976), pp 485–91, for more details. The death-bed scene is gentled in representation of it in texts such as Dormer Creston, *The Regent and His Daughte* (Thornton Butterworth, London, 1933) and Jean Plaidy, *The Regent' Daughter* (Pan, London, 1971).

29 *The Medical and Physical Journal*, 27, 1812, p. 117.

30 For an important study see Patricia Meyer Spacks, *Gossip* (Alfred A. Knopf New York, 1985), referred to briefly at the end of my ch. 5.

31 Gilbert and Gubar, *The Madwoman in the Attic*, p. 182; Alistair Duckworth *The Improvement of the Estate: A Study of Jane Austen's Novels* (The John Hopkins University Press, Baltimore, MD, 1971), p. 3 and pp. 191–2; Susa Morgan, *In the Meantime: Character and Perception in Jane Austen' Fiction* (University of Chicago Press, Chicago, 1980), pp. 177–81. Mr Smith is also the subject of K.K. Collins, 'Mrs. Smith and the Morality o *Persuasion*', *Nineteenth-Century Fiction*, 30, 1975–76, pp. 383–97.

32 Butler, *The War of Ideas*, pp. 280–1.

33 David Spring, 'Interpreters of Jane Austen's Social World: Literary Critic and Historians', Todd (ed.), *New Perspectives*, pp. 53–72. This interpreta

tion may be contrasted with the one advanced by a number of critics that the gentry is revealed to be 'beyond redemption', to quote David Monaghan, *Jane Austen: Structure and Social Vision* (Macmillan, Basingstoke, 1980), p. 143. Leroy W. Smith, *Jane Austen and the Drama of Woman* (Macmillan, Basingstoke, 1983), also goes too far in suggesting that the novel 'blows up', p. 159, the patriarchal order. Other readings of the novel's social messages include Nina Auerbach, 'O Brave New World: Evolution and Revolution in *Persuasion*', *English Literary History*, 39, 1972, pp. 112–28, which has more of a sense of the double vision that I identify. For a useful study of Austen in general that is aware that the texts may be recommending both mobility and a form of stasis see Donald J. Greene, 'Jane Austen and the Peerage', Ian Watt (ed.), *Jane Austen: A Collection of Critical Essays* (Prentice-Hall, Inc., Englewood Cliffs, NJ, 1963), pp. 154–65.

7 *SANDITON*: THE MADHOUSE AND THE GREENHOUSE

1 Warren Roberts, *Jane Austen and the French Revolution*, (Macmillan, Basingstoke, 1979), p. 64. I deal with these post-war rural and urban riots in *English Literature in History 1780–1830: Pastoral and Politics* (Hutchinson, London, 1983).

2 Readers can make up their own minds by consulting B.C. Southam's admirable facsimile edition of the manuscript, *Sanditon: An Unfinished Novel by Jane Austen* (Clarendon Press, Oxford, 1975). He has also written a good critical account of the novel 'Sanditon: The Seventh Novel', Juliet McMaster (ed.), *Jane Austen's Achievement: Papers delivered at the Jane Austen Bicentennial Conference at the University of Alberta 1975* (Macmillan, Basingstoke, 1976), pp. 1–26. Those interested more generally in Austen's manuscripts should also see his *Austen's Literary Manuscripts: A Study of the Novelist's Development Through the Surviving Papers* (Clarendon Press, Oxford, 1964).

3 Alistair Duckworth, *The Improvement of the Estate: A Study of Jane Austen's Novels* (The Johns Hopkins University Press, Baltimore, MD, 1971), p. 210 and Oliver MacDonagh, *Jane Austen: Real and Imagined Worlds* (Yale University Press, New Haven, CT, 1991), pp. 146–7. There is also an essay by MacDonagh that covers the same themes, 'Sanditon: A Regency Novel', Tom Dunne (ed.), *The Writer as Witness: Literature as Historical Evidence* (Cork University Press, Cork, 1987), pp. 114–32. Following the lead of Rachel Bowlby's innovative study, *Just Looking: Consumer Culture in Dreiser, Gissing and Zola* (Methuen, London, 1985), there are now a number of accounts of relationships between advertising and Victorian culture. For examples see Thomas Richards, *The Commodity Culture of Victorian England: Advertising and Spectacle 1851–1914* (Stanford University Press, Stanford, 1991) and Jennifer Wicke, *Advertising Fictions: Literature, Advertisement and Social Readings* (Columbia University Press, New York, 1988). There need to be similar studies on the Regency period itself so that important features of *Sanditon* can be more thoroughly contextualised. I have not done this.

4 John Wiltshire, *Jane Austen and the Body* (Cambridge University Press, Cambridge, 1992), p. 208.

5 Duckworth, *The Improvement of the Estate*, p. 213.

6 Edmund Bartell, *Cromer, Considered as a Watering Place: With Observations on the Picturesque Scenery in its Neighbourhood* (J. Taylor, London 1806), pp. 29–31.

7 Tony Tanner, *Jane Austen* (Macmillan, Basingstoke, 1986), p. 256. The title *Sanditon* appears to have been chosen by the family rather than by Austen herself.

8 Spurrett as detailed in Robin Gard (ed.), *The Observant Traveller: Diaries of Travel in England, Wales and Scotland in County Record Offices in England and Wales* (HMSO, London, 1989), p. 28.

9 William Cobbett, *Rural Rides*, ed. G.D.H. and Margaret Cole (Peter Davies, London, 1967), 3, 2, p. 446. Waterloo Bridge in London was opened in 1817.

10 Charlotte Barnett (ed.), *Diary and Letters of Madame D'Arblay* (Swan Sonnesheim & Co., London, 1893), 4, 2, p. 559.

11 For Eliza de Feuillide's visit see R.A. Austen-Leigh (ed.), *Austen Papers 1704–1856* (Spottiswoode, Ballantyne & Co., London, 1942), p. 164. Jordan as quoted in A. Aspinall (ed.), *Mrs. Jordan and Her Family: Being the Unpublished Correspondence of Mrs. Jordan and the Duke of Clarence . . .* (Arthur Barker, London, 1951), p. 151. See Gwen Hart, *A History of Cheltenham* (Leicester University Press, Leicester, 1965), for further details on the expansion in this period.

12 See William Addison, *English Spas* (Batsford, London, 1951), p. 106 and p. 121. The French émigrés are discussed in Margery Weiner, *The French Exiles 1789–1815* (John Murray, London, 1960).

13 Ruth Michaelis-Jena and Willy Merson (eds), *A Lady Travels: Journeys in England and Scotland from the Diaries of Johanna Schopenhauer* (Routledge, London, 1988), p. 106. These diaries contain a lot of important observations on Regency society. They draw attention to the status of the apothecary in rural areas, p. 48, and provide a good description of the role performed by the master of ceremonies at watering places, pp. 115–17. There is also a passing reference to a performance of a play by Kotzebue, p. 179. I am not qualified to judge some of the scientific research that has been carried out in relation to the properties of spa waters. See for example Noel G. Coley, 'Physicians, Chemists and the Analysis of Mineral Waters: The Most Difficult Part of Chemistry', *Medical History*, supp. 10, 1990, pp. 56–66.

14 Wiltshire, *Jane Austen and the Body*, p. 210.

15 Susan Ferrier, *Marriage* (Oxford University Press, Oxford, 1986), p. 32.

16 For more details see June Rose, *The Perfect Gentleman: The Remarkable Life of Dr James Miranda Barry, The Woman who Served as an Officer in the British Army from 1813 to 1859* (Hutchinson, London, 1977). Barry is also discussed in passing in Peter Ackroyd, *Dressing Up: Transvestism and Drag: The History of an Obsession* (Simon & Schuster, New York, 1979), p. 82, and in more detail in Marjorie Garber, *Vested Interests: Cross-Dressing and Cultural Anxiety* (Routledge, London, 1992), pp. 203–5. Garber's work also relates to some of the themes I discussed in relation to *Mansfield Park*. Although not from the Regency period, *A Narrative of the Life of Mrs. Charlotte Charke, Youngest Daughter of Colley Cibber, esq., Written by Herself* (W. Reeve, London, 1755) has some relevance in relation to Barry since her rebellion took the form of setting herself up when a girl

as a charitable apothecary, before becoming involved in cross-dressing both on and off the stage. I do not know of a modern edition which, once again, is needed.

7 See Park Honan, *Jane Austen: Her Life* (Weidenfeld & Nicolson, London 1987), p. 272 for details.

8 See *Report of the Select Committee on Madhouses in England*, 1814–15, 4, pp. 801–1033, esp. p. 899 for details. Ellen Weeton tells an anecdote that illustrates the way in which bleeding was often regarded as the cure for almost everything by both practitioners and patients in this period. A Miss Davenport who thought that she was overweight made frequent visits to different apothecaries to be bled. They eventually realised what was happening and collectively refused to treat her, Ellen Weeton, *Miss Weeton's Journal of a Governess* (David & Charles Reprints, Newton Abbot, 1969), 1, p. 53.

19 W.R. Martin, 'The Subject of Jane Austen's *Sanditon*', *English Studies in Africa*, 10, 1967, pp. 87–93, p. 90.

20 Tanner, *Jane Austen*, p. 269.

21 Cobbett, *Rural Rides*, 1, p. 30.

22 John Lauber, 'Sanditon: The Kingdom of Folly', *Studies in the Novel*, 4, 1972, pp. 353–63, p. 360.

23 Wiltshire, *Jane Austen and the Body*, p. 218.

24 For Henry's affinities with Lovelace see R.F. Bissenden, 'Mansfield Park: Freedom and the Family', John Halperin (ed.), *Jane Austen: Bicentenary Essays* (Cambridge University Press, Cambridge, 1975), pp. 156–71.

25 For an example of this kind of text see Joan Aiken, *Mansfield Revisited* (Grafton Books, London, 1986). Some of the others are listed in Marilyn Sachs, 'Sequels to Jane Austen's Novels', J. David Grey (ed.), *The Jane Austen Handbook* (Athlone Press, London, 1986), pp. 374–6.

26 Alice Cobbett, *Somehow Lengthened: A Development of Sanditon* (Ernest Benn, London, 1932).

27 James Thompson, *Between Self and World: The Novels of Jane Austen* (The Pennsylvania State University Press, University Park, 1988), p. 161.

28 Edith Holden, *The Country Diary of an Edwardian Lady: A Facsimile Reproduction of a Naturalist's Diary for the Year 1906* (Michael Joseph, London, 1977). This sold roughly two and a half million copies when first published.

Select bibliography

As the notes have been reasonably detailed, the bibliography can be brief. It lists the books on both Austen's writings and Regency England that I would particularly like to recommend to students. It therefore takes the form of an introductory reading list. Full publication details have been provided earlier on, so here only the date of publication, and place if not London, are given.

1 AUSTEN'S WRITINGS

Armstrong, Isobel	*Jane Austen: Mansfield Park* (Harmondsworth, 1988)
Butler, Marilyn	*Jane Austen and the War of Ideas* (Oxford, 1987 edn)
Duckworth, Alistair	*The Improvement of the Estate: A Study of Jane Austen's Novels* (Baltimore, 1971)
Evans, Mary	*Jane Austen and the State* (1987)
Favret, Mary A.	*Romantic Correspondence: Women, Politics and the Fiction of Letters* (Cambridge, 1993)
Fergus, Jan	*Jane Austen: A Literary Life* (Basingstoke, 1991)
Gilbert, Sandra M. and Gubar, Susan	*The Madwoman in the Attic: The Woman Writer and the Nineteenth-Century Literary Imagination* (New Haven, 1979)
Honan, Park	*Jane Austen: Her Life* (1987)
Johnson, Claudia	*Jane Austen: Women, Politics and the Novel* (Chicago, 1989)
Kirkham, Margaret	*Jane Austen: Feminism and Fiction* (Brighton, 1983)
Litvak, Joseph	*Caught in the Act: Theatricality in the Nineteenth-Century English Novel* (California, 1993)
MacDonagh, Oliver	*Jane Austen: Real and Imagined Worlds* (New Haven, 1991)
Mellor, Anne K.	*Romanticism and Gender* (1993)
Monaghan, David (ed.)	*Jane Austen in a Social Context* (1981)
Mukherjee, Meenahski	*Jane Austen* (Basingstoke, 1991)
Poovey, Mary	*The Proper Lady and the Woman Writer: Ideology as Style in the Works of Mary Wollstonecraft, Mary Shelley and Jane Austen* (Chicago, 1984)

Roberts, Warren   *Jane Austen and the French Revolution* (1979)
Spacks, Patricia Meyer   *Gossip* (New York, 1985)
Spencer, Jane   *The Rise of the Woman Novelist from Aphra Behn to Jane Austen* (Oxford, 1986)
Sulloway, Alison G.   *Jane Austen and the Province of Womanhood* (Philadelphia, 1989)
Tanner, Tony   *Jane Austen* (Basingstoke, 1986)
Thompson, James   *Between Self and World: The Novels of Jane Austen* (University Park, Pennsylvania, 1988)
Todd, Janet (ed.)   *Jane Austen: New Perspectives* (New York 1983)
Wiltshire, John   *Jane Austen and the Body* (Cambridge, 1992)

2 REGENCY ENGLAND

Baer, Marc   *Theatre and Disorder in Late Georgian London* (Oxford, 1992)
Clark, Anna   *Women's Silence, Men's Violence: Sexual Assault in England 1770–1845* (1987)
Donnison, Jean   *Midwives and Medical Men: A History of Inter-Professional Rivalries and Women's Rights* (1977)
Hall, Christopher D.   *British Strategy in the Napoleonic War 1803–15* (Manchester, 1992)
Harvey, A.D.   *Britain in the Early Nineteenth Century* (1978)
Hibbert, Christopher   *George IV* (Harmondsworth, 1976)
Lewis, Michael   *A Social History of the Navy 1793–1815* (1960)
Loudon, Irvine   *Medical Care and the General Practitioner 1750–1850* (Oxford, 1986)
Low, Donald A.   *That Sunny Dome: A Portrait of Regency England* (1977)
McKendrick, Neil   *The Birth of a Consumer Society: The Commercialisation of Eighteenth-Century Britain* (1982)
Moers, Ellen   *The Dandy: From Brummell to Beerbohm* (Lincoln, 1978)
Neale, Jonathan   *The Cutlass and the Lash: Mutiny and Discipline in Nelson's Navy* (1980)
Newman, Gerald   *The Rise of English Nationalism: A Cultural History 1740–1830* (1987)
Norton, Rictor   *Mother Clap's Molly House: The Gay Subculture in England 1700–1830* (1992)
Ousby, Ian   *The Englishman's England: Taste, Travel and the Rise of Tourism* (Cambridge, 1990)
Porter, Dorothy and Roy *Patient's Progress: Doctors and Doctoring in Eighteenth-Century England* (Oxford, 1989)
Porter, Roy   *English Society in the Eighteenth Century* (Harmondsworth, 1992 edn)
Porter, Roy   *A Social History of Madness: Stories of the Insane* (1989)
Richardson, Ruth   *Death, Dissection and the Destitute* (Harmondsworth, 1989)

Sales, Roger   *English Literature in History 1780–1830: Pastoral and Politics* (1983)

Smith, Olivia   *The Politics of Language 1791–1819* (Oxford, 1984)

Thompson, E.P.   *The Making of the English Working Class* (Harmondsworth, 1968)

Walton, John K.   *The English Seaside Resort 1750–1914: A Social History* (Leicester, 1983)

Index